Managing
Gender

To Nick and Ben
who grew up with this book

Managing Gender

The State, the New Middle Class
and Women Workers 1830~1930

DESLEY DEACON

OXFORD
UNIVERSITY PRESS

Melbourne

OXFORD UNIVERSITY PRESS AUSTRALIA

Oxford   New York   Toronto
Delhi   Bombay   Calcutta   Madras   Karachi
Petaling Jaya   Singapore   Hong Kong   Tokyo
Nairobi   Dar es Salaam   Cape Town
Melbourne   Auckland

and associated companies in
Berlin   Ibadan

OXFORD is a trade mark of Oxford University Press

© Desley Deacon 1989
First published 1989

This book is copyright. Apart from any fair
dealing for the purposes of private study,
research, criticism or review as permitted under
the Copyright Act, no part may be reproduced,
stored in a retrieval system, or transmitted, in
any form or by any means, electronic, mechanical,
photocopying, recording, or otherwise without
prior written permission. Inquiries to be made to
Oxford University Press.

Copying for educational purposes
Where copies of part or the whole of the book are
made under section 53B or section 53D of the Act,
the law requires that records of such copying be
kept. In such cases the copyright owner is
entitled to claim payment.

National Library of Australia
Cataloguing-in-Publication data:

Deacon, Desley.
  Managing gender: the state, the new middle class and women
workers 1830-1930

  Bibliography.
  Includes index.
  ISBN 0 19 554817 5.

  1. Social classes — New South Wales — History. 2. Elite (Social
sciences) — New South Wales — History. 3. Women — New
South Wales — Social conditions. 4. Bureaucracy — New South
Wales — History. 5. Women — Employment — New South
Wales — History. 6. New South Wales — Social conditions. I.
Title.

305.5'09944

Edited by Sarah Brenan
Designed by Pauline McClenahan
Typeset by Setrite Typesetters, Hong Kong
Printed in Hong Kong
Published by Oxford University Press,
253 Normanby Road, South Melbourne, Australia

HN
850
.Z9
S642
1989

DISCARDED
GARDNER UNIVERSITY

Contents

List of Figures

Preface

For people who supposedly have 'a characteristic talent for bureaucracy', Australians have paid little scholarly attention to
the state. It has been an accepted part of the political landscape,
examined from time to time by curious foreigners, but rarely
by Australians themselves. We have many studies of the development of parties and classes, but almost none that examine
the construction of the state and its relationships to other parts
of the political and social system.

This lack of attention to the state suggests that to the collective Australian mind it remains that 'vast public utility'
described by W.K. Hancock in 1929, 'whose duty it is to
provide the greatest happiness for the greatest number'.
Australian women, however, have never shared this benign
view of the state. If each male citizen is, as Hancock put it, 'a
subject who claims his rights—the right to work, the right to
fair and reasonable conditions of living, the right to be happy—
from the State and through the State', this had demonstrably
not been the case for women. Feminist scholars have been
prominent, therefore, in opening up a new, critical approach
to the state which emphasizes its important coercive and
ideological role.

It is no accident that this study of the development of the
New South Wales public service has grown out of an attempt
to answer a number of feminist questions about female labour
markets in Australia. Every excursion I made into the historical
record led me to some aspect of the state. A simple question
about historical trends in women's labour market participation
landed me in the quagmire of nineteenth-century census

figures and the political preoccupations, concerning both class and gender, of that major public servant and intellectual, T. A. Coghlan. Another question about the employment of married women led me to the public service marriage bars, and once again to Coghlan, this time in his lesser-known role as the leader of a group of public service reformers preoccupied with those same class and gender issues. Further questions about discriminatory pay and attitudes about women's mothering role led me, of course, to the state industrial courts and to the state's role in advising women how to be 'good' mothers—programmes which articulated similar class and gender preoccupations and drew on the strength of the state which the reformers had helped to stabilize. It became obvious that the development of twentieth-century ideas and practices concerning gender, the construction of the modern inter-ventionist state, and the class and family concerns of educated workers were intimately related.

This book is the result of following some of these complex interrelations of gender, class and state in New South Wales from 1830, when the colony began to move away from its convict origins, to 1930, when the shape of its modern political and gender orders was temporarily settled. The book con-centrates on the labour market and family experiences of public service clerical workers—the postmistresses, telegraph operators, typists, shorthand writers, clerks and administrators who were the main protagonists in the struggles over labour market control and access which came to a head in the 1890s. The form of the modern Australian state, with its character-istically strong public bureaucracy, was constructed by men shaped by experience in the clerical labour market, and it was on this labour market terrain that issues of gender were de-cisively fought out.

Although the book is a detailed case study of the develop-ment of the public personnel system in one Australian state, it is also an attempt to provide a new interpretive framework for Australian history. With its emphasis on the independent political role of intellectuals, the process of professionalization and the central role of state institutions in establishing basic Australian ideologies and practices, this book is intended to rescue not just the public servant, but also the small-town lawyer, the suburban school teacher, the upwardly mobile doctor and the aspiring female clerk, from the condescension of a history concerned mainly with whores and ladies, adventurer politicians, an heroic working class and 'Mr Fat' capitalists. H. G. Wells once wrote that 'A time may come when history, grown more penetrating, will have more to tell about clerks and less about conquerors'. Perhaps in Australia that distinction does not have to be so clearly made.

The book is also intended as a contribution to the sociology of the state. As the introductory chapter reveals, recent sociological approaches to the state have neglected the historical and national variety of actual states and the experiences, motivations and powers of their bureaucratic personnel. The Australian experience is useful in documenting so clearly the varying relationship between the backgrounds, interests and resources of public servants and other educated workers and the structure and policies of the state. It suggests, therefore, the usefulness of a more voluntarist and historical approach to the state in which public servants and their class allies are the focus of study.

Finally, a central concern of the book is the construction of gender and gender-differentiated labour markets. The detailed public service records provide an unparalleled opportunity to examine the history of gender distinctions in clerical work—an area of employment which promised both upward mobility and freedom from the restrictions of gender. The unexpected variety of ideas and practice concerning gender-appropriate work indicates the need for more regional-, firm- or occupation-specific studies before we can begin to understand the relationship between gender and work. What this study does show, however, is the way in which the ideas and practices of particular groups can be institutionalized and disseminated through their access to the state.

A book that begins as a doctoral dissertation has a long history and incurs many debts of gratitude. The original research on which this book is based was carried out in the Sociology Department of The Faculties at the Australian National University, where I was a tutor and doctoral candidate from 1980 to 1985. My friends and colleagues there gave me invaluable support and on-the-job training, while the Women's

History Group and other feminist scholars at the ANU provided another source of stimulation, criticism and sisterly
encouragement. Bob Cushing was generous enough to provide
supervision for research that was well outside his own area of
interest, a task to which he brought his own special brand of
intellectual scepticism and enthusiasm. The process of turning
a dissertation into a book was made more difficult by a move
to the United States, but a number of people and institutions
have made it possible. The Social Justice Project at the Research
School of Social Sciences, Australian National University,
and the History Department at the University of Sydney
provided invaluable Australian bases for me in 1986 and 1987,
when most of the rewriting was done, and the American
Civilization Program at the University of Texas at Austin has
given me the new intellectual home I needed to finish the
book. Long periods of research in Sydney were made possible
by Mollie Lenthall's warm hospitality. Critical readings by
Katrina Alford, Marian Aveling, Brian Dickey and Allan
Martin have helped me to clarify my ideas. Bob Connell's
two close readings and incisive suggestions have been invaluable guides for the book's final form. The book is informed
by a continuing intellectual dialogue with Katrina Alford and
by stimulating discussions with Judith Godden, Ann Curthoys,
Ross Curnow and Hilary Golder. Finally, of course, no
scholarly work is possible without the support of family and
friends, whose contribution is not to stimulate, but to soothe,
divert and 'recreate'.

... when we speak of the state's influence we mean the influence that is to be exerted by government officials and government clerks! They are all very fine fellows, to be sure, but however much they have been improved or chastened by their sense of responsibility, by discipline or pride of office, they nevertheless possess all human capacities and all human frailties. Like all men, they have eyes they can open or shut at will and mouths that can on occasion speak, be silent or even eat.* They too can sin through pride, sloth, cupidity and vanity. They too have their sympathies, their friendships and aversions, their passions and interests—and among their interests an interest in keeping their jobs or even slipping into better ones if the occasion offers.

Gaetano Mosca, *The Ruling Class*

*Italian *mangiare* to eat, take 'graft'

Introduction
Rescuing the poor public servant: social theory, state officials and gender

I

It is widely recognized that state policy has played an important part in the construction of the twentieth-century gender order— that set of family and labour market institutions which have denied women access to economic independence.[1] The influence of the state has been particularly important in Australia. Not only has it been central in fostering notions of education, housekeeping and child-bearing which have been prescriptive and confining to women, but it has also given legal force to major restrictions on women's capacities as wage-earners.[2] The state has, therefore, been central in promoting an emphasis on gender differentiation which has helped to make dependency the 'natural' status of women.

Despite the fact that the state has become an object of new scholarly interest in recent years, current theoretical approaches are surprisingly unhelpful in explaining the particular ways in which it intervenes in gender relations.[3] Feminist and Marxist scholars, reacting against liberal views of the state as a neutral arbiter between social groups, have been more concerned to expose its general patriarchal or class nature than to investigate its historical and national complexities. 'The state is male', says Catharine MacKinnon flatly.[4] It is 'never anything other than the materialization and condensation of class relations', says Poulantzas.[5] Drawing on structural models of patriarchy and class, some scholars even deny that their object of study is of any intrinsic interest: they assume that because the state is merely an agent of the dominant group, state actions, no matter how they are perceived by the actors involved, need

1

not be analysed for their immediate and particular outcomes or their instrumental value for particular groups. Even where the actions of states appear to be independent, so the argument goes, this is 'precisely in order to be able to organize the whole of [the ruling] class', a task which can only be carried out when the state is 'relatively autonomous from the diverse fractions of this class'.[6] As R. W. Connell points out in his critique of this 'Althusserian two-step', 'when followers of Poulantzas argue that the state bureaucracy has no power of its own, all they are really saying is that they speak a conceptual language in which whatever the state bureaucracy does, it will not count as "power"'.[7] This approach may provide insight into large-scale constraints within which state institutions, personnel and clients work and make demands, but it fails to elucidate how specific institutions and policies are historically produced.[8]

Reacting in turn against this denial of the independent power of the state, an alternative neo-Weberian approach focusses on the distinctive capacities and characteristics of state structures themselves. Proponents of this position demonstrate how the history, organization and resources of particular states shape client demands, the way clients are organized, the attitudes of personnel and the possible policy options. As Theda Skocpol points out, the very formation and political capacity of classes often depends to a significant degree on the structures and activities of the state.[9] This approach 'brings the state back in' as a real, rather than illusory, object of study, and allows us to understand why, for instance, the New South Wales government could establish a universal and comprehensive system of infant welfare clinics in the 1920s, while the United States federal government struggled unsuccessfully to maintain a much more modest programme. However, the approach is limited by its determined focus on the state itself. It can tell us nothing about the demands made on the state that derive from purely social factors, nor about the attitudes and resources state personnel bring to their actions from their participation in the wider society. It cannot explain, therefore, the dependence of the US infant welfare programme on a well-organized and powerful women's sphere; or why these women-centred policies differed from the more managerial tone of the male-directed NSW programme.[10]

What is striking about these two approaches is their focus on structure—whether constraining or facilitating—rather than on people and practice. This is most obvious in the neglect of the public servant, who is, ironically, almost a forgotten figure in current studies of the state. Like the working class rescued by E. P. Thompson twenty years ago, the 'everyday inhabitants of an important area of the state are treated with 'enormous condescension' by both camps.[11] To one group, state officials are shadowy go-betweens, incapable, either as members of social groups or of state agencies, of contributing to the construction and working of those institutions. According to Althusser, teachers, for instance, 'do not even begin to suspect the "work" the system forces them to do, or worse, put all their heart and ingenuity into performing it with the most advanced awareness'.[12] To the other group, public servants are not puppets or agents: they puzzle and push and negotiate, and sometimes even stage revolutions. But they have no firm roots in civil society, no class or gender, and are defined only by their organizational situation.[13]

More voluntarist accounts have shown promise of avoiding the pitfalls of these two approaches. Conceptualizing the state as an arena open to capture by conflicting groups, they have opened the way for investigation of the social characteristics of state employees. However, these accounts have been limited by their feminist and Marxist frameworks which have assumed unvarying and undifferentiated patriarchal and pro-capitalist stances by state officials. Ralph Miliband, for instance, drawing on his observations of the British case, argues that the state is staffed and controlled by the ruling class and its allies.[14] Australian feminists have argued from the twentieth-century experience that the state is unequivocally '*male* territory'.[15] Whatever the truth of these conclusions for one historical period, they cannot be generalized without losing sight of the actual complexity of class and gender.

It is the contention of this book that the processes of state formation and policy formulation and implementation cannot be fully understood unless the history, interests, resources and effects of public servants are considered seriously. In order to place state employees at the centre of investigation and locate them in a social group which encompasses both state and society, I suggest that they should be looked at as part of the new middle class. A third class standing rather uneasily between the bourgeoisie and the proletariat, the new middle class can be thought of in general terms as consisting of those workers who depend on the sale of educational, technical and social skills, or 'cultural capital'. It is 'new' because its members can be differentiated from the 'old' middle classes, the bourgeoisie and the petty bourgeoisie, by the fact that they do not own the means of production; and it is a 'middle' class because it is differentiated from the working class by the type of labour power it has to offer and by the culture and ideology which surround that work.

Members of the new middle class are, in C. Wright Mills' terms, the handlers of 'paper and money and people'. 'Expert at dealing with people transiently and impersonally', they are 'masters of the commercial, professional, and technical relationship'. They do not make things. They supervise, record and keep track of what others produce. They provide technical and personal services, and teach others how to do things.[16] In addition, they handle ideas, and are the chief interpreters, creators and disseminators of knowledge.[17]

The concept of cultural capital is central to the idea of the new middle class. Alvin Gouldner claims that cultural skills are as much capital as are a factory's buildings or machines. He argues that intellectuals, such as managers, professionals, government officials and journalists, form a New Class whose members monopolize particular cultural skills that unite them, empower them and place them in conflict with the 'old' classes.[18] Similar claims are made by Barbara and John Ehrenreich for what they call the Professional–Managerial Class.

The value of cultural capital for the new middle class is something that is actively created and fought for through the processes of social closure and credentialism. Frank Parkin argues that monopoly of educational qualifications, or credentialism, is a form of exclusionary social closure comparable to property as a basis for class formation. Both, he points out, confer benefits and privileges on the few through denying access to the many, and entail the use of exclusionary rules enshrined in law and upheld by the authority of the state.[19] The creation, evaluation and monopoly of cultural capital is thus a political process, the most obvious and successful example of which is professionalization.

There is considerable debate over the precise boundaries of this new class. The Ehrenreichs' Professional–Managerial Class and Gouldner's New Class comprise only professionals and managers, distinguished by their 'culture of critical discourse' and their control over technical and ideological resources.[20] Anthony Giddens, on the other hand, argues that all white-collar and professional workers share a favourable market situation and are marked off from the working class by the limited social mobility, the physical division of labour and the authority relations between manual and white-collar workers.[21] Poulantzas makes a similar claim, arguing that 'a whole series of rituals, know-how, and "cultural elements"' distinguish what he calls 'the new petty bourgeoisie' from the working class. This ideological differentiation between mastery of the general culture and *savoir-faire* on the one hand and particular manual skills on the other extends from knowing how to write and present ideas to knowing how to speak 'well'.[22]

The unity of this group of educated workers is also hotly debated. Some commentators conclude that it is merely an 'occupational salad'.[23] Others maintain that it is irredeemably divided between managers and professionals on the one hand and clerks, service workers and sub-professionals on the other. This has given rise to considerable discussion as to whether these groups are really part of the capitalist or the working class.[24] Gouldner, on the other hand, claims that his New Class is highly unified, autonomous and powerful, to the extent that it forms a potentially revolutionary class which is 'slowly placing the old moneyed class on the historical shelf'.[25] However, recent studies questioning the continued radicalism and unity of professionals in the United States suggest that Gouldner's claims are exaggerated, even for the highly educated sector he is discussing.[26]

Basic to the question of the unity of the new middle class is the issue of its independence from the bourgeoisie. There is considerable evidence that professionals and managers usurp working class and female skills and disorganize traditional working class life in their efforts to enhance their labour market situation and their sphere of influence. Christopher Lasch, for instance, portrays the traditional family as invaded by the 'so-called helping professions'.[27] Barbara Ehrenreich and Deirdre English describe how experts have taken over many areas of traditional women's work and knowledge and claimed authority over women's domestic activities.[28] In a survey of the progressive era in the United States, Barbara and John Ehrenreich show how engineers and managers used scientific management to diminish workers' collective experience and their mastery over the work process; how public education, charity agencies, experts and public health officials penetrated and undermined working class community life; and how services and commodities which had been supplied by the working class family or community were replaced by those conceived and supplied by other classes.[29]

This evidence has been used to make the argument that the new middle class has no real independence. Instead, its main function is to help reproduce and control a docile workforce for the benefit of capitalism. But these same studies show professionals involved in the much more purposeful activity of constructing their own labour market and the conditions under which they worked. The progressive reforms and ideologies described by the Ehrenreichs created jobs for, and increased the influence of, a variety of specialists, experts, and intellectuals, as did the project described by Lasch.[30] A number of other studies show the large-scale and successful efforts of professional groups to gain labour market autonomy, monopoly of valued knowledge and domination of allied workers.[31] Although these efforts required the support of other influential groups, especially in the state, the reforming zeal of the new middle class was aimed at capitalists as well as the working class. Professionals and managers criticized corporate greed and inefficiency; they attempted to transform the corporation through scientific management; they fought for academic freedom, social reform and consumer issues opposed by capitalists; and the more militant of them advocated government ownership of the means of production and the expansion of social services.[32] Gouldner argues, indeed, that New Class knowledge and expertise give them *de facto* power over the old bourgeoisie, and that their control of ideological resources allows them to 'harass the old, sabotage it, critique it, expose it and muckrake it, express moral, technical, and cultural superiority to it, and hold it up to contempt and ridicule'.[33]

The question of the independence of the new middle class is clarified by Kerreen Reiger in her careful and detailed

examination of the role played by professional experts in
modernizing the Australian family.[34] In a pioneering study of
an emergent class of professionals, technocrats and experts
between 1880 and 1940, Reiger describes their piecemeal but
coherent activities directed at re-forming family life. The
experts, who included doctors, teachers, kindergarten workers
and domestic science and child guidance specialists, were concerned to introduce technology and 'efficiency' into the
household, to control and professionalize reproduction and
child-rearing practices, and to demystify and control sexuality.

Reiger argues that, although these middle class reformers
often worked hand in hand with the bourgeoisie in programmes ostensibly directed at the working class family, their
aims were different and their activities had a profound effect
on the bourgeoisie as well as the working class. In extending
the principles of science and instrumental reason to the household and personal relations, and establishing the professional
as expert, the new middle class helped destroy the bourgeois
ideal of the family as a private and intimate refuge and as a
natural entity based on women's essential femininity. The
new emphasis on mothercraft and domesticity as something
that had to be learned threatened bourgeois assumptions about
the naturalness of women's maternal and household roles,
bringing about a 'disenchantment' of the home and the 'angels'
within it. Reiger concludes, therefore, that the middle class
experts had their own project which actually worked against
the interests of the bourgeoisie, disrupting the division between
public and private life on which capitalism was based.

The separate identity of this network of professional and
technical experts was confirmed for Reiger by their similar
social backgrounds, patterns of training and work experience.
They corresponded extensively with each other, met frequently,
both professionally and socially, and appeared regularly on
the same committees and government inquiries. In all these
activities they emphasized a new ideology which combined a
preoccupation with their own material interests, concern for
the public good, and the enthusiasm for efficiency and the
application of scientific method which is at the heart of the
culture of critical discourse. As Reiger points out:

Not only was [efficiency] the motif of the emerging industrial order
as exemplified by Taylorism, but it was seen as the golden rule of all

social life. The experts' stress on technical efficiency, on the application
of scientific knowledge to practical problems, reflected their own
material interests and became their general pattern of consciousness.
It took form in a variety of ways such as style of language, the
precision of terminology and orderly arrangement characteristic of the
later childrearing literature for example. The emphasis on measurement and regular routine, so typical of the infant welfare movement,
provided organizing principles for the rituals of everyday life... So
the technocratic consciousness was not confined to the public sphere.
The professional middle class aspired to extend it throughout society,
through all social classes and all aspects of life. Management therefore became a favourite term not only in industry and commerce but
in discussion of housework, childrearing and sexuality.

Reiger concludes, therefore, that 'the experts had a particular
message of their own, a representation of reality which meshed
with their own experience of the world, especially their position in the labour market and the skills related to it'.[35]
 Reiger's conclusions that the professionals and experts she
studied were an influential group with a separate project and a
separate identity confirm that the concept of the new middle
class is a viable and useful one. She also suggests that it has
particular relevance to the study of the state. The relationship
of the new middle class to the state is a constant but muted
theme running through the literature on the new middle class.
All the writers on professionalization stress that state support
is vital to the professional project. The Ehrenreichs also point
out that much of the experts' activity they describe was directed towards the state, which supplied many new professional
jobs;[36] however, this relationship is never thoroughly investigated. Reiger considers this special relationship more carefully
than previous writers, though it is again not the focus of her
concerns. She points out that the state not only supported
professional monopoly through licensing legislation, but also
provided experts with a significant institutional base. The
quantitative and qualitative expansion of the state gave the
experts' professionalizing strategy both material support and
legitimacy. By adopting much of the professionals' programme, by providing universal services and disseminating
them widely, the state provided experts with jobs and actively
aided their intervention into many new areas of Australian
life.[37] Because of this support, professionals and like-minded

intellectuals were to some extent *becoming* the state by the second decade of the twentieth century.

The close relationship between intellectuals and the state is also emphasized by R. W. Connell in his work on the construction of hegemony. In a recent essay he notes that 'the ways [intellectuals in the state] jump, the degree of autonomy they can establish, and what they can do with it, are...very important in deciding what is the actual role of the state...'[38] With a fine sense of the process of 'composition' by which cultural practices are constructed and maintained,[39] he acknowledges that intellectuals' role in this process varies considerably according to their conditions of life and work—their 'practical activity'.[40] However, he has not, in his own work, analysed closely the political, economic and social conditions which produce different intellectual stances and which empower or weaken intellectuals. He often seems to suggest, instead, that intellectuals develop appropriate attitudes and power through a massive exercise of will. For instance, discussing the pattern of hegemony in modern Australia, he concludes:

One of the most important things that intellectuals can do through their proper work is to overcome...isolation and prevent...deflections. Being counter-hegemonic is not enough. One must be relentlessly counter-hegemonic, and in sufficient masses to do real damage, and be able to carry through to the actual construction of a human society. In both critique and construction socialist intellectuals have a massive work to do.[41]

This lack of detailed investigation of intellectuals' 'practical activity' has resulted in an approach to the state in Connell's historical work that is uncomfortably close to the 'two-step' he roundly criticizes in Althusser. In his study of class structure in Australian history, written with T. H. Irving, he argues that 'in a great measure, it is the state that is active in [the formation and maintenance of hegemony]; in the routine management of affairs, the state is capable of substituting for the mobilization of the ruling class'.[42] When Connell and Irving talk about 'the autonomy of the state' they are not referring to the independence of other power blocs that is theoretically possible. Instead they are referring to an apparent autonomy which allows the state to reorganize the capitalist class (whose members, it seems, to quote Connell on Althusser's conception of the state, 'can't organise their way out of a paper bag').[43]

Connell and Irving's conception of the state is at odds with their general historical approach and with Connell's later emphasis on the variability of intellectuals' ideas and impact. While the working class is made up, for Connell and Irving, of active subjects, mobilizing and making alliances and compromises, the state remains static in its personnel and impact. Bureaucrats are always 'traditional intellectuals', tied to the ruling class, and, to Connell and Irving, 'the term "public" in public sector really means "system-maintaining"'.[44]

An approach to the state that views public servants as part of a new middle class avoids the assumptions that underly Connell and Irving's early work. It allows us to investigate the implications of Reiger's study that the relationship between the state and intellectuals is an alliance between bureaucratic and professional members of the same class. This provides an entry point to the interests and resources that public servants bring to their activities in the state from the wider society. Several important points are emphasized as a consequence. First of all, the state is not an abstraction for intellectuals. Instead, it is an important part of their labour market, and as such, one of their major preoccupations. Second, questions of social closure, professionalization and definition of cultural capital are central for this class, making public personnel policy an important focus of political struggle. Third, mastery and legitimation of the culture of critical discourse are crucial weapons in this struggle. Consequently the management of impersonal relationships such as bureaucracies, the use of rational criteria of selection such as merit, the faith in rationally derived theory as a guide to action, and the propensity to classification and enumeration are all part of a revolt against traditional authority closely involved with the struggle for labour market control. In addition, the institutionalization of these principles in the practices of the state provides them with a high degree of legitimacy. It is clear, therefore, that there is a potentially close relationship between the construction of state organizations and policies and the construction of the new middle class labour market.

The high level of disagreement about the composition, unity

and autonomy of educated workers suggests, however, that this relationship is not a straightforward one. It is apparent that what Giddens calls 'structuration' is difficult, fragile and volatile for this class, with shifting political loyalties and alliances within the class and with other classes being important sources of fragmentation or strength in the struggle for unity and autonomy.[45] The precarious nature of the process of class structuration makes it necessary, therefore, to look carefully at the details of its historical composition, and to anticipate ambivalences, contradictions, conflicts and disappointments in its class projects.

II

The consequences of the ambivalences and contradictions inherent in the new middle class project are most glaring when we consider gender. Gender divisions constitute a major fault line within the new middle class today. Most comment-ators agree that intellectual workers are seriously divided between managers and professionals, on the one hand, and routine clerical, sales, service, semi-professional and technical workers on the other. The latter categories are predominantly female, and provide a large proportion of women's paid work. Labour market conditions in these feminized categories are substantially inferior to those in the managerial and professional sector: pay is much lower, promotion prospects are poor, and work is routinized. In addition, there are barriers to move-ment from the lower sector of the labour market to the higher. In effect, the new middle class labour market is divided into a primary sector and a secondary sector, and women tend to be confined to the secondary labour market.[46]

As Rosabeth Kanter has shown, the blocked opportunities and powerlessness of secondary labour market workers tend to produce and reproduce low self-esteem, conservatism and limited aspirations—characteristics that have come to be associated with women workers. Women's virtual confine-ment to the secondary labour market places them, therefore, on a downward spiral of disadvantage in which their depend-ency is reinforced by their everyday experience.[47] Despite the emphasis of the new middle class on impersonal and rational personnel principles, somehow merit has become masculinized.

Although clerical and semi-professional work is of such importance for women, there has been little investigation of factors specific to the new middle class in this gendering of professional, managerial and white-collar work. The sophisticated theoretical work of Michèle Barrett and Johanna Brenner and Maria Ramas has demonstrated the complexity of the causes of the sexual division of labour, but these writers draw entirely on the historical experiences of the working class, despite the fact that state policies play an important part in their analyses.[48] Discussions of the sexual division of labour in the new middle class draw in turn upon theoretical approaches based, like those of Barrett and Brenner and Ramas, on considerations of the working class or of women as an undifferentiated whole. A number of feminist writers, for instance, have described attempts by professional groups to exclude women and to subordinate female workers to their authority, but these writers have seen such strategies as part of a general patriarchal oppression of women.[49] Others, writing from a socialist–feminist perspective, have seen the development of a division of labour in professional and clerical work as the result of an articulation of the needs of capital and the power of men in a patriarchal society.[50] However, it is apparent from the previous discussion that members of the new middle class have a particular interest in the organization of their own labour market, an interest separate from capitalist and working class interests, and that they have been capable, in many instances, of dictating their own labour market conditions.

Evidence from recent feminist scholarship on household economies supports this observation. These studies show that attitudes and practices concerning men's and women's employment roles vary significantly amongst different economic groups. In effect, there are a variety of family forms involving different types of family/labour market strategies and ideologies about gender divisions. Louise Tilly and Joan Scott, in their study of the development of the family-wage economy in England and France from the eighteenth to the twentieth century, and Christine Bose, in her study of household composition, resources and distribution of paid work to female adult and younger household members in the United States in 1900, have shown that households exhibit a number of different economic strategies.[51] These include the *family-wage economy*, where the family survives on the wage earned by the adult male, and various forms of the *family economy*. The latter strategy finds its most complete form in the family farm or business, where all members of the household engage in gainful employment, but it has a number of variations, including sending adolescents out to work, the employment of adult women outside the home, adding extended family members to the household to help with support, taking in boarders, and engaging in cottage industry.[52]

Bose demonstrates that where the male householder is self-employed as a farmer or a merchant, female members of the household are not very likely to have gainful employment outside the home. Where he is in high-status professional or managerial employment, the women of the household are even less likely to be gainfully employed. In contrast, in households where the adult male is a labourer, an operative, or unemployed, female family members often have outside employment. Wives and daughters of artisans and clerks are much less likely than those of operatives, etc., to be working outside the home, but a little more likely than those of professionals and managers.[53]

These different household economic strategies have been well documented. The nineteenth-century ideal of the privatized family with the wife confined to the domestic sphere has been associated with the rise of the bourgeoisie in the first half of the nineteenth century. Beverley Kingston has pointed out that behind the rhetoric of the home as a haven and women as 'angels in the house' was the economic reality of bourgeois life. The entertainments, the visits, the paying and returning of calls were functions required to oil the social machinery:

The complex business of maintaining caste, status, and hierarchy in society, of ensuring that marriages were arranged that were suitable or advantageous to the family, the business or the property, of celebrating the birth of heirs, entertaining the right people, or keeping the close-knit circles of family and friends fully functioning, was, in the hands of a capable woman, as important and impressive as her husband's political, diplomatic, or entrepreneurial activity.[54]

A similar strategy has been shown to operate in professional and managerial families. Hanna Papanek uses the term 'two-

person single career' to describe those operations in which the
wife is expected to participate in her husband's career, although
her participation is neither directly acknowledged nor remunerated.[55] A number of studies have demonstrated this
type of family strategy amongst members of the diplomatic
service, corporate executives, academics, politicians and the
protestant ministry.[56]

A variation on the bourgeois/professional family type is
that of the craft worker. Cynthia Cockburn has shown how
the exclusion of women is an important element in the male
solidarity of the craft unionist.[57] Jane Humphries has demonstrated how the exclusion of women from the labour market
is an integral part of the economic strategy of the craft worker's
family, giving the family (though not necessarily the women
within it) greater bargaining power for a higher 'family wage'
and greater resilience to resist pauperization and fragmentation.[58]

Outside these three social groups, however, a different
form of family economic strategy is widespread; it is one in
which all members of the family contribute directly to family
production or family income. Studies of families in the early
colonial period of Australia, of farming families, and of families
in which the adult male does not command high wages and
secure employment show a pattern of improvisation whereby
family members contribute income or labour according to
family needs and individual ability. The selector's wife in
colonial Australia often ran the farm while her husband worked
as a shearer or contractor to make ends meet. Wives of the
urban poor or casually employed often ran boarding houses.
In other cases, mothers worked when children were young,
but retired when children were old enough to substitute for
them in the workforce.[59]

There are, therefore, a variety of ways in which different
economic groups organize family and gender relations. Evidence
of their separate interests and resources suggests that, like the
better-documented working class and bourgeoisie, members
of the new middle class are also likely to approach questions
of family and work from their own unique perspective. This
makes it essential to examine the specific labour market, family
and political situations of new middle class men and women
in order to understand the gendering of intellectual work.

III

This book brings together these themes of gender, class and state in a study of the clerical and administrative labour market of the New South Wales public service from 1830 to 1930. Like other Australian states and private employers, and later the Commonwealth, the New South Wales public service restricted and marginalized women's employment in clerical and administrative work throughout its history.[60] But the story of this process is no Whiggish one of inexorable progress towards or away from discrimination. Instead it is full of the contradictions, ambiguities and vacillations that are an integral part of the history of the new middle class. In addition, it has elements that are unique to the New South Wales case, demonstrating vividly the way that gender and state are constructed in particular historical circumstances.

The book examines changes in women's access to equal pay and opportunity in the New South Wales public service in relation to variations in the job security, political power and perceived family priorities of male public servants and their allies. It has three closely related themes— the struggle for a modern, rationalized public personnel system controlled by public servants themselves, the construction and consolidation of a strong, interventionist state, and the conflict over the definition of men's and women's roles. The book draws on the new middle class perspective for its focus on labour market control and the construction of knowledge, but it is not a study of that class. A definitive work on the larger class context of the public servants who are the book's subjects must await further research on professionals, managers and clerical workers in Australia.[61]

One advantage for the social scientist and historian studying the public service labour market is that it is truly *public*. The historical record provides a rich source of data. The annual *Blue Book* and *Public Service List* published from the late 1850s give almost complete documentation for public service clerical personnel on such important dimensions of labour market experience as age, date of appointment, career progression, salary, numbers and collegial networks. In addition, a continuing commentary is provided on labour market developments in parliamentary debates and inquiries, depart-

mental and public personnel authority reports and public service
union journals. This mass of detailed information, combined
with the invaluable biographical material available in the
Australian Dictionary of Biography and the personal papers and
publications of such central public servants as T. A. Coghlan,
provides the opportunity for the delineation of relatively clear
historical relationships between political, economic and social
developments and labour market changes.

The published public records do, however, have their
limitations, especially for a study centrally concerned with
women. They are almost always written by men or are the
recorded voices of men. In addition, they are usually the
voices of urban, elite men—those who run the public service
or man (literally) its head offices. Some of the innumerable
public inquiries of the period do give us access to the voices of
the ordinary male and female public servants who were scattered
throughout the country areas of the colony. In some almost
unique cases, such as the inquiry into embezzlement in the
early Queensland post office, a woman is one of the main
protagonists. It is only when public service unions begin to
publish their own journals that we hear more from rank-and-
file public servants, though the writers are usually up-and-
coming future public service leaders (and male). Where women
work with the predominantly male unions, their opinions and
activities are preserved in the pages of the union journal. We
can follow Louisa Dunkley's campaign for equal pay in the
pages of the *Transmitter*, and Margaret Hogg's in the *Public
Service Journal*, but the activities of women who work mostly
outside the male organizations, such as Florence Wearne, can
only be pieced together from the records of various women's
groups they are associated with.

The problem of bringing out the women's voices is exacerbated by the lack of detailed studies of most aspects of women's
lives in this period. We still have no definitive study of the
most prominent feminist, Rose Scott, nor of the plethora
of women's organizations that emerged after 1889. Louisa
Lawson's life has, until recently, been the object of extra-
ordinarily misogynist attention from men mainly interested in
her as Henry Lawson's (supposedly) inadequate mother.
Writers such as Mary Gilmore, Barbara Baynton and Miles
Franklin are only starting to be recognized as feminists, and

their feminist activities outside their writings have barely been
investigated. The definitive story of the largest category of
new middle class women, the government schoolteachers, has
yet to be written, although a useful start has been made
towards this goal. Judith Godden's invaluable study of upper
class women and philanthropy is still available only in dissertation form. The lives of middle class women in the suburbs
and country towns are revealed only through glimpses in local
histories, accounts of innkeepers and the occasional fortuitous
literary reference, such as Henry Handel Richardson's description of her mother's life as a country postmistress in neighbouring Victoria.[62]

The consequence of this predominance of men's voices in
the public record and the lack of countervailing accounts of
women's activities and opinions is that men appear to play the
preponderant role in this book's story. This is not an inaccurate
representation of reality. The public service was primarily a
man's world. Men were the major actors in the campaign for
public service reform and in the public service unions. They
did have access to superior resources, and where their interests
differed from those of women, they prevailed. However, the
imbalance in the records does diminish the sense of struggle
that was actually present. It is only good fortune that brings
us the voice of Florence Wearne telling us that she 'never
walk[ed] over a bit of pavement in Phillip St without thinking
of a daily internal argument I had as to whether I would give
up the fight and "let women down" on the first opportunity
they had of getting into the Service by competitive exams; or
fight it out'.[63] I have tried where possible to resurrect such
women as Florence Wearne, and have been helped immeasur-
ably in this attempt by fellow-researchers such as Heather
Radi and descendants of public servants Dora Murphy and
Muriel Swain who have generously shared their knowledge
and memories with me. This book is still based primarily,
however, on published public records and published secondary
material. I hope that it will stimulate others to rescue the
anonymous women and men of the new middle class more
completely.

PART ONE

The Fragmented State and the Blurring of Gender

1

Practical equality: the decentralized state and the family economy

I

When the first ministry responsible to the electors of New South Wales was formed in 1856 it took over from the British colonial authorities a permanent public bureaucracy of about 2500 persons.[1] It is difficult to apply the terms 'state', 'class', or even 'gender', to this scattered, diverse and haphazard group. Perhaps some of the 500 public servants working in Sydney, and even the commissioners for Crown lands and the goldfields, could be seen as forming the beginnings of a separate, autonomous state structure, and as having similar class interests. Certainly they were organized by gender. But the other 2000, distributed throughout the length and breadth of the colony, responsible to a multiplicity of authorities, organized in a variety of ways, often partially independent, were deeply embedded in local and family economies. Among these small-town public officers, community and family loyalties blurred the line between state and society, and took precedence over class and gender as organizing principles.

Of the public servants outside Sydney, almost half were police and gaolers, authority for whom was divided amongst local magistrates, the inspector-general of police, the gold commissioners and commissioners of Crown lands. Two hundred school teachers staffed the two state and religious school systems, each government-subsidized but controlled by its own independent board in conjunction with community groups. Another 200 postal officials, 100 customs officers, a similar number of ports and harbours officials, and about

21

sixty officers of the Surveyor-General's Department administered the posts, customs and shipping and surveyed the land.
Twenty-six stipendiary magistrates (and about 600 unpaid
justices of the peace) presided over the courts of petty sessions,
aided by some sixty petty sessions clerks, while commissioners
for Crown lands and the goldfields settled disputes over land
and mining rights outside the Settled Districts and on the
goldfields. Amongst these officials were a number of women,
married and single, working as matrons in charitable institutions
and gaols, as teachers, and as postmistresses.[2]

This disparate group of provincial officers enjoyed a high
degree of autonomy from central control. The strong British
precedent for decentralized authority led to local, and erratic,
oversight of government functions by unpaid justices of the
peace in many country areas, and to a multiplicity of *ad hoc*
administrative structures. Any attempt at more uniform and
centralized control was hindered by problems of communication
and transport, the attenuated chain of command from London,
and considerations of economy.

The limitations imposed by geography and technology
were formidable. The colony covered an area over two and a
half times that of Great Britain and Ireland, even without
including the Port Phillip and Moreton Bay districts which
became, respectively, Victoria and Queensland in 1851 and
1859. Travel was difficult and dangerous. The first few miles
of railway in this vast territory were not opened till 1855.
Roads were poor or non-existent, and river traffic relatively
undeveloped. In periods of recession, bushrangers preyed on
travellers. The post office was the main means of communication until the first telegraph lines were built in 1858. These
conditions made control by any central authority difficult, and
precluded the development of systems of inspection, even if
money for them had been available.[3]

In any event, the attenuated chain of command from London
did little to ensure the close supervision of scattered departmental officers. The Governor had limited power over major
departmental appointments, which were in the patronage of
the British secretary of state.[4] Once such appointments were
made, the distance between London and Sydney gave appointees great freedom. There was little pressure, therefore,
on men such as the surveyor-general, Sir Thomas Mitchell,
to control their scattered personnel closely. More interested in

exploration and literary and scientific work than in departmental administration, Mitchell spent seven of his twenty-
seven years in office in London and another three in exploration.
His department was left very much to its own devices, unsupervised surveyors neglected their work with impunity, and
there was little check on their corruption by powerful local
interests.[5]

The main potential for control of rural public servants lay
in the office of the magistrate. Magistrates were the central
agents of the government in the country areas except on the
goldfields and outside the Limits of Location, where land and
gold commissioners played an important policing and reporting
role. They presided over local courts, and carried out a
variety of policing and licensing functions. However, the office
of the magistrate never became part of a centrally controlled
public service network. Like their British counterparts, most
served in an honorary capacity, and were subjected to little
outside control. Furthermore, many magistrates carried out
their duties in a desultory manner, and were not anxious
to extend their authority outside their judicial and police
functions.[6]

The lack of centralized control over the rural civil service
was exacerbated by limited finance for more complex organizational structures. This was particularly the case during the
1840s. A severe depression and the struggle between the
Legislative Council and the Governor over the financing of
police and gaols led to tight budgetary control. Attempts to
replace justices of the peace with stipendiary magistrates, and
to bring the disparate elements of the police force under one
central authority, foundered on lack of finance. Instead, many
stipendiary magistrates were retrenched; at their lowest point
in 1846 there were only seven left. Many surveyors were
dismissed and re-employed on licence or a fee-paying basis,
giving them even greater independence than before.[7] In general,
limited government finance led to a very independent provincial service in which many employees had other sources of
income. The post office was run by the local storekeeper; the
policeman was very likely to be a tradesman or farmer as
well; most surveyors had rights to independent work. In
addition, many public officials held several jobs in tandem,
making lines of authority uncertain and tenuous.

In keeping with this pattern of financial stringency and local

control, some government responsibilities were left almost
entirely in the hands of private citizens. Charitable boards,
elected by subscribers, distributed government funds to a
number of institutions.[8] The two school boards, themselves
appointed from the ranks of leading citizens, left considerable
discretion in the hands of local communities, which raised
money for school buildings, certified the salary claims of
teachers, and played a large part in the appointment and
supervision of teachers.[9]

With tenuous links to head offices in Sydney and even more
tenuous ones to other civil servants, these rural officials were
not part of an integrated and organized public bureaucracy.
Instead many public service positions were essentially part of
the local economy. Community notables were called on for
advice on matters of recruitment, remuneration and dismissal,
but incumbents of government positions had, in practice,
considerable freedom to nominate their successors, subject
only to informal community approval. Given that the economy
of the Settled Districts was based on family enterprises such as
the small farm, the store and the inn, this meant that some
jobs tended to become family capital, passed on from one
family member to another in a way that was consistent with
the family economy of the region.

II

The post office, one of the largest public employers in the first
half of the nineteenth century, demonstrates most clearly the
decentralized character of public service employment, and its
integration with the local and family economy. Because of
this, it displays to the highest degree the blurring of state,
class and gender boundaries characteristic of the period.

In 1856 there were 177 post offices in New South Wales
servicing the tiny population of 270 000. These post offices
were scattered over a distance of 1280 miles from Gladstone in
the north to Albury in the south, and over 400 miles from
Sydney in the east to Deniliquin in the west. Prior to 1851 this
vast colony had also included the territory which became
Victoria. There were early attempts by head office to control
rural post office officials, but this proved a formidable task.
One year after the establishment of the Post Office Department in 1828, Sydney postmaster, James Raymond, reported

to the colonial secretary that James Orr, the postmaster at Parramatta, was 'so completely...truant that any attempt on my part to advance the utility of the post office is by him not only rejected, but all communications from this office are treated with contempt'.[10] This was to become a common note of exasperation, and the colonial secretary probably never got a satisfactory answer to his peremptory query of 1841 as to 'why so large a consumption of sealing wax and paper'.[11] There was no major attempt at central organization of the postal department before the appointment of Major Christie as postmaster-general in 1852, following Raymond's condemnation by a Legislative Council select committee for lax management, and for allowing country postmasters and postmistresses to get into serious arrears in their accounting to head office. Christie took a greater interest in the appointment of country officials and decisions about the establishment of new post offices and attempted to institute a system of postal inspection in 1856. He improved the salaries of country officers, and strongly supported the establishment of a public service pension scheme. However, Christie's innovations came too late to change the essential character of early post office organization.[12]

The extreme decentralization of the post office meant that appointments of local postal officials were usually left to the community the post office served, even though the postmaster-general was officially responsible for their nomination. The energetic Major Christie lamented in 1856 that he had to rely on local information because of the difficulties of travelling and the lack of an inspector to be the 'Eyes of the Department'.[13] Giving instructions on how to apply for a postal line, Christie made it clear that such an application should be accompanied by a firm recommendation as to a likely incumbent for the post office.[14] Over a decade later local recommendation was still the crucial factor in deciding who should have charge of the post office. Postmaster-general John Docker pointed out in his *Report* for 1870 that the residents of a town 'generally nominate' and their recommendation 'is for the most part adopted'...[for] 'It is impossible for the head office, at this great distance from most of the country post offices, to exercise any check upon this matter'.[15] Local residents, for their part, closely monitored the conduct of the local post office. In the

small settlement of Upper Manilla, the postmistress, Mary
Ann Nixon, was accused of selling sly grog, and dismissed
after much lively discussion of her merits. The local community were still arguing the case in 1885.[16] They were also
jealous of the privilege of choosing their own postmaster or
postmistress. In 1879 the residents of Lower Gundaroo complained about the removal of an old established resident from
the position of postmaster and the appointment of a 'comparative
stranger' who had only been in the district for a couple of
years.[17] In any event, there was considerable doubt whether
city clerks would be willing to take up positions in the country.[18]
Certainly the relatives of influential city men preferred positions in Sydney. When Sir Charles Cowper's son, Charles,
was looking for a government billet in 1869, he accepted the
police magistracy at Bourke only on condition that he be
transferred to Sydney as soon as possible. He stayed in Bourke
for less than a year before he took up a Sydney appointment.[19]

The first appointments to post offices in the larger country
towns were given to clerks of petty sessions (or clerks to the
chamber of magistrates, as they were then called) in addition to
their other duties.[20] Where there was no bench of magistrates,
other public officials, such as the pound keeper, sometimes
took on the post office.[21] These combined appointments do
not seem to have been satisfactory. Postmasters were paid by
commission, and the extra £50 that a petty sessions clerk in
Parramatta could earn on top of his £150 salary was apparently
not sufficient inducement.[22] Instead, storekeepers and innkeepers quickly became the accepted candidates for post office
duties.

The public house and the store were the central institutions
of the early town,[23] and both provided convenient locations
and suitable personnel for the post office. Prior to 1862 there
were no official post office buildings, so persons assuming
postal duties had to have ample premises in a central street.
Storekeepers and innkeepers had such premises. In addition,
their character and financial soundness were common knowledge. As for the business people involved, the post office
attracted customers to their shop or inn, so the position of
postmaster or postmistress was eagerly sought after.[24] The
Maitland post office was run by publicans for many years.
The *Union Inn* was in 1847 the only substantial building in

town. The Circuit Court was held there, and it was also the place of public worship.[25] Colin Ross, the pioneer storekeeper at Inverell, established the first post office there in 1855.[26] Thomas Dangar, member of the Legislative Assembly from 1861 to 1864, was the first innkeeper, storekeeper and post-master at Scone from 1836 to 1840.[27] George Wickham, the postmaster at Parramatta before his wife, Jemima, took over in 1844, was a chemist and grocer.[28] Arthur Price, storekeeper at Clarence River (Grafton), was the first postmaster in 1840.[29] John Humphries, storekeeper at Gunnedah (Woolshed), opened the first post office in 1856. By 1862, despite the fact that the volume of work at many post offices had grown sufficiently to provide an independent living, 274 of the 368 post offices were run by people with other sources of income. These ranged from publicans to farmers to surgeons, but were most frequently storekeepers and publicans.[30]

III

With post office appointments surrendered to the local com-munity and to central commercial institutions in country towns, the character of the local economy and its sexual division of labour determined the distribution of jobs. These questions have not been studied closely in Australia. The participation of wives and daughters of pastoralists and farmers in the family economy of the region during this period has been well documented, from accounts of small settlers like Sarah Midgley to large pastoralists such as Elizabeth Macarthur at Parramatta and Harriet King at Penrith; but the lives of small townspeople have not received the same attention.[31] We do know, how-ever, that women played an important role generally in com-merce, real estate, manufacturing and retailing in the first half of the nineteenth century. Direct evidence of women's involve-ment in the commercial life of the country town, as opposed to the city, comes from studies of publicans.[32]

Women publicans have been rescued from anonymity by the fact that they had to be licensed. In 1838, thirteen of the 244 country inns were licensed to women. These inns were clustered in the town centres of the older settlements of Parramatta, the Hawkesbury, Maitland and Bathurst. At Campbelltown, two of the seven innkeepers were women and at Bathurst three out of nine. In Parramatta, two of the inns in the main street, including the famous *Red Cow*, were run by women.

These figures reveal only the cases where a woman was the actual licensee of the inn. Even more importantly for our purposes, contemporary advertisements and accounts of local historians and travellers reveal the crucial role of the publican's wife which is hidden behind lists of male licensees and census figures. Many current licensees were widows who had probably worked in partnership with their husbands, or even run the inn themselves while he held the licence. Advertisements for the sale or lease of hotels often specified their suitability for a 'steady industrious couple', and some revealed that the business had been given up because of the ill-health or death of the licensee's wife. Testimonials were often made to 'the excellent conduct and great exertions' of a licensee's wife. At Maitland Elizabeth Muir managed the *Union Inn* from its inception in 1829, even though her husband, the chief constable at Newcastle, was the nominal licensee; after he died in 1833 she continued to run the new *Family Hotel* they had just built. The *Ross Inn* at Penrith was run by John and Susannah Perry, even though it is likely that only John's name appeared on the licence. The *Red Cow* at Parramatta was run from 1800 by the licensee Charles Walker and his wife Hannah. When he died in 1826, Hannah took over the licence and ran the hotel till her death in 1841.[33] Even when Charles Walker was alive, it was acknowledged as Hannah's business. Michael Fitzpatrick, who was born in 1818, claimed in later years that he was born 'just opposite Mother Walker's "Red Cow"'.[34]

These inns were large establishments which supplied an important social focus for the town,[35] and their proprietors were respected. In 1841 the *Red Cow* had a staff of twelve persons.[36] The traveller John Hood testified to its efficient management in 1843 when he described this 'sweet, English-looking, unpretending hostelry ...kept by Mrs Walker'. According to his account there was 'None better in England [and] none so good in Sydney'.[37]

There is little evidence about women as retailers in these large country towns, but the similarities of storekeeping and innkeeping make it feasible to assume that where women were active as hotelkeepers, they were also active as retailers.

An examination of *Brabazon's Town Directory* of 1843 supports this supposition. In Parramatta, a town of about 5000 persons, there were listed three women publicans, a draper, a grocer, a chemist, a dealer, a stationer, a template worker, a bonnet maker and a bonnet cleaner, all married women or widows.

The activities of women in the commercial life of the towns of the Settled Districts before 1856 suggest that men and women worked together as economic partners in this pioneering period just as they did on the land. An examination of the local histories of these large country towns reveals the inhabitants struggling to make a living in a variety of ventures which involved all members of the family. The busy Maitland innkeeper, Elizabeth Muir, for instance, and her police constable husband George, combined these activities with working a farm and running the post office.[38] The same sort of economic partnership is described by a Parramatta resident in a letter to relatives in England in 1820:

Myself and my husband have had many hard struggles to gain the means of an honest livelihood. To accomplish it we have worked night and day. I thank God that he crowned our endeavours with success. I rose early and went to market bringing home my articles on my head, to furnish my shop to the best advantage. With the greatest care of our little profits, and the greatest frugality in housekeeping, we collected together a small sum sufficient to buy a little house. I then applied to the Gentlemen of the Colony, for a Licence; which they not only granted, but said they would assist me and my husband in any way in their power, as they had noticed our industry and that we associated with none but persons of good character...[39]

It is probably important that these family enterprises were generally successful. In the days before the Married Women's Property Acts were passed, these family farms and businesses were ultimately controlled by the husband and father. Even after married women could own property, it was still usually in the husband's name. Marilyn Lake has shown the bitterness, cruelty and division between men and women that could be engendered in family enterprises that failed in the later period of small farming selections and soldier settlement farms in Victoria.[40] In this early period, however, country towns were prosperous and growing, and enterprising families could see the success of their co-operative efforts.

IV

It was not only as partners with their husbands that women were active in the commercial life of the country towns. The prevalence of early widowhood meant that they often played an independent role as heads of families and heads of businesses. Demographic evidence for Victoria in 1881 provides a picture of expectation of life in a society not too far removed from mid-century New South Wales. Where the wife was aged 15—19 there was a one-in-seven chance that her marriage would be ended by the death of one partner ten years later. The proportion rose to one in five for wives aged 30—34 and one in three for wives 45—49. Despite high fertility rates and a high incidence of maternal mortality, husbands were more likely to die than wives, even in women's peak reproductive years: this was the result of the occupational hazards of pioneering life, where death by accident was common.[41]

The high incidence of widowhood was not necessarily compensated for by the well-known fact of the imbalance of the sexes in early New South Wales. In 1846, women made up almost half of the population of the Settled Districts, and it was only in the pastoral districts outside the Limits of Location that seven people out of every ten were males. If the figures for Victoria in the 1880s are even a rough guide to the situation in New South Wales in the earlier period, the possibilities of re-marriage for women over thirty were very low, even though they were higher than in Britain.[42]

Literary evidence reinforces this statistical picture of a life with considerable danger for men and early widowhood for women. In one family history alone, male death and widowhood abound. In *Portrait in a Mirror*, Alexandra Hasluck describes the life of one of her great-grandfathers who lost his son and the husbands of two of his daughters. At an advanced age he was left with responsibility for the three widows and their sixteen children. Her grandmother on the other side of the family saw her husband being swept away in the floods of 1870 as she clung, pregnant with one child, and two small children in her arms, to the roof of their house.[43]

The matter-of-fact acceptance of early male death and the necessity for widows to fend for themselves is conveyed well in a vignette from Florence Nightingale's correspondence. One of the Nightingale nurses who came to New South

Wales in 1868, Bessie Chant, was found making love to a
patient by Lucy Osburn, the lady superintendent. Presumably
she later married the man in question, because Lucy Osburn
subsequently arranged with the Minister of Works to get
Bessie's husband a stationmaster's position in the railways.
But as Bessie put it herself many years later, when she was
matron of the Gladesville Hospital for the Insane, 'shortly
afterwards death intervened and I went back to my profession,
taking up Insanity'.[44]

A consequence of the high male death rate was that the
widow with dependent children was the second most common family type in 1891, when an estimated 10 per cent of
families—a total of 20 000 women and 30 000 children —were
comprised of widows with children under fifteen.[45] Without
the safety net of a social security system, many of these
women had to fend for themselves and their children. Those
who could continue in their family business were the lucky
ones.

V

Women's position as working partners in family economic
activities in the Settled Districts, and their prominence in the
commercial affairs of large country towns, blurred the boundaries between men's and women's work. The system of local
and family patronage in post office employment therefore
benefited women as well as men. As a consequence, in small
towns and hamlets throughout the countryside women such
as Mrs Pearson at Camden and Mrs Kellett at Penrith ran the
post office under the same terms and conditions as men, and
at West Maitland, Parramatta and Brisbane, the three largest
towns outside Sydney in 1856, Mrs Daly, Mrs Wickham and
Mrs Barney presided over establishments of some size and
importance.

The bare bones of these women's careers can be pieced
together from the *Blue Book* after 1858, and the brief official
post office histories tell us a little more about the earlier
period when they first began their post office employment.
However, information about most of these intriguing women
is meagre, and they cannot be fully rescued from history
without detailed local and family histories. The work of many
women is probably hidden, like that of the innkeepers, behind

their husband's official position. Martha Baxter, for instance, the wife of the first postmaster at Port Phillip, took her husband's place unofficially, as he was too busy to carry out his postal duties.[46]

Eliza Burns Daly, who ran the important West Maitland post office from 1853 to 1883, is probably typical of the early postmistresses in terms of family background and experience. Born in 1818 in London, she married Edward John Daly around 1841 in Ireland, and emigrated to Australia, probably with her parents, storekeepers James and Margaret McCarthy Burns. Edward Daly became postmaster at West Maitland in 1843, the year their first son was born. Like many of the postmistresses in this period, she probably ran the office from the beginning, as some accounts speak of her as a shopkeeper. Ten years later, in 1853, Eliza Daly officially succeeded her husband in the post office, probably on his death. She then had at least four children, aged four to ten years. With a salary of £250 a year, plus commission and rent on quarters, she was well provided for.[47]

Less information is available about Jemima Wickham, post-mistress at Parramatta from 1843 to 1870. Like Eliza Daly she was part of the shopkeeping class of this expanding country town. Her husband, George Wickham, was a grocer and chemist. He was listed as postmaster from 1838, but evidence suggests that she actually ran the office. We know nothing about Jemima Wickham's family, but as she was probably about thirty-three in 1838 it is likely that she had children to support. When George Wickham died in 1844, Jemima succeeded him, operating the post office from the eastern end of a long low weatherboard cottage on the south side of George Street, near the *Woolpack Inn*. George Wickham was receiving commissions of £98 a year when he died, and in conformity with changes being carried out at that time, Jemima moved onto a fixed salary of £80 supplemented by a smaller commission which probably brought her salary up to about £100 a year. In 1858 her salary was £160, and in 1860 it had been raised to £190.[48]

Eliza Pearson, postmistress at Camden from 1841 to 1879, was born in 1800, the daughter of William Boardman, who came to New South Wales in 1832 to work for the Macarthurs. Part of the emerging new middle class of the Settled Districts, her husband, James Pearson, became the first clerk of the bench at Camden in 1841. Eliza Pearson had assisted her husband in his previous position in Cawdor for some time, possibly because he was in poor health. On their removal to Camden she established the post office there, with James and William Macarthur acting as her guarantors. As she had a grand-daughter of twenty-one in 1878, she must have had at least one young child at that time. In taking on the work of the post office, she may have been anticipating her husband's death the following year. In any event, this office gave her at least a small income for the rest of her life. In 1858 she earned £40 a year plus commission, and by 1860 her salary was a respectable £90 a year.[49]

Like many of the other postmistresses of this period, Faith Adeline Kellett succeeded her husband, William Kellett, in the Penrith post office and its accompanying stationery shop after his death in 1860. A harness maker by trade, he had been nominally postmaster since 1849, when he was appointed at a salary of £60 a year. Faith Kellett's own evidence suggests, however, that she was the actual occupant of the position. In her late forties when her husband died, Mrs Kellett had two children. Her son, C. H. Kellett, was born in 1847 at Mulgoa, and was thirteen in 1860. Her salary of £100 a year allowed her to support her family and maintain their position as part of the developing new middle class of the country towns. C. H. Kellett became a booking clerk for Cobb and Co. at the age of sixteen, and ten years later, in 1873, he succeeded his mother at the post office as 'her great age rendered her unfit for duty'. Her daughter married Mr G. Davis, who became stationmaster at Strathfield.[50]

The most unusual of these early women officials was Elise Barney, Brisbane postmistress from 1855 to 1865. Unlike Eliza Daly, Jemima Wickham, Eliza Pearson and Faith Kellett, she was not from the petty bourgeois and lower middle class. Instead, she was the widow of an officer, and as such came from an elite background in which most women were expected to be 'ladies'. She was born at Lisbon in 1815, the daughter of Major James Rivers and his wife Mary. She married Lieutenant John Edward Barney, son of Joseph Barney, the drawing master at the Royal Military Academy and his wife, the former Jane Chandler, in 1833. A son, Edward Whiston Rivers Barney was born in 1838 and a daughter, Helena Louise, in 1843. John's brother George, a former major in the Royal Engineers who had acted as civil engineer under Governors Bourke and Gipps, was commissioned in 1847 to establish a new convict colony at Port Curtis. Elise and her family decided to join this expedition, but by the time John resigned his commission and they arrived in Australia, the colony had been abandoned. After an attempt to settle on the Darling Downs, John was appointed in 1852 as the first full-time postmaster at Brisbane, possibly due to the influence of George, who was then chief commissioner of Crown lands and a member of the Legislative Council. Major Christie, a fellow graduate of the Royal Military Academy and former colleague of George's in the Royal Engineers, had just sat on the Legislative Council Select Committee on the Post Office, and was about to take over as postmaster-general, so he may also have helped John Barney secure this appointment.

John Barney died at the end of 1855 after a long illness during which Elise helped him in his post office duties. With two children aged seventeen and twelve to support, the forty-year-old widow took the unusual step for a woman of her position of taking over her husband's office. No doubt George Barney was again influential, as he had just succeeded Sir Thomas Mitchell as surveyor-general the previous month, and he and postmaster-general Christie were fellow Legislative Councillors. With a salary of £175 and £110 in commission in 1858, as well as accommodation for her family, Elise Barney was better off than most other genteel widows who were left to fend for themselves. Her son Whiston assisted her, and in 1859 was formally appointed her clerical assistant with a salary of £91 5s. The following year, after she had become head of the postal department of the newly separated colony of Queensland, her salary was raised to £350 and Whiston became her second-class clerk, with a salary of £200.[51]

Widowhood obviously gave women access to some of the highest-paid positions in the provincial post office. But they could also be appointed in their own right, as Eliza Pearson had been at Camden. Mrs Mary Ann Rutledge, postmistress at Cassilis in 1838, the first woman appointed to a post office position, and Mrs McAlister, postmistress at Stonequarry (later Picton) in 1839, were also appointed directly.[52]

Post office appointments were not confined to married women. A number of single women, such as Anna Holmes, who was appointed postmistress at Cassilis in 1852, were also employed. Miss Holmes was so highly thought of that in 1862, when the Cassilis position was open once more, a local resident wrote to the postmaster-general recommending Miss Mary Agnes McLaren, 'a young girl...born here and extremely reputable in her conduct, who lives with her parents in the centre of the village...remembering how well the duties were performed when Miss Holmes held the office here, I think you cannot do better than give her the appointment'. This the postmaster-general did, preferring Miss McLaren over the male candidate. When she left the position, it went to her sister, Ellen, despite the application of the schoolteacher—a former postmaster—to be reappointed.[53]

The available evidence on these early postmistresses suggests that the practice of families working together in co-operative economic endeavours, combined with the exigencies of young widowhood, gave women a respected place in the commercial community, with a right to responsible, well-paid positions in the post office. This is supported by an examination of the *Blue Book* after 1862, when fuller information is available than we have for the period when these women were appointed. Sometimes wives and daughters worked alongside husbands and fathers; sometimes wives and daughters filled post and telegraph jobs while husbands and sons filled other government positions; sometimes wives or daughters took over from deceased husbands and fathers; mothers and fathers employed their children as assistants. Local residents and post office officials seem to have supported this system. When Robert Browne, postmaster at East Maitland, died in 1871, local residents petitioned successfully for his wife to be given the position. When J. S. Arnott, a later East Maitland postmaster, died in 1880, his wife Anna succeeded him in competition with the acting postmaster (who was also telegraph master), two assistant postmasters from Goulburn, the husband of Dora Browne (the former postal assistant who was the daughter of Robert and Anna Browne), and two other applicants. There was obviously a strong element of compassion in this decision, as Mrs Arnott was reported by the middle of that year to be an invalid whose duties were carried out by her son, and by the end of the year she had resigned. By that time, however, her son, William, had been appointed assistant with a salary of £100.[54] In general, the system of local and family patronage, the need for many women to support themselves and their children, and the visible and respected status of women as participants in the commercial life of the country town, seem to have combined to allow women a place in the post office. Evidence from the *Blue Book* and post office staff lists also confirms that they were treated on equal terms with men.[55]

The positions the leading postmistresses held were of considerable importance in the growing colony. The post office was the principal means of communication before the advent of the railway and the telegraph. Apart from the personal news it carried from one end of the colony to the other and to and from the world outside Australia, it was important for business and for politics. In particular, the post office carried enormous numbers of newspapers all over the colony, extending the influence of the city, and bringing knowledge of the outside world to the country areas.[56] Politicians, newspaper editors and local residents were all anxious to have a reliable and efficient postal service.[57]

The positions that the postmistresses held were much sought after. Thomas Dangar reported to the Inquiry into the Post Office in 1862 that positions in even the smallest hamlets generally had three, four or five applicants for them,[58] and the superintendent of the letter branch of the Sydney office testified in 1858 that there was no problem getting efficient staff in the larger towns such as West Maitland and Parramatta because the salaries there were 'very good'.[59]

The towns in which Eliza Daly, Jemima Wickham and Elise Barney presided over the post office were the largest in the country areas. When Mrs Wickham became postmistress at Parramatta it was already the largest town outside Sydney, with a population of 5000 in 1841. Mrs Daly took over the post office at West Maitland in 1853 when it was a town of over 3000 people. Brisbane had a population of over 2500 people when Mrs Barney became postmistress in 1855, and it had grown to 7000 by 1860. D. N. Jeans calls these towns 'halfway metropolises'; they headed the regional hierarchy with their wide range of government officials and services, cultural occupations, tradespeople and specialist shops.[60]

In keeping with the size of the towns in which they were located, these post offices were among the busiest in the colony. Witnesses at inquiries into the post office in 1858 and 1862 agreed that Mrs Daly at West Maitland had the greatest amount of business in the colony.[61] All of the leading post-mistresses of the period for whom information is available had dependent children, but their maternal responsibilities were apparently not seen as a hindrance to carrying out their postal work. This is despite the fact that they had to receive or meet the mails at all hours of the day and night.

A glimpse of the demanding nature of the work of the post office is given by Henry Handel Richardson in the fictional re-creation of her mother's life in *The Fortunes of Richard Mahony*. Although she is talking about Victoria at a later period, and through the eyes of an early twentieth-century woman, it is probably an accurate, though negative, picture of a post-mistress's work:

Had there been the day's work only to contend with, she would not have complained. It was the nights that wore her down. The nights were cruel. On every one of them without exception, between half-past one and a quarter to two, there came a knocking like thunder at the front door. This was the coach arriving with the night mail: she had to open up the office, drag a heavy mail-bag in, haul another out. Not until this was over could there be any question of sleep for her.[62]

Richardson's mother ran a small country post office. The volume of work at large offices like West Maitland and Penrith was enormous in comparison. Mrs Daly was responsible for 134 incoming mails and 128 outgoing mails a week in 1862; she had to be on duty from 6 a.m. to 10 p.m. three days a week, and from 7 a.m. other days; and her office was open from 9 a.m. to 6 p.m. on weekdays and 1 to 2 p.m. on Sundays. Mrs Kellett at Penrith had, in addition to over 150 daytime mails, thirty that were despatched during the night. She was up at 3 a.m. each day to take in the western mails. She had to be on duty again at 6.30 to receive letters from eight offices and send them on at 7.40. Her office was open from 7 a.m. to 8 p.m. and for two hours morning and evening on Sundays.[63]

The heavy workloads and responsibilities carried by the

postmistresses were fully recognized in 1862 when they were included as a matter of course among the eighteen 'official' postmasters and postmistresses nominated by postmaster-general Christie as part of his plan to upgrade the postal service. With a salary of £300, plus commission and an allowance for rent, Mrs Daly was the highest-paid of this select group. Jemima Wickham at Parramatta and Mrs Kellett at Penrith were also made official postmistresses with salaries of £280 and £200 respectively.

These official post offices were conceived as co-ordinating offices for the surrounding district, and had considerable status and responsibility. Official post office buildings with quarters attached were planned, and many of the substantial and attractive post office buildings still to be seen in New South Wales country towns testify to the standard of housing supplied with these jobs. The work of official post offices was expanded to incorporate the recently established money order office. Official postmistresses and postmasters were considered as part of a career service. They were expected to devote themselves entirely to the business of the post office, and their salaries of £200 to £300, supplemented by commission on stamps and money orders, were meant to compensate for any loss of revenue that had previously been earned in other businesses. They also had to be prepared to move to another locality if required by the department. The fact that three of these eighteen leading post office officials were women demonstrates clearly that Major Christie saw no incongruity between the roles and abilities of country women and the heavy managerial responsibilities of these positions.[64]

None of the official inquiries that investigated the post office in 1858, 1860 and 1862 questioned the fact that the leading post offices were run by women earning high salaries, and with dependent children, even though the volume of work and the salaries of these offices were discussed. Instead, Mrs Daly and Mrs Wickham were singled out for special mention as examples of 'very good' postmasters (sic).[65] Elise Barney's position in the official and commercial community of Brisbane was apparently accepted, even though she was a 'lady'. She won praise for her courtesy, efficiency and hard work, as the population of this provincial town rose sharply, country districts were settled, and her office became the centre of a rapidly expanding postal network. In 1859, when Queensland became a separate colony, she received the following testimonial from Major Christie:

Our official connection so rapidly approaches it termination, that I cannot allow it to close without expressing to you my sense of the very efficient manner in which you conducted the office immediately under your control, and your supervision of the various post offices and mail contractors in Queensland; and I have great pleasure in being able to say that duties of so onerous, and frequently of so difficult a nature, could scarcely be performed more satisfactorily. During the whole tenure of office, I cannot recollect one serious complaint having been made against you, and in postal matters this is saying a great deal. Your accounts were also regularly and correctly rendered, and, in fact, the whole business of your office was performed with zeal and ability, and evidently with a perfect knowledge of postal business.[66]

Elise Barney's acceptance by the 'hard-headed set of English and Scottish merchants and manufacturers' who made up the city's leading citizens[67] is demonstrated by the fact that, as postmistress at the new capital's General Post Office, she automatically became the head of Queensland's postal department. Early in 1860 she described her duties to a Select Committee inquiry in the following terms:

...general supervision of, and responsibility for, all the business of the Office (excepting the accounts); noting and correcting irregularities of other Post Offices; collecting reports of the due performance of the contracts; receiving and replying to all correspondence connected with the Letter Branch of the Department; attending to any complaints that do not require to be referred to the Postmaster-General [who was a minister of the government]; keeping the ship receipt and despatch book of mails, foreign and extra colonial, and the registered letters connected with the same; assisting each and all when they require it, which is very frequently.

The Committee agreed with the acting postmaster-general that 'the working of the Department is at present in every respect satisfactory' and recommended that Mrs Barney's salary be raised to £350 a year. Finding her 'over-burdened with work', the minister did so. At the same time her son, Whiston, was promoted to second-class clerk at a salary of £200.[68]

It was only when a change of regime brought to bear a new set of political and economic factors that Mrs Barney's competence to fill such a role was challenged, and she was dismissed after a long and bitter struggle.[69] In New South Wales, however, no such radical change took place, and the position of women such as Eliza Daly and Jemima Wickham remained unquestioned.

2
Equality by default: selective centralization and the struggle for control

I

It is difficult to discuss most of the New South Wales public service prior to 1856 in terms of state structures or class consciousness, and even, in the case of the post office, in terms of gender. However, a small number of officers in Sydney and outside the Settled Districts did form an increasingly self-conscious, homogeneous and structured group of decidedly masculine composition.

The leading public servants in the co-ordinating departments and head offices in Sydney had always been a powerful group, united by their common British upper class origins and a high degree of interaction and intermarriage within the confines of New South Wales 'society'. These were men of substantial Tory and Anglican background who earned, during Darling's administration, from £1200 to £2000 a year, and were intricately related. Governor Darling and his principal officers, private secretary Henry Dumaresq, colonial secretary Alexander McLeay, and McLeay's assistant, Thomas Harington, were all related by marriage. McLeay's successor, Edward Deas Thomson, was Governor Bourke's son-in-law, and was related through his daughter's marriage to the McLeays, Haringtons and Dumaresqs.[1]

The extraordinary policing requirements brought about by the occupation of the vast lands outside the Settled Districts and later by the goldrushes, allowed these influential officials to extend their reach more effectively into the interior. In 1839, land commissioners were appointed to be 'the eyes and ears of the government at Sydney on practically every aspect of life' in the far-flung districts outside the Limits of Location; and in the early 1850s gold commissioners were appointed on the same model. Earning salaries of £365 to £500 a year in 1839, these men, such as Christopher Rolleston, George Barney and William Mayne, had the same British background and were drawn from the same class as the leading officials.[2]

Attempts to centralize authority in the Settled Districts proved less successful, however. The appointment of varying small numbers of stipendiary magistrates did extend the influence of the Sydney officials somewhat. Edmund Lockyer, for instance, supplemented his unsuccessful land ventures with appointments as police magistrate at Parramatta in 1827 and 1829. Helenus Scott became a stipendiary magistrate in Newcastle in 1853 after the depression of the 1840s and the Bank of Australia failure left him almost penniless. But many of these well-born stipendiary magistrates clustered in Sydney. Scott's brother, David, who was married to Maria Barney, was a police magistrate from 1849, and in 1860 became police magistrate for Sydney. Major Christie, the son of the medical inspector-general of Ceylon, and later postmaster-general, was appointed assistant police magistrate in Sydney in 1840, when failing health forced him to leave the army. When William Manning joined his father John Edye, registrar of the Supreme Court, in 1837 he was immediately appointed magistrate and chairman of the Quarter Sessions at a salary of £800. Charles Windeyer joined his friend Judge James Dowling in 1828, and quickly rose from chief clerk to the Bench of Magistrates to become senior police magistrate in Sydney in 1839.[3]

In the late 1840s and early 1850s the experience of the land commissioners was drawn on in attempts to reorganize the police, the post office, the Surveyor-General's Department and charitable institutions. Despite these strenuous attempts to impose unity and control on the scattered public service, little progress had been made, however, by 1856.[4]

A more important sense of unity came from a newly emerging group in the tiny colony—the new middle class. The emergence of this class has been charted by Michael Roe and George Nadel in their discussions of what Roe called 'the movement for culture' which was, for him, 'the counterpoint of the period' to 'sheep and acres'.[5] We know little about the women of this class except for the rural postmistresses emerging out of the petty bourgeoisie, and scattered references to teachers such as Michael Fitzpatrick's mother, who had a school at Parramatta, and newspaper proprietor Anne Howe. The artist Adelaide Ironside stands out as one woman who was an integral part of the emerging native intelligentsia, but information about her is meagre.[6] The class identity of this group seemed to develop definitively, however, among the male journalists, teachers, lawyers and clerks who gathered in Sydney from the late 1820s to develop a national literature and a local press, and to campaign for public libraries, mechanics' institutes and state secular education.

Unlike the educated gentleman, the public official sent out from London, or even the rural clerk under the patronage of the local gentry, the men of the urban new middle class could not fall back on wealth or social connections. Instead, they had to depend entirely on their literacy and social skills to make a living. Prior to the 1830s, there was a small group of educated men in the colony without wealth or influential connections, who supported themselves by teaching, journalism or clerical work. Many, such as journalist and teacher Laurence Halloran, journalists George Howe and Edward O'Shaughnessy, teachers Henry Fulton and Charles Harpur, and superintendent of convicts and postmaster Isaac Nichols, were convicts or ex-convicts. But free teachers, such as W. T. Cape and J. D. Lang, and journalists, such as Alfred Ward Stephens, began to arrive in the 1820s. The numbers of men seeking to earn a living by their educated skills increased in the 1830s as access to the land diminished with the cessation of land grants and increases in the price of land. The depression of the 1840s brought other educated men to Sydney in a 'push from the bush' when farming ventures failed. They were joined by assisted immigrants of the 1830s and 1840s who, like Henry Parkes, spurned the harsh, lonely and poverty-stricken existence of the rural wage-labourer. To these were added teachers such as W. A. Duncan and Henry Carmichael, whose expectations of major education developments were not fulfilled until mid-century, journalists such as Richard Jones, who arrived as a bounty immigrant in 1838, and young native-born professionals, such as convict's son George Nichols, and groom's son James Martin.[7]

From the early 1840s these teachers, journalists, lawyers and

clerks were an important part of the small radical and literary
circle of Sydney, where they joined the more vocal artisans and
labourers to demand responsible government, the opening up
of squatters' land to small settlers, and the extension of government schools, services and works. Despite internecine battles,
they were a close-knit group. Future politicians James Martin,
John Robertson, Geoffrey Eagar and William Forster had been
at school together. James Martin did his law articles with
George Nichols. Public servant Michael Fitzpatrick studied
with Henry Carmichael at J. D. Lang's Australian College,
and joined him in his new teachers training college in 1835. At
the Australian College, he also knew the gifted artist Samuel
Elyard, one of several brothers who made their mark in the
public service. Martin, Eagar, Forster and Parkes—all budding
politicians—and poets and public servants Charles Harpur,
Henry Halloran and Charles Tompson, wrote for Howe's
Sydney Gazette, Richard Jones' *Maitland Mercury*, J. D. Lang's
Colonist and *Colonial Observer*, Lowe's *Atlas*, Nichols' *Australian*,
W. A. Duncan's *Australasian Chronicle* and *Weekly Register* and
the Anglican *Church Sentinel*, criticizing each other's work and
corresponding extensively. This was a different world from
that of the upper class, British officials, and these men married
within it. James Martin married Isabella Long, the daughter of
a wealthy ex-convict. Her sister married William Dalley, the
brilliant young journalist and lawyer, born of convict parents,
who burst on the political scene in the 1850s. Howe's widow
and proprietor of the *Sydney Gazette* married ticket-of-leave
convict journalist William Watt. Henry Halloran married
Elizabeth Underwood, the daughter of wealthy merchant
Joseph Underwood and niece of ex-convict James Underwood.
W. T. Cape married the daughter of public servant James
Jacques.[8]

It was from these men that the lower ranks of the public
service were filled. The gentlemen who filled the top ranks,
and their superiors and patrons in Britain, would have preferred young men from their own class, but this proved
difficult. Most young gentlemen with ability did not find the
convict settlement attractive; and where they did, they preferred to go onto the land, especially before 1831, when land
grants and good land were available. The administration
quickly lost young men such as Robert Crawford, who came

to the colony with Governor Brisbane in 1821, and James Atkinson, who came out as a free immigrant. Atkinson, chief clerk in the Colonial Secretary's Office from 1820, resigned in 1822 to take up his land grant. His successor Crawford had, by 1825, received a grant of land and was employing forty convicts and running 800 cattle, 600 sheep and eighteen horses on his 2000 acres. By 1826 he had resigned because Darling refused to raise his salary as chief clerk over £365. Instead they had to make do with officers of dubious character, such as John Edye Manning, who was appointed registrar of the Supreme Court in 1828 at a salary of £800, and John Mackaness, who was made sheriff in 1824 at a salary of £1000. Previously insolvent in England, Manning got into financial difficulties in New South Wales, and was suspended in 1842. Mackaness also had financial problems and had, according to Darling, 'as little pretension to the character of a Gentleman of which he boasts, as he has to that of an honest man'. Even worse, they often had to use as clerks educated convicts, such as Charles Nye and Matthew Gregson, who worked in the Colonial Secretary's Office from the 1820s, and Fitzpatrick's father, who became chief bailiff of the Supreme Court.[9]

In despair at having to rely on what was considered un-promising material, Governor Darling attempted to attract well-bred young men of ability by improving the status, stability and predictability of public service employment. In 1826 and 1827 he introduced more generous salary ranges beginning at £150 and going beyond £300, classification by position, promotion by merit, and automatic salary increments. These early measures in the establishment of a career service were supplemented by Governor Bourke in 1838 by a test examination for entrance to the clerical ranks, a board to examine candidates' qualifications for professional appoint-ment in the Surveyor-General's Department, and age limits for appointment. In addition, departmental heads were given greater disciplinary powers through their control of probation and salary increments, Together, the regulations of Darling and Bourke provided checks on outside influence, some pro-tection from arbitrary personnel decisions and uniformity across departments which increased promotion opportunities.

Accompanying this professionalization of the public service was an attempt to mark it off as a special group. Officers were forbidden to engage in private business or to take fees, gratuities or awards, and, in an attempt to inculcate a sense of unity and pride in the service, Darling suggested that 'Officers and Civil Servants' should wear a uniform—'a Blue Coat, lined with white or buff coloured silk' with a button with a crown for heads and deputies of departments, and an unlined coat with no crown on the button for assistants, writers and clerks.[10]

Darling's and Bourke's reforms did not attract many young gentlemen to the service; Darling's lined blue coat with its crowned buttons and £300 a year could not compete with the comfort and status reflected in the mansion James Atkinson was able to build on his land at Berrima.[11] But they did provide enhanced opportunities for the men of the new middle class. Henry Parkes worked in the Customs Department from 1840 to 1845 after his flight from the bush. W. A. Duncan became collector of customs in Moreton Bay when his *Weekly Register* failed in 1846. Henry Halloran, Laurence's son, and the colony's leading poet in the 1840s, joined the Survey Department in 1827. Charles Tompson, who published the first book of poems by a native-born Australian in 1826, worked intermittently in the Colonial Secretary's Office and as clerk to the Legislative Council and the Legislative Assembly from 1829 to 1869. Charles Harpur worked briefly as a teacher for the new National Board of Education and in the post office. Henry Carmichael was a government surveyor for a time, and artist Samuel Elyard worked in the Colonial Secretary's Office from 1837 to 1868.[12]

From 1842 the British authorities bowed to the inevitable, and local male recruitment to clerical positions below £300 a year was actively encouraged.[13] This system of local recruitment from a small radical community, and protection from the worst excesses of favouritism by the reforms of Darling and Bourke, gave unity and independence to Sydney public servants. By the early 1850s the 246 government clerks in Sydney had sufficient solidarity to make collective demands for improved salaries and a public service pension scheme.[14]

Despite the slow progress towards centralization, and the persistence of class divisions between leading officials and the rest of the service, there was by 1856 a clear movement towards a unified and regulated public service. Departmental heads had considerable power over head office personnel within

guidelines which gave rank-and-file public servants some protection from arbitrary decisions. The growing identity of
interests of officials at all levels is demonstrated by the role of
men such as Major Christie, Colonel Barney and Captain
Mayne in attempts to centralize and reform the post office,
land survey and occupation, and the police, and their support
of public service professionalization.[15] It is demonstrated further
by the integration of such models of new middle class entre-
preneurship as William Wilkins, who was recruited with his
wife at a joint salary of £300 to train teachers for the new
national system of education. The son of an English poor law
official, Wilkins attended a school for pauper children and
then trained as one of the first pupil-teachers at the progressive
Battersea College. He arrived in Australia in 1851 alone. His
wife, who had been recruited to train female teachers, died on
the voyage out, leaving us to wonder if the subsequent treatment of women teachers would have been different if she had
lived. At the age of twenty-four, Wilkins set about single-
mindedly to centralize, regulate and unify the education system,
and in the process to raise the status of the teaching profession
and its leading officials and to extend employment opportunities
for teachers. By 1856 he had gained a Legislative Council
Select Committee's support for these goals, extended the pupil-
teacher system into the country areas, opened a training school,
standardized the curriculum and professional qualifications,
and extended the inspectorate.[16] Although the education system
remained divided and heterogeneous, Wilkins' reforms began
a process by which identity of interest developed among scattered teachers throughout the colony and between town and
country. In 1856, however, what unity there was in the public
service emerged amongst city clerks.

The autonomy and power of the service by 1856 was
strengthened by the visibility and influence of leading public
servants under the system of representative government
introduced in 1842. In the Legislative Council of thirty-six
members, twenty-four were elected and twelve nominated,
six of these from among government officials. The Council
was a powerful body. The Governor had to approve legislation
and the imperial government could disallow it. But the Council
could originate and had to approve legislation dealing with
local issues. The six nominated officials had key positions in

this important body, making up the Executive Council, and
thus forming an unofficial cabinet.[17] With their dual legislative
and executive status the officials held positions closer to that
of politician than public servant. The expectations of future
departmental heads about their role were strongly coloured by
the experience of these powerful public servants.

This influential and increasingly unified group were almost
entirely male. Recruitment practices in Sydney were, from the
beginning, controlled by the upper class of officials and military officers, and were established at a time when the urban
bourgeoisie was insisting on a strict division of labour between
men and women, and on 'ladylike' behaviour which did not
include working for profit. As Elizabeth Windschuttle has
shown, Sydney had a formidable group of elite women intent
on moulding the morals and manners of society from early in
the nineteenth century. Their efforts can be most clearly seen
in their philanthropic work directed at guiding working class
women into disciplined and protected domestic pursuits, and
away from the dangers of sexual and economic independence.[18]

Leading government officials and their wives and daughters
led this philanthropic movement. Joined by the clergy, the
military and some merchants and graziers, these families determined the limits of 'good society'. In the small, tightly knit
society of Sydney, there was little room for deviation among
elite women from the role of 'lady', especially when many of
the 'ladies' and 'gentlemen' had a tenuous foothold in polite
society. There was no thought, therefore, of elite women
working for a living or encouraging employment opportunities
for less fortunate women outside domestic service or the
woman's sphere.

These attitudes were embedded in urban public service
employment practices. Although there were 'distressed gentle-
women', impoverished widows and ruined family fortunes
in the city as much as the country, educated women were not
even considered as possible solutions to public service recruitment problems. Clerical work in Sydney head offices developed,
therefore, as a male preserve.

There were ambiguities, however, in this insistence on
women's proper place. Colonel Barney was apparently able to
tolerate, and perhaps even encourage, the employment of his
sister-in-law in the prominent position of postmistress in pro-

vincial Moreton Bay. Major Christie was also quite ready to employ such women and to treat them equitably. Women had always been employed as managers of charitable institutions, and the upper class men and women who supported these organizations increasingly agreed that institutions dealing with women and children were best run by women.[19] The recruitment of William Wilkins and his wife to train male and female teachers respectively shows that the Sydney elite were willing to employ professional women as long as they stayed within this definition of women's sphere. Again, all the initial appointments to the pupil-teacher ranks in the early 1850s were women from artisan, farming and lower middle class backgrounds.[20] The limits of women's sphere in 1856 were obviously negotiable, even in the anxious upwardly mobile society of Sydney.

II

The new system of responsible government radically changed the role and organization of the public service, effectively putting an end to further development of a unified, professional career service. Excluded from the legislature, public officials were also subjected to closer and more effective formal control, as responsibility for executive action passed from the divided authority of the Governor and the imperial authorities to individual ministers drawn from the ranks of elected politicians. At the same time, control of the public service was fragmented among ministers, as whatever unity the Governor's administration had imposed was destroyed, modified only by the workings of cabinet.[21]

The loss of autonomy and unity brought about by these formal changes was exacerbated by political, economic and social conditions in the first thirty years of responsible government. Control of the public service was central to political life during this period. A strong consensus supported a policy of free trade and development involving government provision of railways, roads, public buildings and services funded by revenue from the sale of Crown lands. With few strong differences of principle, belief or interest around which to organize stable political parties, politicians had to rely on personal loyalty, and on their success in bargaining for public works, services and jobs, to secure electoral and parliamentary support.[22]

In the system of factional alignments which resulted, public departments became potential political resources through which ministers could win votes and position, and ministers' success depended, to a large extent, on their effective control of departmental policy and personnel.

One of the first requirements for political control of the public service was the appointment to leading positions of persons likely to be co-operative or who had interests in common with those in political power. The politicians who rose to power by 1860 were upwardly mobile men from new middle class or working class backgrounds who emerged from the radical and literary circles of the 1840s. As founder of the *Empire*, Henry Parkes was the central figure of this group. The son of a failed English tenant farmer and day labourer, and an ivory turner by trade, he worked in the Customs Department and ran a small shop before throwing himself into journalism and politics. James Martin was a successful young lawyer and journalist of working class background. William Forster, who wrote for the *Empire* and the *Church Sentinel*, was, along with James Robertson and Charles Cowper, a prosperous landowner, but Forster's father had been an army surgeon, and James Robertson's a watchmaker; only Cowper's father, the assistant colonial chaplain, could claim membership of the old elite. Robertson, though not an intellectual himself, was a friend and neighbour of Charles Harpur, the poet whom he appointed gold commissioner in 1859 on becoming minister for Lands and Public Works.[23]

Many of the upper class public service leaders retired or went into the legislature after self-government was instituted in 1856, leaving the field free for the appointment of officials chosen by the new political masters for compatibility of outlook and principle.[24] The practice of local recruitment to subsidiary positions in the public service over many years had created a pool of career officers who came from the same literary and political world as the new politicians. Like the politicians, many started their careers as impecunious, though educated, immigrants or were the sons of educated ex-convicts and minor officials.

Typical of the new public service head was Henry Halloran. The son of educated convict Laurence Halloran, he was a close literary and political associate of the great master of the faction system, Henry Parkes. Laurence Halloran had been transported to New South Wales in 1819. He set up the Sydney Grammar School, supported by wealthy emancipists, and was joined by Henry and his mother in 1822. By 1827 Laurence's various educational and journalistic schemes had collapsed, and Henry joined the Survey Department as a clerk. By 1856 he was chief clerk. In the major reorganization of the crucial areas of lands and public works in 1859 he helped Robertson reorganize the Survey Department and the Crown Lands Office. He became 'the Secretary's secretary' in 1866 when Parkes, on forming his first ministry, appointed his old friend principal under-secretary. When the poet Henry Kendall joined them soon after, *Punch* printed verses satirizing the three government poets. Kendall provides a delightful glimpse of the combined literary and public service world in a letter to Harpur, where he describes Halloran calling him into his office each morning to treat him to 'an emphatic recital of his latest'. Halloran remained principal under-secretary until 1878.[25]

Another convict's son was Michael Fitzpatrick, who was appointed to the important new position of under-secretary for Lands and Public Works in 1856. He was born five years after his father (who later became chief bailiff of the Supreme Court) was transported to New South Wales. Educated first by his schoolteacher mother, and then at J. D. Lang's Australian College, he joined progressive educationalist Henry Carmichael at his new teachers training college in 1835. When the education reforms envisaged by Governor Bourke did not eventuate, the school failed, and Fitzpatrick joined the Lands Office in 1837. In 1851 he became clerk of the Executive Council and helped devise the administrative arrangements when responsible government was introduced. When Lands and Public Works divided in 1859, he retained the key position of under-secretary of Lands. Like Halloran, Fitzpatrick had close relations with the new politicians, and in 1869 he moved into politics proper. From 1869 to 1870 he supported the Cowper—Robertson faction in the Legislative Assembly, and from 1872 to 1877 he supported Parkes. He was colonial secretary in the Farnell ministry from 1877 to 1878 and was leader of the opposition against the Parkes—Robertson government until his death in 1881.[26]

A third convict's son was Geoffrey Eagar. Eagar's mother

was deserted by her prominent ex-convict husband when he was a child. She supported her children by running a business which collapsed in the early 1830s, when Eagar started work as a young teenager. He worked his way up in the mercantile world as a clerk and accountant. In 1854 he gained an important position in the emancipists' Bank of New South Wales. Like Halloran, he was active in the literary world, writing for liberal papers in the mid-1830s and editing the radical church paper, the *Church Sentinel*, in 1859. Like Fitzpatrick, his career demonstrated the close relationship between politics and public service in this period. In 1859 he was appointed to the Legislative Council, and became briefly minister for Public Works in the ministry of his old school friend Forster. He entered the Legislative Assembly in 1863 and had a stormy career as treasurer in Martin's ministry from 1863 to 1865 and the Martin—Parkes ministry from 1866 to 1868, during which he tried to fashion a viable economic base for the colony's development policies. He retired from politics in 1868 after a major confrontation with the head of the Customs Department, W. A. Duncan. He began a long career in the public service in 1871 when Martin, again premier, appointed him to the Treasury, and the following year made him under-secretary. He was head of that important department during the boom period of the 1870s and 1880s, and presided over its decline until he died in 1891.[27]

Most other public servants appointed to leading positions in this period were the sons of lesser officials and half-pay officers. William Elyard, the son of one of the numerous half-pay naval and military officers who came to Australia after the Napoleonic wars, was welcomed by the Colonial Secretary's Department when he arrived in 1821. Because he was a free settler of acceptable social background, he was preferred above convict clerks such as Charles Nye. He became chief clerk in 1841 when Harington resigned, and succeeded Edward Deas Thomson as the first principal under-secretary in 1856. His artist brother Samuel, who had attended the Australian College with Fitzpatrick, was in same department from 1837 to 1868, and his brothers Arthur and Alfred also had public service careers.[28]

The Moriarty brothers, Abram and Edward, were sons of Merion Moriarty, portmaster and harbourmaster from 1843 to 1857. Abram joined the Colonial Secretary's Department in 1846. In a long and chequered career which ended in 1896, he replaced George Barney as chief commissioner of Crown lands in 1860, assisted Robertson to draft his land legislation and briefly followed Fitzpatrick as under-secretary of Lands in 1869. Edward went into the Survey Department in 1849 and became engineer-in-chief for harbours and rivers in 1858, a position he held until 1888.[29]

Alexander McLean (*sic*) and Harold Maclean were the sons of Captain John Maclean, superintendent of convicts from 1837 to 1855. Alexander joined the Survey Department in 1842, and was chief draftsman in 1856. When Robertson and Halloran reorganized the department in 1859, Mclean served briefly as surveyor-general until his premature death in 1862. Harold joined the Colonial Secretary's Department in 1844. After a period as senior gold commissioner, he became sheriff in 1864 and comptroller of prisons from 1874 to 1889.[30]

These sons of former convicts, minor officials and half-pay officers helped their politician friends to fashion and administer the economic and developmental policies of the faction period. They gained accelerated promotion in key departments after 1856, while a number of ex-army officers who had had influential connections with the old regime were quickly replaced by career public servants and friends of the new politicians. In the 1859 review of land administration, the veteran surveyor-general and commissioner for Crown lands, Colonel Barney, was replaced by the thirty-five-year-old Alexander McLean. Major Christie, a founder and secretary of the conservative Australian Club, was not allowed to remain in his position as postmaster-general, despite his apparent efficiency, once it was perceived as politically useful. Captain Mayne, the former inspector-general of police and land commissioner who had been auditor-general since 1856, was summarily removed in 1864 when perceived to be obstructive to treasurer Eagar's financial reforms. He was replaced by Christopher Rolleston, the registrar-general and former commissioner for Crown lands. A major pastoralist and company director married to one of the wealthy Leslies, Rolleston was the only highly connected public servant of the period who managed to survive and thrive under the change of political regime.[31]

The final victim of the new political masters was Colonel

Gibbes, the collector of customs. Gibbes, reputedly the son of
the Duke of York, the second son of George III, lived in style
at Admiralty House in Sydney and on his retirement moved
to Yarralumla on the site of present-day Canberra—both
houses now vice-regal residences.[32] Following two critical
reports on his department, the Cowper—Robertson government retired the ageing Gibbes in 1859 and replaced him with
W. A. Duncan, Henry Parkes' friend, who was sub-collector
of customs in Moreton Bay. The position had previously been
offered to Parkes himself, then suffering bankruptcy and
exclusion from the Legislative Assembly after the failure of
the *Empire*. Parkes, however, wanted to re-enter politics, and
the position went to Duncan.

The replacement of Gibbes by one of these two former
radical allies epitomizes the changes that took place in the
public service after self-government. Gibbes had been Parkes'
remote head when he worked in the Customs Department in
his first steady job after his arrival in Australia as a penniless
immigrant in 1839. While engaged on this work, Parkes wrote
the poetry that brought him to the attention of Duncan, then
the radical editor of the *Australasian Chronicle*. Parkes' friendship with Duncan launched him into the small literary and
political world of Sydney and into his long and successful
political career. Duncan , meanwhile, became a public servant
when his *Weekly Register* folded in 1846, and he accepted the
appointment in Moreton Bay which took him out of the
mainstream of New South Wales politics.[33]

One last area where conservative influence had to be removed was from government boards. The Cowper ministry
removed the chairman of the National Schools Board, former
attorney-general Hubert Plunkett, after a noisy confrontation
which seemed to be deliberately provocative on both sides.
One of the men who was to replace Plunkett on the Board
was W. A. Duncan, the new collector of customs, who had
been campaigning, like other members of the emerging new
middle class, for a unified system of national schools since the
early 1840s.[34]

While the new political regime reorganized the top of the
public service to make its personnel more compatible with its
own interests and intentions, it also gathered around it a
number of technical experts from the exclusively masculine

engineering profession. These men were central to the development projects that helped politicians win favour with the
public and hold political factions together—building railways,
roads and telegraphs, and clearing the harbours and rivers.
Edward Moriarty became engineer-in-chief for harbours and
rivers in 1858 after early experience in the Survey Department,
but the other prominent experts were British-trained. They
came as young men to the top positions in expanding departments, and remained there for thirty years or more. William
Bennett, commissioner for main roads from 1862 to 1889,
was recruited by Sir Thomas Mitchell while visiting Sydney
in 1855. Edward Cracknell, superintendent of telegraphs from
1861 to 1893, was one of the young adventurers who came to
Australia with Charles Todd to build the South Australian
telegraphs in 1855. He moved to New South Wales to supervise
the first telegraphs in 1858, and died in office in 1893. John
Whitton was recruited directly from England to the position
of engineer-in-chief of the railways in 1856, and remained in
that position until 1889. The professional interests of these
men usually coincided with those of successive governments
intent on development, except in times of financial crisis,
when friction sometimes occurred. In general, however, they
remained supreme in their departments and retained close
control of their staff.[35]

From 1856, therefore, the new political leaders consolidated
their control over the top echelon of the public service. They
replaced supporters of the old regime with their own men. At
the same time, they imported a number of professional experts
whose interests coincided with their own. These moves were
resisted by the men who were being replaced and by their
patrons, but by the mid-1860s the top of the public service
was effectively transformed.

Paralleling these changes to the top echelons of the public
service in the decade from 1856 was an attempt to centralize
and politicize control of departmental policy and personnel.
Centralization helped ministers gain greater control over policy
decisions such as the disposal of land, the route of a railway,
or the placement of a bridge, a school or a post office. At the
same time it enabled ministers to eliminate departmental, family
and local patronage, placing more jobs at the disposal of the
minister. Through the elimination of independent boards and

commissions and the establishment of hierarchical organizations and systems of inspection, ministers were able to gather control into their own hands.

Expecting that the provision of railways and public works from the sale of Crown lands would be the centrepiece of a political system based on closer land settlement, free trade and development, the new politicians quickly brought the key functions of land, railways and public works under firm ministerial control. This was relatively simple, as a satisfactory system of local government had never been established in New South Wales, and railways were in an embryonic stage. The fledgling Roads, Railways and Telegraphs Commission was brought under closer government control by the Railways Act of 1858 and by the establishment of a Public Works Department, to include the railways, the following year, with central new middle class figure, Geoffrey Eagar, as minister. Captain Ben Martindale, the military engineer recruited from England just prior to responsible government to run the Commission, fought for freedom from political interference, but as under-secretary for public works and commissioner for railways he found himself fully responsible to the minister. He soon resigned in protest, making way for the appointment of career public servant and former town clerk, John Rae, his former secretary and railways accountant. A member of Sydney's artistic community, whom Harpur called rather disparagingly 'the sun or centre of. . . a set of small Scotch wits', Rae fitted well into the reconstructed public service elite.[36]

Despite the land reforms of 1861 and a complete revamping of lands administration by minister Robertson and key officials Henry Halloran, Michael Fitzpatrick, Abram Moriarty and Alexander McLean, revenue from Crown land sales was disappointingly small. Successive governments, guided by Eagar as treasurer, tried to impose unpopular measures such as stamp duty and increased customs duty, and resorted to the unfamiliar expedient of overseas loans in order to continue railway trunk lines and other public works. Without reliable revenue for these developmental projects, it was difficult to forge strong parliamentary alliances and to secure electoral support. Consequently a series of financial crises from 1863 to 1871 contributed to the rapid demise of five faction ministries and to the instability of faction alliances.[37]

During this period of financial uncertainty and political instability, governments turned to a variety of administrative expedients to maintain political support. With railway development barely started, the post office remained an important means of communication, and the provision of reliable postal services was an important vote catcher. Christie's plans for post office reform and regulation were, therefore, briefly supported. The official post offices were instituted and the system of inspection which he had attempted to establish in the 1850s was extended. The post office became a political plum, and when Christie resisted political control of appointments and promotions, a Board of Inquiry recommended in 1862 that his position be removed from the public service and filled by a government minister. Christie retired, under some pressure, in 1865 when the Cowper–Robertson government offered the position to Henry Parkes, who was suffering one of his many political and financial reverses. Parkes never took up the position, but from that time it was held by a minister.[38]

The need to find supplementary sources of finance also gave the Customs Department temporary prominence in this period. Despite W. A. Duncan's membership of the new inner circle of public servants and politicians, he found himself in conflict with his minister, Geoffrey Eagar, over control of policy during the taxation controversies of the 1860s. The enraged minister dismissed his public service head for insubordination, and it was only Duncan's closeness to Parkes, who was then colonial secretary, that enabled him to be reinstated.[39]

Politicians looking for alternative sources of electoral appeal during this period of political and financial confusion also turned to education, improved law and order and a more ordered system of charity. Moves were made to centralize the education system, the police force, the gaols, the magistracy and charitable institutions and bring them under greater political control.[40] The plans of the ambitious and energetic William Wilkins for greater centralization, standardization and professionalization of the education system therefore gained brief support. In 1866 the Parkes–Martin government replaced the two school boards with an appointed Council of Education dominated by politicians. The Council reduced the power of local boards, discouraged denominational schools, established a more comprehensive inspection system, took over the appointment and removal of teachers and the establishment of their salaries and conditions, and imposed a uniform curriculum across the whole school system.[41]

The result of the financial problems of the 1860s was that a wide variety of government functions were centralized and brought under closer political control. Interest in such comprehensive control waned, however, in the 1870s, as revenue from Crown lands began to flow generously. In 1872, when Henry Parkes formed his first non-coalition ministry, he resolved the economic stalemate by vastly increasing the amount of land put up for auction. In 1873, 277 000 acres were sold by auction, compared with 62 000 in 1872. By 1877 six times the 1873 acreage was sold in this way. Revenue from land sales jumped from £436 000 in 1872 to £2.8m in 1877 (see Figure 1). Land sales fell from 1877 to 1879, but revenue picked up again in 1880 when the Parkes–Robertson government allowed large amounts of expensive town and suburban land to be offered at auction for the first time.

During the period of almost continually expanding revenue from public lands from 1872 to 1882, taxation was reduced and government expenditure more than trebled, reaching £10m in 1882 (see Figures 1 and 2). Railways and public works expanded enormously (see Figure 3), providing considerable opportunity for the exercise of patronage.[42] As one parliamentary critic of the system put it succinctly: 'The Minister for Works says, "I shall want £50 000", and the Minister for Lands says, "Here are 50 000 acres"'.[43] T. A. Coghlan, writing in 1918 from the perspective of the cautious public service expert, described the period as one of unbridled log-rolling:

The first years of the operation of the vigorous policy of public works were marked with considerable caution in the choice of works to be carried out, and the Parliaments carefully scrutinized proposals for the expenditure of public money; but presently all caution was thrown to the winds, and Victoria, New South Wales, and Queensland, having money to spend, authorized the construction of many works, the expenditure on which was indefensible from the point of view either of present requirements or of future utility. There was in fact a scramble amongst the parliamentary representatives of country constituencies for as much local expenditure as they could procure for their individual districts. In New South Wales, railways of an expensive character were constructed entirely without regard to any consideration other than satisfying the clamour of the parliamentary representatives of the districts served; while smaller works, like roads, wharves, bridges, and buildings, were also constructed with no more legitimate object.[44]

With railways and public works providing an important element holding factions together, governments could afford to let their control over other activities slacken. Little attention was paid to political control of the post office after the mid-1860s. The district system failed to eventuate, inspection was reduced, and the post office became an unimportant backwater which preserved the recruitment practices and organization of earlier periods. There was little follow-up in the 1870s to the movement towards greater political control of the police and charitable institutions, and it was not until 1880 that the education system was placed under the control of its own minister.

The first thirty years of responsible government were characterized, therefore, by uneven development of the public service, with some departments placed under close political control and others almost untouched by these trends. This process of selective centralization was accompanied by the establishment of a fluid personnel system which allowed

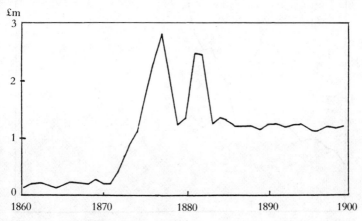

Source: P.N. Lamb, The Financing of Government Expenditure in New South Wales, PhD dissertation, ANU, 1963, pp. 358–9

Figure 1   Receipts from Crown land sales 1860–1900

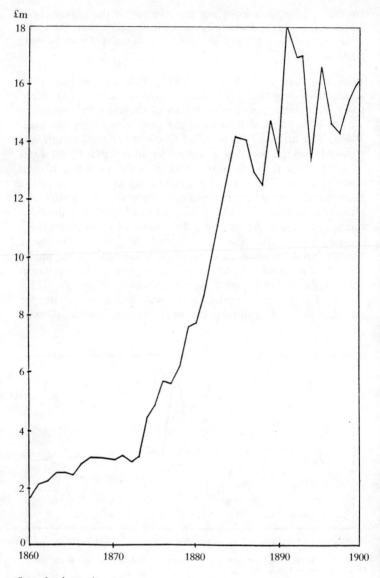

Source: Lamb, op. cit.

Figure 2   Estimated total net expenditure, New South Wales 1860–1900

£m

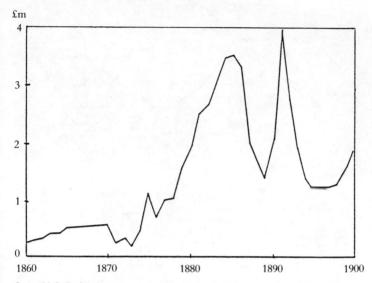

Source: N.G. Butlin, *Investment in Australian Economic Development, 1881–1900*, ANU Press, Canberra, 1964, p. 348

Figure 3   Gross capital formation, railways, 1860–1900

political intervention in appointment, promotion and disciplinary procedures where it was politically useful.

Prior to responsible government, the patronage system had been modified to give departmental heads some control over the quality and discipline of their staff and provide rank-and-file public servants with some protection from the effects of favouritism. The application of these restraints on the excesses of patronage was generally abandoned in 1856.[45] The burden of ministerial interference in personnel matters fell selectively, however, on departments that were politically sensitive or had many relatively unskilled jobs which could be given to political supporters. The Post Office Department in the early 1860s, the Customs Department, and the traffic branch of the Railways Department seemed to bear the brunt of political patronage in jobs, while politically unimportant departments such as the post office after the 1860s, and those requiring educated or professional personnel, such as Whitton's engineering branch in the railways, were left relatively undisturbed.[46]

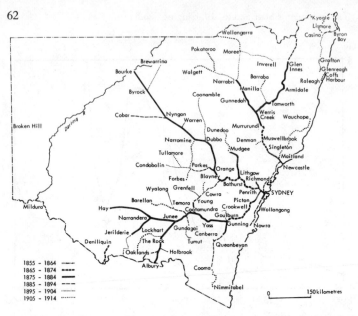

Source: Garry Wotherspoon, 'The "Sydney Interest" and the Rail 1860–1900', in Max Kelly (ed.), *Nineteenth Century Sydney: Essays in Urban History*, Sydney University Press, 1978, p. 13.

Railway construction in New South Wales 1855–1914. The spectacular development of the railways between 1875 and 1885 provided jobs and improved communications

Throughout this period of selective political control, therefore, the public service was highly fragmented, with enormous diversity in departmental organization and personnel practices.

III

Political control of departmental policy and personnel quickly shattered the small degree of public service unity that existed in 1856. Apart from perpetuating a bewildering variety of organizations and personnel systems, political hegemony also divided the interests of the rank and file of the service and leading public servants.

Political control of the public service left all government employees vulnerable to arbitrary recruitment, promotion and dismissal decisions. Although it fell most heavily on the rank and file, it also posed considerable problems for departmental heads. Subject themselves to appointment and removal by their minister, their vulnerability was intensified by lack of control over the quality and discipline of their staff. The potential for conflict inherent in this situation was muted, however, by the political and social closeness of public service leaders and their ministers, the lack of uniformity in the practice of patronage, and the mutual interest of ministers and public servants in the centralization of control that usually accompanied ministerial control of patronage.

If open conflict did flare up, it was in the more vulnerable departments. Major Christie at the post office and W. A. Duncan in Customs in the 1860s, and Richard Moody in the railway traffic branch in the early 1870s, complained bitterly about their loss of, or lack of, effective departmental control. In Duncan's case, the political sensitivity of the Customs Department during the taxation controversies of the 1860s brought the underlying conflict between public servant and minister to tinder point, and his dismissal is a vivid example of the basic insecurity of even leading public servants in this period. However, his swift reinstatement also demonstrates the fact that the close ties of the public service elite with politicians protected them in a way not available to the rank and file.

The accommodation of leading public servants to their political masters and their consequent alienation from their subordinates emerged gradually during the 1860s. In 1863 the rank and file could still look to old-style champions of public service professionalization such as Major Christie, who enthusiastically anticipated a comprehensive Civil Service Bill, probably along the lines of that just passed in Victoria, which would classify officers, confer security of salary, provide protection against patronage, establish rules for leave of absence, and introduce annual salary increments and pension entitlements.[47] However, the influence of Christie and his kind was rapidly waning, and new men such as Michael Fitzpatrick and Christopher Rolleston led subsequent attempts to restore lost public service privileges.

From the sparse evidence available it is difficult to tell what the attitudes of these new public service leaders were to public service autonomy prior to the major financial crises of the late 1860s. Certainly Fitzpatrick played a leading role in establishing a civil service club in 1864; he and Rolleston led a movement of senior public servants for a Civil Service Act in 1866; and he was part of a civil service committee which drafted a Bill that same year in response to public service demands for the amendment of the unsatisfactory Superannuation Act of 1864.[48] However, by 1878 they were remembered as traitors to the public servants' cause.

This ill-will towards the new public service leaders stemmed initially from the 1864 Superannuation Act. Introduced immediately after the announcement of a £5m deficit, this Act was a token gesture to hopes of public service reform which not only confined itself to retirement provisions, but actually limited government liability for pensions, shifting much of the burden onto younger members of the service. Lacking a secure actuarial basis and strong financial backing from the government, the scheme quickly failed. During its lifetime of less than a decade, the Superannuation Act provided generous pensions for retiring public servants at the expense of younger officers, whose contributions were wasted when the scheme collapsed. George Reid, who joined the Treasury soon after the 1864 Act was passed, expressed the sense of betrayal felt by younger public servants when he recalled that it went down in public service memory as the work of 'certain high officials behind the scenes'.[49]

This sense of betrayal was intensified by the failure of senior officers such as Fitzpatrick and Rolleston, who were the government's chief advisers on personnel matters during the 1860s, to amend the Superannuation Act, to bring about a Civil Service Act or to protect the rank and file from retrenchment. From the end of 1865, the financial problems of the government led to strenuous attempts to reduce public service numbers. Despite numerous attempts by successive governments to introduce amendments to the Superannuation Act, and a number of petitions from public servants, hopes of improved provisions faded as the government's financial problems worsened.[50]

By 1870, retrenchments, salary reductions and an actuarial report on the pension scheme were sufficiently alarming to make public servants more militant. As rank-and-file public servants held public meetings and presented petitions, they were championed by opponents of the new politicians who challenged the government's retrenchment policies and demanded major public service reform. This movement was led in the Legislative Assembly by Captain Arthur Onslow, a member of the old elite related to both the McLeays and the MacArthurs. Continuing the alliance between this elite group and the rank and file of the public service epitomized by Christie, Onslow attempted in 1870 to introduce competitive examinations, and the following year managed to persuade the Martin–Robertson government to establish a Select Committee on the Civil Service. As chairman of the inquiry, Onslow drafted a highly critical report and made radical recommendations for the removal of privilege in public service recruitment and promotion, and the opening up of the service to 'the humbler classes', including recruitment by competitive examination.[51]

These challenges to the political control of the public service were not supported by senior civil servants. Instead, the inquiry demonstrated the limited aims of men such as Fitzpatrick and Rolleston, and their lack of commitment to major change. Fitzpatrick was by then a member of the Legislative Assembly, and was an influential member of the Select Committee. He and Onslow had already clashed over the question of competitive examinations, and he had succeeded in introducing test examinations as a compromise in 1871. They clashed again on the Select Committee, where, like the other public service leaders who testified to the inquiry, he opposed competitive examinations and complete independence of personnel matters from political control.[52]

Fitzpatrick's opposition ensured that the final version of the report of the Select Committee was not the radical document Onslow originally drafted. It made recommendations that would only have restored conditions of service enjoyed prior to 1856. If accepted by the government, these recommendations would have curbed the excesses of patronage, but not destroyed it. As it was, however, even these mild reforms were rejected by the Parkes government when it considered the report in March 1873.[53] A month later, the Superannuation Act was repealed, leaving public servants without any pension rights.[54] By that time, government finances were making the dramatic recovery following Parkes' release of more land for auction, and New South Wales was entering a period of unprecedented prosperity.[55] In this new situation, a programme of extensive

political patronage was once more possible, and it was important that politicians retain control of the public service for
this purpose. The only result of this period of turmoil for the
public service itself was an inadequate test examination for
entrance to the service which one candidate who passed it in
1876 characterized as 'puerile'.[56]

Thus the rejection of the mild recommendations of the Select
Committee of 1871–72 and the repeal of the inadequate
Superannuation Act in 1873 marked the successful imposition
of political control over the public service. A system of selective
political hegemony was firmly in place in which ministers
controlled crucial areas of their departments through centralized
bureaucracies with co-operative public service leaders and a
fluid personnel system. During the period of unprecedented
government prosperity fuelled by the land auctions of the
1870s, politicians were able to capitalize on this hegemony to
consolidate political support. The accommodation of leading
public servants to this system left the public service deeply
divided. The unhappy consequences of the Superannuation
Act, the failure to achieve a Civil Service Act, and the complacent attitudes revealed by the Select Committee inquiry
showed the public service elite to be ineffective, if not untrustworthy, guardians of public service conditions. Any confrontation between the rank and file, senior public servants and
the government was postponed, however, by the restoration
of prosperity and the expansion of the public service in 1873.
The resentment and suspicion of junior public servants went
underground, ready to flare again at the end of the decade,
when new financial problems spelled the beginning of the
end of the faction system and the political hegemony that
accompanied it.

IV

By the 1880s the public service exhibited a wide variety of
personnel systems, with public employment controlled sometimes by departmental heads, sometimes by politicians and
sometimes by family and local communities. As a result, no
consistent policy emerged towards the employment of women,
and widely divergent employment practices remained in place.

Head offices in Sydney continued to be exclusively male
preserves. The new middle class men who came to the top of

the public service and politics after 1856 showed no inclination to change this situation, though many came from families where women habitually worked. Michael Fitzpatrick's mother, for instance, ran a school. The mothers of Eagar and Halloran had to support themselves and their families for much of their lives. Even Clarinda Parkes shouldered much of the burden of the Hunter Street shop while Henry talked politics in the back room, and her quiet management of the family farms during his financially precarious political career must often have kept the family fed.[57]

In a society dominated by 'good society', and in an employment situation where they had been considered second best to the gentlemen imported from England, many of these ambitious young men must have felt the scorn of the elite expressed in P. G. King's comment on James Martin:

I am much pleased to see the 'Cowper cum Martin' ministry upset—what a vulgar fellow the latter is. I should think no decent person would ever cross his threshold again or send their cards. I was amused at the use he tried to make of your having once put your feet under his mahogony.[58]

They were anxious, therefore, to acquire the social attributes that would enable them to get on. This desire to conform is clear in the young Henry Parkes. Anxious to put working class ways behind him in his new life as a newspaper proprietor and aspiring politician, he was writing in the *Empire* early in 1850 that 'Every young woman in the Colony ought to be taught that her high and honourable destiny is the destiny of strict duty, and for this she is to live, and in this find her pleasure'. This duty was of course in the home: 'Men rule in commerce, in the market and in the state; but women form the men who are so to govern, and thus are the real, albeit the silent, governors of the whole affairs of human society'. Clearly aware of his and Clarinda's own social deficiencies, Parkes wrote at the same time that they must rear their children 'as respectably as we can—indeed my position now renders it necessary that they should be on a footing with most of the children around'. Whether this was ever achieved is not clear. Certainly their daughter, Menie, felt uncomfortable with the Windeyers and the Mannings in later life, and was a reluctant participant in elite philanthropic activities.[59]

With the ideal of the lady unchanged by the rise of this new social group to political power, there was little response from departmental heads and city politicians to demands for work for women. Young women in struggling households, such as Menie Parkes, were anxious to be economically independent, but got little encouragement from their menfolk. Some women, such as Emily Manning, earned money as writers, but it was considered better that they retreat from society when their husbands were unable to support them in the accepted style than become breadwinners themselves. Only in their 'proper sphere'—in the management of charitable institutions dealing with women and children, in teaching, and in nursing—were women rather nervously conceded the right to employment.[60]

Although the notion of the lady held sway amongst the city elite, the uneven development of the public service left pockets of local and family patronage where women's employment on equal terms with men continued unchanged. The lack of political interest in post office appointments after the brief flurry in the 1860s ensured that women continued to obtain well-paid and responsible positions in country and suburban offices under the old system of local and family recruitment. During the 1860s this system was imported into the new Telegraphs Department.[61]

Like the post office, the Telegraphs Department was never effectively centralized and placed under political control. Although it was part of the Postmaster-General's Department from 1867, it was run as virtually a separate department by its superintendent, Edward Cracknell, until his death in 1893. Cracknell was typical of the professional experts who dominated sections of the public service in this period. He was most interested in the technical aspects of his job and his paternalistic regime never established any systematic personnel policy. He failed to develop any recruitment and training scheme for the large number of telegraph operators required for his expanding service, and he left the country offices to run more or less by themselves. There was no telegraphy school until 1890, so most telegraph operators gained their skills by informal apprenticeships, either as messenger boys or husbands, wives and children of telegraphists.[62] Although Cracknell showed few signs of supporting equal opportunity for women, his personalized administration of the Telegraphs Department left the way open for a system of local and family patronage similar to that of the post office.

Failure to establish central control of country and suburban post and telegraph offices left old ways of doing things unquestioned. It also separated the interests and practices of head office from those of country offices and the suburban offices which mushroomed in the period of rapid suburbanization from 1870 to 1890.[63] In country and suburban post and telegraph offices, community pressure, supported by local politicians, extended opportunities for the employment of women in rural and suburban areas, while at head office resistance to change on the part of departmental heads kept those offices exclusively male.

Country members' concern about employment opportunities for women reflected the fact that a new generation of rural women was now growing to adulthood with the expectation of earning a living and the need to do so. A number of factors contributed to the members' concern. The tradition of family enterprise on farms and small businesses in country towns engendered expectations that each member of the family should contribute to the family economy. As the population of the country towns grew at the expense of the farming community, the number of new middle class managers, government employees and journalists without family businesses in which to employ their children increased. Their children, and those of the petty bourgeoisie who could not be accommodated in family businesses, had to seek work in the paid labour force. To their number were added the children of selectors whose hopes of making a living on the land were beginning to fail by the 1870s.[64]

Evidence of country parliamentarians' concern about women's employment opportunities surfaced clearly in 1871, in parliamentary debates and in the proceedings of the Select Committee on the Civil Service. Committee members showed interest in the British post office's experience of women's employment. Although they made no specific recommendations concerning women in their report, discussion during the hearing of evidence is interesting for a number of reasons. First, there is no indication that parliamentarians introduced the question of women's employment in the interests of economy, despite the current financial straits of the government. The Victorian post office, in contrast, was following British precedent at this time and encouraging the employment of women as cheap labour. Second, there was a marked difference between the apparently positive attitude of the parliamentarians towards the question of female employment and the indifference of the public servants and academics they questioned.

The committee questioned visiting post office official, Anthony Trollope, about the British experience, and, despite Trollope's fairly conservative estimates of women's usefulness as workers, the questioner, William Forster, tended to try to elicit positive answers by such leading questions as:

676. Has it been found that women are more steady in their attention to their duties than men—I have heard that said?

678. Have you ever heard...whether women are considered more efficient or more useful in the particular departments in which they are employed?

The committee's chairman, Arthur Onslow, who maintained a continuing interest in the employment of women, also seemed to be leading his witness in a positive direction when questioning Professor Charles Badham, professor of logic and classics at Sydney University and former examiner for the Indian civil service; but he too failed to elicit much enthusiasm for the employment of women from his witness.[65]

The pattern of positive support from country politicians and indifference from public servants shown in the proceedings of the Select Committee characterizes approaches to women's employment in the service over the next twenty years. Most rural members were still committed to the extension of employment opportunities for women on equal terms with men in 1895, when the question was discussed at length in the debate over the Public Service Bill. William Lyne, the member for Hume, strongly defended women's right to employment, whether they were married or single. In particular he described his attempts to persuade the Post and Telegraph Departments to employ more women in the 1880s. The post office refused to extend women's employment opportunities (presumably as sorters and clerks, as they were already employed as postmistresses in some numbers). The superintendent of the Telegraphs Department had replied that in no circumstances would he agree to their employment (probably as telephonists, who were introduced in the early 1880s), as they could not keep a secret. According to Lyne, Cracknell argued that 'if they were employed...young fellows would be dancing around the windows, and if they wanted to get a secret out of the women they would succeed in doing so'.[66]

Cracknell's statement is extraordinary in view of the fact that women had been employed as operators and station mistresses for at least ten years by the mid-1880s, and in 1886 ran thirteen of the thirty-three suburban telegraph offices and two of the thirteen city branch offices, as well as a number of country offices. It can only be explained by the fact that he viewed the country, suburban and branch offices as quite separate from head office, and that the continued employment of women in these offices was due to inertia. The same was the case with the secretary of the post office who, when asked by the Select Committee on the Civil Service in 1871 whether his department employed any women, made the curious reply that it did not. Like Cracknell, he was obviously referring only to head office.[67]

The combination of decentralized authority, established practice and pressure for employment opportunities for country girls enabled the women of the post office to survive the government's financial crisis of 1870−72 with their equality of pay and conditions intact. The severe salary cuts and dismissals suffered by the public service fell across the board, with no regard for gender. Jemima Wickham was retired from her position at Parramatta, but she had been postmistress there since 1838, and must have been at or beyond what could be considered retiring age. Her male successor took office at a reduced salary of £120. Mrs Daly also had her salary reduced, but so did the postmasters at the twelve other separate official post offices. Faith Kellett at Penrith retained her salary of £200—one of the few incumbents at an official post office to keep her pre-1870 salary and status.

The indifference of department heads to the personnel practices of the country offices, combined with the restoration of government prosperity and relative political stability after 1873, allowed women to infiltrate the Telegraph Department and continue in the post office on the same terms as men more or less by default until Cracknell's death in 1893. For the most part this was done through the operation of local and family patronage. The first woman to become a telegraph operator was Emma Williams who was appointed at Clarence River Heads (Yamba) in 1874. She was probably the daughter of the local clerk of petty sessions. She married customs official A. H. Pegus the following year and, as Emma Pegus, remained post and telegraph mistress at Yamba until 1896, when she was retired at the age of forty-two under the provisions of the 1895 Public Service Act which barred the employment of public servants' wives. The same pattern of family patronage was followed in 1875 when Charlotta Dee was appointed junior operator at the suburban Parramatta Street post office, where her father or husband was postmaster, and Mary Buckley was appointed by her postmaster father as telegraph operator at rural Deniliquin.

A brief period of more positive action in 1875 relieves this pattern of local and family recruitment and training. Probably in response to the pressure of country members and the prosperous conditions of the mid-1870s, fourteen women were appointed to the Telegraph Department as 'perforators' on the new Wheatstone system introduced between Sydney and Tenterfield and Sydney and Albury in 1875. Women penetrated head office for the first time when six of these perforators were appointed to the Chief Telegraph Office in Sydney. Eight others were appointed to the major offices of Tenterfield and Albury. It is not clear why only women were appointed to these positions. They were not employed as cheap labour: the women appointed in Sydney had salaries of £75, considerably more than the £52 that male and female operators of the old telegraph equipment received as beginners; the country appointees received £104, probably including some sort of district allowance. In the absence of further evidence, it must be explained as an attempt at positive discrimination in favour of women. Certainly postmaster-general John Burns claimed that he was the first to employ women in the Telegraph Department, and as an old resident of Maitland, he would have been familiar with the efficient work of postmistresses Eliza Daly and Anna Browne.[68]

If this episode did represent an attempt to discriminate positively in favour of women, it did not last. When the Wheatstone system was abandoned soon after its introduction, due to lack of co-operation from neighbouring colonies, the systematic recruitment of women to the department and their employment at the Chief Telegraph Office ceased. By 1878 city ideas seemed to be penetrating the country areas. When Mrs Pearson at Camden became too ill to continue her post office duties, Captain Onslow arranged that her granddaughter be appointed as her assistant, with the possibility of becoming assistant to the telegraph master when the two offices amalgamated. Both Mrs Pearson and the station master objected. Mrs Pearson 'did not wish either of her granddaughters to acquire a knowledge of the Telegraph business'. The station master considered that 'it would not be advisable for a lady to engage in this office, there being two unmarried young men...employed'. In addition, he felt it would 'imperil the progress of business...to have a lady here as the people in the country do not seem to repose sufficient confidence in the secrecy of female Telegraphists'. When Mrs Pearson died and her granddaughter, Amelia, was appointed in her place, she soon became the target of a smear campaign by a local resident who accused her of talking 'smut' with her young male customers and of being 'on the street'. She was defended by the local constable and other prominent citizens, and by the postal inspector, but nevertheless she lost her position when the telegraph and post offices were amalgamated soon after.[69]

Cracknell himself appears to have opposed any extension of female employment. In 1888, in keeping with his earlier response to Lyne, he informed Post Office head Lambton that he entertained 'a very strong objection to the further employment of females in the capacity proposed':

As far as Telegraph work is concerned, experience here—as elsewhere—does not lead to their being regarded as suitable, the hours are long, their adaptability for office work is in most cases small, and they are not always as amenable as men to the discipline necessary in such a Department as this—:

As there are, in the present day, many fields open for ladies to work in where the kind of employment is more congenial to their tastes, and more suitable to their capacities, I prefer—for the present at any rate—to work our offices with men only as far as possible.

I may add to the foregoing that I have found the ladies who joined the Dep't in the past have done so not with any fixed idea of remaining, in all cases, but merely as a means of employment until

such times as they could change their condition for that of marriage—
Under these circumstances it will easily be understood that they were
not likely to manifest that interest in the work which would be
shown by men who joined the Dept for the rest of their lives if
possible.[70]

Although they did not succeed in penetrating head office
permanently, the women recruited for the Wheatstone system
were used to staff the growing suburban and branch offices in
Sydney. Despite Cracknell's assertions in 1888, many of them
had long careers until their death or retirement in the 1890s
and 1900s. Four of the country recruits resigned, probably
because they could not get appointments in their home towns,
but Henrietta North, Minnie Knott, Angelina Dargin, Mary
Davies, Annie Halloran and Minnie Husing had long careers
ending as post and telegraph mistresses at Edgecliff, Glebe,
Randwick, Hunter's Hill, Lower Botany and Darlington
Point.[71]

Family and local recruitment continued to introduce women
into the post and telegraph offices until the major public
service reforms of 1895. By the 1870s, public service families
were developing, in which jobs were passed on from one
generation to another. The Kibble family illustrates this clearly.
George Kibble, pound keeper at Merton, became postmaster
briefly in 1858. When this office moved to Denman in 1862,
he resumed the position. In 1868, he became telegraph station
master as well. He married in 1865, and at his death in 1879,
his wife Eliza asked to be appointed to his position. She had
been her husband's only assistant during the fourteen years of
their marriage, and, having learnt the Morse instrument, had
done all the telegraph business. She was appointed in her
husband's place, at the same salary, the day after his death.
Soon after she married Mr V. A. de Trevana in 1885, Eliza
Kibble passed the position on to her nineteen-year-old daughter, Annie. Her fifteen-year-old son, James, was then telegraph
operator. In 1888, he was given an additional allowance as
postal assistant. His mother took over these two positions on
his transfer to Sydney, and in 1889 she resumed the position
of post and telegraph mistress on Annie's promotion to the
Waterloo office. Another son, Hervey, stepped into the postal
assistant and telegraph operator positions. Eliza de Trevana

died in 1892, at the age of forty-six. Annie Kibble remained as postmistress at Waterloo until she married in 1909.[72]

The retention of the recruitment practices of an earlier era meant that a small number of women were able to enjoy well-paid and prestigious positions in New South Wales at a time when they were being exploited as cheap labour elsewhere. In 1880 Eliza Daly was one of the highest-paid postal officials in New South Wales. As postmistress at West Maitland, one of the colony's largest towns, her basic salary of £262 per annum was a little less than that of the Dean of Sydney and a little more than that of an assistant professor at Sydney University, who earned £300 and £234 respectively. Mrs Daly's salary was supplemented by commission on the sale of stamps and on money order and savings bank business. This probably increased her earnings to over £400 a year. In addition she was provided with substantial official post office quarters and an allowance for fuel. This comfortable situation was enhanced by her privilege of dispensing minor patronage, enabling her to employ her daughter, Margaret, as her assistant at a salary of £100.

With a family income of over £500 a year, with quarters and fuel provided, Mrs Daly's financial standing compared favourably with the most senior officials in the Postal Department, where the five chief clerks immediately responsible to the secretary earned £400 and £500, and the four postal inspectors earned £450. It also compared well with that of some of the ladies who mixed in the best society. Helen Fell, the widow of businessman David Fell, and an active Sydney philanthropist, had an annual income of £1000. David Fell's will makes it clear, however, that he regarded £350 a year as the minimum she would need to run her household and bring up their two children in an appropriate manner. When her income dropped during the 1890s depression, her brother-in-law advised her that she could live well, but would have to curb her generosity to worthy causes.[73]. Five hundred pounds a year would obviously allow the Daly family to live comfortably.

Henry Handel Richardson's experience in Victoria gives us some insight into the social standing of women such as Mrs Daly. It was apparently acceptable for Richardson's widowed mother, who had led 'the cloistered life of a Victorian lady' as the wife of a successful doctor, and who had some private income, to take up an appointment as postmistress in an 'up-country office'. Although she was apprehensive that it would entail some loss of caste, she found that 'everyone who was anybody' called. The family lived in a six-room brick house with a back verandah and a delightful garden. They kept a servant, and the children had private lessons and later went to boarding-school in Melbourne.[74] Richardson's mother worked in Victoria, where women in the post office were poorly paid and treated unequally. It is probable, therefore, that the social status and standard of living of the New South Wales post-mistresses was quite secure, even if they may not have been considered 'ladies' in the very highest Sydney circles. Arthur Fry, who joined the Postmaster-General's Department in Sydney in 1876, tells us that Mrs Ferris at Waverley 'mixed among good people'.[75] Her membership of the Womanhood Suffrage League and the Women's Political Educational League, along with Rose Scott, confirms that she was acceptable among the more radical Sydney elite.[76]

Although women such as these were able to enjoy access to the highest echelons of the country, suburban and branch post offices under the same conditions as men, they were a select group. Women did not fill nearly as great a proportion of the post and telegraph workforce as they did in neighbouring Victoria; there women were barred from appointment to post and telegraph offices over £100 and were paid much less than men, but they made up over half the suburban and country postmasters and postmistresses, and large numbers were employed as telegraph operators, sorters and minor clerks.[77] In New South Wales, by contrast, women ran only about a quarter of even the lowest level of post office; they managed only about a tenth of the combined post and telegraph offices; they made up only a small proportion of telegraph operators, clustered in branch, suburban and country offices; and there were no women at all employed at head office, as there were in Melbourne. It is obvious, therefore, that although they enjoyed equal pay and had no bars to their careers, they experienced considerable informal discrimination in recruitment practices.

Postmistresses such as Mrs Daly and Mrs Ferris provided the community with examples of independent, capable and responsible women, able to combine marriage and child-rearing with continuing and exacting employment. Despite their small numbers, these country and suburban postmistresses, along with their more numerous schoolteacher sisters, brought a sturdy tradition of working women into the debates on women's labour force participation in the 1890s. This tradition was often carried through public service families. Eliza Kibble's daughter Nita, for instance, who was born five months before her father's death in 1879, refused to accept that she was ineligible for appointment to the Public Library, and pioneered that important avenue of women's work in 1899.[78] Lizzie Isaac, Ellen Pegus and Emma Williams continued their post office careers from their recruitment as single women in their early twenties, through their marriages and continued employment, until their dismissal in 1896 after unbroken careers of over twenty years. Lizzie Isaac, a member of the Isaac family who ran the Scone post office from about 1860 to the late 1890s, was appointed postmistress and junior operator at the Waverley post and telegraph office in 1876 at a salary of £73 . She was then aged twenty-five. In 1878 she married Thomas Ferris, who by 1894 was first clerk in the accounts branch of the Post Office Department at a salary of £313 a year. She was post and telegraph mistress at Waverley until her dismissal in 1896, when she was earning £218. Ellen Pegus was appointed junior operator at South Creek in 1875. In 1878 she married an officer named Cross who rose to a senior position in the railways. They moved to Sydney in 1883, where she became post and telegraph mistress at Leichhardt. She was forty-three years old and earning £180 on her dismissal in 1896. Emma Pegus (née Williams), the pioneer female telegraph operator who was post and telegraph mistress at Yamba from 1874 to 1896, was probably a relation by marriage. Agnes Pegus, who worked at the Leichhardt post office from 1885, was probably her sister.[79]

The situation of women in the post and telegraph offices by 1890 epitomized the disorganized and decentralized nature of the New South Wales public service. They had asserted their need and their right to work on the same basis as their brothers and their husbands, and had succeeded in the country and the suburbs, where no specific discriminatory practices had been instituted. Although they were barred from head office, post and telegraph mistresses were found throughout the country areas, and the city was ringed by offices run by women.

PART TWO

Reorganizing the State

3

Disillusion, division and militancy

I

The spectacular growth of government works, services and jobs which helped maintain politicians' hegemony over the public service during the 1870s was dependent upon a steady flow of revenue from Crown lands. This source of revenue became less reliable after 1877. As land policies became more contentious and the political consensus of the early years of self-government faltered, a period of increasing political and economic instability ensued, in which unemployment and insecurity grew, alternative sources of revenue were bitterly debated, new forms of political support were canvassed and government retrenchment was constantly threatened.[1] In over a decade of crisis and transition, public servants became increasingly militant as repeated attempts to gain greater autonomy and control of their labour market conditions failed.

Throughout this period the divisions between senior and junior members of the service which had emerged in the early 1870s deepened, reducing the effectiveness of the public service constituency. They emerged with great clarity in 1878, when government financial problems loomed for the first time since the boom of 1873, and a bitter public debate flared up over a proposal for a new Superannuation Bill.[2] Ever since the repeal of the Superannuation Act and the rejection of the Select Committee's recommendations in 1873, successive governments had promised a Civil Service Bill. An abortive Bill was introduced late in 1876 by Robertson's new treasurer, Alexander Stuart, a leading merchant and banker who had been a colleague of Eagar's at the Bank of New South Wales and

was a director of that bank through most of the period in
which it had collaborated with the government's loan programme.[3] The contents of this Bill have not survived, but
they were probably influenced by Eagar. He certainly took
the lead early in 1878, when a group of independents led by
Farnell and Fitzgerald formed a government, with Fitzgerald
as colonial secretary. With the support of two up-and-coming
public servants, James Dalgarno, a clerk in the Post Office
Department, and Archibald Fraser, the clerk of the peace in
the Crown Law Office, Eagar took the opportunity to press
for a new Superannuation Act. They drew up a scheme and
had it ratified at a large meeting of public servants.[4]

This action brought a storm of protest from junior public
servants and their supporters who objected to the elitist nature
of the scheme. A long debate ensued in the columns of the
Sydney Morning Herald, with the scheme's opponents even
placing a public notice in the *Herald* warning public servants
that:

THIS SELFISH SCHEME confers on you no advantages WORTH YOUR
HOPING TO REALISE till you are 60 or cripples—no sure promotion, no
guarantee of position, no security for what you now enjoy—but
simply provides for an annual compulsory deduction from your
salaries to support the PROMOTERS, who ought to have provided for
themselves whilst they had youth, health, and ample pay.[5]

Opponents of the scheme accused senior officers of thinking
only of their own security, and urged that the interests of the
service would be better served by insisting on a comprehensive
Civil Service Act which would protect public servants more
completely from political patronage. The concern of public
servants for such an Act was exacerbated by events in neighbouring Victoria. On 'Black Wednesday', 9 January 1878,
Victorian civil servants had been dismissed without warning
in a political crisis, and many had not been re-employed.[6] A
Mines Department officer put the case well in his letter to the
Herald:

One of the avowed objects of the scheme is to secure and promote
the efficiency of the Public service and to ensure to the junior
members a sort of left-hand promotion. Who ever dreams (I scarcely
imagine the House will) of securing these most desirable objects by a
Superannuation Act?...An...immediate effect of such an Act

would be to place the vacant appointments at the disposal of Ministers; and there is at present no security to the general service as to who would be the recipients, no matter what individual claims might be...What the younger officers look and pray to the House for is a Civil Service Act, not a Superannuation Act. They don't want facilities for retiring, but encouragement for working and progress. This is the proper and only way to promote the efficiency of the service, not the other, which would be the 'cart before the horse'. We young officers (by which phrase I mean those who are a long way from thinking or wishing to retire) are 'the horse'. A Superannuation Act and its effects would be the 'cart', which we are to drag.[7]

The divided state of the service and the instability of the Farnell government prevented any action on the question of public service reform in 1878. The conflict left, however, a legacy of disenchantment with the public service elite's perceived weakness and self-interest.

Interest in civil service reform was renewed in the early 1880s as governments faced serious financial problems and threatened public service retrenchment. Widespread dissatisfaction with Crown land policies and the political system they supported brought down the embattled coalition of the two old warriors of the faction system, Parkes and Robertson, in 1882. The new government, led by Alexander Stuart, confirmed the end of a political era with new land policies which drastically cut Crown lands revenue from the 1882 high of £2.5m to £1.3m in 1883, at which level it remained until the end of the century (see Figure 1). Although Stuart maintained government spending by means of major overseas borrowing from 1883 to 1885 and was optimistic that this loss could be quickly replaced by a property tax, the public service remained vulnerable to arbitrary retrenchment.[8]

Public servants were in a favourable position to insist on public service reform in the uncertain situation of the early 1880s. Neither government nor opposition could afford to ignore this large and influential group. By 1884 there were over 11 000 public servants, out of a population of 904 000 and a workforce of about 318 000. Many more worked for the government on contract or as day labourers. T. A Coghlan estimated for 1887 that 24 000 of the 440 000 in the workforce were government and municipal officers and employees. Many of these public employees lived in Sydney, which contained one-third of the New South Wales population in 1884. The public service formed, therefore, a formidable potential voting bloc, especially in the metropolitan constituencies where, it was pointed out in the debate on the Civil Service Bill in 1884, 'the civil servants have great power'.[9]

The political leverage of the public servants was enhanced by their support by members of the new radical press, who often shared the social background and experience of the younger public servants. Chief among these was J. F. Archibald, one of the founders of the *Bulletin*, which was to become the most influential Australian magazine of the period. Archibald, the son of a country policeman, had been a supernumerary clerk in the Victorian Education Department for two years. There his first-hand observations of the effect of 'Black Wednesday' on his fellow workers were the occasion for his first public campaign for justice. His chief clerk, a 'sadly overworked, dyspeptic and irritable, but just and generous man', was dismissed. Archibald was deeply affected by the dismissal:

[The chief clerk] appeared at the office, trembling, in an evident state of deep dejection, and though...there was between us a clear line of official demarcation (and I had never eaten his salt), I ventured, while receiving from him for the last time some official papers, to express my sympathy with him in his illness and misfortune. He looked at me for a moment in a way which made me at first feel I had taken an undue liberty, but tears came into his eyes, his voice faltered, and he shook my hand. I left the room, feeling bitter at the injustice done to this old and weary man, whom all around him knew, despite his occasional impatience, to be an honourable and kindly gentleman. I determined to put in a blow for him.[10]

Not only did Archibald use his newspaper connections to have his chief clerk reappointed, but he continued to fight for the public service when he established his own journal in Sydney two years later. In August 1880, in its first year of publication, the *Bulletin* castigated the government's retrenchment policy as 'an inordinate tax upon a class of people whose voice cannot be raised in their own defence, and who, for this reason, naturally look to the Government for protection':

It is unfortunate that nearly every legitimate and sensible mode of raising revenue by means of new or additional taxation has been tabooed, and consequently the only resource left to mediocrity is the delusive and mischievous cry of retrenchment. Economy in Government expenditure is both proper and necessary at all times, but spasmodic efforts to make ends meet by arbitrarily cutting down the pay of employees is greatly to be deprecated...the first principle of economy in regard to the Civil Service is to secure a good and efficient organization, which can only be effected by reposing confidence in responsible officers, and giving them assurance that they will not be liable to have their domestic arrangements thrown into confusion by capricious and sudden curtailment of their salaries, which it may be fairly assumed have been granted with due regard to the importance of the duties entrusted to them.[11]

In 1882, the *Bulletin*, already a paper with a circulation of 20 000, turned its guns on patronage.

...no one has any right to expect efficiency from a Service in which men are promoted chiefly by favour, and unfriended officers, however efficient, learn by experience that the most strenuous industry has but very subordinate influence upon their fortunes. Every day they know of new men being pitchforked into superior positions which old officers for years hoped some time to attain. Every day they see incapables, who chance to have friends at court, kicked up-stairs into desirable vacancies, on which, according to every rule of justice and fitness, older and abler officers had a distinct claim...Until we have high-minded legislators, who would scorn to solicit billets for their relatives and hangers-on, irrespective of fitness, the service must remain as it is. And until we have constituencies too enlightened to return to Parliament any but men of elevated character, Civil service patronage must still be one of the instruments of corruption.[12]

Public service reform was a major issue in the elections of 1882, and, with an eye to this important constituency, Stuart's new government promised to give first priority to a Civil Service Bill which would remedy 'the serious defects which exist in the regulation of the civil service of the country' in order 'to secure the just recognition of merit and service, and thereby increase the efficiency of the various departments of the Government'.[13] However, the drastic drop in land sales, and Stuart's failure to convince even his own supporters of the need for a property tax and tariff changes, made it impossible to carry out this promise. Civil Service Bills were finally introduced at the end of 1883 and in early 1884, but were lost under the weight of the gathering financial crisis. With treasurer George Dibbs suggesting retrenchment as the only solution to the government's financial problems, it was impossible to press on with a Bill which removed government control of public service salaries and retirement allowances.[14]

This renewed threat of retrenchment gave public servants fresh cause for anxiety and less reason to trust their political patrons. Their immediate interest was in the possibility of a salary freeze or dismissal without adequate pension rights. Salary increments and retirement allowances were subject to the scrutiny of parliament in the annual parliamentary debate on supply. At the best of times this system made public servants dependent on influence, and subject to arbitrary treatment. As premier Stuart characterized the process in 1884,

...there is great inequality in the tangible recognition of [officers'] services [because] the mode of recognition has been marked by fits and starts; influence has been brought to bear in favour of some [while] certain civil servants who discharge their duties faithfully and honorably have not sufficient influence or interest to get their cases brought under the notice of the Minister, who has to recommend to Parliament what the remuneration of the officers under him should be, or to get the attention of members of Parliament directed to them.[15]

In times of budgetary crisis even those with influence were not immune from across-the-board cuts or devastating public attacks on their personal efficiency and integrity under the protection of parliamentary privilege.[16]

The strength of public service feeling and strong popular support for the abolition of patronage probably persuaded Stuart to introduce a third Civil Service Bill on 5 August 1884, despite the fact that the government was still engrossed with the Land Bill.[17] The government needed all the support it could get after a gruelling thirteen-month session, during which it was seriously weakened by the continuing budgetary crisis and divisions over lands policy. Successful loan raisings provided the right political climate to introduce such a Bill. It was also politically advantageous to be seen fighting corruption at a time when the government was allocating a record vote of £13m loan money for public works.[18]

The Civil Service Bill appears to have been pushed through almost solely by the will of the public service. Members paid little attention to it. Under the pressure of the end of an exhausting session, they often barely made up a quorum. Those interested in the measure requested time to study it, but, urged on by petitions from public servants, the government forced the Bill through the committee stage by 1 October. It seemed destined for withdrawal, however, as Stuart suffered a stroke early that month. Public servants continued to press for the Bill to proceed, and it was finally considered in the Council between 14 and 23 October. It was then a race to settle differences between the two houses before parliament adjourned on 1 November. On 31 October the Civil Service Bill was passed.[19]

II

The legislation that emerged from this hurried act of political expediency pleased no one. Although it gave the illusion of transferring authority over personnel matters to an independent board in the interests of removing patronage, and of providing liberal salary increases and retiring allowances independent of parliamentary scrutiny, it was, in fact, an ill-conceived, half-hearted and elitist measure.

The limitations of the Act stemmed from the restricted aims of the public servants and politicians who designed it, the compromises they were forced to make among their divergent interests, and the haste with which these measures were considered. These limitations demonstrated that parliament was not yet ready to relinquish its powers of patronage and its control of the service. More significantly, the circumscribed and limited nature of the Act revealed that leading public servants still had a restricted view of public service reform, a view which separated elite interests from those of the rank and file, and saw each department head as properly the chief of his own domain.

Archibald Fraser and his close friend, Charles Goodchap, the commissioner for railways, appear to have been central figures in drawing up the Bill, although Eagar, as Treasury under-secretary, was no doubt an important adviser to his former minister and colleague Stuart. Fraser was, with Eagar, a leading organizer of the group of senior officers who had tried to steamroll the service and the parliament into an elitist superannuation scheme in 1878. The *Town and Country Journal* asserted in 1889 that it was 'an open secret that the civil

servants owe the Civil Service Act (without its faults, however), chiefly to the exertions of Mr Fraser'.[20] Goodchap was
referred to in the debate on the Bill as the government's chief
adviser.[21] The behaviour and comments of Fraser and Goodchap
after the Act was put into operation, which will be discussed
below, indicate that they had an intimate knowledge of public
service expectations of the Bill.[22] Fraser's dismissal by the
young, reforming Public Service Board in 1896, despite his
criticisms of the 1884 Act and the protests of influential supporters, suggests that he was classed among those senior officers
who, 'though men of ability, were not such as [the Board
members] cared to entrust with the carrying out of the far-
reaching reforms which they felt were necessary'.[23] This
rejection of Fraser as an effective reformer in 1896 suggests
that junior public servants, unlike the *Town and Country Journal*,
blamed him for the limitations of the 1884 Act.

The Bill that emerged from the negotiations between leading
public servants and the Stuart government in 1884 was limited
in conception, although it represented an advance on the proposed Superannuation Bill of 1878. Clerical and professional
staff were to gain guaranteed, specified salaries and increments,
and a secure retirement income, and their interests were to be
watched over by a Civil Service Board. Ministers were to
retain patronage in appointments, as well as complete control
of non-clerical and non-professional staff, except in the railways, where the regulations Goodchap had already instituted
for his large body of employees were to remain in place.[24]

Changes made during the debate on the Bill, however,
eroded the already small powers of the Board in contradictory
ways, sometimes favouring ministers and sometimes heads of
departments, but never the rank and file.[25] In the deteriorating
economic conditions of 1885, when government spending
rose to a peak of £14.2m without a compensating source of
revenue being found, the new Civil Service Board further
narrowed its own powers and the circle of privileged who
benefited from the Act.

The most striking aspect of the Act was its elitist character.
It prescribed generous annual salary increments, but these
benefits were restricted to a small number of clerical and
professional officers. Teachers, police, temporary employees
and non-clerical workers and sub-clerical and sub-professional

staff were excluded from its provisions, leaving most of the staff of large departments like Public Instruction, Railways, Posts and Telegraphs, and the Printing Office outside the effective control of the Act. In all, only 1867 public servants were subject to the appointments, promotions and salary provisions of the Act, out of a total of about 13 000. The compulsory superannuation provisions were hardly less restrictive. Only the 2000 elite, and the 3190 teachers employed by the Public Instruction Department, were automatically covered by the scheme, although all 10 256 permanent public servants could join if they wished. To make matters worse, teachers, who formed the majority of those required to join the pension scheme, did so reluctantly, as it suited their needs poorly.[26]

As well as being elitist, the Act was also ineffectual. It provided for the appointment of a Civil Service Board to classify, prescribe examinations for appointment and promotion, recommend promotions, and limit other discretionary powers of ministers. However, the Board had little actual or potential power. Its members were busy public servants and businessmen who served part-time. Moreover, their powers were severely restricted. In the first place, the Act only applied to a small minority of public servants. Second, in classifying the service, the Board was tied to the divisions, classes and annual increments specified in the Act. More significantly, it was tied to classifying officers according to their current salaries. In addition, it had no power over appointments to the service: it could only prescribe qualifying examinations and report on appointments made without examination or probation. It could comment on decisions concerning increments and make recommendations concerning promotions, but final decisions were made by the relevant minister. The Board could be asked to investigate misdemeanours, but decisions on dismissals and disciplinary action also lay with the minister.

The Board's exclusiveness and powerlessness left both the elite and the rank and file of the service dissatisfied. Over a thousand public servants who had expected to benefit from the Act appealed to the Civil Service Board against their classification outside the General and Professional Divisions, which rendered them ineligible for the generous increments it conferred. Their expectations were not unrealistic, as the Bill was originally intended to apply to 3500 persons—twice as

many as it finally covered. Under pressure to limit the number
of people eligible for the generous increments provided in the
Act, the Civil Service Board had interpreted professional clerical
status narrowly, excluding groups such as telegraphists, draftsmen, and postal officials from the General and Professional
Divisions, despite the fact that these groups considered themselves 'more scientific, intellectual, and professional than
many of the classified officers'.[27]

If many public servants were bitterly disappointed with the
Act, so too were two of its leading advocates, Goodchap and
Fraser. The powers that they expected the Board to gain were
reduced during the debate on the Bill, and were further restricted by the more conservative Board members and the government the following year. The original Bill gave the proposed
Board considerable power to recommend the payment and
disallowance of salary increments, a right which protected the
independence of public servants from political interference.
Stuart showed no commitment to giving the Board such
powers when attacked by opposition leaders Parkes and
Robertson for transferring power from ministers to what they
called an irresponsible board. Assuring the House that 'the
intention was that the board should be an investigating body'
only, he immediately gave way on this question.[28]

More serious as far as the Board was concerned was its lack
of power over salary classification. Fraser and Goodchap had
wanted a Board of Inquiry to work out an equitable system of
classification.[29] They had compromised, however, by accepting current salaries as the basis of classification, expecting that
anomalies and injustices would be dealt with under section 17,
which gave public servants the right of appeal to the Board.[30]
However, the predominantly conservative Civil Service Board,
which comprised Geoffrey Eagar as chairman and John Williams,
the Crown solicitor,[31] businessman W. G. Murray, Archibald
Fraser and Charles Goodchap, decided, on Eagar's casting
vote, that aggrieved public servants did not have the right of
appeal with regard to classification. Fraser and Goodchap
dissented from this decision, arguing that it had been the
intention of the Act that the Board should have the power to
correct anomalies and injustices. They pointed out that, 'as
the Act is now being administered, there are no means whereby
an officer whose classification is unduly low, or whose emolu-

ments are inadequate to the duties of his office, can be raised in the scale of classification or be awarded a higher rate of pay'. 'It is difficult to believe', they go on, 'that such was the intention of the legislature when passing the Act, and it was most assuredly never contemplated by the Civil Servants when they petitioned Parliament for the Bill':

One of the chief purposes for which it was generally understood the Bill was introduced was to provide a remedy for the anomalies and cases of injustice then existing in the Civil Service (certainly not to perpetuate them); and the consent of the Civil Servants to the fixing of their positions according to the salaries of 1884, as an ultimate source of relief would, it is believed, have been withheld had they not relied upon the privilege indicated in the 1/th section, of appealing to the Board against any injustice that might occur in the individual cases through such an indiscriminate mode of classification. They reasonably anticipated that, under the section, the Board would on appeal inquire into the merits of every case and report thereon to the Government, who would confirm or otherwise recommendations made—Parliament of course having the opportunity of becoming acquainted with the result, as provided for under the same section.[32]

By the time this dispute was referred to Stuart for decision, his ministry was in serious financial trouble, internally divided and beset by allegations of corruption and improper practices. In less than two months parliament was dissolved, and Stuart and two of his strongest ministers had resigned.[33] In this situation, Stuart was decidedly unsympathetic to any inter-pretation of the Board's powers which would result in an increase in public service salaries. In his decision he asserted that

it was never intended that the Civil Service Board should have the power of deciding whether the salaries paid were sufficient or insuf-ficient for the services performed. I doubt whether Parliament would have allowed such, even if we had intended to ask for the power. I had no doubt that one of the effects of the Act would be to bring to light many glaring inconsistencies, owing to the mode in which appointments had previously and for so many years been made; and that it was quite possible that eventually some steps might have to be taken with regard to them; but I purposely did not encumber the Bill with any provisions to this effect, because, amongst other reasons, if the Board had been empowered within even strict limits to raise salaries which they deemed insufficient, it would also have been

necessary to invest it with powers to reduce salaries which were in
excess of the value of the services performed...I am quite clear that
the act neither does confer, nor was intended to confer, the power of
rectification upon the Civil Service Board.[34]

It is clear that there had been a serious gap in understanding
between younger civil servants such as Fraser and Goodchap,
influential advisers such as Eagar, and the politicians who
ultimately introduced the Bill. Goodchap and Fraser obviously
expected more of the Bill than Stuart did, and had overestimated
Stuart's commitment to the principle of public service independence. Eagar's casting vote against the right of appeal for
public servants suggests that there was little commitment to
even a mild degree of reform on the part of senior officers
who were closely associated with the previous political faction
system and its public personnel methods. Ten years later,
when Goodchap was a member of the Legislative Council, he
spoke with bitterness about his disappointment with the 1884
Act:

This clause gives power to the commissioners to enter into all the
departments of the public service to make inquiries as to the performance of duties, and for the purpose of thoroughly investigating
and reorganising the service. In connection with the bill which was
passed in 1884 by Sir Alexander Stuart, it was understood by the
majority of the civil service at that time that that measure did give
that power; but after some preliminary investigation had taken place,
the Civil Service Board, of which I was a member, found that this
power was not conferred upon it. A more disappointing, a more
evasive, and more abominable act was never passed to secure the
objects which the then Government had in view. The board, I may
say, was divided as to its powers to affect this good work. The board
consisted of Mr Eagar, the then Under-secretary for Finance and
Trade, Mr John Williams, the Crown Solicitor, Mr Fraser, the
Under-Secretary of Justice, Mr Thomas Littlejohn and myself. By
the casting vote of the chairman it was decided that we did not
possess this power; but we were not content with that. Mr Fraser
and myself persisted and brought the matter before the Attorney-
General, who also determined that however desirable such a power
would be, the act did not give it, and Sir Alexander Stuart ultimately
stated that it was not his intention to grant the power. I have only to
say that if the old 17th section of the act had been interpreted to
mean what is proposed by this bill, the civil service of the country
would have been reorganised in the direction now contemplated ten

years ago, and I have no hesitation in saying that hundreds of thousands of pounds would have been saved to the country. I think it is only right, in defence of the Civil Service Board, that has done so little since 1884, to make this explanation. They tried to do the work, but they were told that the act did not confer the power upon them; in fact, it seems to me that it confers very little power indeed upon them.[35]

The Civil Service Act of 1884, therefore, left ministers and heads of departments with their powers virtually intact. Where the Act applied, in the General and Professional Divisions, ministers could still select persons for appointment from qualified candidates; they could make temporary appointments, appoint specially qualified persons without examination or promotion, disallow increments, make final selections for promotion, discipline officers and grant leave of absence. The Act did provide some guidelines for the exercise of these powers, and the Board had a watchdog role. But as long as members of the Board included public servants whose own security depended on the goodwill of ministers, the watchdog had no effective power. There were some compensations, however. Clerical and professional staff had guaranteed, generous annual increments and retirement provisions which gave them some independence from political influence. Heads of departments, for their part, lost some power over their clerical and professional staff to the Civil Service Board, but their control of other parts of their departments was reinforced.

The privileges won for themselves by the public service elite quickly disintegrated. Deprived of any real power, the Board quickly fell victim to the cost-cutting of the budget crisis of 1885–86. Following the dissolution of parliament in October 1885, the revelation of increasingly higher deficits of £1m and £1.7m led to the swift fall of ministries led by Dibbs and Robertson. When wealthy pastoralist Patrick Jennings succeeded in forming a stable government in February 1886, he promised major financial reform including increased taxation, Civil Service Act and Land Act amendment, local government, and improved surveillance of the Railways Department.[36] With Dibbs as treasurer and colonial secretary the Jennings government recruited the young public servant and journalist, Timothy Coghlan, to the new post of government statistician in an effort to upgrade the colony's image for potential investors; they set in train inquiries into the Lands and Public Works Departments aimed at reorganizing them and reducing their swelling numbers of employees; and they immediately introduced a Civil Service Act Amendment Bill.[37]

This Bill was put aside as the government attempted to introduce amendments to the Stamp Duties Act, a Land Tax Bill, an Income Tax Bill, and a Government Railways Bill. In a stormy session during which political forces behind direct and indirect taxation began to sort themselves out into distinguishable 'parties' for the first time, Jennings and Dibbs were successful only with the stamp duty legislation.[38] With the end of session looming, they pushed a truncated version of the Civil Service Act Amendment Bill through the House in a two-hour session beginning at midnight on 18 October 1886.[39]

This desperate attempt to retrench expenditure in the face of parliamentary refusal to increase taxation was designed purely 'to strike the increments out'.[40] The two previous Bills introduced by Dibbs, the second as late as 22 September 1886, had been more considered. They were intended, according to Dibbs, to:

provide for periodical investigation, reduction and re-organisation of the civil service—for the better regulation thereof—for granting compensation for loss of office—for granting allowances and gratuities—and for other purposes connected with the administration of the said service.[41]

The government's plan to establish regular inquiries into public service numbers and to introduce a compensation scheme for retrenched public servants was shelved, the provisions for automatic increments were repealed, and the Board was left to administer an Act which had been completely emasculated. As parliamentarian John Neild observed when the original amending Bill was introduced: '[The Act] is disliked by the service, disliked by the House, and scouted by the country. And now it is proposed to eliminate from the measure the only thing that commends it to the civil service'.[42]

The fiasco of the hastily conceived, ineffectual and elitist Civil Service Act and its amendment made it clear that governments were not yet ready to surrender control of the public service. It also branded public service leaders as ineffectual as protectors of public service conditions and inextricably tied to the old political order. With only a poorly conceived pension scheme and a toothless Civil Service Board run by such men to safeguard their interests, younger public servants realized that they would have to take matters into their own hands.

III

Militant defensive action seemed very necessary in the years following the almost-total repeal of the Civil Service Act in 1886. The continuing government financial crisis which fore-stalled any hope of radical public service reform gradually dismantled the old political system. The faction system had been successful because the cement which helped hold it together—patronage in jobs, services and resources—had benefits for large segments of the community, including the working class. This hegemonic system of politics depended on a ready and uncontentious supply of government revenue, which only the sale of Crown lands could supply. Once it was clear that there was no ready replacement for Crown land revenue, politicians and their constituencies floundered as they attempted to adjust to this loss and the consequent scarcity of political and economic resources with which to buy support. As resources for patronage became scarce and contentious, interest groups crystallized around country and city interests, alternative policies on taxation and government expenditure, and work- and gender-based interests, and embryo parties, militant trade unions and a feminist movement began to emerge.

Within months of the Civil Service Amendment Act, Jennings had resigned and Henry Parkes had formed a Free Trade government after an election fought for the first time by groups loosely organized around the principles of free trade and protection.[43] Attempting to adjust to the new situation, in which political control of the public service had become a headache and a liability, Parkes made major changes in the administration of railways and public works. He relinquished control of railways administration to an independent commission headed by the youthful Lands Department head, Charles Oliver, forcing Goodchap, who had become too closely identified with the Jennings government, to resign. He retired the ageing John Rae, and placed the separate Public

Works Department under the control of the efficient Joseph
Barling. At the same time he established a parliamentary
committee to supervise the allocation of public money to
railways and public works.[44] He cut public works, made
plans to shift the burden of public works onto local government,[45] and attempted to introduce land and property taxes.[46]

This new regime of austerity proved difficult to maintain.
Parkes was soon forced to resume heavy expenditure on public
works to placate the growing unrest of the working class,
among whom unemployment was becoming a serious problem,
exacerbated by public works retrenchment and increasing
failure on the land.[47] Drawing on cash surpluses built up
during 1887−88, and borrowing from London, his government went on a final spending spree in which expenditure
rose again to its 1885 level of over £14m in 1889 and a new
peak of £18m in 1891 (see Figure 2). Much of this went to
public works, and expenditure on railways rose from £1.4m
to almost £4m (see Figure 3).[48] Meanwhile Parkes had little
success in introducing a land or property tax.[49]

Ignoring the advice of Jennings' Lands Department Inquiry
that 'Nothing less...than a radical alteration in the Civil
Service Act will enable the position of all officers employed in
the Civil Service to be equitably dealt with, while the interests
of the public are also secured', Parkes set up a Royal Commission
on the Civil Service in December 1887 in response to attacks
on public service expenditure and accusations of patronage.
The Commission, made up of ageing members of the old
guard, sat interminably, suspending operations altogether
from January to July 1889. The turnover amongst its seven
members was rapid. Christopher Rolleston, the retired auditor-
general, R. D. Fitzgerald, the former deputy surveyor-general,
and William Wilkins, who had retired from his position as
head of the Public Instruction Department due to ill-health
in 1884, died during the life of the Commission. James
Thomson, the recently retired Treasury official who succeeded
Rolleston, became impatient with the ineffectiveness of the
inquiry and resigned because, he was quoted as saying, 'he
was of the opinion that the results of the Commission's labours
were so small as to be of no practical benefit, and that more
effective and judicious organization could be suggested by a
Board of Public Officers'.[50]

It is unlikely that the Royal Commission was meant to be anything more than window-dressing. Evidence given before the Commission was confidential. Only one report was ever published, and at least one department head, probably the recalcitrant Harrie Wood at Mines, refused to act upon its recommendation on the grounds that non-publication of the evidence made it advisory only.[51] Despite violent denunciations by the *Bulletin* for its supposed retrenchment policies, the government appeared to have no serious intention to cutting back the service with this inquiry.[52] Between 1887 when, as the *Bulletin* put it, 'New South Wales began to have the retrenchment disease badly', and 1893, only about five hundred public servants were retrenched.[53] This was miniscule compared with the increase in public service numbers in that same period. By 1894 there were 32 078 public servants, including 9433 railway workers and 1282 tramway workers.[54] A comparable figure for 1886 is probably the 24 389 quoted during parliamentary debates.[55] With an increase of 30 per cent between 1886 and 1894, there seemed to be considerable basis for belief in the *Bulletin*'s allegation that retrenchment was

merely the art and mystery of discharging a large, sensational batch of able-bodied officials, and recompensating them out of the private savings of the civil servants in general, and then appointing quietly, one by one, a crowd of personal friends and supporters in their stead.[56]

Although public servants did not appear to suffer greatly from actual retrenchment from 1887 to 1891, this was not at all clear to them at the time. As the Royal Commission dribbled out its secret reports, the service was kept in a continual state of anxiety. This was exacerbated by the efforts of a group of protectionists in the parliament, led by E. W. O'Sullivan, W. H. Traill and Thomas Rose, to harass the government by calling attention to the haphazard and ineffectual nature of its retrenchment programme.[57]

In this confused political and economic situation, questions of retrenchment and public service reform were exploited for political advantage. The long-drawn-out Royal Commission, the activities of the 'retrenchment party', and the imminent breakdown of the superannuation fund—the unwanted legacy

of the Civil Service Act—constantly reminded public servants
of their precarious position. The public service became a political football, and public servants joined the numerous groups
who organized militantly during this period.

IV

Rank-and-file public servants began to organize in the early
1880s in response to threats of government contraction and
retrenchment, but the elitism of the Civil Service Act was the
catalyst which stimulated the formation of large-scale, permanent public service associations. In 1881 telegraphists in the
chief telegraph office had elected an informal 'committee of
seven' to mediate between workers and management. This
became a more representative and militant vigilance committee
when telegraphists were excluded from the Professional Division
by the Civil Service Act. In 1886 the telegraphists joined with
the postmasters and postmistresses also aggrieved by the Act
to form a properly constituted Operators Society.[58] Draftsmen,
another sub-professional group who considered themselves
badly treated by the Act, also formed an association during
this period. In 1891 these two white-collar groups were joined
by the Postal Clerks Union.[59] At the same time, political
controversy over the railways prompted the formation of the
mass Railway and Tramway Employees Association in 1886,
and the expanding ranks of the Railways Department provided
a large part of the membership of traditional craft unions
such as the Boilermakers Union and the Australian Society of
Engineers.[60]

These public servants were quickly mobilized into effective
associations with a strong sense of group solidarity. The
communications revolution that had been brought about by
the government's development policies meant that telegraphists,
postal workers and railway workers in particular now moved
constantly around the country, and had access to ready means
of communication among their scattered members. By 1891
the RTEA had almost 3000 members, and its secretary, William
Schey, had been a member of the Legislative Assembly since
1887.[61] The Electric Telegraph Society (ETS), the successor
of the Operators Society, had also grown sufficiently to support a journal, the *Transmitter*, which quickly achieved a wide

circulation and became an articulate platform for the public
service reform movement.

In the last days of the Parkes government in 1891, in the
face of increasing political instability, the precarious state of
the superannuation fund, continuing resentment of the 1884
Act, and the campaigns of the 'retrenchment party', the ETS
joined with the Postal Clerks Union and the Draftsmen's
Association in strenuous efforts to organize a comprehensive
public service association.[62] Early in 1892, as the Dibbs
government threatened retrenchment, a circular was distributed
throughout the service seeking support for the projected
association. The statement of its objects was an interesting
mixture of trade union and professional strategies. Among its
several aims, the association wanted:

C. To promote social intercourse and encourage friendly feeling
among members of the service, and thus sweep away jealousies and
differences which will always prevail when men are disunited and
have no rallying point.
D. To vindicate the rights of the service and uphold its just claims; to
maintain respect for and confidence in the employees of the State, to
seek to obtain recognition of the principle that there is no higher field
of duty for a man than the faithful service of his country, and that
such services should command due consideration and reward.

But it was also meant:

E. To advocate the abolition of patronage and to uphold the principle
of advancement upon the grounds of seniority and merit.
F. To advocate amendment of the present Civil Service Act.
G. To provide a means of united action in the event of the reasonable
interests of the service being endangered by sudden or extreme
changes of policy.[63]

The *Bulletin*, which was supportive of the beleaguered public
service, was sceptical of the more gentlemanly aspects of the
strategy, and advised the association to 'drop everything
except Article E, and to fight for Article E like a cart-load of
wild cats'.[64]

The efforts of the three white-collar unions to establish a
consolidated public service association foundered, like the
Civil Service Acts, on the opposition of some departmental
heads. The immediate stimulus to action was also removed as
immediate danger of retrenchment was postponed by the

government's successful imposition of new customs duties.[65] This proved to be only a temporary reprieve. The 'retrenchment party', led by O'Sullivan, pressed for action to curb the indiscriminate growth of the service. Much to the *Bulletin*'s disgust, they even attacked the salary of the doyen of the public service, Critchett Walker, the chief under-secretary, in a parliamentary debate on supply in February 1892.[66] In November of that year, in anticipation of the budget estimates, they proposed a reduction of 10 per cent on all civil servants' salaries over £300. A compromise 5 per cent cut in salaries over £200 was introduced early the following year. Unable to get its Income-Tax Bill through the Council, the government proposed further cuts as revenue from customs fell in the depressed economy of 1893. Expenditure dropped away precipitously from £17m in 1892 and 1893 to £13.3m in 1894 (see Figure 2), and expenditure on railways fell from almost £4m in 1891 to £1.2m in 1892 (see Figure 3).[67]

In this situation, the superannuation fund once again became the focus of concern, providing a rallying point which unified the service. The retrenchment of even the moderate numbers of officers dismissed after 1887 placed a heavy strain on the fund, which was in danger of collapsing. The Civil Service Board, in its only useful capacity, kept this danger before the public, and individual public service unions provided platforms in which all public servants, including teachers, campaigned strongly for more secure pension provisions. Meanwhile, keeping all of these anxieties on the boil was the *Bulletin*, thundering against 'the Ministerial bushranger' who 'sallies forth with his little budget, gun in hand, and "bails up" the employees, demanding a percentage of their money to pay the debt his weakness has contracted, with the alternative of losing their official lives'.[68]

V

By the end of 1893 a stalemate had been reached. Neither Free Trade nor Protectionist governments had succeeded in introducing a viable source of revenue to replace that lost with the curtailment of land sales. This impasse was a result of the ineffectual character of the two rather misleadingly named 'parties' that had emerged from the collapse of the faction system. Organized around the immediate question of whether the new source of government revenue should be direct or indirect taxation, they were made up of such heterogeneous elements that permanent parliamentary and extra-parliamentary support was difficult to organize.

A more viable basis for party formation was provided by a larger movement for social and political reform amongst 'the democracy'—a miscellaneous group comprising small farmers, skilled and unskilled workers, the petty bourgeoisie, younger public servants and the wider new middle class. Out of this group emerged the Labor Party, which began to organize in 1891, the same year as the public servants were mobilizing seriously.[69] The Labor Party had several advantages over its rivals. It had a more homogeneous group of supporters, although these were by no means confined to the working class. It had a strong organizational base in the union movement, which had grown significantly in both the country and the city in the unstable conditions of the 1880s. In particular, the Trades and Labour Council (TLC), which had been in existence since the early 1870s, provided a central and experienced base for the formation of the new party. In addition, it did not carry the baggage of old political methods which retarded innovation and adaptation to new political realities in the other parties.

Despite these advantages, it took a number of years for the Labor Party to consolidate. During the 1890s the 'democracy' was divided amongst all three parties. It was not until party members accepted a pledge of solidarity in 1894, and Reid resolved the fiscal question with the introduction of direct taxes in 1895, that Labor was able to capitalize fully on its position as an influential third party. By 1904 it had absorbed most of the reform elements in the parliament and the electorate, and an organized conservative group had emerged to oppose it. In the meantime there was a vacuum of effective parliamentary power, broken briefly by Reid's Free Trade Party from 1895 to 1896 and Lyne's Protectionist Party from 1899 to 1901.

In this fluid political situation the new middle class and the working class found common cause as both faced severe and permanent contraction of employment opportunities and deterioration of working conditions as a result of government retrenchment. The newly formed Labor Party and the newly mobilized public service were poised, therefore, to act in concert to avert this crisis.

VI

By 1894 the rank and file of the public service were at tinder-point. In the two decades since Parkes had refused to carry out the mild recommendations of the Select Committee for public service reform, public servants had been constantly frustrated by broken promises from politicians and betrayals by their senior officers. Only in the brief halcyon period from 1873 to 1878 had they been free of the threat of arbitrary retrenchment. The militancy of the public service associations was, at this stage, directed at old-style politicians such as Parkes and members of the public service elite who continued to support political control of the service. Gender was barely an issue. Women had suffered disproportionately from the discriminatory provisions of the 1884 Act, but only because they were chiefly in telegraph and postal offices, whose employees, male and female, were classified as sub-professional and sub-clerical. Because they shared their male colleagues' grievances, women were accepted as a matter of course as members of the new associations. Public service women themselves did not feel a strong need to establish their own associations, as they did in Victoria, where active discrimination made them conscious of their separate interests.[70] Only in 1892 was the first hint given of active discrimination against women in the newly co-ordinated post and telegraph office.[71] The following year women teachers, who had been discriminated against to some degree at least since 1880, felt the first cut of the intense discrimination which characterized their future treatment.[72] It was only among women teachers, therefore, that there was any overt militancy among public service women in this period. Even they did not see their interests as radically separate from those of their male colleagues, and vocal activists such as Annie Golding were listened to with respect as spokespersons for their profession as well as for women.[73]

'Hang your reforms!' said Mr. Chichely. 'There's no greater humbug in the world. You never hear of a reform, but it means some trick to put in new men.'

George Eliot, *Middlemarch*

'COGHLAN'

'Who made the world?' the Master cried.
Young New South Wales, with sense replied:
'COGHLAN'
Who built Australia, can you tell?
You bet my friend I know right well.
'COGHLAN'
Who sacked the Civil Service pray.
Reduced the teachers to half pay?
'COGHLAN'
Now who inspires George Reid, P.C.,
And who went 'home' a coaching he?
'COGHLAN'
And who with quick and practiced hand
Can make a surplus for our land?
'COGHLAN'
Who deals with George's deficits so
That George can a surplus show?
'COGHLAN'
Who from the Board went back to add
Freetrade accounts, and clip and pad?
'COGHLAN'
Who is, just now, from brains and bent,
The top spring of Government?
'COGHLAN'
Who is in fine our rhyme to end,
Reid's mentor, guide, factotum, friend?
'COGHLAN'

4

Remaking the public service

While the politicians and public servants of the old regime staggered through the crises of the 1880s and early 1890s, a quiet revolution had been taking place in the public service. The reorganization of key departments such as Lands, Railways and Public Works, the creation of new offices such as that of government statistician, and the death or retirement of many of the old guard, had allowed a number of young, innovative officers to rise to the top of the service.[1] With new organizational and intellectual skills, and with close ties to the 'democracy', their influence, independence and ideological commitment made them effective representatives of the interests of all public servants. They were well placed, therefore, to take advantage of the vacuum of political power, their closeness to the labour movement, and the threatened militancy of the rank and file to increase the autonomy of the service and ensure its continuing influence and security.

The Department of Public Works provided the conditions under which the new type of public service leader flourished. This large, decentralized department was made up of a number of semi-autonomous branches which employed about 12 000 to 15 000 people in the 1880s. At least 10 000 of these were in the railways. These branches were by far the largest and most complex organizations in the colony, and the bureaucrats who ran them became, through practical experience, the organizational experts of their time. It is not surprising, therefore, that Public Works bred a number of men who became what

Alfred Deakin later called 'the business doctors of the public service'.[2]

The central figures to emerge from the Public Works Department in the 1880s and 1890s were Joseph Barling and Timothy Coghlan, both of whom became members of the Public Service Board established by the Public Service Act of 1895, and Duncan McLachlan, who eventually became the first Commonwealth public service commissioner. Joseph Barling was a key figure linking old and new generations of civil service reformers. Like many public service leaders he had found upward mobility in the expanding public service of the post-1856 period. The eldest of five sons of an English ironmonger, he arrived in New South Wales in 1856. While his father and brothers tried their luck on the land, Barling joined the Public Works Department in 1861 at the age of twenty-one. He worked in both the railways and the harbours and rivers branches, and from 1871 was chief clerk and accountant in harbours and rivers under Edward Moriarty. In the Public Works Department, he came into contact with the older public service reformer, Charles Goodchap, and the two young men who were to become central figures in the remaking of the public service, Duncan McLachlan and Timothy Coghlan. Goodchap was Barling's superior in the railways from 1869 to 1871. McLachlan joined them in 1869 as junior clerk. When Barling moved back to the harbours and rivers branch in 1871 he was administrative chief and patron to McLachlan's friend, Timothy Coghlan, who joined the department in 1873.

The drastic reorganization of public works and railway administration in the mid-1880s opened the way for Barling to become a major influence on public service matters. When the Parkes government divided the Public Works Department and removed administration of the railways from direct political control in 1888, he was placed in charge of the new department. Goodchap had by this time been forced out of the service, but the thirty-four-year-old McLachlan, who had been his chief clerk, joined Barling in the same capacity. Together Barling and McLachlan welded the semi-autonomous branches into a centralized department, and introduced a well-regulated personnel system which was discussed with great interest and approval by the Royal Commission on the Public Service in 1895. In this same reorganization, McLachlan's brother, Hugh, became secretary to the railway commissioners, and Barling's colleagues from harbours and rivers, Robert Hickson and George Tillett, replaced William Bennett, the retiring commissioner for roads, and Edward Moriarty, the retiring engineer-in-chief for harbours and rivers. With Coghlan established in the new and influential position of government statistician since 1886, a network of Barling's colleagues controlled a large part of the public service by 1890.[3]

Close friends and colleagues, with similar petty bourgeois-artisan backgrounds and closely connected with the respectable working class railway community of Redfern, Barling, McLachlan and Coghlan epitomized the new, independent public service leader. All three were committed to the freedom of the public service from political control; all were experts in the manipulation of men and women in organizations and concerned to develop a new science of personnel management; and Coghlan was, in addition, a skilful manipulator of words, ideas and finance.

Much of the strength of this new guard of public servants derived from the fact that they had particular skills that made them useful in the new and volatile political situation. During the faction period, senior public servants had been mainly concerned with administrative and technical tasks as they transferred resources in a relatively straightforward way from land and customs to public works, raising loans where necessary to keep this process on a steady course. As the process was uncontroversial, except in its details, until the late 1870s, manipulation of public opinion was not necessary to make it acceptable to the electorate. With the breakdown of the faction system, however, ideology became important in attracting and consolidating public support, and governments looked for advisers skilled in the manipulation of facts and figures. The old political system had demanded that its public servants be resourceful, but not innovative, as the basic policy of government-led development was clearly laid down, and both politicians and bureaucrats found it suited their interests. The chaotic political situation of the 1880s required new policy initiatives if both bureaucrats and politicians were to survive. The faction system did not require extraordinary organizational skills of its public servants while the supply of government revenue was assured. In a tightening financial situation, however, management became more important than building, economy and efficiency more central than spending, and skills in the manipulation of personnel and organizational forms were demanded.

The new public service leaders had sources of motivation and support that had not been available to the old guard. Identifying more closely with the rank and file of the service, and with strong links to a wider movement for social reform that was still outside the political system, they were not restricted by the close ties of interest and loyalty that kept Eagar's generation under the hegemony of their politician friends. They faced a much more serious and longer-running danger of retrenchment and deterioration of their working conditions than earlier public servants had. Having observed the debacle of the 1884 Civil Service Act and the inefficacy and conservatism of the Civil Service Board and the Public Service Inquiry, they knew that they could not trust politicians or the old guard of public service leaders to protect public servants' rights. The widely discussed removal of Charles Goodchap, the capable and reform-minded commissioner of railways, reminded them that close identification with one government placed even the most powerful public servants in danger. In addition, politicians were more ready to release their hold over the public service as patronage in jobs, services and resources became less feasible as a political strategy.

The new men also had the backing of a mobilizing and unified public service and the support of a wider reform movement. Constant threats of retrenchment, the continuing financial problems of the government, the stacking of the public service for political purposes, and the weakness of the Civil Service Board provided strong motivation for unified public service action. The imminent breakdown of the superannuation fund was an immediate and compelling issue around which the rank and file of the service was organizing, while the longer-term deterioration of public service conditions and the political and social ferment of the previous decade encouraged the development of well-articulated labour market theories amongst its intellectuals. The great size of the public service made it a formidable voting bloc, and its unity was enhanced by the uniform danger of retrenchment faced by all levels of the service, the replacement of many of the old guard of senior public servants by young men who had risen through the ranks, and a strong sense of community enhanced by the centralized nature of the service by the 1890s. Further strength was added to the public servants' campaign for control over their labour market situation by the fact that they were part of the larger movement for social reform amongst 'the democracy'. The splintered nature of this movement gave added importance to the young public service leaders as spearheads of reform from within the bureaucracy. With the size and importance of major government departments providing an unrivalled organizational base and source of managerial expertise, public service leaders had considerable influence in establishing the direction of government policy in a period of political reorganization. This role, and close ties of background and sympathy, made them essential allies during the 1890s of the emerging Labor Party which, by 1904, became itself the focus of the reform movement.

II

Timothy Coghlan (or T. A. Coghlan as he is usually called) was the most important of the new public service leaders who emerged from the Public Works Department in the 1880s. Theoretically sophisticated, ambitious and articulate, he took advantage of the government's need for his particular blend of literary, mathematical and organizational skills to make himself the most influential public servant, if not the most influential political figure, of the period. The professionalization of the public service, its secure position after 1896 and its role in social reform can be attributed largely to his leadership.

Like most new men of the period, Coghlan was an upwardly mobile young man from the working classes. Many of the ideas that went into his remaking of the public service were drawn from this background. He was born in Sydney in 1855, the son of a passionately political Irish Catholic father and a quietly determined Irish Protestant mother.[4] His father poured his energies into the Irish Nationalist cause and the labour movement rather than his trade as a plasterer.[5] In Coghlan's cryptic phrase, he 'neglected his affairs' and did not manage to lift his family out of the poorer sections of the respectable working class suburb of Redfern.[6] When fellow public servant Arthur Fry knew Coghlan as a serious young man in the late 1870s and early 1880s, he notes that the family lived in 'one of the narrowest little back streets of Redfern' and that he 'never heard of the father'.[7]

Coghlan's mother was 'the strength and backbone of the family'.[8] Married at seventeen, she had nine children, born between 1851 and 1876, and was widowed in 1882 when the youngest child, Cecil, was six years old.[9] As Coghlan says, 'the bringing up of her children was left to the mother', and 'were it not for the devotedness of their mother, the lot of the children would have been hard'.[10] Well educated herself, Mrs Coghlan was determined that all her children, male and female, would be trained for professional careers. Despite the family's poverty, she maintained a home where intellectual activity and learning were valued, and where she still found time to read widely and play an active part in the School of Arts.[11] It is a mark of her tenacity that the family was so remarkable. Coghlan's older brother, Charles, became an eminent lawyer; his older sister, Dora, was one of the first female clerks in the public service; another sister, Dorcas, was a noted sculptor; Lucy was a schoolteacher for forty-six years; Iza (always known as Fanny by her family) was amongst the first pupils at the Sydney Girls' High School and one of the first women doctors in New South Wales; and Cecil, the youngest, became a lawyer and Labor member of parliament.[12]

As the third child and second son, Coghlan assumed much of the burden of his family's support as a young man.[13] Neither he nor his brother Charles married until their forties. His own late marriage in 1897, when he was forty-two years old, suggests that he waited until Cecil was established as an articled clerk and Iza had finished her medical degree and was settled as medical adviser to the Australian Mutual Provident insurance company. Of his five sisters, only Dora married, and she found she had to return to work to help support her own family of six children when her husband's business failed.[14]

The Redfern that Coghlan grew up in developed around the railway terminus built in 1855 and expanded with the growth of the railways. When Coghlan's family moved there around 1859, Redfern was, according to W. S. Jevons, a suburb of respectable tradesmen, journeymen and other wage-earners,

living in houses of limited size.[15] There was also a sprinkling
of shopkeepers such as Duncan McLachlan's parents, who
established a general store in the embryo settlement in the
mid-1850s.[16] By the late 1870s much of the movement of
goods and passengers in New South Wales flowed through
the Redfern terminus and most railway repair work was carried
out in its workshops.[17] When Charles Goodchap became railway commissioner in 1878 he purchased the nearby Eveleigh
estate to provide more extensive accommodation for repair
and maintenance workshops.[18] By 1881 Redfern was a crowded
suburb of 10 868 inhabitants, and by 1886 it was second only
to Balmain in size, with over 19 000 people or 10 per cent of
the Sydney suburban population living there.[19]

Redfern's distinctive character as a working class public
service suburb provided both upward mobility and a tradition
of male trade union militancy to its young men. Its workshops and goods yards were strongholds of traditional craft
unionism and the new unionism of unskilled workers. James
McGowen, the future Labor Party leader who taught Sunday
school at St Paul's, Redfern, worked in the railway workshops
from 1875 to 1891 and was secretary of the Boilermakers
Union during that period. The secretary of the Railway and
Tramway Employees Association, William Schey, was elected
to the Legislative Assembly in 1887 as a workingman's representative. Both were associated with the beginnings of the
Labor Party as members of the Redfern Labour League.[20]

The offices of the railways and the nearby Public Works
Department in Phillip Street provided work for the upwardly
mobile sons of Redfern's shopkeepers and artisans who had
excelled at the elementary schooling provided by the national
and church systems. These boys grew up imbued with the
traditions of independence, solidarity and exclusiveness of craft
unionism. They also grew up accepting as a fact of life that
the state played an active part in the economy of the colony,
and that its strength and stability were essential to the well-
being of the working class and the new middle class.

In the small community of early Redfern, Coghlan and the
McLachlan brothers knew each other, though they went to
different schools. The McLachlans attended the school attached
to St Paul's Church of England, where McGowen taught
Sunday school. Coghlan attended the local national school

until he was twelve, and then won a scholarship to Sydney Grammar School.[21] He did not enjoy school and left after two years. After a few false starts he found his niche when he joined the harbours and rivers branch of Public Works as a trainee engineer in 1873. There he came under the influence of chief clerk Joseph Barling. Duncan McLachlan had entered the railways four years earlier, and Fry writes of him and Coghlan 'walk[ing] down on summer mornings from Redfern along the avenue of great figtrees that lined the Elizabeth Street side of Hyde Park'. Through McLachlan, Coghlan was brought into contact with Charles Goodchap during his period of greatest influence. McLachlan lived in Redfern until the 1890s and Coghlan at least until the mid-1880s. When McLachlan moved in the early 1890s to Paddington where his wife's family owned the Barcom Glen estate, Coghlan built his first home there in 1893. The two men remained friends throughout their lives, corresponding regularly and frankly during Coghlan's long period in England from 1905 to 1926.[22]

An ambitious young man who 'allowed no frivolities to interfere with his serious pursuits', Coghlan applied himself vigorously to his career, presenting papers to the Institute of Engineers and accompanying the 1882 expedition to Lord Howe Island to observe the transit of Venus.[23] His enthusiasm for self-improvement led him into the 'debating society, hard-reading crowd' who developed literary, political and intellectual skills in the literary societies which proliferated in the 1870s and 1880s.[24] Coghlan and McLachlan, as young public servants, were founding members and office-holders in the Redfern Literary Society in 1875, and Coghlan was vice-president of the Catholic Literary Society for many years.[25]

Coghlan's literary and debating activities gave him an entree into the burgeoning journalism of the period.[26] In 1880 he contributed to current religious and education controversies in the Catholic *Freeman's Journal*, and the following year he edited the Redfern *Suburban Times* with Arthur Fry, canvassing themes that were to be of enduring interest to him—success, government intervention for 'the comfort of the community', the hardships of the poorer classes, the need for state intervention on their behalf, the need for impartiality in administration, and the better organization of Friendly Societies.[27] Coghlan's literary and journalistic activities introduced him into Sydney's

political world, and it was his close intimacy with the fledgling
politician, James Toohey, that brought Coghlan to Dibbs'
attention for the new position of government statistician in
1886.[28]

Coghlan was only thirty-one and a junior engineer in harbours
and rivers when he was appointed to this controversial position.
As one of Barling's 'stable' in the Public Works Department,
he was part of the group of up-and-coming young men from
Redfern who were making their presence felt in this year of
public service ferment. Arthur Fry says of Coghlan that even
in the Public Works Department, 'whatever way Coghlan
made the figures look swayed the opinion of the majority just
in that direction'.[29] It is obviously this combination of literary,
mathematical and persuasive ability that secured him the position over the head of the more pedestrian officer of the
Registrar-General's Department who had prepared the two
previous census reports. This position provided a springboard
for him to quickly become an indispensable adviser to successive governments on almost every matter of importance,
and a well-known public authority on all policy matters to
which statistics could be applied.

It was indicative of the times that this ambitious young man
chose to become a statistician rather than remain an engineer.
The judicious distribution of jobs, services, and public works
in which the engineer was a central figure was becoming an
unworkable political strategy by 1886. Instead, in a situation
of decreasing abundance, politicians had to make more calculated judgements about expected revenue, government expenditure and the state of the economy and the labour market.
They also had to create the illusion of working in the interests
of all when this was no longer possible. Such illusions needed
skilful creation and manipulation of knowledge. The statistician was the ideal person to carry out this dual role. The
'political arithmetic' of the seventeenth century had become
the 'statistics' of the nineteenth century, the supposedly neutral
facts which formed the basis of the science of government.
The nineteenth-century term 'statist' conveyed the close connection that was made between the work of the state and the
work of the statistician. The statist was, theoretically, the
scientific expert in matters of policy, providing empirical
knowledge on which rational decisions could be made.[30]

The concept of the statistician as a disinterested man of science was useful to both the upwardly mobile intellectual of the nineteenth century and the government who employed him. It provided socially concerned scientists with new careers in the state service which gave them opportunities for intervention and influence. At the same time, governments were able to trade on the authority of the expert to make their policies and administration more attractive to their constituencies.

In appointing Coghlan to this position, the New South Wales government wanted someone who could present facts and figures intelligibly and with authority and could publicize them with flair.[31] Coghlan did not disappoint them. He quickly redesigned the former *Statistical Year Book* as a yearly series entitled the *Wealth and Progress of New South Wales*, an elegantly written exposition of the history, resources and economic characteristics of the colony. This annual production was joined in 1890 by *The Seven Colonies of Australasia*, which presented material on the six Australian colonies and New Zealand. In addition, he provided extensive interpretive comment on the New South Wales census which he conducted in 1891.

These official publications were supplemented by judicious use of the press. By means of press statements, reviews, informal feeds and the publication of articles on social aspects of statistics in his own name as well as under pseudonyms, Coghlan popularized his official publications and the information he gathered. He formed close relationships with the management and writers of the *Bulletin* which gave him ample opportunity to influence public opinion directly and indirectly. He regularly wrote anonymous leading articles and pseudonymous social and economic essays and fiction for the *Bulletin*, and employed a number of *Bulletin* writers in the census office.[32] He also wrote on economic subjects for that 'Journal of the Great Middle Classes', the *Daily Telegraph*.[33]

Almost immediately Coghlan became one of the most respected authorities in New South Wales on social and political issues. An adroit self-publicist, he often inserted into his pseudonymous articles some reference to 'Mr Coghlan, the New South Wales Statist' as the authority on the subject under discussion. The *Bulletin* did likewise, and he soon became a household word.[34] Successive governments found the new statist invaluable as a source of useful information. Soon after he was appointed, Parkes, once again premier, commissioned him to prepare a statement of electorate expenditure in order to meet accusations of government favouritism. He was soon consulted on the government's proposed property tax. Firmly convinced of the necessity of an income tax to place government finances on a stable footing, he persuaded the government that a property tax was not adequate. From that time he became the chief source of advice to governments on taxation, banking and finance, sickness and pension funds, local government and electoral reform. As he himself immodestly remarked in his autobiography (which was written in the third person): 'The government recognised that they had an officer whom they could turn to in difficult matters for which specialists were employed'.[35]

III

As Coghlan's stature grew, his confidence as a social reformer grew also, and he turned increasingly to the subject which engrossed his whole life, 'determining the causes which give the workers so little in the way of comfort'.[36] Evidence of this lifelong interest is manifested in his monumental and authoritative social and economic history, *Labour and Industry in Australia*, which was his main intellectual preoccupation from 1905 until it was published in 1918. Unfortunately there is less evidence regarding the precise nature of his relations with the developing labour movement which he chronicles so well. He does class his knowledge of 'some phases of the Labour movement' with that of the banking crisis of 1893, in which he claims to have been a major participant, and with the statistics he presents, for which, he said, 'I am my own authority'.[37] This suggests a degree of personal involvement in the movement greater than that of merely a contemporary observer. Certainly his family had close connections with the labour movement. His father was a labour activist prior to his death in 1882, and his youngest brother, Cecil, whose upbringing had been his special care, was a Labor nominee to the Legislative Council from 1921 to 1924.[38] He himself was rumoured to be the likely Labor nominee as Governor of New South Wales during the Lang government's 1926 crisis shortly before his death.[39] Coghlan's son recalls that his father would not necessarily have acted as Governor in the way that Lang wished. This independent attitude probably characterized Coghlan's approach to the labour movement—deep sympathy and understanding stemming from his family background and upbringing in a working class suburb, combined with a strong conviction that the solution to labour's problems required authority and expertise such as he himself could provide.

Coghlan's intense interest in the welfare of the working class and his own insecure economic and social background stimulated his development as a theorist of the labour market. His incisive and sympathetic approach to the labour movement and the social problems of his time can be gleaned from two series of articles on political economy he published in 1889 under pseudonyms. The *Daily Telegraph* articles set out his ideas in scholarly fashion, while these ideas are applied to a number of current issues in the *Bulletin*.

Coghlan's political economy was strongly influenced by the respectable working class traditions of craft unionism with which he had grown up, and his own painful experiences of family poverty and struggle for respectability. Blending these traditions and experiences with the most advanced ideas of new middle class reformers in Britain and America, he rejected revolutionary socialism as theoretically misconceived. He borrowed instead from the most recent British and American marginalist economics to elevate to the status of economic 'laws' the necessity of co-operation between capital and labour, the right of labour to strike and combine to maintain a given standard of living, the desirability of intervention in the labour market, and the exclusion of groups such as married women and Chinese from the labour force.[40]

Agreeing with the marginalists' rejection of the theory of value and of the fundamental antagonism of capital and labour, Coghlan embraced a Christian socialism in which 'the basis of Socialism is CHRIST's command—Love thy neighbour'.[41] In economic terms this meant that 'the prosperity of the worker is identical with that of the capitalist'.[42] It did not follow, however, that workers were passively to accept the dictates of capital. It was, rather, an injunction to capitalists to ensure the well-being of workers in their own self-interest. Coghlan maintained that the material prosperity of the entire community depended on the standard of living of the worker;

indeed, free political institutions depended upon the 'industrial condition of the masses'.[43] Therefore a consumption-led economy which afforded the worker a high standard of living was necessary for the well-being of all.

If necessary, active intervention should be used to ensure the workers' prosperity. Rejecting the law of supply and demand, Coghlan emphasized that culture and will played a major part in the determination of wages. Wages, for Coghlan, were based on the cost of production of the labourer, which was determined by cultural practice and active intervention. In a virulent attack on the family economy, he argued that cultures where the whole family worked together, and those where workers were extremely frugal, provided low wages and a poor standard of living. Where male workers expected and demanded high wages sufficient to keep a family, the standard of living of the whole community was highest. In particular, he argued that the competition of married women or partially supported single women for jobs endangered the prosperity of all.[44]

Coghlan appears to have had no explicit theory of the role of the state or of professional experts at this time. However, his rejection of the law of supply and demand left the way open for state and expert intervention. His earliest writings had conceded the necessity for legislation and expert advice to remedy various social problems, and in 1890 he advocated land nationalization.[45] His experience of the potential power of the state to modify the environment of its citizens, his growing concern with the labour market conditions of his own class, and his increasing confidence in his own ability to diagnose and cure current social problems led him to develop a practical approach to the state as a useful base for intervention, as long as it was controlled by independent and able experts.

These provisos were important. Coghlan saw economics as an 'exact science' which worked hand-in-hand with careful investigation.[46] He stressed the importance of empirical investigation of local conditions, criticizing the labour movement where it slavishly followed British precedent. Significantly, he was most critical of the anti-sweating movement and factories and shops legislation, the two areas in which he had carried out investigations and proposed solutions which were not carried out to his satisfaction.[47] He was dismissive of the

ability of politicians and businessmen to maintain the prosperous community he considered so essential to the well-
being of all. His discussion in *Labour and Industry* of the
administration of Crown lands before 1884, the extravagant
government expenditure of the 1880s and the depression which
followed, portrayed politicians and businessmen alike as selfish,
incompetent and short-sighted.[48] He viewed the premiers he
worked with with a jaundiced eye, speaking of Dibbs' venality
and Reid's incapacity for work.[49]

Coghlan did not, however, see the public servant as necessarily any more competent or universal in outlook. He had a
poor opinion of the bureaucrats of the earlier period, especially
those of the Treasury and Lands Departments,[50] and was
contemptuous of his successors at the Public Service Board
who did not maintain their independence of politicians.[51] Nor
was he necessarily approving of all experts. He was quick to
denounce as incorrect or impractical economists who advocated profit-sharing and the single tax as panaceas for social
problems.[52] He was also critical of many public servants who
came to office in New South Wales after he went to London
in the early 1900s.[53] Only when there was a combination of
'correct' theoretical approach and independence could Coghlan
whole-heartedly endorse the reign of the expert. To his friend,
Captain Neitenstein, the penal reformer whose interests were
close to his own, he could write approvingly, 'You of course
are supreme in your act and no minister however powerful
would venture to interfere with you in the performance of
your duties'.[54]

IV

From these ideas on political economy flowed Coghlan's main
concerns as writer, statistician and policy adviser. The nation's
prosperity depended on the maintenance of consumption and
full employment, high wages and good working conditions
for white males. As a statistician, therefore, he concentrated
on the measurement of the prosperity of the colony, the more
accurate description of its labour market, especially of women's
labour market participation, and the improvement of indicators
of prosperity such as infant mortality rates, birth rates, crime
rates and the physical measurement of children. As a policy

adviser, he was concerned with the development of stable financial institutions and the regulation of the labour market.

Equipped with a well-articulated economic philosophy, Coghlan embarked on a period of intense intellectual and political activity from 1889. In his own department he published the first official estimates of national income in the world, blazing a trail which other nations were to follow.[55] He helped devise a new classification of occupations for the 1891 census which was a pioneering work in its field. At the same time, he introduced an industrial census.[56] He also began his studies of life expectancy, maternal mortality, the birth rate and child measurement.[57] As a general adviser to government, he worked closely with treasurers William McMillan and John See on their respective direct taxation proposals. He advised McMillan on bills concerning banking, finance and life assurance, and played an important part on the finance committee of the Federal Convention in 1891.[58] He claimed to have been Dibbs' right-hand man during the bank crisis of May 1893, in moves which he felt saved New South Wales from the catastrophe that occurred in other states.[59] His work on life expectancy led to his additional appointment as registrar of Friendly Societies and trade unions and to his being consulted on the state of the public service superannuation fund.[60] He also drew up a Factories Bill based on his investigations of industrial conditions.[61]

Popular articles in the *Bulletin* on the birth rate, unemployment, women's work, 'superfluous' women, state life insurance and old age pensions, either written by Coghlan or reflecting his influence, brought the more topical aspects of his work to the attention of the public.[62] A more serious audience was tapped through the 1891 census commentary, where he published an address he had given to the Australian Medical Congress on life expectancy, and, in an essay on the employment of women, the substance of one of his 1889 articles on the theory of wages.[63]

When George Reid formed a reform-minded Free Trade government in August 1894, he found Coghlan established as the expert on nearly every aspect of the government's proposed programme. Coghlan quickly became indispensable to Reid, and the combination of Reid's political skill and Coghlan's energy brought into being the new state system that had been gestating since the early 1880s.

George Reid was a former Treasury official who had replaced Henry Parkes as leader of the Free Trade Party soon
after its defeat at the end of 1891. The son of a Presbyterian
clergyman, he joined the public service in 1864 after starting
work at the age of thirteen in a commercial office. He educated
himself through debating societies and the study of law, and
by 1878 was secretary of the Attorney-General's Department.
He was elected to the Legislative Assembly in 1880, where he
supported Alexander Stuart and became a minister in his
government. Although he later supported the Free Trade
Party he differed fundamentally from his more conservative
colleagues and would never accept office under Parkes.[64]

Reid was not habituated to the buying of support through
public works that characterized the old political system, and
quickly showed himself a master of the new politics. His
convincing victory in 1894 and his even greater success in
1895 were the result of his adroit alignment of the urban and
'democratic' vote behind the Free Trade platform of direct
taxation, public service reform, land reform and industrial
legislation. These measures had been the stock-in-trade of
reformers of both major parties since 1887, but Reid managed
to paint the Protectionists as conservatives intent on protecting
the large landowner from taxation.[65]

Reid, the astute politican, and Coghlan, the determined and
opinionated public servant, made a formidable team. They
shared a common interest in the welfare of 'the democracy'—
the worker, the civil servant, the small businessman, the selector
and the miner—and, by virtue of their backgrounds, an understanding of this group denied to more patrician Free Traders
such as B. R. Wise.[66] While Reid organized the political
numbers, Coghlan acted as theoretician, publicist and im-
plementer of a series of measures to defend the combined
interests of the new middle class and the working class.

V

Coghlan's influential position made him well placed to lead
the public service reform movement from within and to help
create a new state system which gave public servants autonomy
and established a secure and independent base for social reform.
Reid was committed to public service reform, having supported the rights of public servants both as a public servant
himself and as a member of parliament.[67] He was also astute

enough to know that political control of the public service had
become an electoral liability, and that the superannuation
question was becoming explosive. He accordingly moved
quickly to establish a Royal Commission on the Public
Service.[68]

The Royal Commission was intended primarily to extricate
the government from the financial chaos it had inherited from
the faction period. Its instructions were 'to inquire and report'
first of all:

- as to the changes necessary for the purposes of placing the Public
  Departments upon a strictly economic and efficient footing;
- as to the present methods of public expenditure, and as to the
  changes necessary to place them upon a sound and economic basis;
- as to the state the Civil Service Superannuation Fund, and the steps
  necessary to place it upon a secure footing, a) with additional
  Government aid, or, b) without such aid.

With these important functions out of the way, it was then
instructed to draw up a scheme 'for the better regulation of
appointments and promotions in the Public Service'.

The report of the Royal Commission, however, turned
these priorities on their head, arguing that 'unless [the question
of public service regulation] be promptly and satisfactorily
determined, whatever other recommendations we make will
be ineffective to free the Civil Service from the influence of
political patronage or control'.[69]

The Royal Commissioners considered that their most
important recommendation was the establishment of an
independent Board with large powers to investigate thoroughly
every branch of the service. They envisaged that this Board
would value the work and responsibility of every officer,
determine salaries, and recommend departmental reorgan-
izations in the interests of economy and efficiency. Political
influence was to be strictly avoided, and the Board was to
have full responsibility for recommending appointments and
promotions. Promotion was to be by merit, from candidates
drawn from the service as a whole. All candidates for appointment were to pass an examination, and to be medically fit.
The Board members were to be liberally paid and were to
devote their full time to their duties. The Royal Commissioners
considered that

by the establishment of such a Board political or other undue influence to secure appointments would cease, the frequent and pertinacious solicitation of members of Parliament by their constituents would be obviated, and Ministers would be relieved of many importunities. The Service would become more honorable and it would certainly possess a higher status than at present.[70]

This change in emphasis to the essentially class concerns of the public servant suggests the influence of Coghlan and Barling. Barling's minister, James Young, who played an important role in the establishment of the Royal Commission, was a strong supporter of Barling's plans for reform, which were highly commended in the Commission's final report.[71] Coghlan was working closely with Reid at the time, and he had just reported on the superannuation fund. He later claimed complete responsibility for the 1895 Public Service Act and the ideas underlying it.[72] This Bill was introduced by Reid on 1 October 1895, as soon as his land and income tax measures had been launched. These three measures and the Act to amend the conduct of the audit, which made government accounts more accessible to public scrutiny—all intimately involving Coghlan—dominated the August to December session.

The Public Service Bill was consciously designed by Coghlan to give large powers to the Public Service Board the Royal Commissioners had suggested,[73] and in some measures, such as competitive examinations and the abolition of the employment of married women, he went beyond the Commissioners' recommendations. The Bill can be considered as a class measure intended to provide public servants and their classes of origin with a high degree of control over the public service labour market. The Bill proposed that control of the service should be moved out of the hands of ministers into the hands of a full-time Board appointed for life. Control was to be centralized and the Board was to have complete responsibility for appointments, promotions, discipline and dismissal, the classification of officers, the fixing of salaries and the organization of departments. Not only was the Board to have much greater powers than the Civil Service Board of 1884, but its jurisdiction was to be much wider. All employees of the service, as well as teachers in the Public Instruction Department and parliamentary officers, were to be subject to the provisions of the new Act.

Only the railways, whose personnel administration was already independent of political interference, were to remain under their own Act.

The Bill passed through both houses of parliament with the basic agreement of most members. Several opposition members expressed some concern about the removal of responsibility from ministers onto an 'irresponsible' board, but they did little to obstruct the Bill. The tenure of Board members was limited to a fixed term by parliament, a change readily agreed to by Reid. Some attempts were made to exclude teachers and the Public Works Department from the jurisdiction of the Board, but these proposals met with little support. There was considerable opposition from members of all political persuasions to the clause barring married women from the service, and a compromise clause was accepted which prohibited the employment of public servants' wives except in the Department of Public Instruction.[74]

The Bill met with the approval of the public service except for the provisions concerning the superannuation fund. The Bill proposed an interim solution only to this perennial problem, and Reid promised a comprehensive measure to deal with it fully as soon as the reorganization of the service was complete. Dismayed public servants rallied to press the government for more decisive action and a deputation including Duncan McLachlan and union activists met Reid the morning before the superannuation clauses were considered by the Assembly. He remained resolute, however, that a satisfactory solution of the matter was not possible until the proposed Board had carried out its investigation of the service.[75]

Coghlan's and Barling's influence became open and decisive when both were appointed early in 1896 to the Public Service Board created by the Act. Coghlan's strong commitment to public service reform is demonstrated by the fact that he chose to accept the Public Service Board position rather than that of commissioner of taxation, which was offered to him at the same time.[76] Their appointment confirmed the transfer of control of public service personnel matters from politicians to public servants themselves. With a token businessman, George A. Wilson, making up a rather reluctant third member of the Board, the two public service reformers set about creating a service in accord with their own ideas.[77]

Within six months they had removed most of the remainder of the old guard and established a network of their own men at the top of the service. The Public Service Act had given the Board the right to retire officers over sixty years of age. It took advantage of this to rid itself of senior public servants it did not consider sympathetic to its purposes. The Board made no secret of this aim. In its first *Report*, it stated clearly that

it was plain that a reform of the Public Service was impossible unless the principal officers of heads of branches were not only competent to perform the duties attaching to their positions, but willing to enter into the spirit of the Board's work.[78]

Archibald Fraser, the architect of the 1884 Act, was one of these marked men. His replacement by the pedestrian George Miller as under-secretary for justice was possibly influenced by his old patron Reid; but this move allowed Coghlan's friend, Captain F. W. Neitenstein, to be appointed comptroller-general of prisons in Miller's place, and another friend, James Williams, to become chief clerk in the Justice Department at the age of twenty-six.[79]

Harrie Wood, the recalcitrant under-secretary for mines, was replaced by Duncan McLachlan, who had briefly replaced Barling as under-secretary for public works. G. A. McKay, the young public service activist who was president of the Draftsmen's Association in 1895, was promoted from the Lands Department to become McLachlan's chief draftsman.[80] This was the beginning of the long association of these two public service reformers. Coghlan's old literary friend, Arthur Fry, was also found a place in McLachlan's department.[81]

The collector of customs, James Powell, was replaced by a young Treasury officer, N. C. Lockyer, and the position amalgamated with that of first commissioner of taxation. Lockyer had been a cadet in the Treasury when Reid was an officer of that department and married Eagar's daughter. His investigation of a major fraud in the Public Instruction Department in 1893 and the recommendations he made concerning changes to the audit system probably brought him to the attention of Coghlan. He worked with Coghlan on the reorganization of the Taxation Department under the new Income Tax Acts of 1895, and they remained close friends until Coghlan's death.[82] Lockyer chose as his secretary and chief clerk John D'Arcy, a thirty-year-old clerk from the Public Instruction Department whom he had probably come in contact with during his investigation of the fraud case in 1893.[83]

William Stephen, the former secretary of lands whom Parkes had saved from dismissal in 1880 by appointing him secretary of the Attorney-General's Department in place of Reid, was retired to make way for a thirty-two-year-old barrister from outside the service, Hugh Pollock.[84] Charles Cowper, the former premier's son who had been sheriff since 1874, was succeeded by the forty-three-year-old Cecil Maybury. Charles Potter, the government printer, was replaced by William Gullick, the young manager of the commercial printing firm John Sands Ltd. Gullick was a school-fellow of Coghlan's colleague and fellow statistician, John Trivett, and a close friend of Barling's brother-in-law, John Vernon.[85]

Only a few members of the older generation of public servants survived this 'massacre of the ancients'. Edmund Fosbery, who was fondly remembered by reformers of the period for his work on charitable boards, remained inspector-general of police until 1903, when he was sixty-nine years old.[86] Stephen Lambton, who had been secretary and then deputy postmaster-general since 1866, did not retire until 1902, despite the fact that James Dalgarno, who had been tainted by his association with the ineffectual reform efforts of the 1870s and 1880s, was waiting in the wings.[87] George Colquhoun, the sixty-six-year-old Crown solicitor who had only been appointed in 1894, was also retained until 1902, but the young son of a former colleague of Barling's and Coghlan's, John Tillett, was appointed managing clerk in his department.[88] Henry Russell, the government astronomer, also escaped retirement until he reached the age of sixty-eight in 1904. The final survivor from the faction days was the principal under-secretary, Critchett Walker. Although only fifty-five in 1896, he had been under-secretary to successive premiers since Halloran retired in 1879. According to a later head of the department, A. G. Kingsmill, Walker was marked for removal by the Board, but was saved by the protests of two of the conservative members of the ministry, chief secretary James Brunker and attorney-general John Want.[89]

The creation of new departments and the reorganization of

existing ones provided the opportunity for further consolidation of Coghlan's and Barling's influence over the top of the service. In 1897, in a reorganization of treasury and audit functions, three of Lockyer's young colleagues, Percy Williams, George Brodie and Ernest Hanson, were moved from Treasury to make up a separate Audit Office with Brodie as assistant auditor–general and chief inspector of public accounts. Barling's brother–in–law, John Vernon, was appointed treasury accountant in place of Lockyer. Barling's former confidential clerk in the Public Works Department, John Holliman, became secretary to the Public Service Board and moved to the new Taxation Department when it was established. [90]

With colleagues who shared their ideas on the role and administration of the service, Coghlan and Barling established a strong system of independent personnel management and provided a secure and receptive organizational basis for a programme of social reform in which the public service played an important part. The young men who were favoured by the new administration ran a large proportion of the New South Wales and Commonwealth public services over the next twenty years. Neitenstein, for instance, carried out the modernization of the prison system in New South Wales and acted periodically as a member of the Public Service Board until his retirement in 1909. [91] James Williams replaced Miller and Pollock as under–secretary for the attorney–general and justice in 1905 at the age of thirty–five, and in 1919 became a member of the Public Service Board. In 1925 he was appointed chairman of the Board, where he remained until 1933. [92] Duncan McLachlan was appointed the first public service commissioner of the Commonwealth Public Service in 1902, and his report as Royal Commissioner in 1920 strongly influenced the direction of public service personnel management for many decades. [93]

With a network of young, innovative officers at the top of the service, Reid and Coghlan made the most of the short period during which Reid controlled both houses of parliament to introduce a number of measures which favoured the working class and at the same time established a new role for the state. The New South Wales government had always been interventionist by virtue of its development policies. It had also shouldered much of the burden of support for the needy and destitute, and from 1884 made *ad hoc* attempts to deal with the problems of unemployment and conflicts between capital and labour. From 1896 the government's intervention into the lives of the people became much more overt. In 1896, two Acts, the Coal Mines Regulation Act and the Factories and Shops Act, regulated the conditions of important parts of the work force. The Coloured Races Restriction Act extended restrictions on immigration of coloured races. A Public Health Act strengthened the control of the government over community health. A State Children's Relief Act provided for the first time a form of state support for widows and deserted mothers with dependent children. A Department of Labour and Industry was established, and a large public works programme was reintroduced which set standards for other employers by extensive use of day labour rather than contract labour and the provision of a minimum wage in government contracts.[94]

More importantly, Coghlan guided Reid through a series of taxation, audit and local government measures designed to ensure a reliable and publicly accountable revenue for the state. Although Reid did not succeed in introducing the local government measures which would have removed much of the responsibility for public works to local authorities, the land and income tax measures of 1895 helped stabilize government finances, and the new cash accounting system made government spending much more accessible to public scrutiny.

These gains proved much more significant than the fairly weak interventionist measures introduced by the Reid government. Reid quickly found that his conservative supporters placed severe limits on the degree to which 'State Socialist' measures, as they were termed, could be smuggled in under the rubric of 'free trade'.[95] His failure to achieve any further reforms lost him the support of 'the democracy' in 1899, and Protectionist governments led by Lyne and then See responded to the 'democratic' constituency for the last time with the introduction of old age pensions, an Early Closing Act and compulsory arbitration of industrial disputes.[96] With the establishment of a clearly class-based two-party system in 1904, the overt influence of the new middle class declined and the independence of its public service members was eroded. Nevertheless, during these few years of 'democratic' hegemony, when new middle class and working class worked hand-in-hand, bureaucratic autonomy had been attained and a pattern of state regulation of civil society was established. This pattern became institutionalized in the first two decades of the new century and had a lasting effect on the relationships between capital and labour and men and women.

Top: The arrival of the mail was eagerly awaited.
Below: Local inns, often run by women, were centres of district life which often doubled as post offices.

Top: Women such as this one in Gulgong c. 1872 were storekeepers, and they often acted as postmistress as well.

Below: The post office was often a family affair. This Penrith Post office List shows Mrs Faith Kellett as postmistress from 1860 to 1873, and her son Charles succeeding her at the same salary.

POST OFFICE at *Penrith*

Record Number.	Persons by whom the Postmaster was recommended.	Name of Postmaster.	Date of Appointment.	Salary. £	Date of Declaration.	Date of Bond.	Names of Suret
		Mrs Faith A. S. Kellett	5 apl 1860	100	24 apl 60	1 July 62	Geo Cox
6948		Do	1 Sep 1862	200			Richd Wm
7215		Do	"	"	"	10 Oct 68	Richd Wm
							Robert Ste
72		Do			8 Feby		Charles Hy
							Robert St
582		Chas Hy Kellett	1 Oct 73	200	19 Sep 73	15 Oct 73	Donald Bea
							Robert Stu
		do			19 Sept 87	1 July 01	Mercantile
18819		"	1 Oct 88	240			
15974		do	1 Jan 90	250			
4032		do	18 Sept 91	270			
1490		do	1 Jan 94	280			
6745		do	1 July 96	240	Less Fee for quarters		
9458		Fredk J. Fowler	28 Sep 97	225	" £30		

Top: As country towns grew, women became postmistresses in post offices such as this one in East Maitland.
Below: Mrs Daly was in charge of this imposing post office in West Maitland built in 1881.

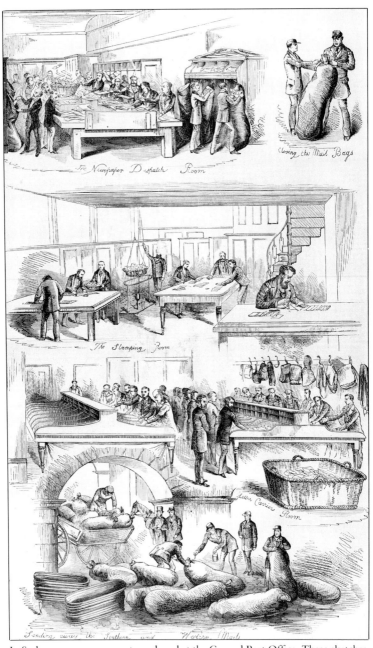

The Newspaper Despatch Room

Closing the Mail Bags

The Stamping Room

Letter Carrier Room

Sending across the Southern and Western Mails

In Sydney women were not employed at the General Post Office. These sketches made in 1879 show only men.

Top: Suburban post and telegraph offices, however, were often run by women. Ellen Cross, postmistress at Leichhardt from 1883 to 1896, moved into this new post and telegraph building in 1888.

Below: Mrs Ada Ford, formerly Mrs Hambly, postmistress at Chatswood in the 1890s, poses with her staff. The young woman on her left is her niece Mary Eliza Hambly.

Left: The grandiose new government buildings in Sydney's city centre were at first exclusively male preserves.   Top: Lands and Mines Offices, 1882   Below: Colonial Secretary's Office, 1882

Young men, anxious for self-improvement, flocked into the reading room of the School of Arts, and sought positions in the swelling public service.

Vol. 1.—No. 7.—New Series.

SATURDAY, JUNE 30, 1883.

Price—6d.

The Bulletin.

SATURDAY, JUNE 30, 1883.

"Down the Harbour," Again!

THE S. M. HERALD has, in its turn, tasted the sweets of our law of libel as interpreted by a N. S. Wales judge. The case ANDERSON V. FAIRFAX did not run on all fours with our own Clontarf action. And the variation has been useful, as climbing previous demonstrations of the iniquity of the law, and of the incompetence of some of our Judges. In THE BULLETIN-Clontarf case, it will be remembered, every allegation in the article which was the cause of complaint was proved and endorsed by an overwhelming array of eye-witnesses. But the Judge ruled that the paper should be tried, not on the particular article merely, but on the contents of previous numbers, even though no allusion were made therein to the subject or point at issue. The purpose of publication was the thing, according to Judge MANNING. Now, in the HERALD case, it is not pretended that the statements in the article which constituted the ground for action were sustained in every detail. There is no doubt that the attempts to verify all that was embodied in the article broke down in several instances. The reporter had not sufficiently distinguished between facts sustainable by his own observation, and inferences which were only patent to his own mind. But that the general purport of the article was made out and sustained by the weight of evidence, there can be no reasonable doubt. The reporter conveyed to the public his impressions that the ANDERSONS' establishment was not what it was represented to be; that the motives of its conductors were not of unqualified purity; that the boys were not so cared for as to justify continuance of public subscriptions; and that it would be a good thing if the whole affair could be quashed. There were evidently sufficient reasons why the reporter should have arrived at these conclusions. But, unluckily, his perceptive faculties were superior to his powers of marshalling his thoughts and giving to causes and inferences their due relation. He jumbled up what he had ascertained with what he had gathered from ex-parte statements and with what he had merely inferred, and in his report failed to discriminate between these essentially different grades of evidence. To his mind, apparently, an inference was as good as a fact, and a personal and internal conviction quite on a par with a matter proved by collation of evidence or by ocular demonstration.

To these defects in the article, the proprietors of the HERALD have primarily to attribute the verdict which has astonished the community and deepened the alarm and uneasiness created by previous interpretations of the law of libel. Not that the article as a whole was not sustained in its essential conclusions, but because opportunity was afforded for the plaintiff's counsel and the Judge to dilute upon the discrepancies between minor details and minor facts. The real question to be decided was embodied in the defendants' second plea, namely, that the publication was for the public benefit. Now, it cannot be contended that it is for the public benefit that exaggerated or unsustained allegations affecting any individual should be published. But it is for the public benefit that impostures, or misrepresentations whereby money intended to support truly charitable institutions are diverted to make-believe establishments, should be freely commented upon. And if representations made in good faith, without malice and with honest purpose, and, broadly

speaking, accurate, should contain a minute infusion of allegations not absolutely correct, it is distinctly for the interest of the community that the representations should be regarded as a whole, and a liberal appreciation of their general import be permitted. It is obviously not possible for any public writer, however excellent his intentions, and however clear his faculties, to assure himself beyond chance of error on every detail in all cases. A reasonable latitude of inference must be conceded; other wise, to describe or comment upon any wrong will be to court a penalty for trying to do the State a service. Now, His Honor Sir GEORGE INNES has been at the trouble to make a special disclaimer on this head. After the verdict had been given, and the Court was about to pass on to

MR. CHAS. A. GOODCHAP, COMMISSIONER FOR RAILWAYS.

other matters, His Honor offered some corrections of the public report, and stated:—

"I did not tell the jury that the article must be shown to be true 'in every particular,' but that all the statements declared on, which in their opinion had not been proved and conveyed serious defamatory charges, must be proved to be true in order to entitle the defendants to a verdict."

Sir GEORGE no doubt believed that this accurately defined his utterances, just as he probably persuaded himself that his summing-up was free from evidence of a strong bias against or for the defendants.

If His Honor's idea of what he did and did not instruct the jury be correct, then the HERALD's report of the trial was certainly inaccurate in a degree quite extraordinary, considering the care with which such matters are habitually presented in that

journal. For in the report we find the very instruction which Sir GEORGE INNES disclaims, conveyed not once, or in a single form, but repeatedly and in a variety of ways. Thus His Honor is represented as putting the case in a nett form in these terms:—

"The question is, Are these statements true? Are these unhappy boys the means of getting a good income from the public and giving ANDERSON a certain hold upon a valuable property—thus attributing to him dishonest motives—and were the boys worked for long hours daily at the severest manual toil, underfed, ordinary education and religious teaching alike neglected, and enjoying none of the play or amusement necessary at their age? Now, are these things true or not? Are they made out to your satisfaction?"

And again:—

"If this article had contented itself with saying

... and, as I said before, the thing has been subjected —and justly—to very strong animadversion and condemnation on many points. But it is for you to say whether these things are proved, and, if they are not proved, then the plaintiff is entitled to a verdict at your hands, with such damages as, under all the circumstances of the case, you may think justifiable."

The above are four separate quotations, culled from different parts of His Honor's summing. They are in perfect harmony each with any and every other, and they all convey precisely the sense which Sir GEORGE disclaims having meant to convey. To dispel the impression that His Honor did actually impress upon the jury that every charge must have been substantiated to their satisfaction before a verdict should be given for the defendants, it would be requisite to suppose that every one of these four paragraphs was inaccurate. It seems more probable that a lawyer of Sir GEORGE INNES' quality had been confused about what he actually did say, than that four separate blunders, each curiously corresponding and dovetailing, as regards the sense and purport, with every other, should have occurred in the report. It is at least quite undisputed that His Honor, whatever he may have meant to leave unsaid, did not at any period of his summing instruct the jury that they should take a broad view of the representations in the article, weigh and consider the general purport, and the ultimate effect from the standpoint as claimed by the defendants, and not denied to them, of public benefit. Sir GEORGE assuredly did not instruct the jury that they were not to split straws and grope among technicalities and petty details, but to decide whether, viewing all the matters comprehensively and in their mutual inter-relations, the article had done the State good service; or that the injury, due to the unsustained fractions of its representations, inflicted upon the plaintiffs had been so considerable as to outweigh the proportion of benefit conferred upon the community at large.

But it cannot be expected that a narrow mind should be the home of a broad conception. The law is vague and faulty. Its administration depends largely upon the interpretation given to it by such Judges as political exigencies or the personal preferences of influential Ministers chance to give us. This has resulted in most unsatisfactory decisions. The intention of the libel laws is that the power of the Press for evil should be curbed. As the law has been administered , the third or fourth-rate men whom accident rather than ability has pitchforked on to the bench of our Supreme Court, its incidence has been to paralyse the influence of the Press for good. Recent rulings have not only been dangerous to the general welfare by restricting the liberty of the public Press, but they have been self-condemnatory in another way. They have added confusion and uncertainty to a general limitation of useful privilege. In the Clontarf-BULLETIN case, it was expressly urged by the counsel for the proprietors of Clontarf that the whole tenor of a journal and any part of the contents of any of its numbers, present or past, might be taken into consideration as affording a test by which to judge of the intention in publishing a particular article. The presiding Judge, Sir WILLIAM MANNING, was at the trouble of consulting the Chief Justice before giving a ruling on this point; and, fortified by consultation with Sir JAMES MARTIN, he ruled that comment on other portions of the paper was admissible, as throwing light upon the spirit in

Top left: Joseph Barling, under-secretary of public works from 1888 to 1896, was an important link between older reformers such as Goodchap and younger ones such as Coghlan and McLachlan.

Top right: T. A. Coghlan, government statistician and creator of the Public Service Act, was appointed to the Public Service Board in 1896.

Below left: Duncan McLachlan was Coghlan's childhood friend and colleague in the Public Works Department. He is shown here on his appointment as under-secretary for mines and agriculture in 1896.

Below right: George Beeby was one of the young lawyers who made a career in the Labor Party and the industrial arbitration system.

Top: Between 1891 and 1904 'the democracy' became a force in New South Wales politics. Delegates to the first interstate Labor-in-Politics Conference in 1900 include New South Wales representatives J. Hepher, MLC (standing middle row) and J. Thomas, James McGowen, Billy Hughes and John Watson (bottom row).

Others in the photograph are:

Top: Queenslanders J. Lesina, A. Hinchcliffe, W.G. Higgs, C. McDonald, J.C. Stewart

Middle: South Australians W.H. Carpenter and T. Price, Victorians J. Barrett and J. Hyman

Below: Sydney women also took advantage of the opportunities for self-improvement provided by the School of Arts.

THE FREE LUNCH   THE BANQUET   ARRIVAL OF THE MINISTERIAL TRAIN   THE BALL   THE PROCESSION

As conditions for many country women deteriorated, the arrival of the railway line gave them an escape route to the city. This illustration from the *Town and Country Journal* in 1880 shows the celebration of the arrival of the line in Wellington.

Rose Scott to T. A. Coghlan, 7 July 1902: 'I feel so grateful to you for all ... your sympathy, with regard to women. ...'

ON PUBLIC SERVICE.

Only 3 Lessons to Write Notes!

And in 2 to 3 months the whole System can be Learned.

Photo. of Pupil's Work at Third Lesson.

TO BE UP-TO-DATE!
TO SAVE TIME!!
YOU MUST LEARN
THE NEW SHORTHAND.

Every Public Servant in New South Wales should avail himself of the opportunity now offered of learning the New Shorthand.

FEES: Full Course, 21 Lessons 21s.

Which may be paid **2s. 6d.** each First and Second Lessons, then **1s.** a Lesson to follow. Postage Extra.

SPECIAL ATTENTION DEVOTED TO COUNTRY PUPILS.

The New Shorthand Business Educational Studios teach **Typewriting, Book-keeping, and Up-to-date Business Methods.** Combined Course, or any Single Subject. Daily Lessons, or when convenient to Pupils. Terms on Application to **W. CHARLTON HUBBLE, Gibbs' Chambers, Moore St., Sydney.**

Top: Along with their brothers, women also learned the New Shorthand, here advertised in the *Public Service Journal* in 1903.
Centre: In 1918 the *Sun* urged women to 'Follow the typewriter route to progress'.
Below: However, this office scene in 1918 shows the gender hierarchy already in place.

Top left: Dora Coghlan Murphy was one of the first women appointed to the public service as shorthand typist. This portrait was taken about 1883.

Top right: Muriel Swain was the first woman appointed as clerk in the public service in 1900.

Below: Rose Scott (seated centre) and the Women's Political Educational League were active in the campaign to open up the public service clerical ranks to women. This picture of members of the WPEL was taken about 1902.

COUNCIL AND COMMITTEES

Public Service . Association . of New South Wales

1913 - 14

To Public Servants

A MASS MEETING

— OF —

Public Servants

WILL BE HELD AT

AARON'S EXCHANGE HOTEL,

— ON —

Tuesday, October 13th,

At 8 p.m.

To consider whether it would be in the interest of the Public Service of this State for the Public Service Association to be registered with a view to Public Servants being brought under the provisions of the Industrial Arbitration Act.

A FREE EXPRESSION OF OPINION is desired

DON'T LEAVE THIS MATTER TO YOUR FELLOW OFFICERS.
Come Yourself and Voice Your Opinions.

PUBLIC SERVICE ASSOCIATION OF N.S.W.
FRED. C. WILLS, Secretary.

To COUNTRY OFFICERS.

If you send your opinion in writing before the 13th inst. it will be read at the Meeting.

Top: By 1924 the image of administrative work depicted by the *Public Service Journal* was exclusively male.

Below left: In 1913 Muriel Swain and Margaret Hogg were on the Council of the Public Service Association.

Below right: In 1914 public servants were considering the advantages of the industrial arbitration system. This advertisement appeared in the *Public Service Journal*.

Top: 'Maternal instinct is useless without mothercraft knowledge' This picture and its message about the relationship between experts and mothers appeared in an article on Health & Baby Week in *Red Tape* in 1927.

Below: Early public service activists such as Muriel Swain turned to other feminist causes in the 1920s. Here she is shown (standing middle row) at the first Pan Pacific Women's Congress in 1928.

PART THREE

Reorganizing Gender

5
Masculinizing work

I

The new middle class project for labour market regulation was not only a battle over class privilege, but also over gender. Women's gradual infiltration into the teaching service and rural and suburban post and telegraph offices had been generally unremarked during the period of colonial prosperity. But the unpredictability of the labour market in the troubled years of the 1880s and early 1890s, and the constant and novel presence of large numbers of unemployed and underemployed, provoked debate over the legitimacy of competition from groups such as Asians and women.

Such questions of gender and race were central to Coghlan's labour market theories. The contention that the nation's prosperity was endangered by the employment of whole families and materially deprived cultural groups was basic to the position he first articulated in his *Daily Telegraph* and *Bulletin* articles of 1889–90. Wages were based on the cost of production of the labourer, and only in societies where the family wage was the cultural norm was the average male labourer able to maintain high wages. Where wife and children contributed to family income, Coghlan asserted, male wages were low and the standard of living poor.

These beliefs about the economic basis of national prosperity led Coghlan to a wholesale attack on the family economy and the employment of married women and partially dependent daughters. He felt strongly that

the condition of a country can in some measure be gauged by the number of such women as are compelled to seek occupations other than in their domestic sphere. When the proportion of such women is large, it may be assumed that the material condition of the country is worse than that of another country were the proportion is small.

'The large employment of women in gainful pursuits', especially the employment of married women, was, therefore, a source of anxiety to Coghlan.[1]

Coghlan's labour market theories and his attitudes to working women derived directly from his working class background and experience. The strength of the craft unions he grew up with in Redfern was based on the restriction of competition in the workplace. Opposition to assisted immigration, exclusion of women and a system of benefits to sick, elderly and unemployed members were designed to protect unionists from competition that might depress wages and conditions.[2] Craft unionism was based also on a very clear ideal of family life and the sexual division of labour. The male breadwinner was expected to be responsible and hardworking, able to support his wife and family. The wife, for her part, was respectable and virtuous, dedicating herself to the physical comfort and moral training of her family.[3] As the son of a politically active tradesman, surrounded by the militant trade unionism of the railway workshops, Coghlan absorbed these ideals, despite the fact that his own father was not able to fulfil this breadwinner role adequately. His mother's devotion and self-sacrifice led him to idealize her nurturing role. The spirit of self-improvement she instilled in him made him ambitious to emulate the family lives of the elite, with their leisured womenfolk. His belief in the transformative power of the Christian ethic allied with science gave him faith in the possibility of a working man's wage adequate to this dream.

In the 1880s and early 1890s the basic tenets of labour market protection became live issues taken up by the wider labour movement. Opposition to continued immigration intensified; Asian workers were subjected to virulent hostility which culminated in restrictions on their entry and regulation of their working conditions; and the admission of women to trades was hotly debated.[4] At the same time, family breakdown became more common; pressure developed for liberalization of divorce laws; the birthrate fell; men and women seemed reluctant to marry; and the more militant women declared their independence of men by training for careers or by organizing their own political groups.[5] In discouraging the workforce participation of women, Coghlan was voicing the attitude of most men of the skilled working class, and of the numerous new middle class men who shared this background, in their urgent attempts to control their deteriorating labour market situation. He was also expressing fear of the loss of the sort of family life he and other men of his class aspired to. It was Coghlan who commented repeatedly on the number of husbands and wives who spent the census nights of 1891 and 1901 apart, and who warned Australians that women were becoming increasingly reluctant to bear children.[6]

II

As government statistician in a period of increasing state power, Coghlan had access to an ideal ideological tool in the struggle for labour market closure against the women he saw as endangering the colony's prosperity. Official statistics, because of their wide dissemination and their disinterested aspect, provide a potent means of labelling groups and of heightening boundaries between them. Occupational statistics in particular have high potential for the manipulation of group images because of the degree of imprecision that is involved in the concept of 'work'.[7] In his yearly account of the *Wealth and Progress of New South Wales* and in his commentary on the 1891 census, Coghlan used his tools of trade to sharpen gender lines and to label women as non-workers during the period of consolidation of the modern Australian labour market.

The collection and interpretation of occupational statistics, even with the relatively objective behavioural criteria used today, provide numerous opportunities for imposing definitions on groups of people and their activities. This was even more so in the nineteenth century, when householders were merely asked the 'profession or occupation' or the 'industry, trade or service' of members of their households, and people were enumerated according to the social perception of their usual occupation rather than what they actually did. The political usefulness of occupational statistics is enhanced by their apparent neutrality, which makes them an effective stalking-horse for ideology. Because of the degree of discretion allowed by the non-behavioural concept of occupation, a study of census data compiled under this system can tell us as much about what householders and enumerators thought about work as it can about people's actual occupations.

Coghlan's census of 1891 and his extensive commentary published in 1894 marked a decisive point in a battle over official conceptions of women as workers. The censuses of Victoria and New South Wales provided the battleground for these rival images. The first, based on the family economy and a *laissez faire* labour market, saw women as essential, productive workers, whether as housewives, as helpers in a family occupation, or outside the home, and presented an image of marriage as an economic partnership. The other, based on the idea of a family wage and a managed labour market, discounted women as legitimate, productive workers, dismissed women's work in the home as unproductive, and regarded women as naturally dependent on their husbands and fathers, the sole legitimate breadwinners.

The Australian colonies had as their models during the late nineteenth century the British censuses which were, from 1851 to 1871, under the direction of the great medical statistician, William Farr.[8] Farr focussed primarily on the size of the population, which he considered a measure of the nation's strength; he assumed that the unit of productive activity was the individual rather than the family; and he assumed a division of labour between men and women in the family that was complementary and equal. Farr's occupational classification of 1851, which he refined in 1861, was the first official attempt to classify such activities scientifically. It was based on a generous conception of productive work which derived from his view of population as 'living capital'.[9] For Farr, the only unproductive classes were children, the infirm and sick, gypsies and vagrants, 'certain ladies' who 'like the lilies of the field, neither toil nor spin', and 'as many gentlemen' who 'would perhaps find equal difficulty in pointing out anything of value which their head or their hand produced'.[10] Class and age rather than gender divided the unproductive and dependent from the workers.

Farr did not value one sort of work over another. He considered the production of human capital through unpaid domestic labour just as important to the nation as other occupations, and he placed such labour in one of the productive classes along with paid work of a similar kind. In 1851 he felt that domestic work should be the extent of women's activities because 'the most important production of a country is its population', and 'where the women are much employed from home, the children and parents perish in great numbers'.[11] But by 1871, he gave his approval to women working outside the home, observing that women's work was becoming 'infinitely diversified' and that 'noiselessly, there has been a rapid increase in the numbers and proportions of women engaged specifically in productive work'. Propounding a *laissez-faire* attitude toward women's access to the labour market, Farr remarked that 'a married woman of industry and talent aids her husband in his special occupation, or she follows different lines of her own...for it is only in a few cases that the whole of a wife's lifetime is filled up with childbearing, nursing and housekeeping'; that 'many of the world's finest children are produced by hard-working women'; and that one of the principal questions of the day was whether women should be excluded from the professions or be allowed 'on the principle of free trade' to compete with men.[12]

In keeping with his conception of women as busy and productive workers, Farr always assumed that the wives and adult children in farming and certain small business households assisted their husbands and fathers. From 1851 they were automatically recorded in their menfolk's occupational category,[13] and even when they were placed in the 'domestic class' in 1871, they were still distinguished from wives and daughters engaged only on household duties.[14] As Farr pointed out, he found 'no evidence of idle women'.[15]

In painting this picture of Britain as a bustling community of workers, all contributing to the size and strength of the nation, Farr presented an image of women as legitimate and productive workers inside and outside the home, and of marriage as an economic partnership. He even went so far as to define the head of a family in one section of his 1851 report as the 'husband-and-wife'. However, Farr's views were always controversial. In the same 1851 report the head of household was designated elsewhere as 'the householder, master, husband, or father', apparently for the purpose of administering the census schedule, and this administrative definition supplanted the other by 1871.[16] His view of housework as an occupation did not survive his resignation from the Census Bureau in 1880. Nor did his automatic classification of female relatives of farmers and small businessmen as workers. However, his successors were unwilling to commit themselves fully to a conception of household workers as dependants, and it was not until 1911 that any uncertainty about the treatment of women working in the home disappeared.[17] The Scottish census officials, who presented independent reports from 1861, were highly critical of Farr's scheme. More Malthusian in their fear of population growth, they wanted to use the census to pinpoint pockets of deprivation. In 1871 they eliminated the 'domestic class' and introduced a breadwinners/dependants distinction which showed how many were dependent on each occupation.[18] A similar scheme was proposed by the social investigator Charles Booth, and a group of economists and social scientists, including Booth, who presented a memorandum to the 1890 Committee on the English Census, but their recommendations were not implemented.[19]

In Australia, census officials in both New South Wales and Victoria adopted Farr's classifications scheme for their censuses from 1861 to 1881, but neither followed the British model completely. The classification of women's work was particularly subject to change, reflecting the variety of attitudes in the community and the various political uses to which census information was put. One important consequence was that classification of the work of female relatives of farmers and small businessmen differed from year to year and from colony to colony, even though the form of inquiry and instructions for recording such work were more or less uniform.[20]

The first principled stand on the issue of the enumeration of women's work was taken in Victoria in 1881 by Henry Heylyn Hayter, the newly appointed government statist in that colony.[21] Influenced by Farr's concern for showing how every member of the population was contributing to its prosperity, Hayter adopted for the 1881 census the practice of automatically counting farmers' wives and daughters and the wives of small businessmen in their menfolk's occupational category. To bring the 1871 statistics into line with those of 1881, he revised the earlier figures rather arbitrarily, transferring 1000 hotelkeepers' wives, 20000 farmers' wives, 500 graziers' wives,

400 graziers' daughters, 400 shoemakers' wives and 400 butchers' wives from the domestic to the non-domestic category. Hayter tried unsuccessfully to persuade the New South Wales statisticians to do likewise, and their refusal drew acerbic comments on their 'peculiar' and outmoded methods.[22]

Hayter's methods were in turn considered outmoded and inappropriate by Coghlan. By 1890, four years after his appointment as government statistician, Coghlan was sufficiently influential to persuade all the Australian colonies to reject Hayter's method and to follow a new system of classification he had devised with the Tasmanian statist, R. M. Johnston.[23] This new classification divided the population unequivocally into two categories, breadwinners and dependants, and it followed the practice of under-enumerating as breadwinners the female relatives of farmers and small businessmen. The new co-ordinated system classified women's work as domestic in the absence of a clear statement to the contrary, and classified women doing domestic work as dependants. Unpaid workers in the home were no longer considered economically active, and instead were placed in the nether world of dependants, a category which embraced 'all persons dependent upon relatives or *natural guardians*, including wives, children, and others not otherwise engaged in pursuits for which remuneration is paid; and all persons depending upon private charity, or whose support is a burthen on the public revenue' (my italics).[24]

The difference that these alternative methods of enumeration made to the image of women conveyed in the census was not small. Hayter's addition of approximately 23 000 women to their male relatives' occupational categories of 1871 represented a major reclassification of women from domestic to non-domestic work in an adult female population of 177 000. In 1891, when Coghlan and Johnston's system was in use, the number of women recorded in the farming sector in Victoria dropped by 32 000 from its 1881 level, in an adult female population of 350 000. The fact that the total number of women recorded as doing non-domestic work fell by only 4000 meant that the 1891 method covered up a sizeable movement of women into paid work. The New South Wales method yielded participation rates of between 24 and 29 per cent for the years 1871 to 1901, whereas Hayter's more generous

138

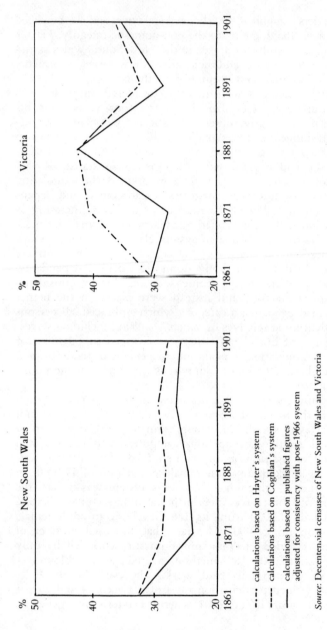

Source: Decentennial censuses of New South Wales and Victoria

- · · · calculations based on Hayter's system
- – – – calculations based on Coghlan's system
- —— calculations based on published figures adjusted for consistency with post-1966 system

Figure 4 Participation rates of women engaged in non-domestic work in New South Wales and Victoria 1861–1901, according to different methods of calculation

method gave participation rates of 41 and 43 per cent in 1871 and 1881 (see Figure 4). By one method women were seen as minor economic actors, and by the other as important contributors to the nation's prosperity.

III

The conflict over the classification of women's work seems to have had as much to do with politics as with science. There was no apparent connection between changes in the organization of work and changes in the type of classification system used. Although Victoria was slightly more industrialized than New South Wales, the two colonies were almost identical in size, culture and politics, yet each espoused a different method. Britain, when at a similar stage of development, had used the method the Australians rejected in 1891, and was now more tentative in taking up the new system. Nor were either Hayter or Coghlan merely following British practice. Instead the colonial statisticians were selecting from the alternatives available those classification systems that served their own interests and fitted with their own ideas about labour markets and gender roles.

The statistical manipulation indulged in by Coghlan and Hayter can be understood at three levels—in the context of colonial rivalry, debates in political economy and conflicts over appropriate gender roles. A major preoccupation of colonial governments during this period was the promotion of their colony to prospective British investors, and an important part of the work of the official statistician was to convince Britain of his own colony's economic soundness. Hayter in Victoria and Coghlan in New South Wales disseminated information and propaganda about their respective colonies in an atmosphere of rivalry exacerbated by their very different social philosophies.[25] In this competition for British investment, each used the classification of women's work that projected what he considered the most flattering image of his colony. At the same time each was able to influence current ideas about the employment of women, helping to turn the desired image into a reality.

The rivalry between Hayter and Coghlan can be seen as a crystallization of the great debate at the end of the nineteenth century between the proponents of *laissez-faire* economics and

individualism on the one hand and state intervention and col-
lectivism on the other. This debate was itself a source of
tension between the colonies and British investors. Many
British journals expressed concern about the increasingly
divergent social and economic philosophies of the Australian
colonies and their mother country. Through protectionist
policies, increasing government intervention, immigration
restrictions, and a general 'excess' of democracy, the colonies
contravened *laissez-faire* doctrines. In the late 1880s, British
distrust of these trends and fears of colonial economic collapse
intensified, in part because of growing unease about the productivity of the worker under 'State Socialism'.[26]

Hayter and Coghlan responded to these British fears in
different ways. A generation older than Coghlan, born into a
well-connected British family and educated at a leading English
public school, Hayter shared the British assumptions. He presented his statistics in conformity with Farr's methods, making
his case for Victoria's progress within the framework of
orthodox liberal economics. Accordingly, he used the discretion he had in the classification of women's work to depict
a large and expanding workforce in which women played
their part. By contrast, Coghlan fitted the *Westminster Review*'s
description of the colonist who demanded 'our own science of
wealth, our own theory of progress'.[27] He was passionate in his
attack on *laissez-faire* assumptions, especially those concerning
the labour market. He was sympathetic to state intervention
and to the collectivist strategies of trade unions, identifying
these strategies with his country's well-being and its superiority over those of Europe. Accordingly he had abandoned
Hayter's and Farr's idea that a nation's prosperity was measured
by the size and activity of its population, and based his case
for the progress of New South Wales on the quality of the
working population and the standard of living they enjoyed.
The discretion allowed by the uncertain occupational status of
farmers' and small businessmen's female relatives was useful
to his purposes, as it had been to Hayter's.

Coghlan's *General Report* on the 1891 census of New South
Wales and Hayter's reply demonstrate the centrality of gender
to this political and economic debate. In his report Coghlan
presents a clear exposition of his new measure of the colony's
prosperity, and shows how it is intimately tied to the image

of women conveyed in the occupational statistics. These ideas were set out in an extended essay on the employment of women in which he reiterated the ideas of his 1889—90 articles, arguing that any contribution by women to the support of their families, or competition for jobs, lowered the wages of men and the standard of living of the whole community.[28] Repudiating Hayter's assumption that 'the sum of the male and female workers compared with the whole population is a measure of the relative advance made by the community in regard to productive or wealth-giving pursuits', Coghlan characterized women's movement into work outside the home as a matter for alarm. He was concerned, therefore, to depict an economy in which few women worked outside the home and where the numbers of such women were not increasing. To this end, he revised figures from previous censuses to show that women had not replaced men as bread-winners and that their participation rate had not grown (see Figure 4); he managed at one point to make female bread-winners disappear altogether through what can only be de-scribed as statistical sleight-of-hand; and, most significantly, he adopted the changes to the classification of female relatives working in family enterprises discussed earlier.[29]

The classification of the work of farmers' female relatives was crucial to Coghlan's argument. In an economy where a quarter of the male workforce was employed in farming, the classification of these women as breadwinners could completely ruin the image of New South Wales he wished to convey. With his method of enumeration, Coghlan could report that only a small number of women assisted on farms, and accounted for this by 'the fact that domestic duties take up the whole of their time'[30] (see Figure 5). That this was not necessarily the case was suggested, however, by the Victorian statist's *Census Report* for the same year. There Hayter revealed that the new method of classifying farmers' female relatives was as much a deliberate act in the service of a particular image of Australia as were his own changes in 1881:

Although no doubt the female relatives of farmers, if living on the farm, attend as a rule, to the lighter duties of the poultry yard and dairy, it was felt by the Conference [of statists] that the statement that so many females were engaged in agricultural pursuits would

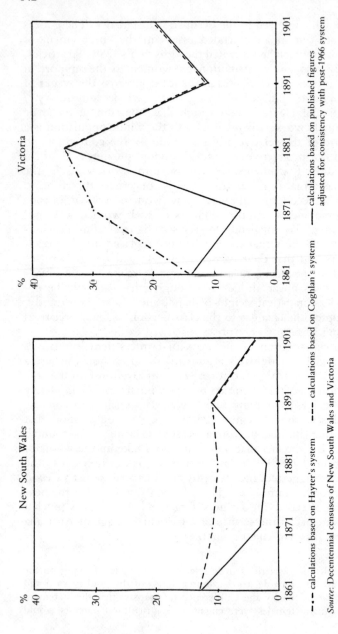

Source: Decentennial censuses of New South Wales and Victoria

Figure 5 Women as percentage of farmers in New South Wales and Victoria 1861–1901, according to different methods of calculation

create an impression elsewhere that women were in the habit of working in the fields as they were in some of the older countries of the world, but certainly are not in Australia. It was therefore decided not to class any women as engaged in agricultural pursuits except those respecting whom words were entered expressing that they were so occupied, the others to be classed in the same way as other women respecting whom no employment was entered—under the head of 'Domestic Duties'.[31]

Coghlan's approach to the nation's prosperity was informed by his sympathy for collective action in the labour market and the quality of working men such action produced. In rejecting the measures of Hayter and Farr, he was abandoning *laissez-faire* faith in the 'invisible hand' and attempting to develop a political economy more appropriate to colonial conditions. In asserting the benefits to all of a political stance by workers, he was effectively seconding for the working class the *Bulletin*'s injunction that 'instead of figuring at the cannibal repast, trussed and roasted on a dish', Australia should 'sit down among the guests—but at the place of honour, with an appetite sharpened by the struggle for existence'.[32]

Among the victims of the 'cannibal repast', however, were working women. In presenting his view of the nation's prosperity, Coghlan established and popularized a number of definitions containing implicit assumptions about women's place and women's economic contribution. By placing much of women's work outside the definition of economic activity at a time when most work was still carried out in family enterprises,[33] he labelled most Australian women as non-workers during the crucial period when important new areas of the labour market were being established.[34] The whole legitimacy of the sort of family economy that fostered the movement of women into post and telegraph work was undermined.

The view of women implicit in these census definitions undoubtedly made an important contribution to the way the larger public viewed women as workers by the early part of the twentieth century. The enormous interest in statistics, their extensive publication in popular form, and Coghlan's powerful position as adviser to governments and expert commentator in public forums meant that his views had considerable influence on elite and popular opinion. Women's contribution to the maintenance and reproduction of male workers became publicly invisible. Ironically, as economic activity moved more and more out of the family, the work of women carrying on the tradition of Coghlan's devoted mother was discounted as consumption rather than production.[35] Informal activities carried out in the home that might have fitted the definition of 'breadwinning' also disappeared from public consciousness. Australian studies suggest that such activities were common, but they were seldom seen as 'work'.[36] As the earlier heroic vision of the 'colonial helpmeet' faded, the work of farmers' wives lost public visibility, even though many worked just as hard.[37] The snowball effect of such a denial is seen in a number of countries where informal economic activities in the home are seldom reported in occupational censuses.[38] As A. J. Jaffe and Charles Stewart conclude, 'If the culture pretends that women do not work, then the women [or the men on their behalf] tend to reply that they have no occupation. . . regardless of what work they may actually do'.[39] In a situation where most women did not officially 'work', the married woman working outside the home was stigmatized as selfish or unfortunate and the single independent woman was an anomaly to be pitied, exploited or ignored.

IV

In his role as a man of science whose name was a household word, Coghlan had considerable power to create knowledge about women. But he was in a position to do much more than that: in his second career as a public personnel manager on the PSB, he had the opportunity to create the conditions that made that knowledge 'true'. As a member of a self-interested and influential new middle class, he had succeeded in moving control of the public service labour market out of the hands of politicians into the hands of public service leaders, giving it a high degree of stability and protection and providing conditions of entry favourable to his own class and their allies, the petty bourgeoisie and the working class. As a creator of the Public Service Act and administrator of its provisions, he was able to regulate the employment of women in line with his own ideas of a prosperous labour market and proper gender relations.

The Public Service Act of 1895 was a paradoxical document. The culmination of many decades of pressure from public servants for uniform and predictable conditions of employment and objective recruitment, promotion and retirement criteria, it was a charter for the merit principle and the abolition of privilege. On the other hand it set formal limits on women's employment in the New South Wales public service for the first time. It gave male public servants a high degree of autonomy from political control and allowed them considerable control over their labour market conditions. At the same time it imposed new controls over women's labour market participation.

The Bill devised by Coghlan and presented to parliament in October 1895 was quite uncompromising on the subject of married women. Coghlan saw married women as a major impediment to a properly constituted labour market because he considered them only partially dependent on their own wages. Current debates over patronage also drew attention to the possibilities for unfair labour market advantage inherent in family favouritism, especially between husbands and wives. Coghlan's Bill therefore proposed that married women be banned from public employment.[40] This provoked an extensive and heated debate which gave little hint of the tenacity with which the family wage concept was to take hold within a decade. Instead the controversy revealed strong support for a *laissez-faire* attitude to women's work not yet influenced by ideas such as Coghlan had published in his census report the previous year. The issue was one of the major questions of principle discussed during the second reading debate on the Bill. Most parliamentarians were shocked by the prohibition against married women. They saw it as a 'barbarous restriction' of women's rights which was out of tune with the meritocratic spirit of the Bill, as well as with custom and progress.

E. W. O'Sullivan, the Protectionist member for Queanbeyan and one of the leading supporters of public service reform, put the countryman's view clearly:

Why should we penalise a woman for fulfilling her natural functions? A woman may be a competent postmistress or teacher, but the moment she takes to herself a partner for life she must leave the service. I am surprised that those who stand up for fair play for women should give their approval to a provision of that character. A woman should not be compelled to leave the service because she gets married any more than a man should be compelled to do so.

O'Sullivan was supported by A. B. Piddington, Free Trade member for Tamworth, and William Lyne, the Protectionist member for Hume. Piddington argued that the prohibition against married women was out of step with the two objects the Bill was designed to achieve—the highest possible efficiency for the civil service and the greatest justice to civil servants and to members of the community who wanted to get into the service. It was also in conflict with the premier's stated aim of promoting the employment of women through this Bill. What is more, he argued, the requirement that women civil servants give up their positions on marriage was a 'peculiar and almost shocking injustice' which could result in women being tied to bad marriages because of lack of access to economic independence. In his opinion marriage made no difference to a woman's ability or right to work. The important point was 'that the state shall be faithfully and well served'. This was not necessarily attained by a policy of one family, one billet:

Of all the instances where the state is, perhaps, more economically, and more thoroughly and happily served, it is precisely the instance where married women are teachers with their husbands. All other things being equal, it is an entirely desirable circumstance.

Lyne joined Piddington in condemning the prohibition as 'an absurdity, a hardship, and a cruelty to women who are willing to provide for their children'. In fact, he argued, 'the married women are those who should be first considered'.

Free Trade members for city electorates based their arguments on the principles of liberalism. Frank Cotton, member for Newtown—Camperdown, urged parliamentarians to 'arouse themselves to something like a sense of dignity, liberalism, and progress, and . . . wipe out this absolutely disgraceful clause'. William McMillan, member for Burwood, and David Storey, member for Randwick, called the clause 'drastic', 'extreme' and 'absolutely revolutionary'. As Storey declared:

Instead of moving forward we are taking a very serious step in the opposite direction. We are moving backwards as the representatives of a free people if we enact in any bill for the better administration of the public service any clause which will be detrimental to the interests of women, whether married or single.

The voices in favour of the prohibition against married women were divided as to their reasons. Only Samuel Whiddon and Jacob Garrard, Free Trade members for Sydney—Cook and Sherbrooke, argued at length that women's place was in the home and associated masculinity and feminity with bread-winning and dependence. Garrard, the minister of Public Instruction, articulated the craft unions' attitude to appropriate sex roles clearly when he expressed contempt for 'so-called men' who live on their wives' salaries and stated flatly that 'when a woman marries she ought to be dependent on her husband'. He described with repugnance the fact that many women combined pregnancy and motherhood with their work as teachers:

It is positively indecent sometimes for big boys and girls in our schools to be taught by married women. For months there are on certain occasions exhibitions that ought not to be put before them..... We have instances where mothers who are teaching in schools, not only go home during the day and attend to their infants, and thus interrupt their ordinary work, but also have their infants brought to the schools.

These lone voices, supported only by a few brief interjections, were quickly silenced. Frank Cotton and William Hughes, the young Labor member for Sydney—Lang, poured scorn on Garrard's 'prurient minded prudery'. Presenting an alternative view of masculinity and feminity, Cotton lauded the gifted, well-trained married woman who attended to her duties as a teacher 'while at the same time wearing the crown of a mother, and occupying what I regard as the highest position of a woman'. As for masculinity, 'if that woman, with all her gifts, were to be thrust out of a school and had to work in a garret...that would be regarded as an outrage on decency and morality, and revolting to one's manhood'.

Most of the support for the clause was couched in terms of opposition to patronage. The question of gender was not central to the argument over patronage, but it could readily be used for political advantage. John McElhone, the Free Trade member for Fitzroy, had been whipping up moral indignation for years by pointing to the case of Sydney Maxted, head of Charitable Institutions, and his wife Sophia, who was matron of the State Children's Relief Board. According to McElhone the two Maxteds together earned about £1000 a year. Other favourite targets were Lizzie and Thomas Ferris, she earning £218 a year as Waverley post and telegraph mistress and he £313 as first clerk in the accounts branch of the post office, and Leichhardt post and telegraph mistress, Ellen Cross and her husband, a senior officer in the railways. McElhone asserted that:

It is an outrage upon public decency that such a thing should be allowed. There are thousands of honest, capable men who are able to fill positions for which these women are receiving their salaries. The sooner these married women are all put out of the service to allow deserving, honest men to take their places the better.

Patronage was obviously the main concern of premier Reid. He seemed to have considered the prohibition on married women seriously for the first time during the debate. Although he was apparently sympathetic to the view that women's place was in the home, he showed no consistent stand on the question beyond some vague commitment to equal opportunity and for the elimination of what he called 'perfect family monopolies'. He was ready to sway with the political wind, and when the *Sydney Morning Herald* joined in the denunciation of this 'unjust and absurd' prohibition, he quickly suggested a compromise amendment to the offending clause which catered to both these concerns. The clause that was finally passed was a considerably watered-down version of Coghlan's original blanket prohibition. It stated that:

Except in the Department of Public Instruction no married woman shall be eligible for appointment to any office in the Public Service if her husband is already in the employment of the State, unless the Board certifies in each case that there are special circumstances which make such appointment desirable.[41]

Although it was not included in the wording of the clause, Reid stated clearly during the debate that the new provisions did not apply to wives already employed in the service.

This debate over the employment of married women suggests that there was little support in the parliament or in the press at that time for Coghlan's position. The main concerns of most supporters of the Bill were the abolition of patronage and the provision of equality of opportunity for all. There was consensus that family favouritism should be eliminated. But at the same time there was agreement that the Bill should provide women with 'fair play in connection with public employment'. 'Fair play' for the dominant voices in this debate meant the recognition that women needed jobs to support themselves and their families, either wholly or partially, and that they had the right to earn their own living, whether married or single, in the same way as men.

The introduction of such an unpopular clause into the Public Service Bill reflected the interests of Coghlan and other new middle class leaders in protecting the public service labour market for men. The provenance of the ideas expressed in the clauses is quite clear. They did not originate from the Royal Commission, which made no special inquiries or recommendations on the question of women's employment. They do not fit with what we know of the attitudes of the women's movement of the time.[42] The approach taken by the Bill was consistent, however, with the ideas about women's employment Coghlan had espoused since his *Daily Telegraph* articles of 1889–90. It appeared also to articulate the less formed concerns of other new middle class men. In 1892 the new leaders of the Post and Telegraph Department who succeeded Cracknell began to discriminate against women by banning the appointment of married women to offices with residence attached. This was greeted with some surprise by the *Transmitter*, but it took up the idea with some enthusiasm.[43] In 1893 the teaching service began to reflect the attitudes expressed by Garrard in the Public Service Act debate by suspending the recruitment of married women altogether.[44]

Despite the fact that there was little public enthusiasm for the prohibition of married women from the service, as a member of the Public Service Board from 1896 to 1900 Coghlan was able to ensure that his original intentions were carried out. Although the stated intention of the parliament was that women already employed in the service should not be affected by the new law, married women in the Post and Telegraph Department were dismissed in August 1896.[45] No further married women were appointed to clerical or professional positions in the service, even though this was not forbidden by the Public Service Act. An official account of post and telegraph policy on the employment of women in 1899 states quite unequivocally that 'New South Wales does not admit married females, and specifies distinctly that any female employee who marries, is obliged to leave the service'.[46] What small evidence we have suggests that exceptions sometimes were made. Coghlan's sister, Dora Murphy, remained in her clerical position although her husband worked in the railways.[47] Twenty years later public service activist Margaret Hogg continued in the service after she married fellow clerk George Duff.[48] In general, however, there was no longer any place for married women in the New South Wales public service.

These administrative actions, announced quietly in the *Government Gazette*, provoked little comment. The *Transmitter* had made a non-committal reference to the debate over married women's employment in November 1895, and it printed a list of male and female officials retired by the Board in August 1896 without commenting on the different grounds for dismissal for men and women.[49] Mrs Ferris gave a dinner party to farewell her staff on 28 July and they presented her with 'a choice silver egg cruet, in appreciation of her many acts of kindness to them'.[50] No one seems to have protested her dismissal, and despite evidence that she was later a member of the Womanhood Suffrage League, there is no public record of either her or the WSL taking up the issue. In this uncertain period of public service reconstruction the women who lost their jobs may have felt that any protest would jeopardize their husbands' positions as well.[51] Certainly there was still considerable tolerance for married women working in public positions. At Sydney Girls' High School Lucy Garvin continued as headmistress through three pregnancies between 1892 and 1897. When she retired in 1919 she had presided over the education of 4000 New South Wales girls to whom she was 'still the source of inspiration'.[52] The employment of married women had been a minor and unnoticed aspect of New South Wales public employment during the nineteenth century. The attack launched by Coghlan and his new middle class and working class allies was unexpected, and despite the strength of the politicians' protest, there was no large and organized constituency to defend the rights of married women. Almost unnoticed, those rights quickly ebbed away.

BALLAD OF MABEL CLARE

A manly independence, born
Among the hills, she had;
She treated womankind with scorn,
And often cursed her datl.
She hated swells and shining lights,
For she had seen a few,
And she believed in Women's Rights
(She mostly got 'em, too).

Henry Lawson, *Along the Western Road*

THE TYPISTS' EXAMINATION

They come from the offices, houses and schools,
Some are writers by practice, some writers by rules,
And some are just sweet unforgivable fools,
But they all want a State situation.
It's a wooden box, or a big tin case,
It's a purse, or a handkerchief edged with lace,
It's parasols all over the place,
At the typists' examination.

It's not a bad salary, two pounds eight,
When you don't start early and don't stop late,
And so there's a yearning to work for the State
In this prosperous federal nation;
Oh. it's typing fancy, and typing plain,
It's printing sentences off the brain,
It's whipping it out and start again,
At the typists' examination

There are many worse things a maiden might do,
Provided of course that *He* isn't in view,
Than pocket a liberal Government screw
At a rather nice occupation;
Oh. it's rickety-tick as the time goes by,
It's tippety-tap as the fingers fly,
It's rattle and ring when the speed is high ·
At the typists' examination

J.A.B. Fry

6

Managing women

I

The problem of single women could be dealt with much less tidily than that of married women. Some single women were supported at least partially by their fathers and brothers, and many could be expected to marry. To Coghlan these were frivolous workers whose labour market participation should be discouraged. However, there were increasing numbers of women who supported themselves, whether by choice or necessity. These women may have thought positively of themselves as independent, but by the logic of Coghlan's economic theories they were what the *Bulletin* cruelly called 'superfluous women'.[1] For new middle class men the permanent presence of these women in the labour market was an obdurate fact that required careful planning and supervision if national prosperity was to be preserved.

The women seeking paid work were the sisters, mothers, widows and daughters of the public servants, journalists, professionals and academics who made up the male half of the expanding urban educated classes. As small selectors failed on the land and wage labour grew at the expense of family farms and small businesses, family members, including daughters, had to find employment outside the family circle. The cry of 'What shall we do with our boys?' was echoed by a similar concern about employment opportunities for girls.[2]

These demands met with little resistance until the second half of the 1880s. At the beginning of that decade the outlook for what became known as the 'New Woman' looked bright. Country and suburban women continued to benefit from the long tradition of equal pay and relative equality of opportunity in post and telegraph offices. Inspectors of rural schools and influential politicians encouraged the employment of female teachers, and by 1880 they were employed in equal numbers, earning salaries of up to £340 (including house), representing from two-thirds to three-quarters of male salaries.[3] High schools for girls as well as boys were set up by the new Education Act of 1880, providing the 'thorough' and 'serviceable' education required to serve the 'urgent needs of the great middle class'.[4] A teachers' training college was established exclusively for women, and in 1881 the University of Sydney was opened to them. A decade later, in 1892, the establishment of a women's college provided accommodation for country women wishing to study at the university.[5] At the same time a burgeoning journal and newspaper press provided work for other women.[6]

The worsening economic situation of the late 1880s changed this optimistic picture. Small farms failed at an increasing rate, families broke up, and the interests of family members diversified. Unemployment and underemployment grew, and resistance developed to women's inroads into the labour market.[7] As the interests of male and female family members diverged and competition for jobs increased, women became more aware of themselves as a disadvantaged group. Feminist organizations emerged to press for equal political, social and economic rights, joining the numerous interest groups which developed during this period of economic instability and political change.

The feminist movement developed out of several forums in response to a variety of grievances. Self-supporting new middle class and working class women such as Mary Gilmore and Louisa Lawson were part of the large floating population, often from the country, who gravitated to Sydney's numerous boarding houses by the end of the decade. Freed from family and sex role constraints, they contributed to the intellectual ferment that characterized Sydney at that time, playing an active part in the variety of 'progressive' causes that engrossed the city's radical intelligentsia. With a long history of independence, they helped establish teachers' associations, worked for labour reform and joined various socialist organizations, working with men for a more humanitarian and rational society.[8]

These women, who had always expected to contribute to their own support, were joined by women from elite families who were suddenly thrown onto the job market. Laura Hogg had been able to devote herself to her philanthropic work as secretary of the Woman's Christian Temperance Union, but in 1891 she found that she had to ask for a 'small salary' because her source of income had been destroyed by the depression.[9] One effect of the economic crisis seemed to be that the definition of 'manliness' no longer included support of unmarried sisters. Margaret Hogg, later a leading public service activist, was apparently forced to earn a living during the 1890s by her male relatives' moral or financial failure.[10] She often referred to the fact that women were forced into the position of breadwinners by what she called 'the delinquencies of men', specifically 'the men related to her by ties of blood to whom she looked in the past to represent her'.[11] In 1914 she wrote, probably referring back to this traumatic period of her life:

The days when the single man supported his women-folk are past... The single man of the present day, paid on a higher scale than the single woman, more often than not uses his surplus for amusements, not for the support of kith and kin.[12]

'Women of spirit are glad of it', she emphasized, and along with many other women she relished her new freedom.

Other elite women associated with philanthropic, cultural and moral organizations were not impoverished by the depression, but were radicalized by the poverty, destitution and exploitation they saw among the women they were trying to help. Already certain of their right as women to diagnose and treat the problems of their own sex, their literary societies, temperance unions, sanitary associations and working girls' clubs became recruiting grounds for feminists who demanded increased political influence through the vote and through active lobbying campaigns.[13]

Louisa Lawson, who started her feminist magazine *The Dawn: a Journal for Australian Women* in 1888 and the social reform club for women, the Dawn Club, the following year, was a typical product of this period of crisis and change. She was a country girl, the daughter of a storekeeper and publican near Mudgee. She married young, and her first son, Henry, was born in a tent on the Grenfell goldfields in 1867. After some years of wandering the goldfields, Louisa and her husband took up forty acres outside Mudgee in 1873. The farm was, in Henry Lawson's words, 'a miserable little hell'. His father was away from home on contracting jobs for long periods of time, and Louisa often ran the farm, supplementing her income with dressmaking and running the local post office.[14] The harsh and lonely life of the selector's wife, and the independent spirit it inculcated, has been given universal form by Henry Lawson in 'The Drover's Wife'. The truth of this story to the experience of women on these selections is indicated by the fact that Henry's wife claimed it as a story from Louisa's life; Henry claimed it was based on one of their childhood neighbours; and Mary Gilmore claimed it as part of her own family history, passed on to Lawson when they were friends in Sydney in the early 1890s.[15]

In 1883 Louisa Lawson gave up the land and her husband. She took her children to Sydney, where she supported them by running a boarding house and then by journalism. As an outsider searching for a new way of life, she entered enthusiastically into the radical literary and intellectual life of the city. In 1887 she ran the short-lived *Republican*, the organ of the Republican Union.[16] The following year at the Progressive Spirtualist Lyceum she met Susannah Gale—a 'sweet gray frocked Quakeress' who was the wife of freethinker Henry Gale, postmaster at Paddington, a member of the reform-minded Windeyer family, and an advocate of equality for women.[17] Encouraged to articulate her developing feminism, Louisa Lawson launched the *Dawn*, the feminist journal which ran until 1905, dispensing, along with more militant flourishes, the sensible advice of the independent country woman.[18]

It is not known how extensive the female 'push from the bush' was. Literary evidence of well-known figures like Louisa Lawson, Mary Gilmore, Barbara Baynton and Miles Franklin, and the examples of political activists and pioneering professionals, such as the Golding sisters and Nita Kibble, suggest it may have been extensive.[19] It is probably not far from the truth to speculate that as soon as the railway line reached one of these remote townships, discouraged wives and daughters flocked back along it to the city, as Louisa Lawson had done when the railway line reached Mudgee.

The women who followed the railway line to Sydney took with them the experience of hard-working, independent women, and they often left behind them an experience of masculine failure, inadequacy or absence. Acutely aware of women's need for well-paid employment, Louisa Lawson argued that 'women must have work, for there are thousands not depending on any man for support, and yet possessing, as far as we know, as good a right to live as any other human being'.[20] Her club and her journal, which employed only women as writers and compositors, encouraged the movement of women into new fields of employment and attempted to assist the unionization of women. She quickly ran into problems with the TLC over her employment of women compositors: the New South Wales Typographical Union, in common with all craft unions, would not admit women as members, and the *Dawn* was therefore boycotted for employing non-union labour.[21] This incident brought into the open the conflict of interest between parts of the trade union movement and women. As the *Dawn* pointed out:

Associated labour seems to be in its own small way just as selfish and dictatorial as associated capital...Trades' unions would dispute, or force out of sight if possible, the right of women to enter the labour market at all.[22]

Throughout the early 1890s the labour movement wrestled with the problem of women's employment, the craft unions generally taking a conservative exclusionary stance, while intellectuals and the AWU, whose predominantly rural members appreciated women's economic contributions, tried to incorporate women into the union movement.[23]

In her campaign to help women to manage their own lives, Louisa Lawson was joined by others of more privileged background who were nonetheless responsive to the increasing divergence of men's and women's interests. Elite women had long been organized for charitable purposes, and had appropriated for themselves a 'woman's sphere' in which women alone were responsible for benevolent work for women and children.[24] They also formed cultural associations such as the Women's Literary Society, formed in 1890, whose more radical members joined the general move towards the organization of political interest groups in 1891 by establishing the Woman-

hood Suffrage League (WSL).[25] Although there was wide
support for women's suffrage, it took over ten years to place
the measure on the statute books. This long-drawn-out campaign helped maintain women's solidarity during the 1890s,
giving them an effective voice on a range of issues of concern
to women. With its roots in the elite women's sphere of
philanthropy, the WSL was never solely concerned with suffrage. Its convenor, Dora Montefiore, and its secretary from
1891 to 1902, Rose Scott, had been drawn into the movement
by their interest in women's custody rights and the age of
consent for girls, and these remained constant concerns of the
League.[26] From its inception the League was also intimately
involved in questions of women's work, pressing for early
closing, shops and factory legislation and increased employment
opportunities for women, and encouraging trade unionism.[27]
In keeping with its aristocratic tradition, it was mainly concerned with the welfare of working class women. It was only
when its own elite members and their friends came up against
prejudice and barriers in the unfamiliar male territory of the
office or the hospital that the League and its successor, the
Women's Political and Educational League (WPEL), began to
fight for employment rights for middle class women.

The WSL was less confrontationist in its approach than
Louisa Lawson and the *Dawn*. Its driving force was the charming and energetic Rose Scott. Although she shared Lawson's
background of masculine failure and female strength and
independence, Scott's experience was cushioned by family
privilege and the less devastating economic conditions of an
earlier period. She was the product of the first flight from the
bush during the depression of the 1840s. Her father was a
large property owner near Singleton, north-west of Newcastle,
who was ruined by the 1843 bank crash. For the next fourteen
years he struggled to keep the family property going while
working at various official positions gained through influential
connections. In 1857 he finally sold the property and moved
his family to Newcastle, where he was police magistrate until
his death in 1879. Rose Scott was born in 1847, four years
after the bank crash, and she left the family property in 1857
when she was ten years old. Her mother, the daughter of the
government chaplain at East Maitland and sister of the historian, George Rusden, probably ran the property during the

years her husband was trying to earn a living elsewhere. Certainly her mother was a dominant influence, and Scott later attributed her feminism to childhood experiences that were 'burnt into' her heart. In any event, she was one of a generation of 'new' women who applied the emerging managerial ethos to their own personal lives, and made a deliberate choice not to marry, preferring to enjoy friendship under less adverse circumstances.

The failure of men like Rose Scott's father was cushioned by the expansion of the towns as commercial and administrative centres. Certainly he was able to keep his family in modest comfort in his position as police magistrate. After his death Scott could live in Sydney with her mother and nephew without having to seek paid work. There she became one of a group of younger upper class women who repudiated the philanthropic tradition of the older generation, and were swept up in an enthusiasm for Christian socialism and state intervention to cure the seemingly intractable social and economic ills of the period. She was ready to apply the new managerial ethos to the larger problems of women as well as to her own life. As Frank Cotton remarked rather deprecatingly, Rose Scott had a 'splendid faith in the efficacy of Government enactments'. During her long career she worked closely with influential public servants such as Coghlan, Neitenstein and Fosbery on a variety of reform issues. More socially secure and influential than Louisa Lawson, Rose Scott set the tone of late nineteenth-century feminism with her well-mannered but indefatigable lobbying of parliamentarians, public servants and opinion leaders by letter, delegation and personal influence, and the Friday 'salon' at her home in Jersey Road, Woollahra was a well-known gathering-place for politicians, intellectuals and reformers of both sexes. [28]

II

New middle class reformers such as Coghlan found themselves in a personal and theoretical quandary when faced with women's demands for increased employment opportunities. Without inherited wealth or assets, and without a family business or farm in which daughters, sisters and widowed mothers could help earn a living, these men did not have the means to support the 'superfluous' women in their families and marry as well. In Coghlan's own family he and his older brother helped support their mother and younger siblings through most of their young manhood. Charles was thirty-nine when he married in 1890. Coghlan himself was close to forty before he could build himself his first house, the lovely 'Clifton' in Paddington, and he was over forty when he married in 1897.[29]

The women in their families were, moreover, anxious to be independent. The sisters and daughters of public service reformers such as Coghlan, John D'Arcy and Charles Fry of the ETS were among the first to take advantage of the new educational and occupational opportunities available to women.[30] Like Rose Scott, four of Coghlan's five sisters did not marry. All but one of them trained for professional careers, and Dora Murphy, the one sister who did marry, began a second career in her forties. John D'Arcy's sister, Constance, graduated brilliantly in medicine in 1904, and went on to a distinguished career as an obstetrician and gynaecologist and deputy chancellor of Sydney University. Active in a variety of women's organizations, she lived with two unmarried sisters. Edith and Millie Fry also excelled while at Sydney Girls' High School, graduated from Sydney University, and had active lives as artist and writer on the one hand and community worker on the other.

In reforming the public service labour market, these men had to find a formula which allowed women like their daughters and sisters to earn their own living, without jeopardizing what they saw as the basis of the nation's prosperity—the family wage paid to the male worker. In trying to reconcile these seemingly conflicting interests in the Public Service Act, Coghlan faced the same dilemma as the trade union movement. He had two options open to him. One was to ban women altogether from male occupations, and to encourage the development of new occupational categories for women with lower pay and fewer opportunities for advancement—in other words to intensify the dual character of the labour market. The other was to admit women to male occupations under absolutely equal conditions. The first was not politically feasible at that time. The need for employment for single women was acknowledged by all. Liberal and egalitarian feeling was strong among Free Trade and radical Labor supporters whose votes were necessary for the public service reform package to succeed. The government was pledged to women's suffrage, which had wide parliamentary support, and any large-scale discrimination against women would be seen as contradictory to the spirit of that commitment. In addition, the long tradition of equality in the New South Wales post and telegraph offices had already spilled over into the new typing and stenographic positions in the Clerical Division, and would have to be publicly repudiated. Exclusion was, moreover, the weaker strategy if it merely led to segregation. That left the way open for women to undercut male wages and for employers to deskill male occupations and employ women in the 'new' occupations thus created. The second option—equal treatment—was preferable practically and politically.

In drafting the Public Service Bill Coghlan seemed reluctant to commit the Board unequivocally to either policy, although his own administration of the Act maintained the principle of equal treatment. The clause concerning the employment of single women merely granted the Board wide discretion to facilitate and make regulations concerning their employment:

The Board may make regulations for facilitating the employment of women in those departments or branches of the Public Service in which it may seem desirable to employ them; and such regulations may determine the salary or wages to be paid to women employed on any particular work or class of work, and may provide generally for all matters relating to the examination of female candidates for employment, which may require special provision.[31]

The principle of extending single women's employment opportunities was so widely approved that little attention was paid by the parliament or the public to the actual wording of this clause. The controversy over the prohibition of married women had exhausted the time and energy parliament was prepared to expend on the question of women's employment. Only Tom Bavister, the independent Labor member for Ashfield, seemed to notice that the Board was being granted large and indefinite powers, and he urged that parliament's intentions concerning the necessity for equal pay should be clearly specified.[32] Bavister's plea, and comments made by other members in the course of the debate, indicate that the clause did not accurately reflect the government's intentions and the wishes of parliament. The whole of the debate conveyed approval of O'Sullivan's declaration that 'What we want is fair play, and a fair field for everybody'.[33] The clause as drafted and passed by parliament, however, did not embody that maxim. It said nothing about equal pay and equal opportunity, and instead gave the Board extraordinary powers to treat women as a separate group in ways that were at the Board's discretion to decide. Rather than freeing women from restrictions, it provided the opportunity for new ones to be imposed. Like the clause referring to married women, this clause reflected the interests of Coghlan and other new middle class leaders in protecting the public service labour market for men. One catered to the general concern to eliminate patronage and the other to the concern for equal opportunity, but both took a much more regulatory approach to the employment of women than that envisaged by most of the Bill's supporters.

III

Although it had a strong charter from parliament and the public, the first Public Service Board made no dramatic difference to employment opportunities and conditions for single women. Young women were actively sought as telephonists, post and telegraph assistants, and shorthand writers and typists, and in 1899, after some delay, as junior clerks and library assistants. Women had always worked in the Post and Telegraph Department, and their increased recruitment to the menial positions of telephonist and post and telegraph assistant hardly represented an advance over the responsible and well-paid jobs women had previously held. Shorthand writers and typists were better paid and had opportunities for advancement, but in appointing more women to these positions the Board was merely expanding on developments already begun in the more progressive departments. The appointment of women as junior clerks and library assistants was more revolutionary, as this gave them clear access to managerial positions in the service; but shorthand writers and typists already had that possibility. What was new was the encouragement women were receiving to enter male territory, both in terms of jobs and space previously dominated by men, and the careful monitoring of this territorial expansion. The Board proceeded cautiously, therefore, with the recruitment of women, and took some pains to continue the practice of appointing women under the same conditions as their male counterparts.[34]

In 1896 women had already been employed for some years in the public service as typists and shorthand writers. Joseph Barling, the innovative manager of the reorganized Public Works Department, had been one of the first to make use of the typewriting machines introduced into Australia in 1885. In 1890 he pioneered the employment of women as typists when he appointed Jane Bennett, the young widow of the late commissioner for main roads, at a salary of £150 a year. In 1893 he began to employ young women in these positions with the appointment of nineteen-year-old Mary Collins. Coghlan's sister, Dora Murphy, then a married woman with four children, joined the Electoral Office as one of the pioneering female shorthand typists the same year, at the age of forty.[35]

The women who entered the public service as typists and shorthand writers in the 1890s had good reason to see it as a career promising good conditions, interesting work and prospects for promotion. Shorthand had long been a well-paid professional skill and a useful accessory for public service clerks.[36] In 1880 the principal shorthand writer, Charles Robinson, earned over £700 a year, placing him among the select few of the service. In 1886 the commercial rate for shorthand and secretarial service was £3 3s per day; for transcription it was 1s per folio.[37] The secretary to the Royal Commission on the Public Service in 1894–95, writer Percy Meggy, received £400 per year for his services. In the public service of the 1870s and 1880s shorthand was a rare skill. Coghlan's friend Arthur Fry, who learnt the art while transcribing free-thought lectures and spiritualist trances—two leading pastimes of progressive public servants—was employed at the post office in 1876 at £100 a year. Despite the fact that he had left school at the age of ten his shorthand made him more valuable than an ordinary clerk starting at £75. Shorthand was not only well paid, but it also gave clerks access to committees of inquiry, delegations with ministers and under-secretaries, and other high-level and confidential work which brought them to the notice of their superiors and gave them useful knowledge and experience. Fry worked for all the postmasters-general, and was even called in to take down a speech for premier Stuart a few days before Stuart died.[38] His friend Hugh McLachlan moved from junior clerk in 1875 to secretary to the railway commissioners in 1889 at a salary of £700 per year with the help of his shorthand.[39] John Holliman's shorthand skills won him a position as head of correspondence and confidential clerk to Barling a few years after he joined the Public Works Department as a temporary clerk in 1884. By 1907 he was under-secretary for Finance and Trade.[40] John Garlick joined the railways in 1890 as a shorthand writer. He was secretary to the Royal Commission on the Birth Rate in 1904 and was appointed under-secretary for Local Government in 1916 at the age of forty-one.[41] Barling insisted that all corresponding clerks, at that time all men, should have shorthand. Fry himself became head of correspondence in Duncan McLachlan's Mines Department in 1896 and declined McLachlan's invitation to become secretary to the federal public service commissioner in 1902. If his claim of making £1000 a year by his extracurricular stenographic activities was true, he hardly needed the job.[42]

In the late 1880s the typewriter was introduced as another useful adjunct to a clerical career. In 1889 it was being advertised as a 'certain source of income and a powerful lever to well paid official and mercantile appointments'. Commercial schools aimed mainly at men had taught shorthand, bookkeeping and correspondence for some time and by 1889 they were including typing.[43] Typewriters were still scarce in the public service in 1895, when the Royal Commission showed great interest in their use. Most of the few typists employed were men. In 1890 there were three typists listed in the *Blue Book*, all males. When Fry went to Mines in 1896 he was placed in charge of eight male typists. These men, like the shorthand clerks, were treated as clerks who typed rather than copied their work by hand, and they had the same salaries and promotion prospects as ordinary clerks. Fry's men earned from £100 to £250.[44]

Women were quick to see the possibilities of typing and shorthand. In 1888 Mrs Dora Armitage, a mother of four young children and wife of a ruined gentleman, opened the first shorthand and typing school in Sydney. She proceeded to sell this new technology to the reluctant businessmen of the city, who felt that they had 'done without typewriting all these years and think we can do without it longer'.[45] Mrs Armitage used the Exhibition of Women's Industries in 1888 to stimulate interest in this work and establish a Lady's Type-Writing Association which, according to the *Dawn* in 1889, had a large number of members who 'have not been slow to see the utility or profit of such work'.[46] In 1896 Mrs Armitage addressed the newly formed National Council of Women (NCW) in her capacity as secretary of a professional association of men and women, the Shorthand Writers' and Typists' Society, which met fortnightly and conducted examinations, and three years later she was secretary of the NCW as well.[47]

Women's response to the possibility of public service employment was overwhelming. Arthur Fry, who was appointed examiner of female typists for the Public Service Board in 1896, writes that:

At the time there were great numbers of young ladies being trained in the Commercial and Correspondence Schools in the city with a view to getting appointments 'in the Government', and the Board, practically under instructions from the Government, had decided to develop that side of the Service, and advertised for applicants accordingly. The first appeal only produced a dozen competitors, but the number soon increased to scores and reached above ninety anxious to show their ability in shorthand and typing.[48]

Only a handful of these applicants gained the coveted government positions over the next few years. Little is known about these women beyond what is supplied in the *Public Service List*. Fry reports that they were 'first class in every way... Four of the ladies were the cream of the schools and colleges in the city and the competition to get their positions was very keen'.[49] If they were trained by Dora Armitage they would have had to meet high standards. She insisted that typing was a profession 'well suited to educated women'. According to Mrs Armitage a typist must have 'a thoroughly sound English education', and 'a knowledge of French, Latin and even of Heathen mythology will not come amiss'.[50]

The little we do know about these women assures us that they met Barling's injunction that 'their characters should be not at all frivolous'.[51] Dora Elphinstone and Dora Coghlan Murphy were both former teachers, and Dora Elphinstone was, according to Fry, an accomplished young woman who spoke French.[52] Florence Wearne obviously took the study of typing and shorthand seriously, winning honours in the exams of the Shorthand Writers' and Typists' Society in 1895 and playing an active part in its activities.[53] May Hickman had joined her father, Harry Hickman, in the Australian Socialist League in 1891, when she was fifteen years old. There she rubbed shoulders with future Labor luminaries, W. M. Hughes, William Holman, G. S. Beeby and J. D. Fitzgerald. The Queensland *Worker* concluded in 1894 that she was 'an ornament to the Australian Socialist movement'. She provided the musical entertainment at the ASL's Sunday evening lectures, wrote the weekly reports of these lectures for the press, and took the minutes at business meetings. Ben Tillett, the British labour leader who visited Australia in 1897 thought she had a really wonderful knowledge of economics—for a young girl. She became a talented public speaker and journalist, writing under the pseudonym of 'May Day'.[54]

Several of these pioneer typists were active members of the women's movement. Florence Wearne was a close friend of Rose Scott's and was, during her lifetime, secretary to the WPEL, a member of the National Council of Women, a committee member of the Peace Society and a member of the Anzac Fellowship of Women.[55] May Hickman probably met Rose Scott when Scott was educating herself in socialism in 1892. She was one of the group working with Hughes and Holman on the Early Closing Bill in 1899–1900. She was vice-president of the WPEL in 1903, speaking at public meetings on women in politics in the company of Scott, Belle Golding and Edith Fry. In 1912 she was living near Rose Scott in Jersey Road.[56] Although she did not identify with militant feminism, Dora Murphy was an admirer of Rose Scott, sharing Scott's belief in the efficacy of the state. She and her daughter Beatrice were two of the first to enrol in the WPEL in 1902, quoting, like a true daughter of Redfern, a motto from Macauley:

None were for a party
And all were for the State.[57]

Dora Murphy's commitment to equal employment opportunities for women is revealed in an enthusiastic letter she

wrote to Rose Scott in 1899 telling her that the clerical examinations were about to be opened to women:

This will open a wide field of lucrative employment to our sex and is
a distinct advance in the industrial position of women workers and
the knowledge will I am sure help to cheer and assist those who are
struggling for the advancement of women, amongst whom dear
Miss Scott you must ever hold a foremost place.[58]

The seriousness of purpose of these women and their activity
in feminist and reform organizations demonstrates their determination to manage their own lives. We can glean something
of the expectations these women had of their new government
positions from the career of Florence Wearne. She was one of
the first appointments by the Public Service Board in 1897,
joining the Board of Health as a shorthand writer and typist at
the age of twenty-four at a salary of £120. Her evidence to the
Women's Clerical Case before the Arbitration Court in 1921
shows that her work was from the beginning that of corresponding clerk and secretary to the Board, a job comparable
in independence and responsibility to that of Fry at Mines,
though on a smaller scale.[59] Her correspondence with Rose
Scott reveals that she interested herself closely in the work of
her department. In 1909, for instance, she read a long paper to
the Toronto Congress of the National Councils of Women on
'Prevention and Treatment of Consumption in the State of
New South Wales Australia'.[60] She had a lifelong career in the
public service, as did three others of the six women appointed
to typing and shorthand positions in 1897−98. By 1929 she
was clerk−librarian and assistant secretary to the medical
board of the Public Health Department at a salary of £421.[61]

Dora Coghlan Murphy's career demonstrates a comparable
seriousness. Two years older than her famous brother, she did
not have his opportunity to join the public service, and the free
secondary education and university medical training enjoyed
by her youngest sister Iza (Fanny) were not yet available. She
entered one of the only professions available to her in the
1860s—that of schoolteacher—and taught at Redfern and
Glebe. She married in 1872 at the age of nineteen, and had six
children over the next twelve years, four of whom lived. Her
husband's business failed in 1884, and in 1891, with children
aged from nine to twenty, she began a new career as a short-

hand typist and clerk. She earned several prizes during her year's course at Sydney Technical College, and after two years running her own shorthand, law reporting and typing office, she joined the public service as a shorthand writer and typist at a salary of £120. In 1900 she was promoted to a clerical position as secretary and accountant at the Botanic Gardens, which paid £175 per annum and provided a house, and involved the supervision of a junior clerk. She remained in that position until she retired in 1917.[62]

In 1899, in an entirely new departure, the Public Service Board opened the newly established examinations for entrance to the clerical division of the service to women. Although there was no discussion on the question, this move implied that the highest managerial levels of the service were now open to women. Even more clearly than the typists and short-hand writers they were recruited on the same terms and conditions as men. The Board's rather tardy action four years after the passage of the Public Service Act and two years after the exams were instituted may have been partly in response to pressure from Rose Scott on behalf of the WSL and from women such as Florence Wearne and Dora Murphy, who were anxious to move into the clerical ranks.[63] The Board excused its tardiness by referring to the lack of 'proper accom-modation' and promised that 'so soon as the required Regulations can be brought into force, and the necessary changes effected in connection with Government buildings, [women's] employ-ment will be considerably further extended'.[64]

Sixty-three women were among the 305 candidates who sat for the clerical examination at the end of 1899. Ten were successful,[65] and over the next three years eight of these were appointed to the service. Early in 1900 Edith (Muriel) Swain was appointed to the Friendly Societies Office, Mary Ryan to the Statistician's Office, and Elizabeth Ambler joined Dora Murphy at the Botanical Gardens. Mary Clouston and Ivy Beattie joined the Public Library and the Statistician's Office in 1901. In 1902 Morna Beaumont, Mabel Bridge and Annie Doherty joined the Central Board of Old Age Pensions. Two more women, Emily Parsons and Annie Vaughan, were appointed to the Friendly Societies Office in 1903 after passing the clerical exam the previous year.

Four other young women, Margaret Armstrong, Nita Kibble,

Bertha Downey and Ida Parsons, circumvented the slow process of appointment from outside the service by sitting for the clerical examination as inside candidates initially appointed to the General Division. Kibble, Downey and Parsons moved up from junior library assistant positions in the General Division which had been opened to women by Kibble's efforts in 1899. Orphaned at the age of thirteen when her postmistress mother died in 1892, Nita tried teaching, and then in 1899 decided to challenge the Public Library's exclusion of women. She enrolled for the examination as N. B. Kibble and came out first in the competition. 'After a great deal of doubt and hesitancy', the library authorities decided to go ahead with her appointment, no doubt encouraged by the Public Service Board. Whatever the case, Nita Kibble paved the way for a number of women who made distinguished careers in the library.[66]

Surprisingly, these women are even more anonymous than their typist colleagues. Muriel Swain was probably typical in her single-minded pursuit of independence. Her nephew recalls that 'during her entire lifetime [she was] an enthusiastic advocate of many aspects of woman's interests'. Born in 1880, she was the eldest of nine children of a struggling merchant who later became relatively well-to-do and 'most conservative'. She and her two oldest brothers bore the brunt of the family's hardships in the 1890s. There was no question of Muriel not seeking employment, an option chosen by two of her younger sisters born in 1890 and 1894. The family put a high value on learning. Muriel's brother, Harold, writes that 'having been taught my letters by my elder sister (Muriel), I was engaged, between customers, . . . in a tedious struggle to begin the library which occupied the rear of the shop; whilst my father took the Shakespeare to bed, of nights, to read to my mother . . .'. Harold subsequently became dux of Fort Street Model School and Muriel matriculated from the Parramatta Convent of Mercy with the highest pass in the state. Three years older than Harold, Muriel went on to Sydney University. By the time she was due to graduate and Harold to matriculate, the Public Service Board had begun its competitive examinations. As Harold points out, his mother was 'concerned to get us jobs'. He became one of the first forestry cadets. Muriel sat for the first public service clerical examination open to women, and was the first woman appointed as clerk. By 1910 she was a compiler in the Statistics Department at a salary of £170. In 1912 she became the first woman to be elected to the council of the Public Service Association, a position which her nephew thinks would not have pleased her family. In 1914 she completed an additional degree in economics, a course that had just been introduced by former Public Service Board member, Robert Irvine, whose aim was 'not to turn out cheap clerks; its aim is rather to turn out lieutenants and the future masters of industry'. This was obviously to apply only to men. Although Muriel Swain was by 1920 sub-editor of the *Industrial Gazette*, the Department of Labour and Industry's meticulous chronicle of industrial matters, and by 1929 was earning £321 a year, her brother, in contrast, had, without benefit of any degree, become director of forests in Queensland in 1918, chairman of the Forestry Board in 1924, and commissioner of forests in New South Wales in 1935.

Muriel Swain lived with her parents and several of her brothers and sisters until they died or married, and with her youngest sister, Audrey, until she died in 1964. Her youngest sisters felt it was not 'the done thing' to go to work, even though one did not marry until late in life and the other married at thirty. Like many of the women who joined the public service at this time, she was active in a wide variety of scientific, philanthropic, feminist, sports and international peace organizations, but she was considered by at least part of her family as 'wasting her life. She was seldom home before midnight any night'.[67]

Like the women who joined the clerical division as typists and shorthand writers in this period, female clerks such as Muriel Swain were seeking permanent careers in the service. They showed tenacity in getting their appointments in the first place, and several made lifelong careers. Of the fourteen women who became clerks, two transferred to the Common-wealth public service in 1902 and five remained in the state service for many years. In addition to Muriel Swain, Nita Kibble was, by 1929, earning £510 as principal research officer in the Public Library. Mary Ryan earned £590 as compiler of statistics and literary assistant in the Statistical Department.

Emily Parsons was a compiler of statistics at a salary of £321 a year, and her sister Ida was a senior cataloguer in the Public Library in 1920 at £283.

IV

The employment policies of the Public Service Board at the end of the 1890s and this brief period of experiment with the equal treatment of men and single women can be attributed to three main factors. First, the employment of women was a major social issue which Coghlan and his colleagues were aware of through their personal experiences and the pressure of women's organizations with whom they had close dealings. No plan for labour market regulation could ignore the question of women's work. Coghlan had the example and, no doubt, the lobbying, of his own sisters to bring home to him the need for work for single women. He was reminded of this by Rose Scott, who worked closely with a number of his influential public service colleagues on social welfare measures concerning women.[68] She probably came into contact with Coghlan in connection with their common interest in women's industrial conditions, and was careful to cultivate him. In 1902 she wrote to him in gratitude for 'all your kindness and [indecipherable], and all your sympathy with regard to women'.[69] He, for his part, respected her abilities and aims and shared her managerial and humanitarian approach.[70]

The issue of equality of pay and opportunity in the public service gained especial prominence between 1900 and 1902, when the Victorian Women's Post and Telegraph Association, led by Louisa Dunkley, drew on the New South Wales example to campaign for equal pay and opportunity for women in the newly constituted Commonwealth public service. Louisa Dunkley's active participation in the inter-colonial conferences of telegraphists held in those years, her eloquent exposition of the women's cause in the pages of the *Transmitter*, and her close relationship with the leading New South Wales union activist, Edward Kraegen, kept the issue before the service and won the support of many of its leaders.[71]

Second, the ascendency of the new middle class in both politics and public service from 1895 to 1903 gave free play to the social engineering bent of men such as Coghlan, evident in attempts to implement a well-integrated plan involving income and land tax, local government, factory inspection, early closing regulation, old age pensions and public service regulation; in this plan the new middle class would become moderators between capital and labour. Regulation of the labour market and women's employment according to theoretical principles was an important part of this plan.

Third, the Public Service Board was, in these early years, strongly identified with the interests of the service as a whole. Coghlan and Barling were the creators of the Act which gave the public service security. In their implementation of the Act, they took great pains to balance the interests of the public with those of public servants in fair and reasonable pay and conditions. They were close friends and colleagues of most of the public service leaders. Although the beginnings of rank-and-file dissatisfaction with the more high-handed actions of the Board were demonstrated by the formation of a viable Public Service Association (PSA) in 1899, the closeness of purpose of the Board and the public service union leaders was illustrated by the way in which union leaders moved into top personnel authority and departmental positions in this period.[72] With political and public service support to back them, men such as Coghlan were able to maintain their strong commitment to theoretical principle to promote the extension of equal employment opportunities for single women.

Despite these factors favouring the establishment of equal pay and opportunity for female clerical workers, and the Board's optimism in 1900 that there would be little difficulty in utilizing the services of women clerks,[73] harbingers of its failure were apparent from the beginning. The Board vacillated in its treatment of women, never making a clear statement of its policy. This may have indicated disagreement among its members, or merely ambivalence or uncertainty. The tentativeness of its approach was particularly evident in the case of female typists and shorthand writers. It was never clear whether these women were to enjoy the same opportunities as their male counterparts, though they entered the service on the expectation that they would. The Board did not discriminate against women in their starting salaries, but they were ready to treat women differently in other ways. In 1896 they were already stereotyping typewriting as appropriate women's work,[74] and a special examiner, Arthur Fry, was appointed for female typists. The Board seemed only too ready to treat typing and shorthand as temporary work for women who would soon marry. At some early stage they fixed an informal ceiling of £125 for women doing this work. The female short-hand typists and their feminist friends had other ideas.[75] When Dora Coghlan Murphy wrote to Rose Scott in 1899 about the opening of clerical positions to women, Scott scrawled indignantly across the top of the letter '. . . even tho' the area in which they are allowed to compete may not extend as yet to the highest positions in the Public Service'.[76] Dora Murphy's promotion from shorthand typist to clerk in March 1900, just before Coghlan resigned from the Board, and the promotion of four of the senior shorthand–typists to £140 the same year, confirmed the intention of the Public Service Act and the first Board that men and women be treated alike, but no firm statement of this principle was written into the regulations.[77]

Male public servants, who were not accustomed to working with women, greeted the new female recruits with suspicion, hostility and incomprehension. The *Transmitter* declared rather defensively that men did not have a great deal to fear from the introduction of women into the service: 'The objectionable thing is that in the matter of employment male and female do not meet on equal terms'.[78] Florence Wearne found her first months a trial by fire. Thirty years later, they were still vivid in her memory:

It is nearly 30 years since I joined the Service in a very conservative office where the men had banded together and decided they would make things so unpleasant that a woman would be glad to resign. Well I didn't take any notice of the unpleasant happenings, just went on as though they didn't exist or were every day occurrences. After a couple of months the men decided they were rather beasts, and abandoned their opposition—in my case; although I might say I never walk over a bit of pavement in Phillip St without thinking of a daily internal argument I had as to whether I would give up the fight and 'let women down' on the first opportunity they had of getting into the Service by competitive exams; or fight it out.[79]

Even Arthur Fry, who was full of praise of the superior qualities of 'his' typists, did not appear to take their career ambitions seriously. His condescending verses ('There are many worse things a maiden might do/Provided of course that *He* isn't in view,)[80] hardly provide an accurate reading of Florence Wearne, May Hickman or Dora Elphinstone. Nor does the *Public Service Journal* writer who noted in 1900:

...the apparent intention of the Public Service Board to pass little detachments of nice Australian girls into the Department occasionally, causes no misgivings. The dainty typists, who are to come our way, will, no doubt, make 'After Office Houris' a popular pursuit.[81]

The women's strongest supporter seems to have been Coghlan. The evidence suggests that his influence was decisive in what positive action was taken to carry out the mandate to improve employment opportunities for single women. The year when the clerical examination was finally opened to women was the one period when Coghlan was not heavily engaged in other government tasks or out of the country. More tellingly, almost all of the appointments of female clerks were to his own Statistician's Office, to the offices of the Friendly Societies and Old Age Pensions, which were partly his creations, or to the Botanic Gardens, where his sister worked. Yet even Coghlan's views were clearly ambivalent. At the same time as he was working for the expansion of opportunities for single women, he was promoting the idea that women's place was in the home in his opposition to the paid employment of married women and his concern about the decline of the birth rate.[82] He himself had married in 1897 a woman who described herself on her marriage certificate as a 'lady'.

At base the tentativeness of even the Board's most decisive member reflected the fact that he was working on principles which conflicted with deep-seated fears (of women as labour market competitors) springing from the deeply masculine urban working class tradition. The contradictions inherent in this were not lost on one public service wit who commented in verse on Coghlan's role in the birth-rate controversy of 1904:

Dear! let me tell you the world is discovering,
Actually thinks, that you've got off the track;
Something far worse than a war-cloud is hovering
Over the country unless you turn back;
Well meaning men in a mild sort of fury are

At your behaviour, entering their sphere...
Bookkeeper fair, who are working so busily,
Maid, with stenographer's pencil and book...
Haven't you heard the State's pitiful call?
Why won't you marry, and—keep up the average?
Coghlan is waiting to hear from you all![83]

In view of this ambivalence, Coghlan's attitude was probably close to that of the *Bulletin*, which moved from a virulent anti-feminist stance in 1887 to a reluctant concession in 1889 that 'the evil is evidently becoming unavoidable and must be endured in the best way possible'.[84] In the intense dialogue of the period about appropriate gender roles, the voices of principled male public servants such as Coghlan were weakened by their ambivalence. Although they seemed at times to be speaking with the same voice as their sisters, their concerns were different and their commitment more shallow. It was the tentativeness of their commitment that allowed their work to be swiftly undermined in the changing political climate of the new century.

7
Masculinizing merit

I

By the time the first women clerks were appointed in 1900, it was already too late for this innovation to succeed. A change of government in 1899 ushered in a long period of political stalemate. Caught between the demands of organized male labour for better wages and services and of conservatives for government economy, governments quickly brought the Public Service Board to heel. The brief experiment with expanded equality of opportunity for women was swiftly terminated, leaving in place machinery which allowed gender distinctions to be reintroduced as the rationale for a new and virulent form of discriminatory cost-cutting.

The power of the new middle class during the 1890s depended on its members' judicious management of policies which appealed to a precarious alliance of radical and conservative groups. A swift realignment of radical and conservative forces between 1899 and 1904 led to a new and permanent political polarization around labour and capital which undermined the unity and influence of the new middle class. This brief period of political reorganization was dominated by the struggle for the working class vote. Reid's Free Trade Party fell in 1899 because it could no longer deliver the progressive measures expected by the more radical sections of the labour movement. Under the influence of the radical democrat E. W. O'Sullivan and the liberal intellectual B. R. Wise, Lyne's Protectionist government tried to woo the labour vote from 1899 to 1901 with increasingly interventionist state policies which aroused anti-state sentiments among its conservative

175

opponents. Despite the efforts of Lyne's successors to cut government projects, the election of 1904 was fought on the issues of government expenditure and 'socialist' policies. 'The issue', said conservative leader Carruthers, 'is against the State persisting in its endeavours to reduce the people to the condition of an army of State employees, dependent upon political patronage for work, and upon foreign money-lenders for loans to pay the wages'.[1] His Liberal—Reform Party's victory and the success of the Labor Party in forming a viable opposition ended the new middle class—working class hegemony of the previous decade. The new focus on the opposition of capital and labour provided little opportunity for the promotion of the separate interests of the new middle class. It was no longer essential to Labor's political success; indeed, sometimes their interests clashed. Moreover, state interventionist policies were viewed with suspicion, if not hostility, by the newly mobilized conservatives.[2]

The effect of this process of realignment on the Public Service Board was evident from the beginning. In its scramble for the labour vote the Lyne government capitalized on the consolidation of the public service carried out by Reid and Coghlan to introduce a compulsory arbitration system and to revive heavy expenditure on public works.[3] At the same time it was unwilling to allow the Public Service Board the autonomy and centralizing role that was essential to Coghlan's conception of an effective public bureaucracy. While its expensive and interventionist policies aroused anti-state sentiments among conservative opponents, it set out to break the power of the Board.

Within days of taking office, the Lyne government moved to discredit Coghlan, Reid's chief financial and public service adviser, and to remove him from the Public Service Board. This campaign was led by B. R. Wise, who, as attorney-general, took over ministerial responsibility for the public service. Wise was a barrister whose father had been a Supreme Court judge and friend of Parkes. A member of the New South Wales elite, he was educated at Rugby and Oxford, where he was strongly influenced by the social reformist ideas of J. A. Hobson and Arnold Toynbee. Known by his contemporaries as a brilliant but untrustworthy 'twister', Wise was a member of the Free Trade Party from 1887 to 1895, when he backed Parkes against Reid and lost his seat. Returning to politics in 1898, he intrigued with Labor radicals to bring down the Reid government and, despite apparent political differences, took office in Lyne's Protectionist government.[4]

Wise had been alienated prior to taking office by Coghlan's strong stand on the financial aspects of Federation.[5] He was also anxious to cast suspicion on anyone associated with Reid's financial arrangements in order to place the extravagance of his own government in a better light. In addition he shared Parkes' suspicion of an independent public service, and by association felt some hostility towards its architect. Believing that ministerial responsibility had been lost in the Public Service Act, 'in one of those pathetic outbursts of mistrust of its own honesty and capacity which is characteristic of modern democracy when in certain moods', he had consistently opposed the Public Service Board since his return to parliament.[6] Once in power, Wise immediately tackled Coghlan, the mastermind of Reid's financial and public service policies, calling on him to choose between his Public Service Board and statistician positions, and questioning the legality of arrangements Board members had made with Reid concerning their pension rights. At the same time, accusations of malpractice were made against Coghlan by the assistant statistician, J. R. Martin, who later moved to Lyne's Treasury Department and spearheaded a further attack on Coghlan over the accounts of the Reid government.

The effect of this attack on the ambitious Coghlan was devastating. He took leave from the end of November and was incapacitated with what was probably a nervous illness for some time. After a protracted correspondence with Wise, he resigned from the Board in March 1900. He was cleared of the charges made against him by Martin, but remained under a political cloud for most of Lyne's administration.[7]

With Coghlan out of the way, the government attempted to undermine the legal powers of the Public Service Board. Two days after Coghlan went on leave, Wise moved the second reading of a Public Service Act Amendment Bill to exempt under-secretaries from the Board's control and to establish an appeal court against Board decisions. The Bill was lost with the close of the session, and a further Bill introduced in August of the following year was not proceeded with in a crowded session.[8]

Unable to bring about legislative changes in the Board's jurisdiction, the government moved to re-establish control over public service expenditure by overseeing the allocation of annual increments. With Coghlan gone, and his successor, stipendiary magistrate Cornelius Delohery, not appointed until mid-1900, the Board was in no state to fight off this incursion.[9] In a brief period of reaction, the Board observed that 'the administration of [the Public Sevice Act] has been subjected to the most crucial examination' and questioned the government's right to override its recommendations.[10] By 1901, however, the Board had given way, conceding that automatic increments were too costly.[11]

The Board's surrender to government pressure to cut public service expenditure had immediate repercussions for women. With Coghlan no longer on the Board to insist on theoretical correctness, they embarked on a policy of separating 'skilled' from 'routine' clerical work, and of distinguishing these by gender. This policy allowed at least the show of economy on salaries and conditions of female 'unskilled' workers without endangering those of male 'skilled' (and organized) workers. Despite the earlier victories won by Florence Wearne and her colleagues, formal ceilings of £100 were placed on the salaries of typists and £150 on those of shorthand typists in 1901.[12] From mid-1900 women were invariably appointed to the poorly paid position of typist, even though many, such as May Hickman, were accomplished and experienced shorthand writers. Able to point to these efforts at government economy, the Board had restored the attractive increment scales of male clerks by 1903.[13]

The same gender-specific thinking led to the early demise of the plan to employ women as clerks. Reporting in 1900 on the success of their plan to recruit female clerks, the Public Service Board presented it in terms which emphasized the replacement of men by women, arguing that:

No doubt the employment of women in such places as are suitable for them, will have the effect of curtailing to some extent the employment of men; but this will produce a result beneficial to the State, because an equal number of men will be compelled to seek positions which women cannot occupy, and therefore will be available to engage in occupations tending to develop the resources of the Colony.[14]

Understandably this approach had little appeal to male public servants already feeling the pinch of government economy. The *Transmitter* had emphasized in 1896 that male and female employees must 'meet on equal terms'.[15] The implication in 1900 that they were actually intended to replace men in clerical positions prompted a long and hostile editorial in the *Public Service Journal* suggesting separate and limited career avenues for women 'in industries [such as teaching, typewriting and telephony] for which they are well-adapted, and in which they do not come into undesirable competition with the other sex'.[16]

The antagonism of the PSA was probably enough to discourage further action on the part of the already reluctant Board in the atmosphere of retrenchment and recession of the years 1901 to 1904. In fact, it is probable that no action at all would have been taken without Coghlan's continued intervention despite his political eclipse. Of the ten women who passed the clerical examination at the end of 1899, only three were given positions in 1900, all to his own or allied departments. Once Lyne—always a supporter of women's increased opportunities—moved to the Federal sphere early in 1901, no more appointments of female clerks were made. By the end of that year, attempts to place the female clerks and to change the Board's policy on the advancement of female typists and shorthand writers had apparently come to an impasse. Coghlan, by this time making a comeback to political influence, had not given up his commitment to these women. In November he wrote to Rose Scott:

I have been anxious to call on you for some weeks past, but have not so far been able to spare the time from my office duties and I am averse to letting you call on me first.

You have done so much for the women of the state that everyone looks to you to do more. I had an idea I could help you in your good work by certain suggestions for the amelioration of the condition of working women, in regard to which you might be able to make effectual representations and if you will permit me to call some evening next week I shall be glad to explain myself further.[17]

We do not know what Coghlan and Rose Scott discussed, but a deputation from the Womanhood Suffrage League to the

Public Service Board soon after canvassed the problems of placing women and the question of equal pay,[18] and Rose Scott began a lengthy correspondence on the problem of sanitary arrangements for women in the public offices.[19]

Farcical as it seems in the late twentieth century, sanitary arrangements seemed to be a major stumbling-block to the further employment of women. Rose Scott ·wrote to the *Sydney Morning Herald* early in 1902 in reply to their leader criticizing the Public Service Board's lack of progress in placing women clerks that 'Women have often had reason to thank the Board for justice and courtesy...the reasons given by the Board are obvious, and speak well for their sense of justice'.[20] The reasons referred to were apparently the lack of lavatory facilities for women and the reluctance of the Public Works Department to provide them. One consequence of 'ladies' trying to invade male territory in a time of economic belt-tightening was that they had to endure the embarrassment of possibly shared bathrooms. Rose Scott wrote with some emotion to Coghlan after almost a year of negotiations with Public Works:

I may tell you that in the Mines Department there is no decent or *private* lavatory for women— in consequence one girl employed there has been *very ill* the Dr says in consequence & the other has to risk all decency poor girl to save her health. I spoke to Mr Kidd last week—& he said he will see about it *at once*—will he? I hope so—It is really dreadful that Factory Inspectors can expose manufacturers [indecipherable], but must not speak of what goes on in govt buildings—[21]

Coghlan had been concerned with this problem since his investigation of sweating in 1891−92, when he found the 'chief abuse' to be 'the almost uniform absence of provision for sanitation and for the preservation of decency'.[22] He now supported Rose Scott in her current appeal to E. W. O'Sullivan, the minister for public works, for help.[23] Despite their efforts, the Board reported the abandonment of recruitment of female clerks by 1903:

Owing to the absence of proper accommodation in the Public Offices, and for other reasons, it has not been found possible to employ women to any extent on clerical work, other than as shorthand and typing clerks, for which, as is well known, women have shown special aptitude.[24]

Why 'the absence of proper accommodation' was a problem
for clerks and not for typists is unclear. No doubt the 'other
reasons', which were not spelled out, were equally compelling.
In any case, the mandate of the Liberal—Reform government
in 1904 to cut the public service led to a total cessation of
junior clerical recruitment, male or female, from 1904 to
1907, ensuring that the recruitment of female clerks came to a
definite end.[25] The Carruthers government also removed
Coghlan to London where he acted as agent-general for New
South Wales for most of the period from 1905 till his death in
1926, waiting in vain for the call to some higher office from a
grateful Holman or Deakin. He was rewarded instead by the
appointment of the indolent Reid as high commissioner over
his head and his old enemy Wise in his place as agent-general.[26]
Meanwhile the women of the public service had lost even this
ambivalent champion.

II

The retirement of Wilson and Barling in 1906 and 1907 marked
definitively the end of the 'strong Board' contemplated by
the 1895 Act.[27] The *Public Service Journal*, in summing up the
Board's administration, concluded that it had, in recent years,
been too complacent in its relations with the government, and
that it had 'more than tolerated' government interference.[28]
Attorney-general Charles Wade followed Wise's precedent in
appointing a legal officer, E. H. Wilshire,[29] to the Board in
place of Wilson, and he chose former under-secretary of the
treasury and commissioner of taxation, C. J. Saunders, to replace Barling.[30] These appointments confirmed the Board's
metamorphosis from an autonomous instrument of social engineering to a passive administrative tool. The Public Service
Act had given the Board large discretionary powers which had
been appropriate to the political climate of the time, but with
ministers no longer supportive of its independence and members not in tune with its creators' original intentions, the Board
had lost its effectiveness as a watchdog of public servants'
rights. Personnel decisions lost their principled and positive
quality and became *ad hoc* responses to government pressure.

Coghlan's friend, Captain Neitenstein, who spent a year on
the Board in 1906 and 1907, wrote to Coghlan in 1909 about
the lack of respect commanded by the new members. This

came as no surprise to Coghlan, who considered that Saunders and Wilshire were 'almost impossible' and that Saunders was 'quite unfit by temperament and training' for the PSB post.[31] As he commented to Neitenstein in 1909, 'When I drew up the Public Service Act it did not seem possible that any but a strong board would ever be appointed and accordingly I proposed great powers for it'. Coghlan had not anticipated that different political circumstances would reduce the Board's power, and he was critical of ministers such as Wade who, he implied, improperly interfered with departmental administration.[32]

The *Public Service Journal* shared Coghlan's concern about the weakness of the Board. In 1910, when Delohery was about to resign at the age of seventy, it expressed the hope that the service would see 'a young energetic and fearless man appointed to the office, who will not be liable to infection from political pressure, ancient, unjust precedents, and short cuts to avoid difficulty.[33] For a short period of time, it seemed as if this might happen. In the closely fought election of that year, both parties courted public servants with promises of salary increases and reform.[34] In this conciliatory mood, Wade appointed Coghlan's old protégé, G. A. McKay, to the Board in Delohery's place, and when McKay found the position impossible, [35] the progressive economist, R. F. Irvine, was appointed in his place by the victorious Labor government.[36] Amid 'an [indecipherable] feeling that he should never have been on the Board at all', Saunders retired at the age of fifty after twelve months sick leave.[37] However, Irvine resigned after only a year in office, and, with the honeymoon with the public service over, two lacklustre colleagues were eventually found for Wilshire at the end of 1912.

The goverment's choice—W. J. Hanna, the former undersecretary of public works, and J. M. Taylor, a former Board officer[38]—did nothing to inspire public servants' confidence as economic problems caused by the outbreak of war threatened their conditions. The 'prevailing gerontocracy' was, according to a writer in the *Public Service Journal*, powerless, imperceptive and pedestrian.[39] Doubts about the Board's ability to safeguard the service were well founded. As the cost of living escalated, public servants suffered reductions in their salary and a deterioration in conditions of service.[40] At the end of 1916, the Nationalist government, formed by former Labor premier W. A. Holman in coalition with the former Liberals, reduced public works, dismissed hundreds of state employees and promised not to increase state income tax during the war.[41] In a situation reminiscent of the early 1890s, public servants were once more aware that they were a target for expenditure cuts. A letter to the *Public Service Journal* in 1916 warned:

...let the Public Service Association be alert. The shadow lurks, but the Public Service should not be the sufferers for the pass to which, not merely war conditions, but also mis-management and lack of organisation have brought industrial and public life today.

The writer urged the members of the Public Service Board to 'rouse themselves out of the old grooves' because while they allowed the service to 'rumble along in the old ruts...there must necessarily be a great deal of expenditure which would be avoided if the Service was organised'.[42] The Board, however, made no attempt to press the government on behalf of the service.[43]

Faced with the Board's inability to protect public servants in this crisis, the Public Service Association withdrew its support. Recommending sweeping democratization of personnel administration, it advocated the abandonment of the Board as the wage-fixing tribunal for the service and argued that public service wages and conditions should be decided in the same way as those of other workers—by the industrial arbitration system, that other new middle class legacy of the 1890s.[44]

Deprived of the support of the public service, the Board was also abandoned by the government. Despite, or perhaps because of, its docility, the emasculated Public Service Board was no longer an effective instrument for the government in the difficult political situation of 1917. The government's economy measures since the beginning of the war, combined with deliberate pegging of wage awards by the Industrial Court below cost-of-living increases, and conscription, were provoking considerable industrial unrest which paralleled the public servants' dissatisfaction. The defection of the moderate Holman from the Labor Party strengthened its more militant industrial wing, and trade unionists, including public servants, began to take a more truculent stance opposing their deteriorating conditions. At the same time, as leader of the Nationalist Party, Holman had to respond to a conservative constituency which opposed increased taxation and government spending.[45] In the face of these contradictory demands, the government needed a more innovatory and flexible public personnel authority than the Board provided.

The announcement just prior to the elections of March 1917 of a Royal Commission on the Public Service gave Holman the breathing space he needed to deal with the growing problem of the public service. The Commission began in September in the middle of the general strike which started in the railways workshops. Its first report issued late in 1918 condemned the Board for its mismanagement of the public service. In a bitter confrontation the Board members were forced to resign and a new Board with expanded powers was established, with former businessman J. S. Marks as chairman, and W. D. Loveridge of the Board's office and J. L. Williams, Coghlan's old friend, as members.[46]

The political turbulence of 1917 and 1918 demanded, however, speedier solutions than a shake-up of the Public Service Board could provide. The Board's new strength proved illusory as the government handed control of public service salaries to the lawyers and statisticians of the Board of Trade and the Industrial Court. These changes inaugurated a new phase of public personnel management. Without control of public service salaries, the Public Service Board became increasingly the government's instrument, effecting petty economies in response to alarming wage increases caused by the Board of Trade's declarations. The Public Service Board lost its residual role as guardian and regulator of public service conditions, and was reduced during the 1920s to a mere shadow of the body that Coghlan had conceived and instituted in 1896.

III

The continued weakness of the Board meant that any principled approach to the employment of women was completely abandoned, and the small number of female public servants fought a rearguard battle to preserve their rights. Women were, according to the *Public Service Journal*, 'entirely neglected' in the salary regrading of 1906. The women of the public service and the *Journal* protested against this injustice, but by the time economic prosperity returned in 1907 and junior clerical recruitment had recommenced, the question of equality for women was entirely forgotten by the Board.[47] Carruthers promised women 'eventual' equal pay in the elections of 1907,[48] but this had little relevance to the women of the public service. Women were no longer appointed to the same jobs as men, and when they were recruited to the increasingly female job of typist, it was often on a 'temporary' basis, despite the fact that many of these women made permanent careers in the service. The few pioneer women tried to press premier Wade to deliver on his predecessor's promise immediately following the elections of late 1907, but they got nowhere as the government lowered taxes.[49] Rose Scott wrote indignantly to the Board in 1908 that 'This was the ground work of the Public Service Act, that men and women were to be treated equally. . . Was the provision in the act only introduced then to oblige one lady sister to a high official?'—but the Board remained unmoved, except to make yet another exception of Florence Wearne and promote her from shorthand typist to clerk, following Dora Murphy's example, in October 1908.[50]

When Labor gained office in 1910 it was also pledged to equal pay, thanks to the efforts of party activists such as public servants Annie and Belle Golding and their sister, Kate Dwyer, the first president of the Women's Organising Committee of the Political Labor League.[51] However, its precarious majority in the Legislative Assembly, the hostility of the Legislative Council to any new industrial legislation, and the disaffection of the left-wing of the labour movement severely restricted the Labor government's ability to act on principle, even if it wished to.[52] In order to maintain the support of the larger and more organized part of its constituency, it continued the policy of improving the pay and conditions of male workers at the expense of female workers. The groundwork for this strategy had been laid in the public service since 1903, and it was increasingly legitimated by the emphasis on the different roles and responsibilities of men and women made by the new industrial courts, the emerging infant welfare movement, advocates of domestic science education for girls, and alarmists concerned about population decline.[53]

In January 1911 the government granted all adult male

public servants a minimum wage of £110 per annum.[54]
Despite pious sentiments from attorney-general Holman, it
was only after strong representations from the Public Service
Association, urged on by public service women, that the
minimum wage was extended to a limited number of female
public servants. Women in occupations covered by current
industrial awards were denied this minimum wage, however,
and were left with annual salaries as low as £50 a year.[55]
Announcing the extension of the public service minimum
wage to women, Holman spoke stirringly of the government's
commitment to equal pay:

> The principle we have acted upon is, as we believe, the sound one of
> equal pay for equal work. No operative ought to be sweated on the
> score of sex. If a woman really does a man's work she should be paid
> a man's wage, and the minimum is now fixed.[56]

The operative word was 'really', and the Board proceeded,
immediately the minimum wage for women was implemented,
to ensure that women did not 'really' do the same work as
men. With new income tax legislation increasing government
revenue, the Board was able to raise the starting salary and
increment range of male clerks to £60 and £200 respectively in
1912. In compensation, however, the Board intensified its
policy of deskilling women, writing the ceiling on women's
careers into the regulations for the first time and announcing
its intention to employ women to do 'work of more or less
mechanical nature' which was being performed by higher-
salaried men. The Board considered this beneficial to the
service, as it released men for 'more important duties'.[57]

Following the outbreak of war, demands for economy became
more urgent. Accordingly, at the end of 1915 the Board opened
clerical positions to women for the first time since the turn of
the century. In contrast to the equality they had enjoyed at
least in principle at that time, female clerks were now to have
a lower starting salary, a smaller increment range, and an
inferior entrance examination which was used as an excuse for
the inequality of conditions governing male and female labour
markets.[58] In responding to their male trade union constituents
within the constraints of a powerful opposition, the Labor
government had little hesitation in sacrificing the cause of
women's equality.

These moves to intensify the dual labour market were fiercely resisted by a wide range of public service women, supported by feminist organizations and Labor women who felt betrayed by their party. In 1910 women made up about 27 per cent of the 12500 permanent public servants. Most of these 3500 women were teachers, almost two hundred were poorly paid cleaners, nurses, asylum attendants and printing office employees, and a small group of about fifty filled a tiny 2 per cent of all professional and clerical positions. Women such as Annie Golding had been office bearers in the Public School Teachers Association for many years,[59] and the other newly mobilized public service women followed the teachers' lead in trying initially to work through the established union, the Public Service Association.

The militancy of public service women was first aroused by the denial of the minimum wage to those women most in need of wage justice. In September 1911, Margaret Hogg, a typist in the Stores Supply Department, began her long campaign to improve the pay and opportunities of women in the service with letters to the *Sydney Morning Herald*, the Public Service Association and the *Public Service Journal* protesting the decision not to extend the minimum wage to public service women already covered by wages boards.[60] The following year, the formal restriction of most women's career mobility and the revival of the question of superannuation mobilized Margaret Hogg and others to seek a more prominent part in the Association's affairs. From 1912, Margaret Hogg, Muriel Swain, May Matthews and Belle Golding were active members of the PSA council, until a change from departmental to divisional representation in 1918 made it more difficult for women to gain election to the council.

All of these women were active feminists. Belle Golding, the first female factory inspector appointed under the Early Closing Act in 1900, had worked for many years in the suffrage movement and a variety of reform movements under the umbrella of the Women's Progressive Association she established with her sister Annie.[61] May Matthews, a former teacher who had transferred to the Registrar-General's Office as a typist, was also involved in campaigns by the National Council of Women and the Women's Progressive Association to widen women's political and economic participation.[62] Both were Labor Party members of long standing, May Matthews becoming president of the Women's Central Organizing Committee in 1918. Margaret Hogg, an old friend of Rose Scott's and later treasurer of the Feminist Club, had joined the service as a temporary typist in 1908 and had finally secured a permanent position in 1911 at the age of forty-one.[63] Muriel Swain, now a compiler in the Statistician's Office, was one of the first women clerks appointed in 1900. By 1912, when she became the first woman to be elected to the PSA council, she had been in the service for twelve years and was just over thirty years old. Like the other female councillors, she was involved in a wide variety of women's organizations.[64]

These four activists were responsible for persuading the Public Service Association to take up the female public servant's cause. They argued that women had to earn their living just as men did, that they often had similar obligations to support others, and that they should therefore enjoy equal pay and opportunity with men. 'In this twentieth century', wrote Margaret Hogg with characteristic rhetoric:

When woman takes her part in the battle of life and into which economic conditions have brought her to stay, it is only a fair demand that all disabilities which prevail under the public service regulations and which hamper her progress should be eliminated and placed in the Archives of the Museum of Antiquity, where future generations may gaze and marvel that such impediments should ever have been placed in the pathway of versatile, conscientious, industrious woman.[65]

Margaret Hogg argued that women sought equality because 'men related to her by ties of blood to whom she looked in the past to represent her' had failed her. But women's equality could only be beneficial to the state and to men:

The argument that woman will neglect her home ties for higher education and political work is no more true than that she has and does neglect it for pleasure and social functions. The wider woman's outlook the greater her understanding of the word duty—or, again,

That women will become unwomanly—well, leave that to nature, which has given woman instincts peculiar to herself and has guarded them for centuries. To be less frivolous, less empty-headed, is not loss of womanliness, it may be less pleasing to certain types of man—but not less womanly.[66]

The Public Service Association responded to the appeal of its women members in 1911, and pressed their case with the Public Service Board and the attorney-general, D. R. Hall.[67] There was no doubt a degree of self-serving in this support, as the Association had always been concerned at the possibility of under-cutting by women. However, its president, J. S. D'Arcy, was one of the young men who had been associated with Coghlan in the 1890s, and he was the brother of Dr Constance D'Arcy, a pioneering woman doctor. In any event, he supported Margaret Hogg's election as a delegate to the first interstate conference of public service associations in December 1913, and together they secured a resolution from the conference advocating equality of pay and opportunity for women.[68]

Despite the efforts of D'Arcy and the women councillors, the Association's major push for improvement of women's conditions in 1914 proved to be too late. Their representations to attorney-general Hall were made a month before the outbreak of war, and were lost sight of in the ensuing financial anxieties of the government.[69] Margaret Hogg was incensed by Hall's off-hand reference during this interview to the 'fair sex':

The 20th century is not the epoch in which women desire to be called by such an empty title. This is the period which has brought them into the industrial world to face the serious fact of earning their living. In doing so they have discovered that they are just as capable, industrious and conscientious as men. Having come to this self-knowledge in spite of the obstacles which have been strewn in their path for the last fifty years, they ask for equal opportunities and equal remuneration.

The days when the single man supported his women-folk are past, and women of spirit are glad of it. The single man of the present day, paid on a higher scale than the single woman, more often than not uses his surplus for amusements, not for the support of kith and kin...

I would suggest that single men and single women be remunerated on the same scale, and married men and married women on the same basis, positions being equally open to both sexes.[70]

Aware that wartime economies posed special dangers for their cause, public service women formed their own section of the Association in 1915 to add greater weight to their demands.

190   Managing Gender

They were still, at this stage, anxious to co-operate with their
male colleagues. Margaret Hogg, who convened the meeting
to form the women's section, assured *Public Service Journal*
readers that:

There is no desire to dissociate the Women's Section from the PSA,
which, in spite of the remarks of the unenthusiastic, has done, and is
doing, so far as lies in its power, all that it can do to rectify any
grievances and disabilities of the officers of the service.[71]

Those who took an active part in the women's section represented a wide cross-section of rank and occupation. Muriel
Swain, now editor of the Department of Labour and Industry's
Industrial Gazette, was president, and Belle Golding, who had
been a factory inspector for fifteen years, was vice-president.
Both earned over £200 a year. Annie Frank and Florence
Wearne, two of the original female shorthand typists appointed
in 1897, and Mary Ryan, who was one of the 1900 cohort of
female clerks along with Muriel Swain, earned £150 and £170
a year. Caroline Byrne earned only £70 as sister at the Coast
Hospital after twelve years service. Rachel Hill, forewoman in
the Government Printing Office with thirty years experience,
Louisa Sibthorpe, sewer in the same office for twenty-nine
years, and Mrs Annie Todd, court keeper at the Water Police
Court with twenty-six years service, all earned between £52
and £100.

The women on the Association council, supported by the
women's section, tried to press their male colleagues into
greater activity on their behalf. By this time, however, the
Public Service Board and public service men were feeling the
effects of the government's economies. The Association dragged
its feet in protesting against the opening of clerical positions to women in September 1915 on unequal terms. Special
meetings arranged by the women's section were obstructed
by some male members of the Association, with the result
that the new regulations were a *fait accompli* before deputations
to the attorney-general and the PSB were organized.[72] A
deputation including Belle Golding, Margaret Hogg, May
Matthews and six male council members finally met the Board
in December, but Margaret Hogg was sceptical about its
results. Reporting that the deputation received 'the blandest
and most charming reception from the Board and assurances

for the future', she warned that 'We are not sure whether there is any analogy between the hopeful assurances and the ostrich hiding its head from the facts in the illusiveness of promises'.

In anticipation of such an attitude on the part of the Board, the public service women had already drawn the wider women's movement into the battle. The Feminist Club, of which Margaret Hogg was a member, made representations to the premier and sought the assistance of the Public Service Association to make up a joint deputation to the Board. John D'Arcy, Muriel Swain, and factory inspector Grace Scobie formed an Association committee to work with the Feminist Club. The Board responded negatively to the demands of the resulting delegation, stating, much to the indignation of the women public servants, that the employment of women as clerks was only in 'the initiatory stage'. As Margaret Hogg exclaimed in the *Public Service Journal*, 'Sixteen years ago women entered the Public Service [as clerks], and the Board say that their employment is still in the Initiatory Stage'.[73]

With its more restrained interventions ignored, the Feminist Club stepped up its activities on behalf of public service women. Other interested organizations were invited to join the campaign,[74] and in July 1916 representatives of the Public Service Association, the Feminist Club, the Women Teachers' Club, the Women's Progressive Association, the Women's Liberal League and the Technical College were received by the Board. The women put their case eloquently and logically. Miss Chandler of the Public Schools Teachers' Association laid to rest the Board's spurious argument about the experimental nature of the employment of women: 'As a public servant who has nearly forty years' service', she commented, 'I cannot agree that we are in the initiatory stage'. Belle Golding appealed to justice and equity:

The question of equal pay for equal work is the same old question that has been agitating the public mind year in and year out. We cannot dress it up in new garments...Equal pay for equal merit should be the battle-cry of the Board. We, as women, should not be compelled to wait on deputations for justice, to wait on this Board, to wait on the Government of the State, or the Commonwealth, or anyone else. The Government of this State has equal pay for work of equal merit on its platform. The Government of the Commonwealth

has it on their platform. The Liberal League also has it on its platform. . . .
We should not have to ask for that which is our right and our justice. . . .

Our expenses are high; the cost of living is high; it is as high to
the woman as to the man. We have to pay the same rates and taxes,
and we have to pay the same travelling fares. . . We have to attend to
our duty just the same hours as the man. . . We ask you to value
our work on the results, and to lose sight of the fact that we are
women.[75]

However, this last request seemed to be impossible. At the
conclusion of the meeting, Margaret Hogg observed: 'I know
Mr Taylor and Mr Hanna are shivering on the brink of great
reforms, but I think Mr Wilshire is a long way off. I would
like to see Mr Wilshire give in'.[76] He apparently did not, as
the decision of the Board was a concession only to men:
female and male clerks were to compete on equal terms by
sitting for the same examination from the end of the following
year; but the principle of equal pay was not accepted. The
Board would only concede that the large discrepancy between
men's and women's pay should be reduced.[77]

Incensed at this outcome, Margaret Hogg attempted to
capitalize on current public service discontent to have the
Board reconstituted. She initiated Association moves to obtain
direct employee representation on the Board, and argued that
one of these should be a woman. She and Belle Golding were
members of the committee appointed to consider these questions, but they did not carry the day, and the committee
reported against both recommendations.[78] Undeterred, the
two women continued to press the Association, the Board
and the premier for the acceptance of complete equality of pay
and opportunity, pointing out that 'the principle of equal pay
is not justice to women, but a safeguard to the interests of
men as well'.[79]

The whole question was shelved by the government early
in 1917. With a difficult election approaching premier Holman
announced to the delegation including Belle Golding in February
that he was commissioning an inquiry into the public service.[80]
The question of equal pay and opportunity had to wait on the
results of this inquiry. In the meantime Margaret Hogg's
warning to her male colleagues proved timely. As soon as the
election was over the Board announced an austerity programme which included the substitution of female for male
clerks. As she pointed out in the *Public Service Journal*,

One cannot emphasise too emphatically the call to all right thinking
men not to emphasise, but to sink sex discrimination as the only
means of attaining that Ideal State, that Democratic State for which
the world upheaval is preparing the way.[81]

The revised regulations of August 1917 confirmed the continued use of female clerks as cheap labour, making only the
minor concession of granting women the same starting salary
as men. However, their automatic annual increments remained
£5 less than men's; their increment range was £45 less; and
women with Leaving Certificate qualifications did not get the
£15 increase in starting salary enjoyed by men.[82]

   In October 1917 Margaret Hogg gave evidence on behalf of
the women's section of the PSA before the Royal Commission.[83]
This was her last official service for public service women.
The Public Service Association was reorganized along divisional rather than departmental lines, and she lost her place
on the council in February 1918.[84] A few months later she
married fellow clerk George Duff. Even though she continued
in the service and expressed 'no desire to relinquish my advocacy of any principle or movement for the improvement of
the status of women', she no longer played an active part in
the affairs of the Association or the women's section.[85] Con-
firming that this was the end of an era, Belle Golding resigned
from the Association at the end of 1917, and the women's
champion, John D'Arcy, died a premature death.[86]

IV

A new phase began for the public service in 1919. The previous
year Holman had established a Board of Trade to assist the
Industrial Court which had been operating in different forms
since 1901*. The Board of Trade was empowered to declare
'from year to year after public inquiry as to the increase and
decrease of the average cost of living, what shall be the living
wages to be paid'. Holman hoped by this means to dampen
prevailing conflict over wages and the cost of living.[87] Workers
gained a considerable wage increase from the first declaration
of the Board of Trade in September 1918, and public servants
stepped up pressure for their inclusion under its jurisdiction.
Following large public meetings during 1919, the government

---

*The name also varied—sometimes 'Arbitration Court' was used.

finally gave way and allowed public servants access to the arbitration system.[88] In the same month, the members of the Public Service Board resigned.

Further pressure from public servants forced the government to allow them to benefit immediately from the living wage declaration of the Board of Trade. As no declaration had yet been made of the living wage for women, the Public Service Board decided that female employees should receive three-quarters of the male increase, despite the request of a mass meeting of public servants for equal treatment of the sexes, a petition signed by 860 female public servants, and the statement of the Royal Commission that 'for absolutely equal work there should be no question about equal pay for women'. To make matters worse, even this small increase was not given to the poorly paid women in the Government Printing Office who did not receive the adult minimum wage after as much as twenty years service. Nor did it apply to junior officers, who earned as little as £60 a year.[89]

In response to this setback, and in anticipation of arbitration proceedings, public service women organized once more. By now, however, they were divided over tactics. Florence Wearne proposed the reformation of the women's section of the Public Service Association, which had lapsed with the reorganization of the Association in 1918. Belle Golding, on the other hand, argued for a women's association having no connection with the Association. Yet another group opposed both proposals, considering that it was 'inadvisable to make any mention of sex in connection with our claims before the Arbitration Court'. Finally the Association was asked to admit three women to the log committee to represent the women's interests. Florence Wearne also went ahead with her plan to establish a women's branch of the Association, although her attempt to place two of its representatives on the council initially proved unsuccessful.[90]

The female clerical case was heard separately from the male case in the Industrial Court from 30 May to 7 June 1921. By that time there were about four hundred female clerical workers in the service, making up about 15 per cent of the clerical division.[91] Florence Wearne was the opening witness, her presentation was well prepared and eloquently argued when she was given a chance to speak, and her evidence was followed by that of a number of other women with long careers in the service. Despite the evidence they presented on the range and value of their work, the scales awarded by the Court were a bitter disappointment. An appeal was lodged, but this was dismissed by the Full Court comprising Mr Justice Edmunds and Judges Rolin and Beeby.[92]

In fixing the wage scale for women clerks, Judge Curlewis refused to take seriously the Association's claim for equal pay, asserting that he had no power under the Act to consider such a claim.[93] He was bound, he asserted, to base his decision on the living wage declaration of the Board of Trade. This was £4 5s for males and £2 3s for females. In the male clerical case, he had fixed the maximum salary at £421 after twenty years service. In fixing the maximum for women clerks the judge retained the Board of Trade margin of £2 2s between men's and women's salaries, and derived a maximum for female clerks of £312. At the base of the scale, for age twenty-one, a weekly allowance of 17s was made for the fact that female clerks had greater expenses for education and dress than female industrial workers. The salary was therefore fixed at £156. With a starting salary of £156 per year, compared with £221 for men, women were to receive £12 increments each year, while men received £20.

Female shorthand typists fared even worse. Their salaries were fixed on a scale from £154 at age twenty-one to £224 after ten years service or six years adult service. This meant that they received only £10 for each additional year of service, and ended up with a salary of little more than that of a twenty-one-year-old male clerk. The low ceiling of £224 was based on the assumption that women did not make careers of sec-retarial work, and was copied from an award previously made in the Water and Sewerage Board case, where there were no shorthand typists of more than six years experience. In the public service case, however, the Judge had heard evidence from witnesses with up to twenty-five years service.

In a further denial of the career aspirations and realities of shorthand typists, Judge Curlewis refused to recognize the general principle that shorthand typists gained training just as valuable as junior clerks, and that they should be allowed to proceed into the senior clerical ranks. In the face of evidence from Florence Wearne, Alice Thompson and others with long

service and large responsibilities, he treated these 'girls', as he
persisted in calling them, as special cases who could be dealt
with by the Board on an individual basis.[94] Otherwise the
principle was confirmed that shorthand typing was not the
beginning of a career; instead it was treated as a temporary
occupation for 'girls' who would quickly marry. With a salary
ceiling equal to that of a young male clerk, this was a self-
fulfilling prophecy.

V

The female clerical award marked the beginning of a rapid
deterioration of the conditions of women's work in the public
service. The family wage principle on which the living wage
declaration of the Board of Trade was based was the crucial
element in this process of deterioration. This principle had
evolved out of attempts of earlier arbitration court judges to
establish guidelines for their decisions. Judges such as Mr Justice
Heydon of the New South Wales court and Mr Justice Higgins
of the Commonwealth court brought to their positions the
amateurism and biases that many participants in the debate
on the Trades Disputes Bill of 1892 had feared from a judicial
president of the court. With closer identification with 'the
classes' than with 'the masses', they knew little of working
class life, even though they were sympathetic with male
workers' aspiration for a decent standard of living.

Charles Heydon was the son of a printer and publisher and
had been in practice since 1875. He became president of the
Arbitration Court in 1905 and was retired in 1918 at the age of
seventy-three. As a Roman Catholic familiar with the 1891
papal encyclical on the conditions of labour, which urged that
remuneration should be enough to keep a man, his wife and
his children in 'reasonable and frugal comfort', he was receptive
to similar claims from the male unionists and labour lawyers
such as George Beeby and W. A. Holman who appeared
before him.[95] Early in his jurisdiction he formulated the rough
principle that there should be a living wage below which
wages should not fall. This living wage should allow every
worker, however humble, to receive enough 'to lead a human
life, *to marry and bring up a family* and maintain them and
himself with, at any rate, some small degree of comfort'.[96]
Neither Heydon nor Higgins, in his famous judgement of

1907 in the Commonwealth court, calculated this amount with any degree of accuracy, if indeed this was possible. In practice, they accepted one of the ruling rates paid by reputable employers as their baseline.

When Commonwealth statistician G. N. Knibbs began publishing cost-of-living figures regularly in 1912, the courts came under pressure to calculate the living wage more accurately and objectively. Heydon undertook an extensive investigation in 1913–14 to determine the size of the average family and its actual expenditure. He based his decisions from that time on the needs of a family of two adults and two children, assessed at 8s a day in 1914. The whole question of the accuracy of the calculation of the living wage became a matter of major political concern during the war years, as Heydon deliberately lagged increases in wages behind cost of living rises. By the end of the war, a considerable sense of injustice had built up amongst workers, fuelled by inconsistencies between Commonwealth and state awards. Holman's attempt to defuse this unrest by establishing the Board of Trade as a 'neutral' authority to calculate the cost of living almost destroyed the arbitration system. The first living wage based on the calculations of the Board of Trade statistician, D. T. Sawkins, in 1919 was 28 per cent higher than that of 1918—a spectacular rise of 17s per week.

The wage explosion for male workers caused by the 'scientific' calculation of a family wage was, in Sawkins's words, 'viewed with apparent consternation by employers'.[97] It caused no less consternation to the Holman government. In a period of intense controversy, all interested parties focussed attention on the implications of such a formal adoption of the family wage principle.

The 'scientific' calculation of a family wage posed a major threat to the male wage-earner unless he could maintain his right to control all elements in the total wage. The statisticians broke the wage into components, with set amounts allocated to the expense of a wife and a specified number of children. Previously, the worker had won a wage by the process of bargaining, and once gained, it was his to dispose of as he wished. Now the wage was, in theory, allocated by a tribunal for specific purposes. Accordingly, employers could argue that men without dependants should not be paid that proportion of the wage meant for family maintenance. Women could argue that portion of it should be paid directly to the mother. They could also argue that single men and women should be paid equally, where each had no dependants. Whatever the argument, it implied less money in the pocket of the male wage-earner.

When the size of the living wage based on the Board of Trade's calculations was revealed to the Holman government, it attempted to take advantage of the theoretical structure of the family wage to reduce the cost of the wage rise to its employer constituency. The government proposed that the living wage should be calculated on the basis of a man and wife only, and that mothers should be paid directly for the maintenance of children from a tax on employers. As 35 per cent of adult males were bachelors, and the average family had one dependent child rather than two, this proposal would cut the wages bill considerably.[98]

The Maintenance of Children Bill, which embodied these proposals, was opposed by unionists and employers alike, and was rejected by the Legislative Council. Unionists objected to what amounted to a major cut in male wages. Employers were suspicious that the endowment tax would escalate and involve them in unknown future expenses. The full wage, calculated to cover the needs of a man, his wife and two children, was therefore gained by all male workers, irrespective of their marital status or family needs. This large increase in the living wage engendered a spiral in prices and unemployment which led the Board of Trade to grant less than the full cost of living increase in 1920. Over the next few years the living wage was reduced, but the effective level of average wages remained higher than that of 1907 until at least 1926.[99]

It was in this atmosphere of uncertainty and confrontation that women public servants were trying to maintain their struggle for equal pay and opportunity. The first declaration of a living wage for women in 1918 based on the 'needs' criterion awarded women half the male wage. The decision was justified on the grounds that women had no family responsibilities. This justification of women's poor pay had built up gradually as the concomitant of the family wage concept for men. Heydon himself was not in favour of women going out to work—it might interfere with women's desire to marry and it might keep men out of work. He also thought that most women worked from choice rather than necessity. Employers' advocates such as Tom Rolin (who was on the Full Court which dismissed the female clerks' appeal) argued that most women did not have to keep themselves fully, and that they could therefore be paid *less* than a living wage. Labour lawyers such as Beeby at least convinced Heydon that single women did need to pay for their own keep, and that their contributions were an essential part of family income.[100] None, however, argued as the women public servants did, that single men often had no responsibilities and single women often maintained other family members.

By 1918 it had become an entrenched industrial court attitude that women were worth no more than 'two-thirds of a man'.[101] This evaluation was based, like that of the male living wage until 1919, on current rates of pay, rather than factual judgements about women's productivity or needs, despite rhetoric to the contrary. As the living wage was the basis of all other wages determined by the court, the weakness of the bargaining strength of the unskilled female worker was imported into the fixing of female public service wages. The poor standard of comfort provided to unskilled women by the low wages they could command became institutionalized as the 'needs' of all women. In effect, the small gains won so painfully by the militant organization of women clerical workers were wiped out completely by tying public service wages to the arbitration system.

VI

The adoption of the living wage declarations as the basis of public service salaries had an immediate impact on the gap between the wages of male and female clerical workers.[102] This was confirmed and intensified by the clerical award, which dealt a death blow to hopes of equal pay and opportunity for women in the service. The clerical award provided a basis for the rapid intensification of a dual labour market in the Clerical Division. The members of the reconstituted Public Service Board used the discrepancy between the salaries of male and female clerks to extricate themselves from their difficulties.[103] Charged with the duty of running an economical public service, they had no control over the major cost factor, salaries. With male salaries skyrocketing, the Board resorted to employing more women at cheaper rates in order to cut costs.

The determination of the Fuller government of 1922 to 1925 to reduce the expenses of the public service encouraged this trend.[104] From 1922 no further entrance exams for female clerks were held.[105] The PSB reported in 1923:

Girls are being employed wherever possible on minor office work, such as typing, which is not appropriate for boys qualified by examination for permanent employment. This is found to be both convenient and economical, as, in most cases, the girls do not enter the Clerical Division of the Public Service with the object of making it their life's career, as educated boys do.[106]

In 1923 a new classification of temporary office assistant (female) was introduced for girls between the ages of sixteen and nineteen.[107] As the Board explained in 1924:

By a careful sorting out of the work and by the employment of female office assistants on the least valuable type of clerical work... the Board has been able to manage with a greatly reduced number of qualified junior clerks.[108]

With a commencing rate of £65 and a maximum salary of £117 at age twenty-one, this was cheap, disposable labour compared with male clerks who had in 1921 been awarded a starting salary of £92, a minimum of £222 at twenty-one and an increment range up to £421. Women's lack of rights and prospects meant that there was a high turnover which kept the wages bill low. Public service women objected to the assumption that they were uninterested in a career, stating in the *Public Service Journal* that

Exception was...taken to the Public Service Board's report which stated that women of the Service do not desire to do anything but the easy and mechanical work of the Service.[109]

In June 1924 over 30 per cent of the 700 women clerks and shorthand typists in the service were temporary employees. By 1929 the Board was able to boast that

The whole of the increase in the Clerical Division was in the number of females employed on clerical work as typists, office assistants, etc., with comparatively low rates of pay...The number of male employees in the Clerical Division *decreased* during the eight years by 69.[110]

By 1930 so-called 'temporary' employees made up 56 per cent of the 1300 women in the Clerical Division. By 1944, such 'temporary' employment was the norm for women clerks, with 86 per cent of the 3327 female clerical employees working without rights to security of tenure, upward career mobility or wage justice.[111]

VII

The female clerical award and the Public Service Board's policy of separating women into a secondary labour market drove a wedge between the interests of male and female clerical workers. The support of male unionists for equal pay and opportunity had always been equivocal because Public Service Board and government policies towards women were never unambiguous, and the danger had always been present that women would be used to replace men. This uneasiness had developed into outright hostility from some Public Service Association members during the difficult war years. The female clerical award gave male unionists more freedom to express opposition to women's equality and to press for the exclusion of women. At the interstate conference held in December 1923, A. J. Trollope, the new president of the Association, voted against the usual motion endorsing equal pay, arguing that it was not in the interests of the race to have women in jobs while the family breadwinner could not find work.[112]

The Association tolerated the employment of women as cheap labour, however, because temporary office assistants were in a separate designation and thus removed from competition with men for the better Clerical Division jobs. As the Association's general secretary reported to its executive in 1924 after discussions with the Board,

The object of employing these girls is to relieve junior clerks of work of the most elementary character, such as typing. The number employed is limited and there is no intention on the part of the Board to extend the system.

Seeing that only 45 boys are available this year for appointment as junior clerks, the Board is anxious to so arrange the work as to avoid the necessity of putting educated juniors out to work that can be performed by these female assistants. I was assured that the employment of these girls is not to be regarded as a menace but rather should be looked upon with favour as a means of freeing educated officers from merely routine work.

The result of the discussion...satisfies me that the Association had nothing to fear in this regard.[113]

Women public servants had little support from the Association, therefore, when the Fuller government revoked public servants' access to the Arbitration Court and authorized the PSB to make agreements with public service unions on pay and conditions. The women's cause was further weakened by the fact that the reorganization of the Association along divisional lines made it more difficult for them to be elected to council. Attempts to gain representation for the women's section were initially unsuccessful, and the status of the section remained unclear during much of the 1920s.

There continued to be some support in the Association for equal pay and opportunity, however. When access to the Arbitration Court was restored in 1925 with Labor's defeat of the conservative Fuller government, the PSA did support the women's section's request that a clause be inserted in the new Industrial Arbitration Bill authorizing the court to deal with the question of equal pay. Ironically, this clause was worded so badly it actually excluded public service women from its jurisdiction.[114]

By 1929 there was open division in the Association over the question of equal pay and opportunity for women. It was supported in an editorial in *Red Tape*, the successor of the *Public Service Journal*, in February of that year, and in a paper presented by F. C. Wills at the conference of the Australian Public Service Federation in Perth in October.[115] However, the usual conference motion in favour of equal pay and opportunity was opposed by the president of the New South Wales Association, W. A. Flynn, whose unflattering remarks about women drew the wrath of feminist writers and women public servants.[116] Although other members of the council dissociated themselves from their president's remarks, Flynn continued his campaign to sever the links between the interests of the men and women of the service by setting up a completely separate women's organization.[117] By the following year he

had established a women's auxiliary as a means of 'affording
the (almost) 1,000 women members an opportunity of managing their own concerns within the Association, and so to
obviate intervention by outside organisations in the affairs of
women members of the public service'. Repudiating all the
work women activists had done from within the Association
he exhorted them to organize separately if they wanted to
improve their conditions of employment. 'Women aspire to
the wage level which men attained only after long years of
intensive organisation', he informed them condescendingly.
'Be it said to them, in all sincerity, "Go thou and do likewise"'.[118]

VIII

By 1930 women clerical workers were set apart as a separate
category by employer and union alike. After thirty years of
struggle, a dual labour market had been established in the
Clerical Division which placed women in a powerless position
in the workplace and the industrial arena. The small gains
made by the first Public Service Board had been wiped out
almost completely by changes in political, economic and social
conditions which resulted in weak Labor governments willing and able to protect only male workers, weak boards who
used their large statutory powers to the detriment of women
workers, and an industrial arbitration system run by lawyers
which used women as sacrificial lambs to maintain their cred-
ibility as peacemakers between capital and labour. The net
effect was to reinforce the stereotypes of male and female
workers which were beginning to break down at the end of
the nineteenth century, to identify male workers as breadwinners and female workers as current or potential dependants
working for 'pin-money' only, and to create circumstances
which forced men and women into those roles.

> There is a very close connection between *employment* as experts and the enthusiasm for human welfare.
>
> Samuel Gompers

> Look, woman, in the West, there wilt thou see
> An amber cradle near the sun's decline:
> Within it, featured even in death divine,
> Is lying a dead infant, slain by thee.

Lines attributed to Meredith, quoted by Dr. H. B. Allen, presidential address to the Australasian Medical Congress, 1908

8
Managing gender

I

In handing over public service wage fixing to the Board of
Trade and the Industrial Court, the government ended definitively the career of the strong Public Service Board envisaged
by Coghlan in 1895. At the same time it confirmed a wider
managerial role for the state and the influence of the professions
within it. Public service reform had been part of a general
movement at the end of the nineteenth century to open up
professional work to 'the democracy' and to upgrade it materially and ethically. Like public servants, members of the established professions had, during this period, lobbied successfully
to standardize and democratize professional training and admission and to gain state recognition of professional monopoly
and autonomy. These professionalizing projects were not only
similar in style and purpose, but were also closely interrelated.
Public service professionals were active organizers and lobby-
ists in all these campaigns, and the state's enlarged role as a
medium of social reform provided new jobs and an ideological
platform for the newly strengthened professions.[1]

During the first thirty years of the twentieth century, this
partnership between the state and the professions grew in
scope and intensity. The Labor and Nationalist governments
from 1910 to 1920 were crucial in this process. Without funds
or reliable support for more radical and independent programmes, these governments turned increasingly to reforms
through bureaucratic organizations set up in the wake of the
public service reforms of the 1890s and to partnership with
the professions. With the support of ministers belonging to

these professions, such as W. A. Holman, J. D. Fitzgerald,
George Beeby and D. R. Hall, and with the guidance of
professionals in the bureaucracy, a variety of government
programmes were established which were dependent on expert
advice and support.[2]

The institutionalization of professional influence in the state
helped make the language of science, technology and expertise
one of the dominant discourses of early twentieth-century
Australia, and rational, scientific practice the model for order-
ing a variety of social arrangements. From daylight saving
to hydro-electricity to 'scientific motherhood', the ability of
engineers, economists, doctors and lawyers to harness and
manage nature and society 'efficiently' became an article of
faith.[3] Australia shared this faith in the efficiency of the 'scientific way' with other comparable countries during this period.
Proponents of what became known as the efficiency movement believed that social problems could be systematically
eradicated by the organized application of science and expertise,
especially through the state bureaucracy. In the United States,
government scientists were the standard-bearers of the movement which sought 'a political system guided by the ideal of
efficiency and dominated by the technicians who could best
determine how to achieve it'. In Britain, public health officials
in particular supported the movement led by Beatrice and
Sidney Webb which aimed to create 'an efficient bureaucracy,
directed from above by an "intelligence department" of
"experts"—social investigators, economists, scientists and
statisticians'.[4]

The efficiency movement presents a confusing mixture of
altruism, benevolence and self-seeking on the part of its adher-
ents. Drawing on scientifically validated knowledge, couched
in the rhetoric of the national good, and in terms of education
rather than supervision, the movement was in part a genuine
attempt to apply what was seen as new and reliable knowledge
for the public welfare. But its practice quickly slid into co-
ercion, regimentation and self-interest. This was because it
was, at base, a movement by rising and embattled social
groups to enlarge and make more secure their labour market
opportunities. Sincere as their impulses to social reform may
have been, their choice of means was often dictated by the
need to encourage the adoption of measures which depended

on their particular marketable skills. In the process, they often
denigrated the skills of the persons they purported to help in
order to make their own services seem essential. In addition,
they could not afford to genuinely educate their clients, as
their continued prosperity depended on the establishment of
a power relationship in which they were dominant and indispensable to their clients. The movement's most famous pro-
ponent, and possibly its most influential, was the inventor of
scientific management, Frederick Winslow Taylor. Taylorism
provides the starkest example of the self-interested motive at
the heart of the efficiency movement. Though couched in the
usual rhetoric of scientific rationality, the general good and
the education of the worker, Taylorism was, at heart, a systematic attempt to deprive the craft worker of knowledge of
his craft and control over his work process in order to make a
place for a new breed of professional manager.[5]

The Australian state provided a sympathetic environment in
which the ideology and practice of efficiency could flourish. In
New South Wales, for instance, the reforms of the mid-1890s
had restored faith in the state, strengthened its institutions,
and established its role as a reliable agent of social reconstruction.
There were, however, subtle differences in approach between
the architect of this reconstituted state, T. A. Coghlan, and
the professionals who built on his foundations in the early
years of the twentieth century. The quarrels between Wise
and Coghlan over the Public Service Board and compulsory
industrial arbitration illustrate these differences. Looking at
the state partly through the eyes of the craft worker, Coghlan
was concerned with establishing the economic, political and
social conditions necessary to strengthen workers' control of
their own situation, which he identified with the common
good. He disapproved of indiscriminate spending on public
works and unemployment relief where they did not contribute
to workers' self-reliance, and worked to increase workers'
autonomy through his support of the Labor Party, the Public
Service Act and self-help organizations such as Friendly Societies.
He saw strikes as an effective and necessary sign of working
class people's desire and ability to fight their own battles, and
did not support compulsory arbitration schemes which placed
responsibility for conciliation outside the participants themselves. Coghlan's approach to the state and the role of profes-

sional experts was, therefore, a limited and cautious one. Where he most closely resembled his progressive successors, in his managerial approach to women's employment, he did so because he believed this was necessary for a strong labour movement and a prosperous nation.

Wise, on the other hand, had a paternalistic approach to the problems of the working class and the new middle class. An Oxford liberal, a Queen's Counsel, and a member of the established elite, he believed that enlightened professionals should act as arbiters between capital and labour, if necessary with the support of the state.[6] In practice this meant that he was in favour of state intervention where upper class liberals such as himself could make decisions on behalf of workers, but violently opposed it when they could not. He was a prime mover, therefore, in the plan for compulsory state arbitration in which lawyers would play an important part, but disapproved strongly of a Public Service Board run by public servants such as Coghlan and did his best to weaken it. These differences between Coghlan and Wise were essentially class differences, both approving of state intervention when it was controlled by people of their own background and informed by attitudes and theories derived from their own experience. Because Coghlan's theories derived from the experience of the working class, his approach emphasized worker self-determination, while Wise's was more managerial.

The conditions of professional organization and the exigencies of politics in the early years of the twentieth century ensured that Wise's managerial approach prevailed. All levels of the professions participated in the associations that developed in this period, and there were no major issues dividing the senior ranks from the junior as there were in the public service. Their new unity and strength derived partly from the smooth integration of men from a wide variety of class backgrounds. In 1887 the *Bulletin* was thundering at 'the monopoly which the members of the close corporation of the law... enjoy' and 'the curled darlings of fortune whose sires possess fat banking accounts and mansions near Sir Frederick Darley's at Edgecliff Road, or in some equally aristocratic location',[7] but by the early 1900s a number of young men from working class, petty bourgeois or new middle class backgrounds had entered the profession and were rising to prominence in politics and the public service. Despite this democratic trend, the very ease with which the professions assimilated men (and women in the case of medicine) from a variety of class backgrounds left the established elite with much of its influence intact.[8]

This elite influence in the professions was strengthened by the ascendancy of a political partnership between upper class liberals such as Wise and young socialist intellectuals such as W. A. Holman and W. M. Hughes. Already committed to a version of socialism that favoured state intervention and eager for upward mobility through the newly accessible legal profession, the two young Labor politicians quickly came under Wise's influence when he returned to politics in 1898. Holman stated in his tribute to Wise on his death that 'there are probably no men in the public life of this state who are under a deeper debt of gratitude to [Wise] than I am myself':

Both as a beginner in the world of politics, and also as an aspirant for admission to the world of law, in my early days as a law student, seeking admission to the Bar, I was placed under deep obligations by the immediate personal intervention of the then Attorney-General of the State, Mr B. R. Wise. That I myself have arrived at any position of distinction in the public life of this State is, to a degree, greater than I can express, due to the help—I shall not merely say encouragement—but the definite and tangible help I received from the Attorney-General of fifteen years ago...I came into this House as a bitter political opponent of Mr. Wise's and of all his views...I sat here and, by the mere force of the most brilliant intellect I have ever seen displayed in this House, I was converted...to a recognition of Mr. Wise as a man born to be an intellectual leader of his generation.[9]

Holman and Hughes readily supported Wise's plan for compulsory state arbitration of labour disputes and there is evidence that Holman shared Wise's hostility to the Public Service Board. Holman and his fellow socialist, journalist and law student during the 1890s, George Beeby, struggled throughout their careers to preserve and improve the arbitration system in the face of employer and left-wing hostility. In return the new field of industrial law proved a useful source of work for these young Labor lawyers. Holman built up his legal reputation as an industrial lawyer. Beeby's specialization in industrial matters launched his career on the state Industrial Court in 1920, the Commonwealth Conciliation and Arbitration Court in 1926 and finally as chief judge of the Commonwealth court in

1938.[10] Despite Coghlan's assiduous cultivation of Holman and his fellow progressive, Alfred Deakin, Holman's continued identification with Wise rather than Coghlan is demonstrated by his appointment of the ailing Wise as agent-general in London in 1915 in place of Coghlan. The refusal of Holman and Deakin to give Coghlan the recognition he felt was due to him no doubt stems from their fundamental, though subtle, differences in outlook, and Coghlan's acerbic comments on men such as George Knibbs, the Commonwealth statistician during this period, were motivated as much by ideological differences as by jealousy.[11]

II

The professionals in the state programmes set up by Holman's governments between 1913 and 1920 were concerned with the same problems of class conflict and inequality as Coghlan and Reid had been, and the management of gender roles remained central to their solution. Guided by expediency rather than theoretical rigour, they made increasingly radical attempts to re-form the family and male—female relationships in line with both craft union and upper class ideals. With the resources of the state at their disposal, they were able to present a consistent— and Procrustean—view of a desirable gender order, to disseminate it widely, and to encourage and force its universal adoption.[12]

The infant welfare programme established by the Labor government illustrates this process well. Without adequate funds to carry out its ambitious plans for better health services for its working class constituency, the government supported, amongst other projects, a programme to educate mothers in the 'scientific' principles of infant welfare. Designed and controlled by the medical profession, it brought together issues of health, education, population control, child care, labour market control and gender role management which were central to the joint professional—state project.[13]

The programme began in a modest way in the early years of the twentieth century in response to widespread anxiety about the decline in Australia's population growth, the fall in the birth rate and the high rate of infant mortality. Powerful opinion leaders such as Coghlan discussed these matters extensively, and interest was brought to a high pitch in 1903—04

by the publication of Coghlan's second study of the birth rate
and the appointment of a Royal Commission to investigate
the problem.[14] Commentators began to speak of children as
having a calculable economic value, and of child bearing and
rearing as a duty rendered to the state for which mothers
should possibly be paid.[15] The endowment of motherhood by
the state became an important question throughout Australia
over the next thirty years, becoming entangled in the debate
over the family wage in 1919, and culminating in the Commonwealth Royal Commission on Child Endowment in 1929.[16]

The idea that women were performing an important economic service for the nation in bearing and rearing children,
and the concern that this task be carried out efficiently, gave
rise to a number of measures designed to coerce, instruct,
encourage or subsidize women in this work.[17] The infant
welfare programme was one of the most influential of these.
It was set firmly in train by the Labor government in 1914
when the efforts of feminists to help mothers in the poorer
suburbs and of public health education programmes were
combined in a new system of baby clinics. Over the next
decade the medical profession, public health officials and
voluntary association leaders worked out an accommodation
by which the clinics were run by the Public Health Department on behalf of the profession as a whole.[18]

By 1927 the infant welfare programme had become a universal means of disseminating medical influence. The establishment of clinics in more affluent areas and intensive publicity
for the movement exposed women of all classes to its ideas.[19]
Eventually almost every mother patronized the clinics, and
this patronage continued long after the concern about population size and high infant mortality rates disappeared.

The strategy of the infant welfare programme was over-
whelmingly managerial. This had not been the case with the
labour programme in its early years, when, influenced by
the Women's Organizing Committee of the Labor Party, it
emphasized the economic basis of infant mortality and advocated the payment to mothers of maternity and child allowances
and the provision of medical services for childbirth and sick
babies. The New South Wales Labour League attempted in
1909 to introduce maternity allowances,[20] which were successfully introduced in 1912 by the Federal Labor government.[21]

These provisions assumed that women would do the best for their children provided they had the means to do so. In contrast, public health officials focussed their campaign on the 'ignorance and carelessness' of parents—especially the mother.[22]

Doctors had always agreed that mothers needed to be educated to their tasks.[23] The infant welfare movement incorporated this elitist approach and was, therefore, 'a plan for the exercise of a control over the home conditions'[24] in order to 'help mothers to rear their infants that they might become— first, healthy children, and later, worthy citizens of the State'.[25] This campaign was based on the assumption that mothers had little or no knowledge of mothercraft and that the medical profession, and its agent, the health visitor, were the repositories of such knowledge. As one Australian public health official (who has been described as 'childless and impatient of domesticity'[26]) pointed out, 'the whole question of infant life is a highly technical one, involving very skilled supervision and closely disciplined execution'. In order to overcome the problem of the 'vast ignorance' and 'prejudice' of mothers, who brought only 'fondness and an uninstructed intelligence' to their task, infant welfare officials advocated the issuing of simple instructions to mothers which they should follow unquestioningly.[27] Maternity was, according to this ideology, no longer a matter of instinct supplemented by common sense, but an unskilled trade which should and must subordinate itself to the dictates and authority of medical and para-medical experts.

The analogy with Taylorism, that supreme example of the appeal to science, technical expertise, efficiency, and the 'one best method', is irresistible. But it is unlikely that the infant welfare movement actually deskilled women as mothers, despite the widespread influence of the clinic system. The mother's craft could never be destroyed to the degree that Taylorism could strip a worker of his skills, because mothers had ultimately to carry out their day-to-day work unsupervised by the medical profession except by the weight of their moral authority.[28]

Nevertheless, the infant welfare movement is likely to have had considerable influence on ideas and ideals about women. In promoting the superior efficiency of the 'scientific way', the programme had to denigrate the knowledge and efficiency

of mothers. The image of women conveyed by this enormously successful movement was of ignorance, inefficiency
and lack of responsibility. 'Refractory' mothers who did not
avail themselves of the services of the baby clinics were castigated as 'indifferent and apathetic to their responsibilities'.
With the link between poverty, large families and infant mortality obscured by this focus on inadequate mothering, it was
assumed that all mothers needed advice, because 'the maternal
instinct alone is not sufficient equipment for the proper feeding
and rearing of babies' and 'mothers in every grade of life. . . may
need mothercraft instructions and guidance'.[29]

This aspect of the infant welfare movement—its condescension to mothers and its constant denigration of women's
skills—contributed to the stereotype of women as incompetent
and capable of working only under supervision which was
being disseminated by the Public Service Board during the
same period. This demeaning stereotype undoubtedly affected
women's employment opportunities adversely. Through an
insistence that women were basically rather silly, unskilled
creatures, the perception of female wage-earners as 'secondary'
and marginal was reinforced.[30]

By insisting that motherhood was a full-time and demanding
occupation, exclusive of any other occupation and commitment,
publicists of the infant welfare movement also took a coercive
stance towards women's education and workforce participation.
Like Taylorism, the infant welfare movement advocated
specialization of function and training, and attempted to
coerce women into what was considered their proper role.
The considerable discussion in the *Australasian Medical Gazette*
surrounding the Piddington Royal Commission into the
'Hours, etc., of Females and Juveniles' in 1911–12[31] revealed
this at its starkest. An editorial emphasized that it was the
duty of the medical profession to ensure that 'the mother shall
be fully equipped for her responsible position'. It argued that,
'Biologically speaking, a woman's whole life is centred round
that one function—childbearing. . .'.[32] For this reason, it was
argued,

the present conditions of the female labour market are in many
ways injurious to the growth and healthy development of the race
[because] women are employed in a large number of factories at

work...which is absolutely useless in fitting them for a future life of wifehood and motherhood.

The writer went on to argue that girls would be better in domestic service where 'a girl is trained and better fitted in every way for childbearing and rearing' and where they could indirectly boost the birth rate by providing domestic help to women of the wealthier classes. He recommended therefore that:

the employment of female labour in any trades or factories except those which can only be carried out by women should be prohibited by law, and every girl should be compelled to serve a training in domestic economy, just as young men are compelled to train for military service.[33]

The coercive aspect of the infant welfare movement was further demonstrated by a resolution moved at the Australasian Medical Congress in 1914 by Dr Truby King, the New Zealand doctor whose name is synonymous with the movement. King urged the state to provide an education for girls which ensured 'complete fitness for maternity and the practical care of the home', and asserted that

even where marriage does not take place, the education which gives the girl the best all-round equipment in body, mind, morals, and inclination for home life and potential motherhood, also gives her the soundest and surest foundations for future health and happiness, and for a sustained power of earning an independent living....[34]

Women were, therefore, to devote their whole lives to 'that one function—childbearing' in the interests of 'the breeding of a stronger and sturdier race'.[35] If they did this, they would, despite King's assurances, find themselves untrained for participation in anything but the secondary labour market.

III

In her survey of the 1920s, Heather Radi remarks of women's participation in public affairs that 'Against an almost solid wall of disapproval...they seemed to give up'.[36] The coercive and condescending aspect of the infant welfare programme and a variety of related 'educational' domestic science and school health programmes contributed to this 'solid wall of disapproval'. By stressing women's duties as mothers, this managerial approach strengthened the ideology of women's place in the home; by stressing their need for supervision, it built up an image of women as lacking in responsibility and resourcefulness. To the degree that these ideas were accepted by women, or imposed on them through restrictive practices and legislation, the efficiency movement discouraged labour force participation and ambition, and encouraged trained incapacity for primary labour market work. To the degree that its ideas were accepted by others, the movement strengthened prejudices against women's participation in the workforce and in positions of responsibility, and encouraged policies of exclusion from such work.

The marginalization of women as legitimate participants in the workforce, and the concomitant emphasis on women's exclusive roles as wives and mothers, was, therefore, both capitalized on and reinforced by professionals within the state administration. The 'educational' programmes directed at mothers and potential mothers allowed the professionals to increase their labour market opportunities and to establish their influence in areas of expertise that had formerly been the province of individual women and families. The coercive and condescending rhetoric and practice of these programmes strengthened the ideology that women's place was in the home, and that women were lacking in the responsibility and resourcefulness necessary for independence, even, ironically, in what had previously been considered their 'natural' sphere.

This emphasis on women's exclusive roles as wives and mothers, had, of course, its counterpart in an increasingly Procrustean view of the male role as breadwinner. Although this had always been an important part of the construction of masculinity, the imposition by the state of the family wage concept gave increased legitimacy, consistency and practical effect to the symbolic identity of paid work and maleness. A. B. Piddington, an archetypal progressive of the period who was in many ways sympathetic to women's independence, could speak of work as 'the energetic tissue in a nation's virility', and could recommend the iron and steel industry as 'specifically deserving of encouragement' because of 'the masculine character of the industry itself'.[37]

By 1930, therefore, an integrated set of ideas and practices had developed in New South Wales which identified breadwinning exclusively with masculinity and made dependence the 'natural' status for women. This dependent status was by no means settled before the turn of the century. Throughout the nineteenth century, labour market practices with regard to women in New South Wales were diverse, and during the 1890s, although the right of married women to economic independence came increasingly under attack, attempts to extend the independence of single women had widespread support, and were part of the state's policy towards its own clerical workers. Within thirty years, however, the prescription for women was uniformly based on their definition as dependants and potential dependants. This definition made them, at best, marginal and temporary workers, and at worst, illegitimate usurpers of jobs rightfully belonging to others. All women were expected to marry, and the unmarried career women whose rights Coghlan was ready to recognize and protect became an anomaly who could not be fitted into the assumptions and categories of the industrial courts. Women had the right to paid work only after men's need for such work was satisfied. They should not compete with men for work, especially if it was well paid and had prospects for career advancement. As temporary workers, women did not require career structures. As potential dependants, they had no right to high wages or equal pay. Women had higher and exclusive duties as wives and mothers, so they should not work if they were married, and definitely should not do so if they had children. But even in what was termed their separate sphere, women were not independent. Instead they were subject to the authority of the expert in the very work it was supposedly 'natural' for them to fill.

The prescription for women's dependence was not only ideological, but coercive as well. It was embodied in the family-wage decisions of the state Industrial Court and in the regulations and practices of the state public personnel system, and was disseminated through state resources such as the infant welfare programme and the reports of the census. In short, the ideological and coercive resources of the state were deployed to construct and uphold this particular view of women's place in the family and the labour market.

Many of the ideas that went into the prescription for women's dependence, and the strength and consistency of its application, owed much to the new middle class, working through its members in the state bureaucracy and the industrial relations system. T. A. Coghlan, as government statistician and member of the Public Service Board, had consistently worked to remove married women from the workforce by redefining many such women as non-workers in his census reports, and by excluding them from the public service workforce by legislation and administrative practice. He also did much to popularize an emphasis on the exclusive duties of women as mothers in his publications on the birth rate. In addition, he instituted a discretionary state personnel system for women whereby the employment of single women by the state was regulated separately from that of men, and though his intentions and practice in this sphere were supportive of women he unwittingly opened the way for massive discrimination against women which was contrary to the intentions of the legislators who passed the Public Service Act in 1895.

Not only did new middle class men such as Coghlan play an active part in the construction of ideas and practices which contributed to women's dependence in the early twentieth century, but, possibly more importantly, they also laid the basis for the use of state resources for their implementation and dissemination. Without the strong and relatively independent administrative base established by Public Service Board leadership in the mid-1890s, and the relationship built up between the public service and the labour movement on the one hand and the feminist movement on the other, it is unlikely that powerful ideological and coercive institutions such as the state Industrial Court and the infant welfare programme would have been so firmly established.

These projects for managing gender and managing the state were intimately related. The motivation for intervention into women's family and working lives and the determination to gain autonomy and security in their own working lives both stemmed from new middle class labour market—and probably family experiences as well—in a particular period of history, and they drew on ideas current in their particular cultural milieu. Persistent threats to public servants' security and standard of living during the 1880s and early 1890s generated protective labour market strategies which culminated in Coghlan's Public Service Bill of 1895, with its provisions for appointment and promotion by measurable qualifications, a form of public service self-government, the exclusion of married women, and the regulation of the employment of single women. The contradictory character of the Bill's advocacy of a universalistic merit principle on the one hand, and the exclusion of some workers on ascriptive grounds on the other, demonstrated an accommodation of the labour market ideas of craft unionism with which many of the reforming public servants had grown up, the need to dismantle political patronage, and the economic realities of new middle class families, where sisters and daughters had to, and wished to, support themselves.

New middle class men had not only the motivation to manipulate the labour market in their favour, but also the power to do so from the mid-1890s. The size of the public service, the experience of its personnel in organizational management, the newly found unity between rank-and-file and leaders, and the well-developed theoretical stances of some of those leaders, all contributed to new middle class strength within the state bureaucracy in the early 1890s. The vacuum of power caused by the breakdown of the faction system of politics, and the slow development of a viable party system between 1882 and 1904, made the new middle class a powerful voting bloc, and gave public service leaders considerable personal influence, a combination which allowed the latter to insist on a high degree of autonomy for the state bureaucracy. This autonomy, combined with the political importance of the new middle class at that time, its close links with the labour movement, and its influence through the press, helped consolidate the position of the public service as an important medium of social reform.

The new middle class labour market projects of the 1890s and early twentieth century were primarily projects by men for men. This reflected both the anxieties about their labour market situation experienced by male workers in the period and the relative powerlessness of women workers at that time. Women were not sufficiently integrated into the influential clerical and professional areas of the workforce to be considered reliable allies of male workers in the face of deteriorating conditions. On the other hand, a number of factors inhibited women's organization as a powerful and militant separate group, and left them unprepared to counter the surge of discriminatory practices which overwhelmed them in the early years of the twentieth century. In the first place, New South Wales female clerical workers were disarmed by the long tradition of relatively equal treatment in the country and suburban post offices, a tradition that was apparently being extended into other areas of work by the reforming public service leaders of the 1890s. Second, the close working relationship between feminist leaders and public service leaders, and the absorption of some feminist activists into the public service on apparently favourable terms, built up a relationship of trust between men and women of the new middle class. Finally, the scattered nature of women's clerical employment throughout the countryside and the suburbs, and the relatively small numbers involved, meant that there was little organizational basis for militancy amongst female clerical workers, even if there was the motivation.

The situation of female clerical workers in the New South Wales public service contrasts with that of women in the Victorian public service. In Victoria, the gross discrimination suffered by female post and telegraph workers, and their employment in large numbers in the central post and telegraph office, provided the incentive and the opportunity for militant organization in the 1890s which won them important concessions and the legislated right to equal pay in the Commonwealth Public Service Act of 1902.[38] The rights won by the Victorian women were subsequently lost as the set of discriminatory ideas and practices described in this book became entrenched throughout Australian society.[39] However, the contrast between Victoria and New South Wales does help explain why the labour market campaigns of the 1890s were left largely in the hands of men, giving them the power, as circumstances dictated, to pursue the interests of male workers at the expense of women.

The ideas and practices of new middle class men from the 1890s to the 1930s concerning women as workers, and their power to transform them into accepted conventions of thought and behaviour, were the product of a particular time and place and cannot be attributed to some essential quality of either men or the state. The contrast with previous attitudes towards the employment of women in the country regions is marked.

Wherever local autonomy was high, the system of family patronage gave men and women virtually identical interests in the labour market. Economic security depended on the family, and it was in the interests of men to pass jobs on to other family members rather than to men outside the family. Once control of public personnel policy was centralized, men's labour market interests lay in collective solidarity with other male workers. The management of class, therefore, led to the management of gender.

The management of class itself was no inevitable process. Between 1856 and the mid-1880s the possibilities for collective action by public servants were present once large segments of the public service were centralized. However, there was little motivation for organization and militancy while the labour market position of most public servants was secure. Even in the early 1870s, when public servants began to feel the effects of the government's economic problems, these insecurities did not persist long enough to stimulate the formation of public service unions or the formulation of labour market strategies directed against women, and any possibility of greater militancy was forestalled by the sudden improvement in government prosperity in the mid-1870s. It was only when the labour market position of the new middle class was seriously threatened in the mid-1880s and early 1890s that the state began to intervene overtly to regulate women's labour market participation and to actively manage gender roles.

Even when members of the new middle class were strongly motivated to promote state intervention into women's working lives, the type and scope of intervention varied according to the relative strength of the new middle class or its various sections. For a short period between 1896 and 1900 it seemed possible for the Public Service Board to introduce a labour market policy towards single women that would prevent the development of a separate and cheaper workforce among women, thus avoiding the dangers of undercutting of male wages and fragmentation of class unity. This proved impossible, however, after 1900, as the demands of capitalists, on the one hand, for lower taxes and wages, and organized male labour, on the other hand, for the maintenance of their standard of living, forced the Public Service Board and the industrial courts to sacrifice the rights of all women to independence. In order to continue to manage the state, the new middle class also had to manage class, and in the conditions of an industrializing nation, this meant the management of gender on a scale not envisaged by the architects of public service reform in 1896.

Notes

Abbreviations

ACA	Articled Clerks' Association
ACJ	*Articled Clerks' Journal*
ADB	*Australian Dictionary of Biography*
AEHR	*Australian Economic History Review*
AGPS	Australian Government Publishing Service
AJE	*Australian Journal of Education*
AJS	*American Journal of Sociology*
AJPH	*Australian Journal of Politics and History*
AJPA	*Australian Journal of Public Administration*
AMG	*Australasian Medical Gazette*
AMP	Australian Mutual Provident Society
ANL	Australian National Library
ANU	The Australian National University
ANZJS	*Australian and New Zealand Journal of Sociology*
ANZAAS	Australian and New Zealand Association for the Advancement of Science
APSA	Australian Political Studies Association
ASE	Amalgamated Society of Engineers
ASR	*American Sociological Review*
AWU	Australian Workers Union
BPP	*British Parliamentary Papers*
CPP	*Commonwealth Parliamentary Papers*
CPD	*Commonwealth Parliamentary Debates*
CSB	Civil Service Board
CUP	Cambridge University Press
DGPH	Director-general of public health

DT	*Daily Telegraph*
Ed.	Editor
ETS	Electric Telegraph Society
GG	*Government Gazette*
HS	*Historical Studies*
IMJA	*Intercolonial Medical Journal of Australia*
JAHS	*Journal of the Australian Historical Society*
JRAHS	*Journal of the Royal Australian Historical Society*
LC	Legislative Council
LH	*Labour History*
ML	Mitchell Library
MJA	*Medical Journal of Australia*
MOH	Medical Officer of Health, Metropolitan Combined Sanitary Districts, Sydney
MRP	Monthly Review Press
MUP	Melbourne University Press
NLB	New Left Books
NSW	New South Wales
NSWUP	New South Wales University Press
NY	New York
NYUP	New York University Press
OUP	Oxford University Press
PA	*Public Administration*
PD	*Parliamentary Debates*
PLL	Political Labour League
PMG	Postmaster-general
PSA	Public Service Association (of New South Wales)
PSB	Public Service Board (of New South Wales)
PSC	Public Service Commission
PSJ	*Public Service Journal*
QPP	*Queensland Parliamentary Papers*
RCPS	Royal Commission on the Public Service (1895)
RCPSNSW	Royal Commission on the Public Service of New South Wales (1918)
RKP	Routledge and Kegan Paul
SMH	*Sydney Morning Herald*
SUP	Sydney University Press
TCJ	*Town and Country Journal*
TLC	Trades and Labour Council
UQP	University of Queensland Press

V & P   Votes and Proceedings of the New South Wales
             Legislative Assembly
Vic.   Victoria
VPP   *Victorian Parliamentary Papers*
WOC   Women's Organising Committee, Political Labour
             League
WPEL   Women's Political Educational League
WSL   Womanhood Suffrage League

Introduction: Rescuing the poor public servant: social theory, state officials and gender

1 For comprehensive summaries of theoretical approaches, see
  Michèle Barrett, *Women's Oppresion Today: Problems in Marxist
  Feminist Analysis*, Verso, London, 1980, C. 7 and R. W. Connell,
  Gender and Power, Stanford University Press, Stanford, 1987.
  The term 'gender order' is used by Jill Julius Matthews in *Good
  and Mad Women: The Historical Construction of Femininity in
  Twentieth Century Australia*, George Allen & Unwin, Sydney,
  1984.
2 Cora V. Baldock, 'Public Policies and the Paid Work of Women',
  also Bettina Cass, 'Redistribution to Children and to Mothers; a
  History of Child Endowment and Family Allowances', and
  'Population Policies and Family Policies: State Construction of
  Domestic Life', in Cora V. Baldock and Bettina Cass (eds),
  Women, Social Welfare and the State, George Allen & Unwin,
  Sydney, 1983, pp. 20–53, 54–84, 164–85; Bob Bessant, 'Domestic Science Schools and Women's Place', *AJE* 20, 1, 1972, pp.
  1–9; Jenni Cook, 'Housework as Scientific Management: the
  Development of Domestic Science in Western Australian State
  Schools 1900–1914', in Lenore Layman (ed.), *The Workplace*
  (*Time Remembered* special issue, no 5), Murdoch University, Perth,
  1982, pp. 84–102; Desley Deacon, 'The Employment of Women
  in the Commonwealth Public Service: The Creation and Reproduction of a Dual Labour Market', *AJPA*, 41, 3, 1982, pp. 232–50,
  and 'Women, Bureaucracy and the Dual Labour Market: an
  Historical Analysis', in Alexander Kouzmin (ed.), *Public Sector
  Administration: New Perspectives*, Longman Cheshire, Melbourne,
  1983, pp. 165–82; C. Larmour, 'Women's Wages and the WEB',
  also Penny Ryan and Tim Rowse, 'Women, Arbitration and the
  Family', in A. Curthoys, S. Eade and P. Spearritt (eds), *Women at
  Work*, Society for the Study of Australian History, Canberra,
  1975, pp. 47–58, 15–30; Jill Julius Matthews, 'Education for

Femininity: Domestic Arts Education in South Australia', *LH* 45, 1983, pp. 30–53; Paige Porter, 'The State, the Family, and Education: Ideology, Reproduction, and Resistance in Western Australia', *AJE* 27, 2, 1983, pp. 121–36; Rosemary Pringle, 'Octavius Beale and the Ideology of the Birthrate', *Refractory Girl* 3, 1973, pp. 19–27; Jill Roe, 'The End is Where We Start From: Women and Welfare Since 1901', in Baldock and Cass, pp. 1–19; Edna Ryan and Anne Conlon, *Gentle Invaders: Australian Women at Work 1788–1974*, Nelson, Melbourne, 1975; Edna Ryan, *Two-thirds of a Man: Women and Arbitration in New South Wales 1902–08*, Hale & Iremonger, Sydney, 1984; Anne Summers, *Damned Whores and God's Police: The Colonization of Women in Australia*, Penguin, Melbourne, 1975; Dominica Whelan, 'Women and the Arbitration System', *Journal of Australian Political Economy* 4, 1979, pp. 54–60. For first-wave feminism and the state see Judith Allen, 'Breaking into the Public Sphere: The Struggle for Women's Citizenship in NSW 1890–1920', in J. Mackinolty and H. Radi (eds), *In Pursuit of Justice: Australian Women and the Law 1788–1979*, Hale & Iremonger, Sydney, 1979, pp. 107–17; Carol Bacchi, 'First-wave Feminism: History's Judgement', also Marian Simms, 'The Australian Feminist Experience' (for the current women's movement) in Norma Grieve and Patricia Grimshaw (eds), *Australian Women: Feminist Perspectives*, OUP, Melbourne, 1981, pp. 156–67, 227–39.

3 For examples of recent work on women and the state, see Baldock and Cass; Nancy Schrom Dye, *As Equals and as Sisters: Feminism, the Labor Movement, and the Women's Trade Union League of New York*, University of Missouri Press, Columbia, 1980; Alice Kessler-Harris, *Out to Work: A History of Wage Earning Women in the United States*, Oxford University Press, New York, 1982; Diane Kirkby, 'The Wage-Earning Woman and the State': The National Women's Trade Union League and Protective Labor Legislation, 1903–1923, unpubl. paper; Jane Lewis, *The Politics of Motherhood: Child and Maternal Welfare in England 1900–1939*, Croom Helm, London, 1980; Mary Ruggie, *The State and Working Women: A Comparative Study of Britain and Sweden*, Princeton University Press, Princeton, 1984.

4 Catharine MacKinnon, 'Feminism, Marxism, Method and the State: Toward Feminist Jurisprudence', *Signs* 8, 4, 1983, p. 644.

5 Nicos Poulantzas, *Classes in Contemporary Capitalism*, New Left Books, London, 1975.

6 Louis Althusser, 'Ideology and Ideological State Apparatuses (Notes Towards an Investigation)', in *Lenin and Philosophy and Other Essays*, Monthly Review Press, New York, 1971, transl. Ben Brewster, pp. 127–86; Nicos Poulantzas, 'The Problem of

the Capitalist State', in Robin Blackburn (ed.), *Ideology in Social Science: Readings in Critical Social Theory*, Fontana, Glasgow, 1972, pp. 238–62, esp. 247.

7 R. W. Connell, 'Complexities of Fury Leave...A Critique of the Althusserian Approach to Class', in *Which Way Is Up? Essays on Class, Sex and Culture*, George Allen & Unwin, Sydney, 1983, pp. 98–139, esp. 124.

8 See, for example, Lucy Bland, Trish McCabe and Frank Mort, 'Sexuality and Reproduction: Three "Official" Instances', in Michèle Barrett, Phillip Corrigan, Annette Kuhn and Janet Wolff, (eds), *Ideology and Cultural Production*, Croom Helm, London 1979, pp. 78–111; Elizabeth Wilson, *Women and the Welfare State*, Tavistock, London, 1977.

9 'Bringing the State Back In', in Peter B. Evans, Dietrich Rueschmeyer and Theda Skocpol (eds), *Bringing the State Back In*, CUP, New York, 1985 gives a comprehensive overview of this approach. See also Bertrand Badie and Piere Birnbaum, *The Sociology of the State*, transl. Arthur Goldhammer, University of Chicago Press, Chicago, 1983; Roger Davidson, 'Llewellyn Smith, the Labour Department and Government Growth 1886–1909', in Gillian Sutherland (ed.), *Studies in the Growth of Nineteenth-Century Government*, Routledge & Kegan Paul, London, 1972, pp. 227–62; John Ikenberry and Theda Skocpol, 'From Patronage Democracy to Social Security: The Shaping of Public Social Provision in the United States', in Gosta Esping-Andersen, Martin Rein and Lee Rainwater (eds), *Stagnation and Renewal*, Armonk, New York, M. E. Sharpe, 1987; Ann Schola Orloff and Theda Skocpol, 'Why Not Equal Protection? Explaining the Politics of Public Social Spending in Britain, 1900–1911, and the United States, 1880s–1920', *ASR*, 49, 6, 1984, pp. 726–50; Martin Shefter, 'Party and Patronage: Germany, England, and Italy', *Politics and Society*, 7, 4, 1977, pp. 403–51 and 'Party, Bureaucracy, and Political Change in the United States', in Louis Maisel and Joseph Cooper (eds), *The Development of Political Parties: Patterns of Evolution and Decay*, Sage Electoral Studies Yearbook, no. 4, Beverly Hills, 1979, pp. 211–65; and 'Regional Receptivity to Reform: The Legacy of the Progressive Era', *Political Science Quarterly* 98, 3, 1983, pp. 459–83; Stephen Skowronek, *Building a New American State: The Expansion of National Administrative Capacities 1877–1920*, CUP, 1982.

10 For the US see Molly Ladd-Taylor, *Raising a Baby the Government Way: Mothers' Letters to the Children's Bureau 1915–1932*, Rutgers University Press, New Brunswick, 1986. The New South Wales situation is described in Chapter 8.

11 E. P. Thompson, *The Making of the English Working Class*, rev. edn, Penguin, Harmondsworth, 1968, p. 14.

12 Althusser, 'Ideology and Ideological State Apparatuses', p. 157.
13 For example, Skocpol, 'Bringing the State Back In'.
14 Ralph Miliband, *The State in Capitalist Society*, Basic, New York, 1969. For a critique by Poulantzas, and Miliband's reply, see Poulantzas, 'The Problem of the Capitalist State'. For succinct exposition and critique see Stewart Clegg, 'The Politics of Public Sector Administration', in Kouzmin, pp. 1–36, esp. 20–22; for an earlier example of this approach outside a Marxist framework see J. D. Kingsley, *Representative Bureaucracy: An Interpretation of the British Civil Service*, Antioch Press, Yellow Springs, 1944; for Australia see P. Boreham, M. Cass and M. McCallum, 'The Australian Bureaucratic Elite: The Importance of Social Backgrounds and Occupational Experience', *ANZJS* 15, 2, 1979, pp. 45–55; Stuart Macintyre, 'Labour, Capital and Arbitration 1890–1920', in Brian W. Head (ed.), *State and Economy in Australia*, OUP, Melbourne, 1983, pp. 98–114; for an overview of literature see Marian Simms, 'The Political Economy of the State in Australia', in Kouzmin, pp. 37–56, esp. 46–56; for a critique see R. W. Connell, *Ruling Class, Ruling Culture: Studies of Conflict, Power and Hegemony in Australian Life*, CUP, 1977, pp. 57–9; for the US see Gabriel Kolko, *The Triumph of Conservatism: A Reinterpretation of American History, 1900–1916*, Free Press, New York, 1963; James Weinstein, *The Corporate Ideal in the Liberal State, 1900–1918*, Beacon Press, Boston, 1968; for an exposition and critique see Fred Block, 'Beyond Corporate Liberalism', *Social Problems* 24, 3, 1977, p. 352–61, 'The Ruling Class Does Not Rule: Notes on the Marxist Theory of the State', *Socialist Revolution* 33, 1977, pp. 6–28, and 'Beyond Relative Autonomy: State Managers as Historical Subjects', *Socialist Register*, 1980, pp. 227–42; Theda Skocpol, 'Political Response to Capitalist Crisis: Neo-Marxist Theories of the State and the Case of the New Deal', *Politics and Society*, 10, 2, 1980, pp. 155–202; for a discussion taking the new middle class into consideration see A. Gould, 'The Salaried Middle Class in the Corporatist Welfare State', *Policy and Politics*, 9, 1980, pp. 401–18.
15 Ryan and Conlon, p. 175; Ryan; Summers, esp. p. 373; for a critique of current feminist attempts to penetrate the state see Ann Game and Rosemary Pringle, 'Women and Class in Australia: Feminism and the Labor Government', in Graeme Duncan (ed.), *Critical Essays in Australian Politics*, Edward Arnold, Melbourne, 1978, pp. 114–34.
16 C. Wright Mills, *White Collar: The American Middle Classes*, OUP, New York, 1951, pp. 65–6.
17 Barbara and John Ehrenreich, 'The Professional–Managerial Class', in Pat Walker (ed.), *Between Labor and Capital*, South End Press, Boston, 1979, pp. 5–15.

18 Alvin Gouldner, *The Future of Intellectuals and the Rise of the New Class*, OUP, New York, 1979.
19 Frank Parkin, *Marxism and Class Theory: A Bourgeois Critique*, Tavistock, London, 1979, esp. p. 58.
20 Gouldner, pp. 28–42; Ehrenreich and Ehrenreich.
21 Anthony Giddens, *The Class Structure of the Advanced Societies*, 2nd edn, Hutchinson, London, pp. 107–12, 177–97.
22 Poulantzas, *Classes in Contemporary Capitalism*, pp. 209–10, 235–7, 258.
23 Mills, p. 17.
24 See Nicholas Abercrombie and John Urry, *Capital, Labour and the Middle Classes*, George Allen & Unwin, London, 1983, Chapters 4, 5, for a review of the literature; for influential formulations see G. Carchedi, *On The Economic Identification of Social Classes*, Routledge & Kegan Paul, London, 1977; George Ross, 'Marxism and the New Middle Classes: French Critiques', *Theory and Society* 5, 2, 1978, pp. 163–90.
25 Gouldner, esp. p. 12. For similar views from a conservative viewpoint see B. Bruce-Briggs (ed.), *The New Class?* Transaction, New Brunswick, 1979.
26 Steven Brint, '"New-Class" and Cumulative Trend Explanations of the Liberal Political Attitudes of Professionals', *AJS* 90, 1, 1984, pp. 30–71.
27 Christopher Lasch, *Haven in a Heartless World: The Family Besieged*, Basic, NY, 1977, esp. p. xx.
28 Barbara Ehrenreich and Deirdre English, *Witches, Midwives and Nurses: A History of Women Healers*, Feminist Press, New York, 1973; and *For Her Own Good: 150 Years of Experts' Advice to Women*, Pluto Press, London, 1979, esp. p. 4.
29 Ehrenreich and Ehrenreich; see other articles in the same book for critiques and the Ehrenreichs' reply; also Magali Sarfatti Larson, *The Rise of Professionalism: A Sociological Analysis*, University of California Press, Berkeley, 1977; Evan Willis, *Medical Dominance: The Division of Labour in Australian Health Care*, George Allen & Unwin, Sydney, 1983. For critiques of neo-Marxist perspectives on the professions see Mike Saks, 'Removing the Blinkers? A Critique of Recent Contributions to the Sociology of the Professions', *Sociological Review*, 31, 1, 1983, pp. 1–21; Terence C. Halliday, 'Professions, Class and Capitalism', *European Journal of Sociology*, 24, 1983, pp. 321–46.
30 Ehrenreich and Ehrenreich; Lasch.
31 Eliot Freidson, *Professional Dominance*, Aldine, Chicago, 1970; J. L. Berlant, *Profession and Monopoly: A Study of Medicine in the United States and Great Britain*, University of California Press,

Berkeley, 1975; N. and J. Parry, *The Rise of the Medical Profession*, Croom Helm, London, 1976; Larson; Willis.

32 Ehrenreich and Ehrenreich.

33 Gouldner, p. 17.

34 Kerreen Reiger, *The Disenchantment of the Home: Modernizing the Australian Family 1880−1940*, OUP, Melbourne, 1985.

35 ibid., pp. 212−15.

36 Ehrenreich and Ehrenreich; see also Berlant; Freidson; Parry; Larson; Willis.

37 Reiger, pp. 212−13.

38 R. W. Connell, 'Intellectuals and Intellectual Work', in *Which Way Is Up?* pp. 231−54, esp. p. 246.

39 R. W. Connell, 'Crisis Tendencies in Patriarchy and Capitalism', in *Which Way is Up?*, pp. 33−49, esp. 39; R. W. Connell and T. H. Irving, *Class Structure in Australian History: Documents, Narrative and Argument*, Longman Cheshire, Melbourne, 1980, pp. 22−4, 201−207.

40 'Intellectuals and Intellectual Work', esp. p. 241.

41 R. W. Connell, 'The Pattern of Hegemony', in *Ruling Class, Ruling Culture*, pp. 221−2.

42 Connell and Irving, p. 23.

43 ibid, pp. 111−12; for Connell on Althusser, see 'Complexities of Fury Leave', p. 126.

44 Connell and Irving, pp. 112, 201.

45 For structuration see Giddens, pp. 107−112.

46 Abercrombie and Urry, pp. 34−63; R. D. Barron and G. M. Norris, 'Sexual Divisions and the Dual Labour Market', in D. L. Barker and S. Allen (ed.), *Dependence and Exploitation in Work and Marriage*, Longman, London, 1976, pp. 47−69; Harry Braverman, *Labor and Monopoly Capitalism: The Degradation of Work in the Twentieth Century*, Monthly Review Press, New York, 1974.

47 Desley Deacon, 'The Employment of Women in the Commonwealth Public Service'; Rosabeth Moss Kanter, *Men and Women of the Corporation*, Basic, New York, 1977.

48 See Michèle Barrett, *Women's Oppression Today*, the review and critique of Barrett in Johanna Brenner and Maria Ramas, 'Rethinking Women's Oppression', *New Left Review*, 144, 1984, pp. 33−71, and Barrett, 'Rethinking Women's Oppression: A Reply to Brenner and Ramas', *New Left Review*, 146, 1984, pp. 123−8. For an overview of the literature see Ann Curthoys, 'The Sexual Division of Labour: Theoretical Arguments', in Norma Grieve and Ailsa Burns (eds), *Australian Women: New Feminist Perspectives*, OUP, Melbourne, 1986, pp. 319−95.

49 J. Donnison, *Midwives and Medical Men*, Heinemann, London,

1977; Ehrenreich and English, *Witches, Midwives and Nurses* and
For Her Own Good; M Hutton Neve, *'This Mad Folly': The
History of Australia's Pioneer Women Doctors*, Library of
Australian History, Sydney, 1980; Ann Oakley, 'Wisewoman and
Medicine Man: Changes in the Management of Childbirth', in
Juliet Mitchell and Ann Oakley (eds), *The Rights and Wrongs of
Women*, Penguin, Melbourne, 1976, pp. 17–58; Mary Roth
Walsh, *'Doctors Wanted: No Women Need Apply': Sexual
Barriers in the Medical Profession, 1835–1975*, Yale University
Press, New Haven, 1977.

50 Margery W. Davies, *Woman's Place is at the Typewriter: Office
Work and Office Workers 1870–1930*, Temple University Press,
Philadelphia, 1982; Willis.

51 Louise Tilly and Joan Scott, *Women, Work, and Family*, Holt,
Rinehart and Winston, NY, 1978; Christine Bose, 'Household
Resources and U. S. Women's Work: Factors Affecting Gainful
Employment at the Turn of the Century', *ASR*, 49, 4, 1984, pp.
474–90.

52 ibid, p. 475.

53 ibid., pp. 487–9.

54 Beverley Kingston, *My Wife, My Daughter and Poor Mary Ann:
Women and Work in Australia*, Nelson, Melbourne, 1977, pp. 24–5;
also Jean I. Martin, 'Marriage, the Family and Class', in A. P.
Elkin (ed.), *Marriage and the Family in Australia*, Angus & Robertson,
Sydney, 1957.

55 Hanna Papanek, 'Men, Women, and Work: Reflections on the
Two-Person Career', *AJS* 78, 4, 1973, pp. 852–72.

56 Hilary Callan, 'The Premiss of Dedication: Notes Towards an
Ethnography of Diplomats' Wives', in Shirley Ardener (ed.),
Perceiving Women, Malaby, London, 1975; Kanter; Papanek;
Rosemary Whip, 'The Parliamentary Wife: Participant in the
"Two-Person Single Career"', *Politics*, 17, 2, 1982, pp. 38–44.

57 Cynthia Cockburn, *Brothers: Male Dominance and Technological
Change*, Pluto, London, 1983.

58 Jane Humphries, 'Class Struggle and the Persistence of the Working Class Family', in Alice H. Amsden (ed.), *The Economics of
Women and Work*, Penguin, Harmondsworth, 1980, pp. 140–65.

59 Shirley Fisher, 'The Family and the Sydney Economy in the Late
Nineteenth Century', in Patricia Grimshaw, Chris McConville
and Ellen McEwen (eds), *Families in Colonial Australia*, George
Allen & Unwin, Sydney, 1985, pp. 153–62; Martha Norby
Fraundorf, 'The Labour Force Participation of the Turn-of-the-
Century Married Woman', *Journal of Economic History*, 39, 1979,
401–17; Patricia Grimshaw and Graham Willett, 'Women's
History and Family History: an Exploration of Colonial Family

Structure', in Grieve and Grimshaw, pp. 134—55; Marilyn Lake, 'Helpmeet, Slave, Housewife: Women in Rural Families 1870—1930', in Grimshaw *et al.*, pp. 173—85; Ray Markey, 'Women and Labour, 1880—1900', in Elizabeth Windschuttle (ed.), *Women, Class and History: Feminist Perspectives on Australia 1788—1978*, Fontana, Sydney, 1980, pp. 83—111. For a first- hand description of Australian family economy see Ryan, pp. 10—11. For comparable studies of English experience, see Sally Alexander, 'Women's Work in Nineteenth-Century London: A Study of the Years 1820—50', in Mitchell and Oakley, pp. 59—111; Leonore Davidoff, 'The Separation of Home and Work: Landladies and Lodgers in Nineteenth and Twentieth Century London', in Sandra Burman (ed.), *Fit Work For Women*, Croom Helm, London, 1979, pp. 64—97.

60 Deacon, 'The Employment of Women in the Commonwealth Public Service'; Carol Chambers Garner, 'Educated and White-Collar Women in the 1880s', also Claire McCuskey, 'Women in the Victorian Post Office', in Margaret Bevage, Margaret James and Carmel Shute (eds), *Worth Her Salt: Women at Work in Australia*, Hale & Iremonger, Sydney, 1982, pp. 112—31, 49—61; Claire McCuskey, The History of Women in the Victorian Post Office, unpubl. MA thesis, La Trobe University, 1984; Carol O'Donnell, *The Basis of the Bargain: Gender, Schooling and Jobs*, George Allen & Unwin, Sydney, 1984; Gail Reekie, 'Female Office Workers in Western Australia, 1895—1920: The Process of Feminization and Patterns of Consciousness', in Layman, pp. 1—35; Lachlan N. Riches, 'The Struggle for Equal Pay in the Australian Private Banking Industry 1966—1975', in Bevage *et al.*, pp. 343—57.

61 J. M. Bennett (ed.), *A History of the New South Wales Bar*, Law Book Co., Sydney 1969; Wilfred Blacket, *May It Please Your Honour*, Cornstalk, Sydney, 1927; and Stuart Woodman, Lawyers in New South Wales 1856—1914: The Evolution of a Colonial Profession, unpubl. PhD thesis, ANU, 1979 provide partial or anecdotal accounts of the legal profession. Sylvia Lawson, *The Archibald Paradox: A Strange Case of Authorship*, Kingswood, Allen Lane, Melbourne, 1983; Mrs Macleod, *Macleod of the "Bulletin": The Life and Work of William Macleod by his Wife*, Snelling Printing Works, Sydney, 1931; and R. B. Walker, *The Newspaper Press in New South Wales, 1803—1920*, SUP, 1969 provide survey, biographical and anecdotal accounts of journalism. Bruce Mitchell, *Teachers, Education and Politics: A History of Organizations of Public School Teachers in New South Wales*, UQP, 1975; and R. M. Pike, The Cinderella Profession: The State School Teachers of New South Wales 1880—1963, unpubl. PhD thesis, ANU, 1966 discuss teachers. A. G. McGrath, The Evolution of the Medical Association

in Terms of the Concurrent Social Conditions, unpubl. PhD thesis,
University of Sydney, 1975 is the only, inadequate, account of
the medical profession in NSW but T. S. Pensabene, *The Rise of
the Medical Practitioner in Victoria*, Health Research Project and ANU
Press, 1980 and Willis are guides to probable developments. George
Nadel, *Australia's Colonial Culture. Ideas and Institutions in Mid-
Nineteenth Century Eastern Australia*, Cheshire, Melbourne, 1957;
Michael Roe, *Quest for Authority in Eastern Australia 1835–1851*,
MUP, 1965, 'The Establishment of the Australian Department of
Health: Its Background and Significance', *HS* 17, 67, 1976,
pp. 176–92 and *Nine Australian Progressives: Vitalism in Bourgeois
Social Thought 1890–1960*, UQP, 1984; and Tim Rowse, *Australian
Liberalism and National Character*, Kibble, Melbourne, 1978 pro-
vide useful accounts of the intellectual milieu. A. W. Martin,
Political Developments in New South Wales 1894–6, unpubl.
MA thesis, University of Sydney, 1952; R. J. Parsons, Lawyers
in the New South Wales Parliament, 1870–1890, unpubl. PhD
thesis, Macquarie University, 1973 provide the only accounts of
political activities of the new middle class. The large literature on
writers of the period rarely considers them as part of a sociological or political group.

62 Ann-Mari Jordens, 'Rose Scott: Making a Beginning', in James
Walter and Raija Nugent (eds.), *Biographers at Work*, Institute for
Modern Biography, Griffith University, Brisbane, 1984,
pp. 26–35 and unpublished work by Judith Allen provide the
only material on Rose Scott. For women's organizations see
Allen, and Dianne Scott, 'Woman Suffrage: The Movement in
Australia', *JRAHS* 53, pt 4, 1967, pp. 299–322. See Manning
Clark, *In Search of Henry Lawson*, Macmillan, Melbourne, 1978
for a typical treatment of Louisa Lawson—cf. Brian Matthews,
Louisa, McPhee Gribble, Melbourne, 1987. For writers see Verna
Coleman, *Miles Franklin in America: Her Unknown (Brilliant)
Career*, Angus & Robertson, Sydney, 1981; Lucy Frost, 'Barbara
Baynton: An Affinity with Pain' and Frances McInherny, 'Miles
Franklin, *My Brilliant Career*, and the Female Tradition', in Shirley
Walker (ed.), *Who Is She? Images of Women in Australian Fiction*,
UQP, 1983, pp 56–70, 71–83. Noeline Kyle, *Her Natural Destiny:
The Education of Women in New South Wales*, NSWUP, 1986;
Noeline Williamson (Kyle), 'The Employment of Female Teachers
in the Small Bush Schools of New South Wales, 1880–1890: a
Case of Stay Bushed or Stay Home', *LH* 43, 1982, pp. 1–12; and
'The Feminization of Teaching in New South Wales: A Historical
Perspective', *AJE* 27, 1, 1983, pp. 33–44 give an account of
conditions from 1880 but neglect union and political activity.
Judith Godden, Philanthropy and the Women's Sphere, Sydney,

1870–circa 1900, unpubl. PhD thesis, Macquarie University 1983 gives an excellent account of elite women; Henry Handel Richardson, *The Fortunes of Richard Mahoney, Book 1*, Heinemann, London, 1954; and *Myself When Young*, Heinemann, London, 1948 provides a useful picture of the work of a postmistress.
63 Florence Wearne to Mary Booth, 2 December 1924, Anzac Fellowship of Women papers, ANL MS 2864, courtesy Heather Radi.

1 Practical equality: the decentralized state and the family economy

Where not otherwise stated, information on careers and salaries comes from the *Blue Book*.

1 Arthur McMartin, *Public Servants and Patronage: The Foundation and Rise of the New South Wales Public Service, 1786–1859*, SUP, 1983, pp. 293–4.
2 Figures from McMartin; Alan Barcan, *A Short History of Education in New South Wales*, Martindale, Sydney, 1965, p. 93; Select Committee on the State of the Magistracy, *Final Report*, V & P 1858, vol. II; *Blue Book* 1860. The exact number of women and men employed is difficult to determine throughout the nineteenth century, as auxiliary staff are often given in the *Blue Book* as an aggregate number and counter post office staff were not listed until 1883. The Settled Districts or Limits of Location stretched in an arc of about 200 miles around Sydney and comprised the original nineteen counties of the colony.
3 For difficulties of inspectors over a decade later see Rodney I. Francis, 'Schooling Under the Council of Education, 1867–1880: The Inspector's Lot was Not a Happy One', *JRAHS*, 66, 1, 1980, pp. 39–46. For dangers of travelling in the early period see James Dalgarno, 'Development of N.S.W. Postal Inland Service', *JAHS* 2, 7, 1908, pp. 149–61, esp. 157; Gwendoline Wilson, *Murray of Yarralumla*, OUP, Melbourne, 1968.
4 For personnel practices before 1856 see McMartin; S. G. Foster, *Colonial Improver: Edward Deas Thomson 1800–1879*, MUP, 1978; Brian Fletcher, 'Administrative Reform in New South Wales under Governor Darling,' *AJPA* 38, 3, 1979, pp. 246–62.
5 D. W. A. Baker, 'Sir Thomas Livingstone Mitchell', *ADB* 1788–1850; The Origins of Robertson's Land Acts, unpubl. MA thesis, ANU, 1957.
6 McMartin, pp. 6–7, 75–9, 84–92, 220–21, 290–91. For role of 'gentry' as magistrates see Michael Roe, *Quest for Authority in*

Eastern Australia 1835—1851, MUP, 1965, pp. 41—2, 48. For the reluctance of unpaid magistrates to carry out duties see Lorraine Barlow, '"A Strictly Temporary Office?" N. S. W. Police Magistrates 1830—1860', paper delivered to Law in History Conference, La Trobe University, May 1985, p. 6.

7 R. W. Connell and T. H. Irving, *Class Structure in Australian History: Documents, Narrative and Argument*, Longman Cheshire, Melbourne, 1980, pp. 33—4; Hazel King, 'William Colburn Mayne', *ADB* 1851—1890; 'Some Aspects of Police Administration in New South Wales, 1825—1851', *JRAHS* 42, 5, 1956, pp. 205—30; John Kennedy McLaughlin, 'The Magistracy and the Supreme Court of New South Wales, 1824—1850: a Sesqui-Centenary Study', *JRAHS* 62, 2, 1976, pp. 91—113; McMartin, p. 236.

8 Brian Dickey, *No Charity There: A Short History of Social Welfare in Australia*, Nelson, Melbourne, 1980, pp. 30—66.

9 Barcan, pp. 83—4, 94.

10 Parramatta Post Office History, Aust. Post, NSW, mimeo.

11 Vann L. Cremer, Camden Post Office History, Aust. Post, NSW, mimeo.

12 David Haworth, 'William Harvie Christie', *ADB* 1851—1890; Vivienne Parsons, 'James Raymond', *ADB* 1788—1850; McMartin, p. 219; PMG, *Report* 1855, V & P 1856—7, vol. II, p. 24; *Report* 1856, V & P 1857, vol. I, pp. 5—12; *Report*, 1857, V & P 1858—9, vol. II. pp. 12—13; Select Committee on the Post Office, *Report*, LC V & P 1851, 2nd sess., p. 517.

13 PMG, *Report* 1856, pp. 5—8.

14 PMG, *Report* 1855, p. 24.

15 PMG, *Report* 1870, V & P 1870—71, vol. III, p. 35. For the role of justice of the peace 1834 see Denman Post Office History, Aust. Post, NSW, mimeo. For details of process 1876 and role of local community and member of parliament see Vann L. Cremer, Upper Manilla Post Office History, Aust.Post, NSW, mimeo.

16 Cremer, Upper Manilla.

17 *Removal of Late Postmaster, Lower Gundaroo*, V & P 1880—81, vol. III, pp. 11—15.

18 Board of Inquiry into the Post Office Department, *Minutes of Evidence*, V & P 1862, vol. III, p. 83.

19 Pamela Moore, 'Charles Cowper', *ADB* 1851—1890.

20 e.g. Parramatta, Penrith 1828, Maitland 1829, Cassilis 1839.

21 e.g. Denman 1858.

22 Parramatta Post Office History.

23 James Jervis, *The Cradle City of Australia: A History of Parramatta 1788—1961*, Parramatta City Council, Sydney, 1961, pp. 96—101; R. B. Walker, *Old New England: A History of the Northern Tablelands of New South Wales 1818—1900*, SUP, 1966, p. 44; W.

Allan Wood, *Dawn in the Valley: The Story of Settlement in the Hunter River Valley to 1833*, Wentworth, Sydney, 1972, p. 248.

24 Board of Inquiry 1862. Shopkeepers and innkeepers were sometimes willing to forego payment of rent for use of premises; see Cremer, Camden.

25 Wood, pp. 254, 271, 303; Maitland Post Office History, Aust. Post, NSW, mimeo; Maitland file, Aust. Post Historical Section.

26 Walker, p. 56.

27 Nancy Gray, 'Henry Dangar', *ADB* 1788–1850, p. 281.

28 *Brabazon's NSW General Town Directory*, 1843; Jervis, p. 160. Both give George Wickham as postmaster 1843 but the *Blue Book* gives Jemima's date of appointment as 1838; see Parramatta Post Office History.

29 *Grafton Post Office Souvenir*, 1978.

30 *Return of all the Deputy Postmasters and Postmistresses in NSW*, V & P 1862, vol. II, pp. 735–45.

31 Hazel King, *Elizabeth Macarthur and Her World*, SUP, 1980; Ruth Teale (ed.), *Colonial Eve: Sources on Women in Australia*, OUP, Melbourne, 1978, pp. 69–70.

32 Alan Atkinson, 'Women Publicans in 1838', *Push from the Bush* 8, 1980, pp. 88–106; Helen Heney, *Australia's Founding Mothers*. Nelson, Melbourne, 1978, p. 110; Katrina Alford, *Production or Reproduction? An Economic History of Women in Australia, 1788–1850*, OUP, Melbourne, 1984, pp. 195–7; Monica Perrott, *A Tolerable Good Success: Economic Opportunities for Women in New South Wales 1788–1830*, Hale & Iremonger, Sydney, 1983; Teale, pp. 32–6, 61–3.

33 Atkinson, pp. 89–104; Jervis, pp. 98–9; Wood, pp. 248, 254, 297.

34 *SMH* 6 June 1878, p. 5.

35 Jervis, pp. 98–9.

36 Atkinson, p. 89.

37 John Hood, *Australia and the East*, John Murray, London, 1843, p. 120.

38 Wood, pp. 248, 254, 297.

39 Teale, p. 34.

40 Marilyn Lake, 'Helpmeet, Slave, Housewife: Women in Rural Families 1870–1930', in Grimshaw *et al.*, *Families in Colonial Australia*, George Allen & Unwin, Sydney, 1985, pp. 173–85.

41 Peter McDonald and Patricia Quiggin, 'Lifecourse Transitions in Victoria in the 1880s', in Grimshaw *et al.*, pp. 64–82, esp. 66–7.

42 Alford, p. 233; D. N. Jeans, *An Historical Geography of New South Wales to 1901*, Reed Education, Sydney, 1972, p. 135; McDonald and Quiggin, pp. 72–5; Peter F. McDonald, *Marriage in Australia: Age at First Marriage and Proportions Marrying, 1860–1971*,

Department of Demography, ANU, Canberra, 1975, pp. 96–113.

43 Alexandra Hasluck, *Portrait in a Mirror: An Autobiography*, OUP, Melbourne, n.d., pp. 12–13, 36. The child born soon after was Evelyn Hill, one of the first Australian women graduates.

44 Kay Daniels, Mary Murnane and Anne Picot (eds), *Women in Australia: an Annotated Guide to Records Edited for the National Research Program* vol. II, Australian Government Publishing Service, Canberra, 1977, pp. 189–90.

45 McDonald and Quiggin, pp. 78–9.

46 *History of Postal Services in Victoria*, p. 112. There were no staff lists published before *Country Postmasters*, V & P 1858, vol. III, pp. 1026–8. Further lists are in PMG, *Report* 1860, V & P 1861–2, vol. II, pp. 12–15; *Return* 1862; and *Report* 1867, V & P 1868–9, vol. II. The *Blue Book* published details of official postmasters and postmistresses from 1862. After Posts and Telegraphs began to amalgamate offices in 1867, Posts gave only the staff of *separate* official offices while Telegraphs gave a complete list; a full list of post and telegraph positions in 1882 (without names) is in PMG, *Report*, V & P 1883–4, vol. IX, pp. 25–51. From 1883 all staff in official post offices were listed in the *Blue Book*. Birth dates were not given until the *Public Service List* replaced the *Blue Book* in 1898. Thus women's post office careers and the succession of family members can be followed only haphazardly until 1882.

47 Maitland Post Office History; Maitland file, Aust. Post NSW Historical Section; death cert. January 1895. This salary may be incorrect; *Country Postmasters* 1858 gives the salary as £200, though the commission would have raised it to at least £250.

48 Parramatta Post Office History; Alan G. Morschell, Seven Country Post Offices: A Study of Nineteenth Century Post Office Architecture in New South Wales, unpublished B Arch. thesis, University of NSW, 1976. *Returns* 1862 give Jemima Wickham's date of appointment as 1 April 1838. She was still alive in 1890 when listed in the *Blue Book* as pensioner.

49 Cremer, Camden; Camden file, Aust. Post NSW Historical Section.

50 Penrith Post Office History, Aust. Post, NSW, mimeo; Penrith file, Aust. Post NSW Hist. Section; *Transmitter*, 17 July 1899.

51 Australian Post Office, *Centenary of the Brisbane General Post Office 1872–1972*; Manfred Cross, 'Mrs Elise Barney—Pioneer Postmistress', paper given to Postal-Telecommunications Historical Society of Queensland, courtesy Shirley Kingston, Aust. Post Qld; 'George Barney', *ADB* 1788–1850; Select Committee on Government Departments, *Final Report, QPP* 1860; *Papers and Correspondence Concerning Defalcations in the General Post Office*, *Evidence Taken Before Commission to Inquire into Defalcations in the*

General Post Office and Select Committee on the Post Office and Money Order Department, *Minutes of Evidence, QPP* 1865, pp. 901—31, 1061—107; death cert. July 1883; see Desley Deacon, 'Elise Barney', *200 Australian Women*, Women's Redress Press, Sydney, 1988 for concise details.

52 Vann L. Cremer, Cassilis Post Office History, Aust. Post, NSW, mimeo.

53 ibid.

54 Maitland Post Office History.

55 Copies of staff lists from 1862 in Aust. Post NSW Historical Section files. For male/female succession at same salary see Kellett, Penrith 1873, Chape, Balmain 1874, Browne, East Maitland 1871, Arnott, East Maitland 1880, Isaac, Scone 1884, Kibble, Denman 1879.

56 Alan Atkinson, 'Postage in the South East', *Push from the Bush* 5, 1979, pp. 19—30.

57 Select Committee on Retrenchment in the Public Expenditure, *Progress Report*, V & P 1858, vol. III; Board of Inquiry 1862.

58 Board of Inquiry 1862, p. 83.

59 Select Committee on Retrenchment 1858, p. 112.

60 G. J. R. Linge, *Industrial Awakening: A Geography of Australian Manufacturing 1788 to 1890*, ANU Press, Canberra, 1979, pp. 62, 66, 383 for figures; Jeans, p. 130.

61 Select Committee on Retrenchment 1858, p. 112; Board of Inquiry 1862, p. 25.

62 Henry Handel Richardson, *Australia Felix*, Heinemann, London, 1954, p. 798. For Mrs Richardson see also Henry Handel Richardson, *Myself When Young*, Heinemann, Melbourne 1948; and Claire McCuskey, 'Women in the Victorian Post Office', in Margaret Bevage *et al. Worth Her Salt: Women at Work in Australia*, Hale & Iremonger, Sydney, 1982, pp. 49—61, esp. 52.

63 *Return* 1862, pp. 8—11; Penrith file, Aust. Post NSW Historical Section.

64 *Correspondence Concerning Official Post Offices*, V & P 1862, vol. II; PMG, *Report* 1862, p. 7; 1863, p. 10, V & P 1863—4, vol. III.

65 Select Committee on Retrenchment 1858, p. 112.

66 *Minutes of Evidence*, p. 30; letter from secretary Sydney office based on Christie's minute.

67 Governor Bowen, quoted in S. Lane-Poole, *Thirty Years of Colonial Government*, Vol. 1, Longman, Green, London, 1889, p. 111.

68 Select Committee on Government Departments, *Final Report, QPP* 1860, pp. 344—5, 389.

69 An understanding of the attack on Elise Barney requires study of politics and economy of Queensland which this book cannot pursue. It is probably connected with the failure of pastoralist

ventures at that time, and the political influence of these pastoralists in the reorganization of power following the separation of Queensland. As a woman of the colonial upper class occupying a well-paid public position in the rapidly developing colonial capital, Elise Barney was more vulnerable than her NSW counterparts to patronage politics. By 1862 the work of the postal department had expanded sufficiently to require a full-time head and a postal inspector. A member of the emerging squatter faction, Thomas Murray-Prior, was appointed to the combined position. Mrs. Barney remained as Brisbane postmistress, but Murray-Prior became increasingly anxious to consolidate his uncertain control over his office by removing the Barneys, with whom he had to share an office building in which they had lived and worked for many years. Whiston Barney resigned under pressure in the middle of 1863. A year later Mrs Barney was removed to a separate money order office where soon after a clerk nominally under Mrs Barney's supervision embezzled money order funds. She was placed on leave of absence and never returned to her position. A public service inquiry found both Murray-Prior and Mrs Barney to blame, but a parliamentary select committee exonerated them. Mrs Barney was retired, while Murray-Prior was appointed to the Legislative Council, became postmaster-general several times and chairman of committees. Mrs Barney was granted a pension at her then rate of salary and died in 1883; see *Papers and Correspondence Concerning Defalcations, Evidence Taken Before Commission*, Select Committee on the Post Office and Money Order Department, *Minutes of Evidence*; H. J. Gibbney, 'Thomas Lodge Murray-Prior', *ADB* 1851−1890.

2 Equality by default: selective centralization and the struggle for control

1 S. G. Foster, *Colonial Improver: Edward Deas Thomson 1800−1879*, MUP, 1978; Arthur McMartin, *Public Servants and Patronage: The Foundation and Rise of the New South Wales Public Service, 1786−1859*, SUP, 1983; M. E. Osborne, 'Sir Edward Deas Thomson', 'Alexander McLeay', 'Sir Ralph Darling', *ADB* 1788−1850; Elizabeth Windschuttle, '"Feeding the Poor and Sapping Their Strength": The Public Role of Ruling-Class Women in Eastern Australia, 1788−1850', in Windschuttle (ed.), *Women, Class and History: Feminist Perspectives on Australia, 1788−1978*, Fontana, Sydney, 1980, pp. 53−80.

2 'George Barney', *ADB* 1788−1850; Chris Cunneen, 'Christopher

Rolleston', Hazel King, 'William Colburn Mayne', *ADB* 1851—1890; McMartin, pp. 203—8, 216, 278—81.

3 Nancy Gray, 'Robert and Helenus Scott', 'Edmund Lockyer', J. B. Windeyer, 'Charles Windeyer', *ADB* 1788—1850; David Haworth, 'William Harvie Christie', Martha Rutledge, 'Sir William Montagu Manning', *ADB* 1851—1890; Ann-Mari Jordens, 'Rose Scott: Making a Beginning', in James Walter and Raija Nugent (eds.), *Biographers at Work*, Institute for Modern Biography, Griffith University, Brisbane, 1984, pp. 26—35.

4 J. Bach, 'William Spain', D. W. A. Baker, 'Sir Thomas Livingstone Mitchell'; 'George Barney', Vivienne Parsons, 'James Raymond', Hazel King, 'Francis Nicholas Rossi' and 'John McLerie', *ADB* 1788—1850; Hazel King, 'Mayne', ibid, and 'Some Aspects of Police Administration', *JRAHS* 42, 5, 1956, pp. 205—30; Brian Dickey, *No Charity There: A Short History of Social Welfare in Australia*, Nelson, Melbourne, 1980, pp. 45—7; McMartin, pp. 205—90; PMG, *Report* 1855, V & P 1856—7, vol. II, p. 24; *Report 1856*, V & P 1857, vol. 1 pp. 5—12; *Report* 1857, V & P 1858—9, vol. II, pp. 12—13; Select Committee on the Post Office, LC V & P, 1851, 2nd sess.

5 George Nadel, *Australia's Colonial Culture: Ideas, Men and Institutions in Mid-Nineteenth Century Eastern Australia*, Cheshire, Melbourne, 1957; Michael Roe, *Quest for Authority in Eastern Australia 1835—1851*, MUP, 1965, pp. 65—9.

6 Sandra J. Blair, 'Patronage and Prejudice: Educated Convicts in the New South Wales Press, 1838', *Push From the Bush* 8, pp. 75—87; Brian Dickey, 'Michael Fitzpatrick', Ruth Teale, 'Adelaide Eliza Ironside', *ADB* 1851—1890.

7 A. G. Austin, 'Laurence Halloran', D. W. A. Baker, 'John Dunmore Lang', J. V. Byrnes, 'Edward O'Shaugnessy', 'George Howe' and 'Alfred Ward Stephens', K. J. Cable, 'Henry Fulton', V. W. E. Goodin, 'William Cape', *ADB* 1788—1850; and 'Public Education in New South Wales before 1848', *JRAHS* 36, 1—4, 1950, pp. 1—14, 65—108, 129—210; Elizabeth Guildford, 'Richard Jones', Arthur McMartin, 'Isaac Nichols', *ADB*, ibid., and *Public Servants and Patronage*; A. W. Martin, *Henry Parkes: a Biography*, MUP, 1980, pp. 25—124, esp. pp. 28—30; Nadel; J. Normington-Rawling, 'Charles Harpur', *ADB*, ibid., and *Charles Harpur, An Australian*, Angus & Robertson, Sydney, 1962; Roe, *Quest* and 'William Augustine Duncan', *ADB*, ibid; Bede Nairn, 'Sir James Martin', G. P. Walsh, 'George Robert Nichols', *ADB* 1851—1890; S. H. Roberts, *History of Australian Land Settlement (1788—1920)*, Macmillan and MUP, Melbourne, 1924; C. Turney (ed.), *Pioneers of Australian Education: a Study of the Development of Education in New South Wales in the Nineteenth Century*, SUP, 1969, esp. pp. 68—72 for Carmichael.

8 For interactions of politicians and public servants in the literary
   and political world see Martin; Nadel; Normington-Rawling,
   Harpur, Roe, *Quest*. For the 'middling-class' nature of liberal and
   radical politics in the 1850s and 1860s see D. W. A. Baker, 'The
   Origins of Robertson's Land Acts', *HS*, 8, 30, 1958, pp. 166–82;
   C. N. Connolly, 'The Middling-Class Victory in New South
   Wales, 1853–62: a Critique of the Bourgeois-Pastoralist Dichot-
   omy', *HS* 19, 76, 1981, pp 369–87; and T. H. Irving, 'Some
   Aspects of the Study of Radical Politics in New South Wales
   Before 1856', *LH* 5, 1963, pp. 18–25; Martin, pp. 46–199, esp.
   47–8. See Baker, 'Origins', p. 172 for Robertson; Blair; K. J.
   Cable, 'Sir Charles Cowper', *ADB* 1851–1890, pp. 475–82;
   Dickey, 'Fitzpatrick' and 'Henry Halloran', ibid, p. 327; Goodin,
   'Cape', D. R. Hainsworth, 'Joseph Underwood', 'James
   Underwood', *ADB* 1788–1850; 'Charles Tompson', ibid.; P. N.
   Lamb, 'Geoffrey Eagar and the Colonial Treasury of New South
   Wales', *Australian Economic Papers*, 1, 1, 1962, pp. 24–41, esp.
   29–30; Bede Nairn and Martha Rutledge, 'William Bede Dalley',
   'Sir James Martin', and 'William Forster', Bede Nairn, 'Sir John
   Robertson', M. J. Saclier, 'William and Samuel Elyard', *ADB*
   1851–1890; Normington-Rawling, *Harpur*, esp. p. 23 for Eagar,
   p. 232 for Robertson.
 9 Dickey, 'Fitzpatrick'; McMartin, *Public Servants and Patronage*,
   pp. 72–3, 153; R. J. M. Newton, 'John Edye Manning', 'John
   Mackaness, *ADB* 1788–1850.
10 B. T. Dowd, 'Appointments to the Surveyor-General's Depart-
   ment in the 1830's', *JRAHS* 45, 4, 1959, pp. 212–13; Brian Fletcher,
   'Administrative Reform in New South Wales under Governor
   Darling', *AJPA* 38, 3, 1979, pp. 246–62, esp. pp. 249–52, 260;
   McMartin, *Public Servants and Patronage*, pp. 179–80; Select
   Committee on the Civil Service, *Progress Report, Addendum to
   Halloran's Evidence*, V & P 1872, vol. 1, pp 97–8.
11 *Historic Homesteads of Australia*, Vol. 1, Aust. Council of National
   Trusts, Canberra, 1985, pp. 56–63.
12 Dickey, 'Halloran'; Martin; Normington-Rawling, *Harpur*, Roe,
   'Duncan'; Saclier, 'Elyard'; 'Tompson'; Turney.
13 McMartin, *Public Servants and Patronage*, pp. 246–8.
14 ibid.; Martin, p. 82; 'Provisions for Incorporation in Proposed
   Pension Bill', in PMG, *Report* 1857, V & P 1858–9, vol. II, p. 13.
15 See note 3.
16 Alan Barcan, *A Short History of Education in New South Wales*,
   Martindale Press, Sydney, 1965; A. R. Fraser, 'The Authorship
   of the Final Report of the New South Wales Education Commission,
   1854–1855', *JRAHS* 52, 3, 1966, pp. 169–79; Goodin, 'Public

Education'; Martin, pp. 89—90; Nadel pp. 185—270; Turney, pp. 193—215; and Turney, 'William Wilkins', *ADB* 1851—1890.

17 Foster, pp. 64—125; McMartin, *Public Servants and Patronage,* p. 256.

18 Windschuttle, pp. 53—80.

19 J. Godden, Philanthropy and the Women's Sphere, Sydney, 1870—circa 1900, unpubl. PhD thesis, Macquarie University, 1983.

20 Noeline Kyle, *Her Natural Destiny: The Education of Women in New South Wales,* NSWUP, 1986, pp. 134—6.

21 Brian Dickey, 'Responsible Government in New South Wales: The Transfer of Power in a Colony of Settlement', *JRAHS* 60, 4, 1974, pp. 217—42; Foster, pp. 142—4; McMartin, *Public Servants and Patronage,* pp. 251—92.

22 R. W. Connell and T. H. Irving, *Class Structure in Australian History: Documents, Narrative and Argument,* Longman Cheshire, Melbourne, 1980, pp. 105—35; Connolly; Irving; Peter Loveday, 'Patronage and Politics in New South Wales 1856—70', *PA*(Sydney), 18, 4, 1959, pp. 341—58; Peter Loveday and A. W. Martin, *Parliament, Factions and Parties: the First Thirty Years of Responsible Government in New South Wales, 1856—1889,* MUP, 1966; A. W. Martin, 'The Legislative Assembly of New South Wales, 1856—1900', *AJPH* 2, 1, 1956, pp. 46—67; and *Parkes.*

23 Cable; Martin, *Parkes*; Nadel; Normington-Rawling, *Harpur,* p. 232; Nairn and Rutledge, 'Martin', and 'Forster'; Nairn, 'Robertson'; Roe, *Quest.*

24 C. E. Smith, 'F. L. S. Merewether', *JRAHS* 59, 1, 1973, pp. 1—15, esp. 9.

25 Austin; Dickey, 'Halloran'; McMartin, *Public Servants and Patronage,* p. 281; Martin, *Parkes*; Normington-Rawling, *Harpur,* pp. 264—5, 290. He married the first woman graduate of Melbourne University, Bella Guerin (MA 1885) when he was 79, after writing a poem to her achievement.

26 Dickey, 'Fitzpatrick', and 'Responsible Government', pp. 228—36; Foster; E. J. Lea-Scarlett, 'Columbus Fitzpatrick', *ADB* 1851—1890; Loveday, pp. 346—7; McMartin, *Public Servants and Patronage*; Martin, *Parkes.*

27 R. F. Holder, *Bank of New South Wales: A History,* Angus & Robertson, Sydney, 1970; Lamb, 'Eagar', pp. 29—30, The Financing of Government Expenditure in New South Wales, unpubl. PhD thesis, ANU, 1963, and 'Early Overseas Borrowing by the New South Wales Government', *Business Archives and History,* 4, 1, 1964, pp. 44—62; N. McLachlan, 'Edward Eagar (1787—1866): A Colonial Spokesman in Sydney and London', *HS*

10, 40, 1963, pp. 431−56; Normington-Rawling, *Harpur*, p. 23.

28 Foster, pp. 139−40, 144; McMartin, *Public Servants and Patronage,*
    passim; Saclier, 'Elyard'.

29 Baker, 'Origins', p. 173; J. T. Maher, 'Abram Orpen Moriarty',
    Alan Powell, 'Merion Marshall Moriarty' (incl. Edward), *ADB*
    1851−1890; V & P 1870−71, vol. III, pp. 781−806.

30 C. Davis, 'Alexander Grant McLean'; Suzanne Edgar, 'Harold
    Maclean', *ADB* 1851−1890; McMartin, *Public Servants and*
    Patronage, pp. 280−2; M. L. Sernack Cruise, Penal Reform in
    New South Wales: Frederick William Neitenstein 1896−1909,
    unpubl. PhD thesis, University of Sydney, 1980 (for Harold).

31 Board of Inquiry into the Post Office Department, *Report*, V & P
    1862, vol. III, esp. pp. 5, 6, 31−2, 57, 68, 72; *Correspondence*
    Concerning Official Post Offices, ibid., vol. II, pp. 922−4; Cunneen;
    Haworth; King, 'Mayne'; Lamb, 'Eagar', p. 34−5; McMartin,
    Public Servants and Patronage, p. 281; Martin, *Parkes*, p. 211;
    PMG, *Report* 1860, V & P 1861−62, vol. II, p. 10.

32 A. F. Pike, 'John George Nathaniel Gibbes', *ADB* 1788−1850;
    Board of Inquiry in connection with the 'Louisa', *Report*, V & P
    1858−9 vol. II; Select Committee on the Customs Department,
    Report, V & P 1858, vol. III, Gwendoline Wilson, *Murray of*
    Yarralumla, OUP, Melbourne, 1968.

33 For Duncan see Martin, *Parkes*, pp. 30−41; Nadel; Normington-
    Rawling, *Harpur*; Roe, 'Duncan', and *Quest*.

34 Connell and Irving, pp. 147−8; Martin, *Parkes*, p. 38; J. N.
    Molony, *An Architect of Freedom: John Hubert Plunkett 1832−1869*,
    ANU Press, Canberra, 1973; Roe, 'Duncan'.

35 J. L. Affleck and Martha Rutledge, 'Edward Charles Cracknell';
    Robert Johnson, 'William Christopher Bennett'; C. C. Singleton,
    'John Whitton', *ADB* 1851−1890; N. G. Butlin, *Investment in*
    Australian Economic Development 1861−1900, CUP, 1964, pp. 352−6;
    I. M. Laszlo, Railway Politics and Development in Northern
    New South Wales, unpubl. MA thesis, University of New England,
    Armidale, 1957.

36 G. J. Abbott, 'Ben Hay Martindale', Nan Phillips, 'John Rae',
    ADB 1851−1890; F. A. Larcombe, *A History of Local Government*
    in New South Wales, SUP, 1973; Normington-Rawling, *Harpur*,
    pp. 117−18, 121−7; R. L. Wettenhall, 'Early Railway Manage-
    ment Legislation in New South Wales', *Tasmanian University Law*
    Review 1, 1960, pp. 446−74.

37 Baker, 'Origins', pp 166−82; Butlin, pp. 323−5; Lamb, 'Eagar',
    pp. 24−41, Financing, 'Early Overseas Borrowing', and 'Crown
    Land Policy and Government Finance in New South Wales,
    1856−1900', *AEHR* 7, 1, 1967, pp. 38−68.

38 Board of Inquiry into the Post Office Department; *Correspondence*

Concerning Official Post Offices; PMG, *Report* 1862, V & P 1863—4, vol. III, pp. 7, 27—8; 1863, V & P 1863—4, p. 10; 1865, V & P 1866, vol IV, pp. 2—4, 6, 11; and 1866, V & P 1867—8, vol. III p. 11. Official post offices were listed for the first time in the 1862 *Blue Book*. By 1871 interest in centralization had receded and the number of separate official post offices had been reduced from eighteen to five—see PMG, *Report* 1870, V & P 1870—71, vol. III, p. 15; *Report* 1871, V & P 1872, vol. I, p. 4; *Blue Book* 1871; Martin, *Parkes*.

39 G. E. Caiden, 'The Study of Australian Administrative History', paper delivered at APSA Conference, Melbourne, August 1963, p. 9; *Correspondence Respecting Removal of W. A. Duncan, Esq. from the Office of Collector of Customs; Further Correspondence; and Correspondence Respecting Removal of Messrs Berney and Jones, and Reinstatement of Mr Duncan*, V & P 1868—9, vol. II; Lamb, 'Eagar', pp. 27, 37—9; Martin, *Parkes*, pp. 245—6.

40 Select Committee on Unpaid Magistracy, *Report*, V & P 1861, vol. I; Select Committee on Public Prisons in Sydney and Cumberland, *Report*, V & P 1861, vol. I; *Report of Progress of Formation of the Police Establishment Since the New Police Act Came into Operation*, V & P 1862, vol. II.

41 Barcan; E. J. Payne, 'The Management of Schools in N. S. W. (1846—1866): Local Initiative Suppressed', *Journal of Educational Administration*, 6, 1, 1968, pp. 69—86; Turney, *Pioneers*, pp. 193—215; and Turney, 'Wilkins'.

42 Figures from Lamb, 'Crown Land Policy', and Financing.

43 Farnell, quoted Lamb, 'Crown Land Policy' p. 55.

44 T. A. Coghlan, *Labour and Industry in Australia: From the First Settlement in 1788 to the Establishment of the Commonwealth in 1901*, Macmillan, Melbourne, 1969 [first published OUP, London, 1918], pp. 1419—20.

45 See Loveday for details of regulations and practice; McMartin, *Public Servants and Patronage*, pp. 274—8, 289—92.

46 PMG, *Report* 1860, p. 10; Board of Inquiry, evidence of Christie, p. 6; and *Correspondence Concerning Official Post Offices*; Caiden; *Correspondence Respecting Removal of W. A. Duncan*; Lamb, 'Eagar', pp. 27, 37—9; Martin, *Parkes*, pp. 245—6; Select Committee on the Civil Service, *Minutes of Evidence*, V & P 1872—3, vol. I, evidence of Moody, pp. 9—13, 31—4, 44—5.

47 PMG, *Report* 1862, p. 1285.

48 G. Kilminster, 'Fifty Years Ago III', *PSJ*, November 1918, p. 9; Loveday, pp. 346—7; PSB *Report* 1899, V & P 1900, vol. II, App. XXII; Select Committee on the Civil Service, evidence of Rolleston, pp. 17—18.

49 *PD*, 1885—6, p. 1011, 30 March 1886. Reid, later premier, joined

Treasury as a temporary replacement for accountant James Thomson; see Sir George Houston Reid, *My Reminiscences*, Cassell, London, 1917.

50 Amending Bills introduced July 1865, February 1870, May 1871, November 1872; only the 1871 Bill reached a second reading. For retrenchment see V & P 1866, vol. I, p. 324; 1870, vol. I, pp. 1009−40, 1044.

51 George Black's actuarial report April 1870, V & P 1870, vol. I, pp. 1047−53. For public service petitions re proposed salary reductions see V & P 1870−71, vol. II, pp. 1115−9; for salary reductions in Public Works see pp. 1085−114, and V & P 1872, vol. I, pp. 1299−315.

52 Bede Nairn, 'Arthur Alexander Walton Onslow', *ADB* 1851−1890; Select Committee on the Civil Service, *Report* and *Proceedings of Committee*, esp. p. 9; V & P 1872, vol. I. pp. 67, 288.

53 For evidence of public service leaders see Select Committee on the Civil Service, *Progress Report*.

54 4 April 1873. See V & P 1872−3, vol. 1, p. 281.

55 For finances see Lamb, 'Crown Land Policy'.

56 Arthur Fry, 'Forty Years in the Civil Service', Fry family papers, ML MSS 1159/2, p. 3.

57 Dickey, 'Fitzpatrick, and 'Halloran'; Lamb, 'Eagar'; A. W. Martin, *Letters from Menie: Sir Henry Parkes and His Daughter*, MUP, p. xvi.

58 Nairn, 'Martin'.

59 Martin, *Letters from Menie*, pp. xvi−xvii.

60 ibid, pp. 5−15, 56−8; Godden; Kyle; Sally O'Neill, 'Emily Matilda Manning', *ADB* 1851−90.

61 *Cyclopaedia of New South Wales*, p. 251; PMG, *Report* 1874, V & P 1875, vol. III, pp. 6, 43.

62 Public Service Inquiry Commission, *Report on General Post Office, Money Order Office and Electric Telegraph Department*, V & P 1890, vol. II, pp. 11−12; PMG, *Report* 1890, V & P 1891−2, vol. VI, p. 19; *Transmitter*, 21 February 1893, pp. 3−4.

63 Sydney's suburban population rose from 63 000 in 1871 to 276 000 in 1891; see Max Kelly, *Paddock Full of Houses: Paddington 1840−1890*, Doak Press, Sydney, 1978, p. 197.

64 The proportion of the population living outside municipalities and towns of over 500 declined from 53% in 1871 to 42% in 1881 and 35% in 1891 (calculated from N. G. Butlin, 'Colonial Socialism in Australia, 1860−1900' in Hugh G. J. Aitken [ed.], *The State and Economic Growth*, Social Science Research Council, New York, 1959, pp. 26−78, esp. 29). Workers on the land fell from one-third to one-quarter of total employers and employees in the years 1861−1901; see D. N. Jeans, *An Historical Geography of New*

South Wales to 1901, Reed Education, Sydney, 1972, p. 297. The rate of selector failure was high: of 170000 conditional purchases made to the end of 1882, resident selectors numbered less than 20000 (see Coghlan, p. 1358).

65 Select Committee, Minutes of Evidence, p. 24; Q. 745, p. 27; Onslow, PD 1879—80, p. 1185, 18 February 1880. Attorney-General Martin replied to Edward Greville, journalist member for Braidwood, that there was no objection to women's employment as telegraph operators; see V & P 1870—71, vol. 1, p. 873. For Victoria see Claire McCuskey, 'Women in the Victorian Post Office', in Margaret Bevage et al., Worth Her Salt; Women at Work in Australia, Hale & Iremonger, Sydney, 1982.
66 PD 1895, pp. 1629—30.
67 Select Committee on the Civil Service, Minutes, p. 39.
68 Cyclopaedia of New South Wales, p. 251, Martha Rutledge, 'John Fitzgerald Burns', ADB 1851—1890.
69 Vann L. Cremer, Camden Post Office History, Aust. Post, NSW, mimeo.
70 Cracknell to Lambton, May 1888; folio held Aust. Post NSW Historical Section from original file B88/5821 [376/10]; previous and following folios not held, so exact issue and outcome unclear.
71 In 1891 Glebe had a population of 17000, Randwick 6000, Hunter's Hill 3600, Botany 2000; see Kelly, pp. 8, 197—8; G. J. R. Linge, Industrial Awakening: A Geography of Australian Manufacturing 1788 to 1890, ANU Press, Canberra, 1979, p. 383; Census of NSW 1881, Summary Tables.
72 Denman Post Office History; Waterloo Post Office History; Jean Arnot, 'Nita Bernice Kibble', ADB 1891—1939; Transmitter, 20 February 1892, p. 3.
73 Judith Godden, 'Portrait of a Lady: A Decade in the Life of Helen Fell (1849—1935)', in Bevage et al.; information Judith Godden.
74 Henry Handel Richardson, Myself When Young, Heinemann, London, 1948, pp. 25—41
75 Fry, pp. 59—60.
76 Rose Scott refers to Mrs Ferris as part of a WPEL delegation in a letter to T. A. Coghlan, 7 July 1902; see Coghlan papers, ANL MS 6335. Her name appears on WSL and WPEL membership lists.
77 PMG, Report 1880, VPP 1880—81, vol. IV, p. 22; McCuskey. Overseas experience emphasizes NSW's uniqueness; see Cindy S. Aron, '"To Barter Their Souls for Gold": Female Clerks in Federal Government Offices, 1862—1890', Journal of American History 67, 4, 1981, pp. 835—53; and Ladies and Gentleman of the Civil Service: Middle-Class Workers in Victorian America, OUP, New York, 1987; Susan Bachrach, Dames Employees: The

Feminization of Postal Work in Nineteenth-Century France, *Women & History*, 8, 1983; Samuel Cohn, *The Process of Occupational Sex-Typing: The Feminization of Clerical Labor in Great Britain*, Temple University Press, Philadelphia, 1985; Lee Holcolmbe, *Victorian Ladies at Work: Middle-Class Working Women in England and Wales, 1850–1914*, Anchor Books, Hamden, Connecticut, 1973.

78 Arnot.
79 For Mrs Cross and Mrs Ferris see *PD* 1895, pp. 1827–8, 17 October.

3 Disillusion, division and militancy

1 N. G. Butlin, 'Colonial Socialism in Australia, 1860–1900', in Hugh G. J. Aitken (ed.), *The State and Economic Growth*, Social Science Research Council, New York, 1959, pp. 26–78; G. L. Buxton, '1870–90', in Frank Crowley (ed.), *A New History of Australia*, William Heinemann, Melbourne, 1974, pp. 165–215, esp. 175–6; T. A. Coghlan, *Labour and Industry in Australia: From the First Settlement in 1788 to the Establishment of the Commonwealth in 1901*, OUP, London, 1918, pp. 1346–63; C. J. King, *An Outline of Closer Settlement in New South Wales. Part I: The Sequence of Land Laws*, Department of Agriculture, NSW, 1957, pp. 83–105; P. N. Lamb, 'Crown Land Policy and Government Finance in New South Wales, 1856–1900', *AEHR* 7, 1, 1967, pp. 38–68; esp. 58; A. W. Martin, *Henry Parkes: a Biography*, MUP, 1980, pp. 331–6, and 'The Legislative Assembly of New South Wales, 1856–1900', *AJPH* 2, 1, 1956, pp. 46–67, esp. 62.
2 For finances see Lamb.
3 Dalley, *PD* 1883–5, p. 3718; Kenneth W. Knight, The Development of the Public Service of New South Wales from Responsible Government (1856) to the Establishment of the Public Service Board (1895), unpubl. MA thesis, University of Sydney, 1954, p. 58. For Stuart see Bede Nairn and Martha Rutledge, 'Sir Alexander Stuart', *ADB* 1851–1890; P. N. Lamb, 'Geoffrey Eagar and the Colonial Treasury of New South Wales', *Australian Economic Papers* 1, 1, 1962, pp. 24–41, esp. 31.
4 For Dalgarno see *Illustrated Sydney News*, 26 December 1889, p. 18; *PSJ*, June 1900, p. 6; *Transmitter*, Nov. 1895, p. 9; Jan. 1904, p. 5; Sir George Houston Reid, *My Reminiscences*, Cassell, London, 1917, p. 24. For Fraser see Bruce Mitchell, 'Archibald Colquhoun Fraser', J. H. Forsyth, 'Charles Augustus Goodchap', *ADB* 1851–1890; *DT*, 26 October 1896; *Evening News*, 26 October 1896; *SMH*, 18 April 1871, p. 5, 26 October 1896, p. 4; *TCJ*, 9 February 1889 p. 28; CSB, *Report* 1885, V & P 1885–6, vol. II, pp. 46–51; *PD*, 1896, pp. 1009–38, 24 June.

5 *SMH*, 8 June 1878, p. 10; see also 27, 29—31 May; 1, 3—5, 7—8, 12—13, 15, 19, 24—28 June; 1, 6, 8 July.

6 G. E. Caiden, 'The Study of Australian Administrative History', paper delivered at APSA Conference, Melbourne, 1963, p. 4.

7 P. Drummond, *SMH*, 1 June 1878, p. 3.

8 *DT*, 27 March 1880, p. 6; Lamb, 'Crown Land Policy', pp. 41, 62, and The Financing of Government Expenditure in New South Wales, unpubl. PhD thesis, ANU, 1963, pp. 23A, 27; Martin, *Parkes*, pp. 356—7.

9 *Wealth and Progress 1886—87*, pp. 130, 140, 488; Young, *PD* 1883—4, p. 5350, 23 September 1884.

10 Sylvia Lawson, *The Archibald Paradox: A Strange Case of Authorship*, Allen Lane, Melbourne, 1983, esp. pp. 23—5, and 'Jules Francois Archibald', *ADB* 1851—1890.

11 *Bulletin*, 28 August 1880, p. 1.

12 ibid, 15 April 1882, p. 2.

13 See *PD* 1882, p. 2, 22 August 1882; PD 1883—4, p. 5364, 23 September 1884; *PD* 1883, p. 46, 17 January; Caiden, pp. 4—5.

14 See *PD* 1884, pp. 1446—64, 1909, 2040—41; Peter Loveday and A. W. Martin, *Parliament, Factions and Parties: The First Thirty Years of Responsible Government in New South Wales, 1856—1889*, MUP, 1966, p. 129. For tax see *Wealth and Progress 1886—87*, pp. 387—80; A. W. Martin, 'Free Trade and Protectionist Parties in New South Wales', *HS* 6, 23, 1954, pp. 315—23.

15 *PD* 1883—4, p. 5076, 3 September 1884.

16 E.g. McElhone, *PD* 1880—81, pp. 600—601, 24 February 1881.

17 Cf. Dalley, *PD* 1883—4, p. 5719, 14 October 1884.

18 Loveday and Martin, p. 128; Martin, *Parkes*, p. 346.

19 *PD* 1883—4, pp. 4655—61, 5075—6141 *passim*. Stuart resigned a year later.

20 9 February 1889, p. 28.

21 *PD* 1883—4, p. 5474 (Goodchap was not named but can be identified by V & P 1864, vol. I, pp. 167—78). Goodchap succeeded John Rae (who remained under-secretary of public works) as commissioner in 1878; a bachelor, he lived at the Reform Club, of which Robertson was a member. For additional information see Forsyth; *Bulletin*, 5 May 1880, 30 June 1883; *Illustrated Sydney News*, 30 September 1882; *TCJ*, 2 March 1889, p. 13.

22 See also Fraser's evidence to Royal Commission on the Civil Service (RCPS), *Minutes of Evidence*, V & P 1894—5, vol. III, p. 105.

23 RCPS, *Minutes*, pp. 108—112; PSB, *Report* 1896, V & P 1896, vol. II, p. 3; *PD* 1896, pp. 1009—38, 24 June. Fraser died soon after, predeceased by four days by Goodchap.

24 *PD* 1883—4, p. 5448, 25 September 1884. Stuart explained he had arranged with Goodchap to increase the increments provided in

the Railway regulations in conformity with the Bill's provisions. Lyne gave a figure of 10 921 railways employees when introducing the Railways Bill 1886; see *PD* 1885—6, p. 3850, 5 August 1886.

25 Clauses 4, 5, 6; see *PD* 1883—4, pp. 5352—5, 23 September 1884; pp. 5440—41, 5448, 25 September.

26 Figures calculated from CSB, p. 3 (an estimated 1700 police have been added to 11 371 given for public servants—see *Wealth and Progress 1886—87*, p. 488). For teachers see V & P 1885—6, vol. I, p. 220; vol. II, p. 381. Police had their own fund.

27 *PD* 1883—4, p. 5079, 3 September 1884; CSB, pp. 2—4, 8—45, esp. 17. The Board's *Report* refers to 1725 in the General (clerical) Division and 142 in Professional; they automatically received annual increments of £20 to £30 until they reached the top of the range; after four years they moved to the next range. Section 7, designed to exclude departments with existing regulations such as Railways from the provisions of the Act, covered 3214 sub-clerical and sub-professional workers. Regulations usually provided for annual increments for £5—£10 and promotion only when a vacancy occurred; see CSB, App. VI, pp. 52—65. Section 8 covered 1539 non-clerical workers whose salary increases were subject to scrutiny of parliament and restricted to a maximum of £10 a year. The CSB could allocate officers to the general and professional divisions even if they were in departments excluded by section 7.

28 See note 25.

29 RCPS *Minutes* (Fraser's evidence), p. 105.

30 CSB, pp. 46—51, esp. 49—50.

31 For Williams see *Bulletin*, 31 October 1891, p. 11; *SMH*, 6 June 1878, p. 10, 21 October 1891, p. 5; V & P 1889, vol. II, p. 399.

32 CSB, pp. 46—51, esp. 49—50.

33 Loveday and Martin, p. 129.

34 Minute, 24 August 1885, CSB, App. V, p. 51.

35 *PD* 1895, pp. 2736—7, November 1895.

36 *PD* 1885—6, p. 930, 24 March 1886. For Jennings see Martin, *Parkes,* pp. 356—60. For Dibbs see L. F. Crisp, *George Richard Dibbs 1834—1904: Premier of New South Wales Prophet of Unification*, ANU, Canberra, 1980.

37 All agreed on need for a statistician but Coghlan's appointment on 5 July 1886 and his ambitious plans were controversial in the tight financial climate. For the breach between Jennings and Dibbs, who supported Coghlan fully, see T. A. Coghlan, 'Autobiography', Coghlan papers, ANL MS 6335; Joan M. Cordell, T. A. Coghlan: Government Statist of New South Wales 1886—1905, unpublished MS, pp. 23—9; *PD* 1885—6, 10 June, 15, 22, 23, 24 July, 18, 19, 24, 25 August 1886. For the lands inquiry

see V & P 1887, 2nd sess., vol. II, pp. 57–101; B. G. Andrews, 'William Henry Traill'. For earlier attempts at reform of lands see Kenneth W. Knight, 'William Houston', *ADB* 1851–1890; Suzanne Edgar, 'William Wilberforce Stephen', ibid.; King, esp. p. 103. For the Public Works inquiry see, V & P ibid., pp. 107ff. For the Public Service Bill see *PD* 1885–6, p. 1007, 30 March 1886.

38 Loveday and Martin, pp. 131–42.

39 See *PD* 1885–6, pp. 5778, 5834.

40 ibid., p. 1009, 30 March 1886.

41 ibid., p. 5034, 22 September 1886.

42 ibid., p. 1010, 30 March 1886.

43 For the tax dispute see Martin, *Parkes*, pp. 356–60; Loveday and Martin, pp. 136–42; for a definitive account of party development see Loveday and Martin, Ch. 6; Peter Loveday, A. W. Martin and Patrick Weller, 'New South Wales', in Peter Loveday, A. W. Martin and R. S. Parker (eds), *The Emergence of the Australian Party System*, Hale & Iremonger, Sydney, 1977, pp. 172–248.

44 Government Railways Act (51 Vic. No. 35), 17 May 1888; Public Works Act (51 Vic. No. 37), 5 June 1888. For the railways see I. M. Laszlo, Railway Politics and Development in Northern New South Wales 1846–1889, unpubl. MA thesis, University of New England, Armidale, 1957, esp. p. 74; for Oliver see King. For Goodchap see *TCJ*, 2 March 1889, p. 13. Goodchap's feud with engineer-in-chief Whitton contributed to this confusing episode. For Barling see Jill Robinson, 'Joseph Barling', *ADB* 1851–1890; V & P 1887–8, vol. II, pp. 97–100.

45 *PD* 1887, 2nd sess., pp. 137–8, 22 & 28 September; similar Bills were introduced on 7 May 1890, 5 August 1891.

46 Lamb, 'Crown Land Policy', p. 42; Loveday and Martin, pp. 142–3. The Land Tax Bill was introduced on 3 May 1888; the Property Tax Bill on 3 July.

47 E. A. Boehm, *Prosperity and Depression in Australia 1887–1897*, OUP, Oxford, 1971, p. 3; Buxton, pp. 165–215, 187–90; Coghlan, pp. 1442–54.

48 Lamb, Financing, p. 38.

49 The 1888 Land Tax Bill was blocked in the Council; the Property Tax Bill was lost when parliament was prorogued. No serious attempts were made in the next two years despite a budget deficit of £2.6m in 1889; see McMillan's financial statement, *PD* 1889, pp. 534 ff., 10 April.

50 V & P 1887, 2nd sess., vol. II, pp. 57–101, esp. 73; 1887–8, vol. I, pp. 13–14; 1894, vol. II, pp. 487–8; *PD* 1887–8, pp. 373–84, 11 October 1887; CSB, *Report* 1887, V & P 1887–8, vol. II, p. 2. The Commission's original members were J. Watson MLC,

J. Garrard, W. McMillan and J. See MLA, T. A. Dibbs,
R. Fitzgerald, C. Rolleston. Watson was succeeded by S. Joseph,
A. Renwick, E. Lamb; McMillan by B. Wise; See by J. Burns,
W. Wilkins; Rolleston by J. Thomson.

51 RCPS, *Report*, p. 50. The House was informed on 6 December
1894 that the recommendations had been carried out as far as
possible in Post Office, Treasury, Mines and Justice; see V & P
1894, vol. II, p. 488. See *PD* 1888–9, 1st sess., p. 207, 30
November 1888 for Treasury retrenchments following the inquiry;
Mitchell for Justice; Post Office Inquiry *Report*, V & P 1890, vol.
II, p. 281; RCPS, p. 332 for Registrar-General's Department
1893, p. 335 for Customs 1889; and *Minutes of Evidence*,
pp. 189–211 for Mines 1889; Attorney-General's Department
Inquiry *Report* 1891; R. J. Parsons, Lawyers in the New South
Wales Parliament, 1870–1890, unpubl. PhD thesis, Macquarie
University 1973, appendix.

52 *Bulletin* 3 December 1887, p. 5.

53 *Bulletin*, 20 October 1894, p. 7. The *Bulletin* quoted figures from
a recently published CSB *Report* (1893).

54 RCPS, *Report*, pp. 78–80.

55 CSB, *Report* 1886, V & P 1887, 2nd sess., vol. II, p. 2; V & P
1885–6, vol. I, p. 419 (O'Sullivan); *PD* 1885–6, p. 1012, 30
March 1886 (Davies). Coghlan gives 24 000 government and
municipal officers and employees in *Wealth and Progress* 1885–6,
p. 488, so is probably the source of these figures.

56 *Bulletin*, 20 October 1894, p. 7.

57 *PD* 1890, pp. 5681–5, 27 November; Bruce Mansfield, *Australian
Democrat: The Career of Edward William O'Sullivan 1846–1910*,
SUP, 1965, esp. pp. 113–15 and 129, 163, 192; C. N. Connolly,
Biographical Register of the New South Wales Parliament 1856–1901,
ANU Press, Canberra, 1983; Andrews; R. B. Walker, *The
Newspaper Press in New South Wales, 1803–1920*, SUP, 1976,
pp. 88, 93–4, 120; Lawson.

58 J. S. Baker, *Communicators and Their First Trade Unions: A History
of the Telegraphist and Postal Clerk Unions of Australia*, Union of
Postal Clerks and Telegraphists, Sydney, 1980, esp. pp. 9, 51, 65;
PMG, *Report* 1885, V & P 1885–6, vol. VII, p. 6; *Transmitter*, 20
February 1892, p. 12, 18 September 1896, p. 3.

59 ibid., 10 August 1891, p. 4; 1 December 1891, pp. 5–6.

60 K. D. Buckley, *The Amalgamated Engineers in Australia, 1852–1920*,
Department of Economic History, RSSS, ANU, Canberra, 1970;
J. C. Docherty, The Rise of Railway Unionism: A Study of New
South Wales and Victoria c. 1880–1905, unpubl. MA thesis,
ANU, 1973, esp. pp. 25, 49–52.

61 ibid.; Connolly; Bede Nairn, *Civilising Capitalism*, ANU Press,

Canberra, 1973; John Rickard, *Class and Politics: New South Wales, Victoria and the Early Commonwealth, 1890–1910*, ANU Press, Canberra, 1976, pp. 137–8.

62 *Transmitter*, September 1891–February 1892. For difficulty arranging loans from London 1890–91 see Lamb, Financing, p. 330; Coghlan, pp. 1647, 1669–70. For the 'retrenchment party' see *PD* 1890, pp. 5681–5, 27 November; Mansfield, pp. 114–5. For superannuation and 1884 Act see *Transmitter*, November 1891–February 1892.

63 ibid., 9 January 1892, p. 6. The other objects were:

A. To establish unity throughout the service, whereby its interests might be protected and advanced.

B. To provide a representative organisation for the purpose of thoroughly discussing all matters affecting the service, and which shall be an acknowledged authority qualified to express the voice thereof.

H. To collect statistics and other data in which the service might be in any way interested, and to establish a library where all such information would be accessible to members.

For Dibbs see *PD* 1891–2, pp. 3201–20, 1 December 1891.

64 Quoted *Transmitter*, 9 January 1892, p. 6; see also 27 February, p. 7.

65 ibid., 9 June 1892, pp. 5, 8; 10 August, p. 6; 14 November 1895, p. 9. For customs see *Wealth and Progress 1898–9*, p. 176.

66 *PD* 1891–2, pp. 5359–80, 17 February 1892; 1892–3, pp. 1557–602, 1 November 1892; *Bulletin*, 27 February 1892, p. 6; Mansfield, pp. 112–7.

67 For cuts see *PD* 1892–3, pp. 4947–65, 5580–1. For the economy and the financial crisis see Coghlan, pp. 1673–80. For revenue see *Wealth and Progress 1898–9*, p. 887; Lamb, 'Crown Land Policy', pp. 40, 65–6, Financing, p. 38.

68 CSB, *Report* 1889, V & P 1890, vol. II, pp. 2–3. *Bulletin*, 18 January 1893, p. 6 comments on Board's 1891 *Supplementary Report*; 10 October 1894, p. 7 on 1893 *Report*; quotation from *Bulletin*, 3 December 1887, p. 5.

69 Loveday, Martin and Weller; for a contemporary account see W. H. Traill, 'Protection and Democracy', *DT*, 5, 9 February 1898, in Brian Dickey (ed.), *Politics in New South Wales 1856–1900*, Cassell, Melbourne, 1969, pp. 185–90; for Labor see Robin Gollan, *Radical and Working Class Politics: A Study of Eastern Australia 1850–1910*, MUP, 1960; Ray Markey, 'Women and Labour, 1880–1900', in Elizabeth Windschuttle (ed.) *Women, Class and History: Feminist Perspectives on Australia 1788–1978*, Fontana, Sydney, 1980, pp. 83–111, and 'The ALP and the Emergence of a National Social Policy, 1880–1910', in Richard

Kennedy (ed.), *Australian Welfare History: Critical Essays*, Macmillan, Melbourne, 1982, pp. 103–37; Bede Nairn, *Civilising Capitalism*, ANU Press, Canberra, 1973.

70 J. S. Baker, 'Louisa Margaret Dunkley', *ADB* 1891–1939, and *Communicators*; Judith Biddington, The Role of Women in the Victorian Education Department, unpubl. MEd thesis, Melbourne University, 1977.

71 *Transmitter*, 9 July 1892, p. 2.

72 *Regulations Under the Public Instruction Act of 1880*, V & P 1892–3, vol. III, pp. 1259–82, esp. 1263, 1 July 1893.

73 *Transmitter*, 13 April 1895, p. 2 notes: 'perhaps the most attentive hearing to any speaker [at a public meeting on superannuation November 1894] was secured by Miss Golding, a public school teacher'; see Beverley Kingston, 'Annie Mackenzie and Isabella Theresa Golding', *ADB* 1891–1939; Bruce Mitchell, *Teachers, Education and Politics: A History of Organizations of Public School Teachers in New South Wales*, UQP, Brisbane, 1975, p. 25.

4 Remaking the public service

1 Halloran retired in 1878 at 67, Duncan in 1881 at 70; Eagar died in office in 1891 at 73; Cracknell in 1893 at 62.

2 *CPD*, 1901, p. 1302, 19 June, quoted Frank Crowley, '1901–1914', in Crowley (ed.), *A New History of Australia*, William Heinemann, Melbourne, 1974, pp. 260–311, esp. 273. Public Works employed 4901 persons, Railways 9344, Tramways 1282, Post Office, Public Instruction about 5000 each, while the two largest private engineering companies employed barely 1000 each in 1894; see RCPS, *Report*, V & P 1894–5, vol. III, pp. 79–80; G. J. R. Linge, *Industrial Awakening: A Geography of Australian Manufacturing 1788 to 1890*, ANU Press, Canberra, 1979, p. 473.

3 For Barling see Jill Robinson, 'Joseph Barling', *ADB* 1851–1890; for his appointment as chief clerk in 1887, see V & P 1887–8 vol. II, pp. 97–100; for his reforms see RCPS, *Report*, pp. 28–9, 38 and *Minutes of Evidence*, pp. 225–37. For Duncan McLachlan see Ross Andrews, 'Father of the Public Service', *Canberra Times*, 30 November 1980, p. 7; G. E. Caiden, 'The Early Career of D. C. McLachlan', *PA* 22, 2, June 1963, pp. 199–201; Desley Deacon, 'The Employment of Women in the Commonwealth Public Service: The Creation and Reproduction of a Dual Labour Market', *AJPA*, 41, 3, 1982, pp. 232–50; *PSJ*, June 1902, p. 13, April, p. 6, December 1915, p. 17; *Transmitter*, May 1902, pp. 6–7; R. L. Wettenhall, 'Duncan Clark McLachlan', *ADB* 1891–1939. For

Hugh McLachlan see *TCJ*, 20 October 1909; Coghlan to McLachlan, 5 October 1909, Coghlan papers, ANL MS 6335; Wettenhall. For Hickson see J. M. Antill, 'Robert Rowan Purdon Hickson', *ADB* 1851–1890, and 'Robert Rowan Purdon Hickson: Civil Engineer (1842–1923)', *JRAHS* 55, 3, September 1969, pp. 228–44. For upward mobility among public service clerks see Shirley Fitzgerald, *Rising Damp: Sydney 1870–90*, OUP, Melbourne, 1987.

4 For basic facts of Coghlan's life and family see Austin Francis Coghlan and Eden Willats [son and daughter], 'Reminiscences', transcription from tape recording, 1969 and T. A. Coghlan, 'Autobiography', Coghlan papers; Joan M. Cordell, T. A. Coghlan: Government Statist of New South Wales 1886–1905, unpubl. MS, 1960; J. A. B. Fry, 'Forty years in the Civil Service', Fry family papers, ML MS 1159/2; E. C. Fry, 'T. A. Coghlan as an Historian', paper presented at ANZAAS Congress, Hobart, 1965, and 'Review Article: Labour and Industry in Australia', *HS* 14, 55, 1970, pp. 430–9; Neville Hicks, 'Sir Timothy Augustine Coghlan', *ADB* 1891–1939; personal communication, Miss Beatrice Proust [granddaughter Dora Coghlan Murphy], 27 October, 18 November 1987.

5 Proust.

6 Coghlan, p. 1.

7 J. A. B. Fry, p. 169.

8 Proust.

9 Lilith Norman, *The Brown and the Yellow: a History of Sydney Girls' High School*, OUP, Melbourne, 1983, p. 208.

10 Coghlan, p. 1.

11 Proust.

12 ibid.; for Cecil see Heather Radi, Peter Spearritt and Elizabeth Hinton, *Biographical Register of New South Wales Parliamentarians 1901–1970*, ANU Press, Canberra, 1979; for Iza (Isa) see M. Hutton Neve, *'This Mad Folly': The History of Australia's Pioneer Women Doctors*, Library of Australian History, Sydney, 1980, esp. pp. 141–2; Norman, p. 208.

13 Coghlan, p. 1; Coghlan and Willats, p. 3; J. A. B. Fry, p. 169.

14 Proust.

15 Coghlan, p. 1; Max Kelly, *Paddock Full of Houses: Paddington 1840–1890*, Doak Press, Sydney, 1978, p. 10. For Jevons see Kelly, p. 12, n. 7.

16 Caiden, p. 199; Wettenhall; Sydney directories.

17 Alan Roberts, 'Planning Sydney's Transport 1875–1900', in Max Kelly (ed.), *Nineteenth Century Sydney: Essays in Urban History*, SUP, 1978, pp. 24–36, esp. 24–5.

18 V & P 1888–9, vol. II, p. 599.

19 *Wealth and Progress 1886−7*, pp. 142−4.
20 Radi *et al.*; H. V. Evatt, *The Story of W. A. Holman and the Labour Movement: Australian Labour Leader*, Angus & Robertson, Sydney, 1940; Robin Gollan, *Radical and Working Class Politics: A Study of Eastern Australia 1850−1890*, MUP in association with ANU, Canberra, 1960; Bede Nairn, *Civilising Capitalism*, Canberra, ANU Press, 1973, esp. p. 72; John Rickard, *Class and Politics: New South Wales, Victoria and the Early Commonwealth, 1890−1910*, ANU Press, Canberra, 1976.
21 Coghlan to McLachlan, 5 October 1909, Coghlan papers.
22 J. A. B. Fry; Caiden, p. 199; Wettenhall; Sydney directories. Goodchap became MLA for Redfern in 1889; see J. H. Forsyth, 'Charles Augustus Goodchap', *ADB* 1851−1890.
23 J. A. B. Fry; Coghlan, pp. 1−2; Cordell, pp. 23, 25; *SMH*, n.d., Coghlan papers.
24 George Black, *A History of the N. S. W. Political Labour Party*, Sydney, 1926, p. 22, quoted in B. Mansfield, 'The Background to Radical Republicanism in New South Wales in the Eighteen-Eighties', *HS* 5, 20, 1953, pp. 338−48, esp. 338.
25 Coghlan, pp. 1−2; Cordell, pp. 23, 25; *SMH*, 5 July 1875, p. 5.
26 E.g. *DT* began 1879; *Bulletin* 1880, see Sylvia Lawson, *The Archibald Paradox: A Strange Case of Authorship*, Allen Lane, Melbourne, 1983, pp. 47, 65−90.
27 Coghlan, p. 4; Cordell, p. 25; J. A. B. Fry. Copies of pseudonymous and anonymous articles probably from *Suburban Times* and presumed to be his work are in a clippings book, Coghlan papers.
28 Coghlan, p. 3. For Toohey see C. N. Connolly, *Biographical Register of the New South Wales Parliament 1856−1901*, ANU Press, Canberra, 1983; G. P. Walsh, 'John Thomas Toohey and James Matthew Toohey', *ADB* 1851−1890.
29 J. A. B. Fry.
30 M. J. Cullen, *The Statistical Movement in Early Victorian Britain: The Foundations of Empirical Social Research*, Harvester Press, Hassocks, Sussex, 1975, esp. pp. 10−11; John M. Eyler, *Victorian Social Medicine: The Ideas and Methods of William Farr*, Johns Hopkins University Press, Baltimore, 1979, esp. pp. 9, 15−16.
31 See Parkes, *PD*, 1886, p. 2557, 10 June.
32 Archibald sought him out immediately he became statist; see Archibald to Dr (Charles) Coghlan, 19 May 1886, Coghlan papers. He formed close friendships with Archibald and business manager William Macleod, with whom he corresponded while in Britain 1905−26; see Coghlan, pp. 4, 8; Lawson, *Archibald Paradox*, and 'Jules François Archibald', *ADB* 1851−1890; Mrs Macleod, *Macleod of the Bulletin: The Life and Work of William Macleod by His*

Wife, Snelling Printing Works, Sydney, 1931; Ailsa Zainu'ddin,
'The Early History of the *Bulletin*', in Margot Beever and F. B.
Smith (eds), *Historical Studies: Selected Articles*, MUP, 1967,
pp. 199–216. Coghlan's son recalls that Archibald tried to persuade
Coghlan to become editor-in-chief of the *Bulletin*; see Coghlan
and Willats, p. 6. What Coghlan considered his 'best articles',
when not leaders, were published under the name of Henry
Siebel; see *Bulletin*, 5, 12, 19, 26 October, 2, 16, 23, 30 November,
14, 28 December 1889, 4, 18 January, 8 February, 3 March, 17
May 1890. The contribution of the writer F. J. Broomfield to the
1891 census report is acknowledged in the preface. Critic John Le
Gay Brereton worked with Coghlan in the 1890s; they corresponded until Coghlan's death. Henry Lawson had a short-lived
sinecure in Coghlan's office in 1898; see T. A. Coghlan, *General
Report on the Eleventh Census of New South Wales*, Sydney, 1894,
preface; Coghlan papers; Fry, 'Review Article', p. 433; Bertha
Lawson, *My Henry Lawson*, Frank Johnson, Sydney, 1943,
pp. 66–7.
33 Coghlan, p. 4; R. B. Walker, *The Newspaper Press in New South
Wales, 1803–1920*, SUP, 1976, p. 86. Coghlan wrote under the
pseudonym Peter Barkis; see *DT*, 1, 8, 22 June, 6, 13 July, 7, 14
September 1889.
34 Coghlan, p. 4.
35 Coghlan, pp. 5–7.
36 Coghlan to Deakin, 12 April 1906, Coghlan papers, referring to
his social and economic history of Australia published as *Labour
and Industry in Australia: From the First Settlement in 1788 to the
Establishment of the Commonwealth in 1901*, OUP, London, 1918.
37 ibid., preface.
38 Coghlan and Willatts, p. 18; Proust; Radi *et al.*
39 Coghlan and Willatts, pp. 22–3; Fry, 'Review Article', p. 449.
Lang married Henry Lawson's wife's sister, so was part of a circle
Coghlan would have known in the 1890s.
40 The currency of Coghlan's reading is demonstrated by his reference to 'an American writer', probably Stuart Wood or J.B.
Clark, who had recently debated the question of basis of wages
'with great ability'; see 'The True Basis of Exchange: A Correction
... II', *DT*, 8 June 1889, p. 9.
41 'The Socialism of Christ', *Bulletin*, 28 December 1889, p. 5.
42 'The True Basis of Exchange: Labour and Capital', *DT*, 22 June
1889, p. 9.
43 'Material Prosperity and Political Wellbeing', *Bulletin*, 2 November
1889, pp. 6–7.
44 ibid. These arguments run through all his articles; see esp. *DT*,
8 June, 13 July, 7 September 1889.

45 *Suburban Times* articles, Coghlan papers; 'The New Panacea', *Bulletin*, 18 January 1890, p. 6.
46 'The True Basis of Exchange: A Correction...II', *DT*, 8 June 1889, p. 9.
47 *Labour and Industry*, pp. 1835–6, 2092, 2095–7.
48 ibid., vol. III, esp. pp. 1351–2, 1361–2.
49 ibid., p. 1947; Coghlan to Lockyer, 29 April 1910, Coghlan papers.
50 ibid., pp. 1217, 1352, 1361–2.
51 Coghlan to Neitenstein, 5 March, 19 March 1909; Coghlan to McLachlan, 29 April 1910, Coghlan papers.
52 *Bulletin*, 16 November 1889, p. 6, 18 January 1890, p. 6.
53 Coghlan papers, *passim*.
54 Coghlan to Neitenstein, 19 March 1909, Coghlan papers. For a general discussion, see Sandra Stanley Holton, 'T. A. Coghlan's *Labour and Industry in Australia*. An Enigma in Australian Historiography', *HS* 22, 88, 1987, pp. 336–51. For Coghlan's interest in criminology see *Bulletin*, 23 and 30 November 1889, pp. 6–7, p. 6; Cordell, pp. 64–5.
55 H. W. Arndt, 'A Pioneer of National Income Estimates', *Economic Journal* 59, 1949, pp. 236–45; Paul Studenski, *The Income of Nations. Theory, Measurement, and Analysis: Past and Present*, NYUP, 1958, pp. 136–7.
56 Coghlan, 'Autobiography', pp. 4, 5.
57 Cordell, pp. 69–98.
58 Coghlan, 'Autobiography', p. 5. His imminent appointment as taxation commissioner was widely rumoured in 1893; see Hayter to Coghlan, February 1893, Coghlan papers.
59 Coghlan, ibid., pp. 6–7; *Labour and Industry*, pp. 1675–80.
60 RCPS, pp. 42–3.
61 Coghlan, 'Autobiography', p. 7.
62 *Bulletin*, 14 December 1889, p. 6; 3 March 1890, p. 6; 2 February 1892, pp. 6–7; 12 March, p. 6 (anon.); 12 August 1894, pp. 6–7 (anon.); 18 July 1896, p. 6 (ed.).
63 *General Report*, pp. 14–15, 276–9.
64 A. W. Martin, *Henry Parkes*, MUP, 1980, pp. 406–9; Sir George Houston Reid, *My Reminiscences*, Cassell, London, 1917.
65 A. W. Martin, 'Free Trade and Protectionist Parties in New South Wales', *HS* 6, 23, 1954, pp. 315–23.
66 J. Tighe Ryan, 'The Political Leaders of N. S. W.', *Review of Reviews*, 20 July 1894, wrote that 'although [Wise is] an advanced democrat [he] cannot get the ear of democracy' (quoted in A. W. Martin, Political Developments in New South Wales 1894–6, unpubl. MA thesis, University of Sydney, 1952, p. 80).
67 See Reid's letters to the editor *SMH*, 6, 8 July 1878 during the

superannuation dispute. He was out of parliament during the passage of the 1884 Civil Service Bill but defended the rights of public servants during a debate on amending Bills 1886; see *PD*, 1885–6, p. 1011, 30 March 1886; pp. 5835–45, 18 October.

68 November 1894.

69 RCPS, pp. 25, 30.

70 ibid., pp. 30–32, 45, esp. 31.

71 RCPS, *Minutes of Evidence*, pp. 225–37; *PD* 1894–5, pp. 3129–30, 6 December 1894. For commissioners Thomas Littlejohn, James Robertson, Richard Teece, F. T. Humphery MLC and J. H. Storey, see *John's Notable Australians* 1906; Ken Knight, 'Patronage and the 1894 Royal Commission of Inquiry into the New South Wales Public Service', *AJPH* 7, 2, 1961, pp. 166–85, esp. 169; *SMH*, 13, 25 June 1878; Ruth Teale, 'Frederick Thomas Humphery', *ADB* 1851–1890.

72 Coghlan, 'Autobiography', pp. 7–8. He spoke of the creation of the Board in letters to Neitenstein, 5 March 1909, Deakin, 1909 (draft not sent), and McKay, 3 March 1910, Coghlan papers.

73 Coghlan to Neitenstein, 3 March 1909, Coghlan papers.

74 *PD*, 1895, pp. 1578–9, 9 October.

75 *Transmitter*, 14 November 1895, pp. 7–12; *PD*, 1895, pp. 2095–2108, 29 October.

76 Coghlan, 'Autobiography', p. 7.

77 Kenneth W. Knight, The Development of the Public Service of New South Wales from Responsible Government (1856) to the Establishment of the Public Service Board (1895), unpubl. MA thesis, University of Sydney, 1954, pp. 153–4.

78 PSB, *Report* 1895, V & P 1896, vol. II, p. 3.

79 For Miller, Fraser, Neitenstein, and Fraser's dismissal see M. L. Cruise Sernack, Penal Reform in New South Wales: Frederick William Neitenstein 1896–1909, unpubl. PhD thesis, University of Sydney, 1980, pp. 69–101, App. 21; see also S. Garton, 'Frederick William Neitenstein' *ADB* 1891–1939.

80 Wood utterly opposed public service reform; see RCPS, *Minutes of Evidence*, pp. 189–211; *Report*, p. 40; and *Report on Evidence Before Civil Service Commission by Mr. H. C. L. Anderson*, V & P 1896, vol. II, pp. 87–156. McKay accompanied McLachlan on the public service delegation to Reid on the superannuation question in 1885. For McKay see *PSJ*, June, October 1902; *Transmitter*, 14 November 1895, pp. 9–11, 17 July 1902, p. 6.

81 J. A. B. Fry, p. 87.

82 See Coghlan papers; D. I. McDonald, 'Sir Nicholas Colston Lockyer', *ADB* 1891–1939; 'Edmund Lockyer', *ADB* 1788–1850; *PSJ*, December 1900, p. 6; RCPS, p. 33.

83 For D'Arcy see *PSJ*, April 1891, pp. 17–18; Sernack, App. 21;

Hutton Neve; Heather Radi, 'Dame Constance Elizabeth D'Arcy', *ADB* 1891–1939.

84 For Pollock see V & P 1896, vol. II, p. 16.

85 Gullick founded the Ethnological Society with John Vernon and Percy Williams in 1902. See PSB, *Report* 1897, V & P 1898, vol. I, p. 2; *PSJ*, January 1906, p. 14 for Potter and Gullick; April 1919, p. 41 for Trivett; January 1903, p. 6 for Vernon; February 1900, p. 4 and September 1904, p. 6 for Williams.

86 Fosbery was a member of the Old Age Pensions Board in 1900, of which Coghlan was chairman—see Brian Dickey and Martha Rutledge, 'Edmund Walcott Fosbery', *ADB* 1851–1890; Rose Scott papers, ML MSS 38/27, f. 347.

87 For Lambton see *Transmitter*, 21 February 1893, p. 11.

88 For Colquhoun see *PSJ*, May 1900, p. 6; for Tillett see *PSJ*, May 1902, p. 6.

89 Kingsmill claims that 'had Mr Walker chosen he might have been a member of the [PSB] from the commencement'. This seems unlikely but may indicate dissension between old guard Free Traders represented by Brunker and Want and new represented by Reid; see A. G. Kingsmill, 'Richard Cornelius Critchett Walker', *ADB* 1851–1890, and *Witness to History: A Short Study of the Colonial Secretary's Department*, Alpha Books, Sydney, 1972, pp. 37–8; *PSJ*, April 1900, p. 6, July 1903, p. 14.

90 For Brodie see *PSJ*, March 1905, p. 6. For Hanson see *PSJ*, 1901. For Holliman see RCPS, *Minutes of Evidence*, p. 231. For reorganization of audit see PSB *Report* 1897, p. 28.

91 *PSJ*, March 1922, pp. 21–2. For Neitenstein's membership of PSB, see Coghlan to Neitenstein 5, 19 March 1909, Coghlan papers.

92 For Williams see *PSJ*, August 1905, p. 6, April 1919, pp. 3–4; *Red Tape*, December 1933, p. 90; *TCJ*, 9 June 1915, p. 45, 19 March 1919, p. 5. He was a witness at Coghlan's wedding in 1897; he and Coghlan corresponded regularly during Coghlan's period in London; Coghlan papers.

93 McLachlan retired in 1915; Royal Commission on Public Service Administration, Report, *CPP* 1920–21, vol. IV. McKay joined McLachlan as Commonwealth public service inspector for New South Wales in 1902, and employed ETS activist Charles Kraegen as his chief clerk. McKay returned briefly to the New South Wales service in 1910 as a member of the Public Service Board, but returned to the Commonwealth as the first federal commissioner of land tax. Kraegen became New South Wales inspector in place of McKay in 1910. Lockyer became head of the Commonwealth Taxation Department in New South Wales in 1901. John D'Arcy became under-secretary for navigation in 1910, and was

an active member of the Public Service Association (PSA) which
was formed in 1899, acting as chairman for most of the period
from 1907 to his early death in 1918. Percy Williams, one of
D'Arcy's fellow councillors on the PSA in 1903 and chairman in
1904, became comptroller of the Government Savings Bank in
1902. George Brodie and Ernest Hanson helped to reorganize the
Charities Department following the Public Service Board inquiry
of 1898 and the retirement of the long-time director, Sydney
Maxted. Hanson was appointed director of government charities
in 1901. In 1906 he returned to the Audit Office as chief inspector,
and George Brodie became inspector-general of charities. John
Vernon became auditor-general in 1903, and John Holliman became under-secretary of the Treasury and commissioner of taxation
in 1907. John Tillett succeeded the ageing Colquhoun as Crown
solicitor in 1902 at the age of thirty-four. For McKay see PSB
Report 1898, V & P 1899, vol. I, p. 15; Brian Fitzpatrick, *The
British Empire in Australia: An Economic History 1834–1939*, MUP,
1941, p. 369; Coghlan papers. For Kraegen see J. S. Baker,
'Edward Charles Kraegen', and 'Louisa Margaret Dunkley'
(Kraegen's wife, a prominent woman activist), *ADB* 1891–1939,
and *Communicators*; *SMH*, 22 October 1895; *PSJ*, December 1902,
p. 6; *Transmitter*, 17 January 1903, pp. 4–5.
94 See Coghlan, *Labour and Industry*, pp.1442–68, 2018–41,
   2097–108, 2191–9; Rickard, *Class and Politics*, p. 134.
95 Martin, 'Free Trade and Protectionist Parties', p. 323.
96 Coghlan, *Labour and Industry*, pp. 2096, 2109, 2201–17; Jill Roe,
   'Old Age, Young Country: The First Old Age Pensions and
   Pensioners in New South Wales', *Teaching History*, 15, 2, 1981,
   pp. 23–42; R. B. Walker, 'Australia's Second Arbitration Act',
   LH, 19, 1970, pp. 17–25.

5 *Masculinizing work*

1 Coghlan, 'The Employment of Women', in *General Report on the
  Eleventh Census of New South Wales*, Sydney, Government Printer,
  1894, pp. 276–9, esp. 276, 278.
2 K. D. Buckley, *The Amalgamated Engineers in Australia, 1852–1920*,
  Department of Economic History, RSSS, ANU, Canberra, 1970,
  esp. pp. 3–4; Cynthia Cockburn, *Brothers: Male Dominance and
  Technological Change*, Pluto Press, London, 1983.
3 Jane Humphries, 'Class Struggle and the Persistence of the
  Working Class Family', in Alice H. Amsden (ed.), *The Economics
  of Women and Work*, Penguin, Harmondsworth, 1980, pp. 140–65.
4 For assisted immigration see T. A. Coghlan, *Labour and Industry
  in Australia: From the First Settlement in 1788 to the Establishment of*

the Commonwealth in 1901, OUP, London, 1918, pp. 1285–7, 1837; for opposition to Asian migration and regulation of Asian workers, pp. 1331–45, 1846, 1943–4, 2187, 2317–25; for Coghlan's contemporary views see 1889–90 *DT* series and his articles in the *Bulletin* of 12 October, 2 November 1889, and 3 March 1890. For women in trades see W. Nicol, 'Women and the Trade Union Movement in New South Wales, 1890–1900', *LH* 36, 1979, pp. 18–30.

5 Anne Summers, *Damned Whores and God's Police: The Colonization of Women in Australia*, Penguin, Melbourne, 1975; Hilary Golder, *Divorce in 19th Century New South Wales*, NSWUP, Sydney, 1985.

6 *General Report*, p. 169; *Childbirth in New South Wales: a Study in Statistics*, Government Printer, Sydney, 1900; *The Decline of the Birth-rate of New South Wales and Other Phenomena of Childbirth: an Essay in Statistics*, Government Printer, Sydney, 1903; Neville Hicks, *'This Sin and Scandal': Australia's Population Debate 1891–1911*, ANU Press, Canberra, 1978.

7 The accepted measurement of 'working' population today is that adopted for the Australian census of 1966; it comprises employed (persons fifteen years and over who worked for wages, salary, payment or profit in the week preceding the census and those who had a job, business, profession or farm, full-time or part-time during the period, even if temporarily absent) and un-employed (those who did not work during preceding week and either looked for work or were temporarily laid off without pay for entire week, 'looking for work' being indicated by certain specified activities). For a detailed discussion see Desley Deacon, 'Political Arithmetic: The Nineteenth-Century Australian Census and the Construction of the Dependent Woman', *Signs*, 11, 1, 1985, pp. 27–47.

8 For Farr see *Dictionary of National Biography*, pp. 1090–91; Michael J. Cullen, *The Statistical Movement in Early Victorian Britain: the Foundations of Empirical Social Research*, Harvester Press, Hassocks, Sussex, 1975, pp. 29–43; John M. Eyler, *Victorian Social Medicine: the Ideas and Methods of William Farr*, Johns Hopkins University Press, Baltimore, 1979.

9 *Census of Great Britain* 1851, *Population Tables* II, vol. I, *BPP* 1852–3, vol. 88, pt. I, pp. lxxxii–c for Farr's 1851 classification; pp lxix-lxxv for history of occupational statistics; for 1861 classifi-cation and ideas on productivity, 'The New Classification of the People According to their Employments', in *Census of England and Wales* 1861, *BPP* 1863, vol. 53, pt. I, pp. 225–248; for economic ideas, Eyler, pp. 90–96; B. F. Kiker, *Human Capital: In Retrospect*, University of South Carolina, Bureau of Business

and Economic Research, Columbia, 1968, pp.5—11; quotation William Farr in Eyler, p. 95. The British census was introduced primarily because of interest in population size; there was little interest in activities of the population until 1831, and then no clear differentiation on grounds of productivity; see *Census of Great Britain* 1851, *Population Tables* I, vol I, *BPP* 1852—3, vol. 85, pp. ix-xi.

10 *Census of England and Wales* 1861, p. 225.

11 *Census of Great Britain* 1851, *Population Tables* II, p. lxxxviii.

12 *Census of England and Wales* 1871, vol. IV, *BPP* 1873, vol. 71, pt. 1, pp. xli—xlii.

13 *Census of Great Britain* 1851, *Population Tables* II, pp. lxxxviii—lxxxix, xci, xciv.

14 *Census of England and Wales* 1871, vol. III, p. xxxv; vol. IV, pt. 2, p. 81.

15 *Census of England and Wales* 1871, vol. IV, pp. xli—xlii.

16 *Census of Great Britain* 1851, *Population Tables* I, p. xli, xxxiv.

17 In the census of 1881 housewives and small businessmen's female relatives not reported assisting were included among 'Persons without Specified Occupations' in 'Unoccupied Class'; however the reports of 1881 and 1891 stressed this classification as a technicality; if such women were counted, the proportion of occupied women was similar to men's. The census of 1891 encouraged reporting of women in family enterprises as occupied. See *Census of England and Wales* 1881, vol. IV, *BPP* 1883, vol. 80, pp. 29, 49; *Census* 1891, vol IV, *BPP* 1893—4, vol. 106, pp. 57—8, 138; Catherine Hakim, 'Census Reports as Documentary Evidence: The Census Commentaries 1801—1951', *Sociological Review* 28, 3, 1980, pp. 551—80, esp. 557—8.

18 *Census of Scotland* 1861, vol. II, *BPP* 1864, vol. 51, pp. xl, xlii—xlvii; *Census* 1871, vol. II, *BPP* 1873, vol. 73, pp. xxxvi—xlviii. The Scots returned to the England and Wales system in 1881; see F. L. Jones, 'Is It True What They Say About Women? The Census 1801—1911 and Women in the Economy', Department of Sociology, RSSS, ANU, Canberra 1983, mimeo.

19 Charles Booth, 'Occupations of the People of the United Kingdom 1801—81', *Royal Statistical Society Journal*, 49, 1886, pp. 314—435; Committee to inquire into the Census, *Report*, *BPP* 1890, vol. 58, p. 119.

20 Australians gave more explicit instructions about recording relatives' work in family enterprises and required specific statement of wives' and daughters' employment on domestic duties, but many householders still failed to do this; see *Census of Victoria* 1861, *Population Tables*, pt. I, *Report*, Melbourne 1862, p. xxi. Pt. II, *Report*, 1862—3, p. ix states that 'Agricultural and Pastoral

Class' included farmers' wives, etc., if assisting on farm' and 'male and female relatives of farmers living on farms if above 15 years of age and not otherwise described'. *New South Wales Census* 1871, *Report*, Sydney, 1873, p. XXVII claims that most female relatives of food and drink sellers and of farmers were included in 1861 in menfolks' classification but note table 46 (p. LXIX) indicates this was only assumed; comparison of the figures for 1861 and 1871 suggests that in 1861 NSW practice was the same as Victoria's. From 1871 NSW was concerned with over-enumeration of female workers possibly because of depressed employment; censuses then assumed no female relatives were assisting in family enterprises.

21 I. J. Neeson, *ADB* 1851—1890.

22 Henry Heylyn Hayter, *Census of Victoria* 1881, *General Report*, Melbourne, 1883, pp. 105—20 *passim*, 140—1.

23 *Tasmanian PP*, 1890, vol. 21, no. 146, pp. 1—19; Coghlan, *General Report*, pp. 270—5; Henry Heylyn Hayter, *Census of Victoria* 1891, *General Report*, Melbourne, 1893, pp. 190—2. For Johnston see R. L. Wettenhall, 'Robert Mackenzie Johnston(e)', *ADB* 1891—1939; Robert Mackenzie Johnston, *The R. M. Johnston Memorial Volume: Being A Selection of the Principal Writings in Connection with Geology and with Economic and Social Problems of the Day*, Government Printer, Hobart, 1921. For Johnston and Coghlan see Craufurd D. W. Goodwin, *Economic Enquiry in Australia*, Duke University Press, Durham, NC, 1966; and *The Image of Australia: British Perception of the Australian Economy from the Eighteenth to the Twentieth Century*, Duke University Press, Durham, NC, 1974.

24 Coghlan, *General Report*, pp. 270—75, esp. 272.

25 See Goodwin, *Economic Enquiry* and *Image* for the rivalry.

26 ibid., pp. 122—35, 160—84.

27 'Democratic Government in Victoria', *Westminster Review* 33, 2, 1868, pp. 481—523, quoted ibid., p. 130.

28 'The Employment of Women', pp. 276—9, esp. p. 278.

29 ibid., pp. 276, 279, 281.

30 ibid., pp. 280—81.

31 *Census of Victoria* 1891, p. 192.

32 'Protection—a National Necessity', *Bulletin* 9, 433, 1888, p. 4, quoted Goodwin, *Economic Enquiry*, p. 344.

33 Coghlan, *General Report*, p. 280 notes the number of small employers and people working on their own account.

34 The problem that New South Wales encountered in recording women's work is paralleled today in developing countries: see Ruth B. Dixon, 'Women in Agriculture: Counting the Labor Force in Developing Countries', *Population and Development Review* 8, 3, 1982, pp. 539—66.

35 The nature of productivity and productivity of housework are continuing subjects of debate; see Paul Studenski, *The Income of Nations: Theory, Measurement and Analysis: Past and Present*, NYU Press, 1958, pp. 11—12, 177; Simon Kuznets, *National Income and Its Composition 1919—1938*, National Bureau of Economic Research, New York, 1941, p. 6—21; John Kenneth Galbraith, *Economics and the Public Purpose*, Houghton Mifflin, Boston, 1973, pp. 29—37; Heidi Hartmann, 'The Unhappy Marriage of Marxism and Feminism: Towards a More Progressive Union', in Lydia Sargent (ed.), *Women and Revolution: A Discussion of the Unhappy Marriage of Marxism and Feminism*, South End Press, Boston, 1981, pp. 1—41. A renewed interest in valuation of household work is demonstrated in Milton Moss (ed.), *The Measurement of Economic and Social Performance*, National Bureau of Economic Research, New York, 1973; Martin Murphy, 'Comparative Estimates of the Value of Household Work in the United States for 1976', *Review of Income and Wealth*, 28, 2, 1982, pp. 29—43.

36 Jill Julius Matthews, 'Deconstructing the Masculine Universe: The Case of Women's Work', in *Third Women and Labour Conference Papers*, South Australian College of Advanced Education, Salisbury, 1982, pp. 474—82; Patrick Mullins, 'Theoretical Perspectives on Australian Urbanisation: 1. Material Components in the Reproduction of Australian Labour Power', *ANZJS* 17, 1, 1981, pp. 65—76; Anne Aungles, 'Family Economics in Transition: Adelaide Women in the Depression', paper delivered at ANZAAS Congress, Perth, 1983.

37 E.g. Lino, 'Women Who Work', *Argus*, 13 January 1902, pp. 5—6.

38 Leonore Davidoff, 'The Separation of Home and Work? Landladies and Lodgers in Nineteenth and Twentieth Century England', in Sandra Burman (ed.), *Fit Work for Women*, Croom Helm, London, 1979, pp. 64—97; Martha Norby Fraundorf, 'The Labor Force Participation of Turn-of-the-Century Married Women', *Journal of Economic History* 39, 1979, pp. 401—17, esp. 402—3; D. Ian Pool, 'Changes in Canadian Female Labour Force Participation, and Some Possible Implications for Conjugal Power', *Journal of Comparative Family Studies* 9, Spring 1978, pp. 41—52, esp. 43—5, 50—51.

39 A. J. Jaffe and Charles D. Stewart, *Manpower Resources and Utilization: Principles of Working Force Analysis*, Wiley, New York, 1951, pp. 452—3.

40 *PD* 1895, p. 1821, 17 October. The following account of discussion on the Bill draws on ibid., pp. 1642—3, 1650, 1821—9 and 1877—88.

41 59 Vic. No. 25, s. 36.

42 There is, however, evidence of some support among women by the 1900s. Louisa Dunkley of the Victorian Women's Post and

Telegraph Association agreed married women should resign and
did so herself when she married Edward Kraegen in 1903; she
may have been influenced by Kraegen as the NSW committee
originated the motion banning married women from assistant
and telegraphist positions; see *Transmitter*, 17 September 1901,
p. 10, 21 December, p. 7, 18 February 1904, p. 5. Bruce Mitchell,
*Teachers, Education and Politics: A History of Organizations of Public
School Teachers in New South Wales*, UQP, Brisbane, 1975, p. 26
claims single female teachers agreed with Education Department
chief Peter Board on ban on married women; that they campaigned for a ban imposed in 1910 by the Teachers Association
conference; but that Kate Dwyer, married sister of the feminist
teachers Belle and Annie Golding, opposed it.

43 *Transmitter*, 9 July 1892, p. 2.
44 *Regulations under the Public Instruction Act of 1880*, V & P
    1892–3, vol. III, pp. 1259–82, esp. 1263, 1 July 1893.
45 *GG*, 30 July 1896 for postal assistants, 7 August for postmistresses,
    operators, assistants; *Transmitter*, 27 July 1896, p. 3, 18 August,
    pp. 6–7.
46 'Translation of information relative to New South Wales appearing
    in Berne Telegraph Bureau Circular No. 505 (Employment of
    females)', extract from Post and Telegraph official file 376/10,
    B99–18706, ff. 40–41, Aust. Post NSW Hist. Section.
47 Personal communication, Miss Beatrice Proust, 18 November
    1987. When Dora Murphy's promotion was questioned in 1900
    the concern was with nepotism not marital status; see *Public
    Service. (Information Respecting Clerk at the Botanic Gardens.)*, V &
    P 1900, pp. 693–4.
48 *PSJ*, October 1917, p. 8, December, p. 41.
49 *Transmitter*, 14 November 1895, p. 13.
50 *Transmitter*, 18 November 1896, p. 7.
51 This suggestion from P. Grimshaw and M. Lake's honours class,
    Melbourne University, 1987.
52 Jennifer Rowse, 'Lucy Arabella Stocks Garvin', *ADB*
    1891–1939.

6 *Managing women*

1 12 March 1892, p. 6.
2 For the superior situation of farmers' widows see Patricia
   Grimshaw, Charles Fahey, Susan Janson and Tom Griffiths,
   'Families and Selection in Colonial Horsham', in Patricia Grimshaw
   et al. (eds), *Families in Colonial Australia*, George Allen & Unwin,
   Sydney, 1985, p. 118–37, For girls' employment see *PD*,
   1879–80, pp. 1184–93, 18 February 1880.

3 Noeline Kyle, *Her Natural Destiny: The Education of Women in New South Wales*, NSWUP, Sydney, 1986, pp. 134—45; Public Instruction Department, *Report*, V & P 1882, vol. II, pp. 6—7.

4 43 Vic. No. 23, 16 April 1880, s. 25, 26; W. Vere Hole and Anne H. Treweeke, *The History of the Women's College within the University of Sydney*, Halstead Press, Sydney, 1953, p. 29; Lilith Norman, *The Brown and Yellow: A History of Sydney Girls' High School*, OUP, Melbourne, 1983. The quotation is from C. H. Spence (referring to SA) in *South Australian Register*, 18 September 1879, quoted Alison Mackinnon, 'Educating the Mothers of the Nation: The Advanced School for Girls, Adelaide', in Margaret Bevage, Margaret James and Carmel Shute (eds.), *Worth Her Salt: Women at Work in Australia*, Hale & Iremonger, Sydney, 1982, pp. 62—71, esp. 63.

5 Australienne, 'Women's Hope From Women's Higher Education', *Melbourne Review* 7, 1882, pp. 308—14; Hole and Treweeke, pp. 28—35; M. Hutton Neve, *'This Mad Folly!' The History of Australia's Pioneer Women Doctors*, Library of Australian History, Sydney, 1980, pp. 49—57; Kyle pp. 147—8; Public Instruction Department, *Report* 1882, p. 9.

6 E.g. Frances Holden, Emily Manning ('Australie'), Louise Mack, Ethel Turner, Ina Wildman; see Sally O'Neill, 'Emily Matilda Manning', *ADB* 1851—1890; Sylvia Lawson, *The Archibald Paradox: A Strange Case of Authorship*, Allen Lane, Melbourne, 1983, pp. 179, 203 for Louise Mack; pp. 167, 201—4, 243—4 for Wildman; Philippa Poole, *The Diaries of Ethel Turner*, Lansdowne, Sydney, 1979.

7 For the effect on families in Victoria see Grimshaw *et al.*, p. 133; Marilyn Lake, 'Helpmeet, Slave, Housewife:' Women in Rural Families 1870—1930' in Grimshaw *et al.*, pp.173—85. For the employment problem see T. A. Coghlan, *Labour and Industry in Australia: From the First Settlement in 1788 to the Establishment of the Commonwealth in 1901*, OUP, London, 1918, vol. 3 *passim*; Shirley Fisher, 'The Family and the Sydney Economy in the Late Nineteenth Century', in Grimshaw *et al.*, pp. 153—62; and 'An Accumulation of Misery?' in Richard Kennedy (ed.), *Australian Welfare History*, Macmillan, Melbourne, 1982, pp. 32—50.

8 Verity Burgmann, *'In Our Time': Socialism and the Rise of Labor 1885—1905*, George Allen & Unwin, Sydney, 1985; Graeme Davison, 'Sydney and the Bush: an Urban Context for the Australian Legend', *HS* 18, 71, 1978, pp. 191—209, esp. 193—7; B. Mansfield, 'The Background to Radical Republicanism in New South Wales in the Eighteen-Eighties', *HS* 5, 20, 1953, pp. 338—48; Bruce Mitchell, *Teachers, Education and Politics: A History of Organizations of Public School Teachers in New South*

Wales, UQP, Brisbane, 1975. For Mary Gilmore see W. H. Wilde, 'Dame Mary Jean Gilmore', *ADB* 1891−1939.

9 Judith Godden, Philanthropy and the Women's Sphere, Sydney, 1870−circa 1900, unpubl. PhD thesis, Macquarie University, 1983, p. 257.

10 M. D. Hogg to Rose Scott, 31 January 1904, Rose Scott papers, ML MSS A2277, f. 253a. It is not clear if Laura and Margaret were related. Information on the two Hoggs from *Women's Suffrage Journal*, 15 September 1891, p. 3 and Judith Godden.

11 *PSJ*, 12 September 1911, p. 7; 10 December 1913, p. 29.

12 'New Era', *PSJ*, 1 September 1914, p. 11.

13 Godden.

14 Brian Kiernan, *The Essential Henry Lawson: The Best Works of Australia's Greatest Writer*, Currey O'Neil, Melbourne, 1982, pp. 1−40, esp. 4; Bertha Lawson, *My Henry Lawson*, Frank Johnson, Sydney, 1943, esp. pp. 149−54; Brian Matthews, 'Henry Lawson', Heather Radi, 'Louisa Lawson', *ADB* 1891−1939; records Eurunderee (Pipe Clay) post office, Aust. Post NSW Historical Section.

15 Story reprinted Kiernan, pp. 85−90; see Bertha Lawson, p. 11.

16 Sylvia Lawson, p. 136; Mansfield, p 340

17 See J. A. B. Fry, 'Forty Years in the Civil Service', Fry family papers, ML MS 1159/2, p. 1; News cuttings concerning Mrs Louisa Lawson, ML; information Judith Godden; 'Sir William Charles Windeyer', *ADB* 1851−1890.

18 First edition 15 May 1888; for sympathetic analysis see Brian Matthews, *Louisa*, McPhee Gribble, Melbourne, 1987.

19 Jean F. Arnot, 'Nita Bernice Kibble', 'Barbara Jane Baynton (Janet Ainsleigh)', Viva Gallego, 'Catherine Winifred Dwyer' (née Golding), Beverley Kingston, 'Annie Mackenzie and Isabella Theresa Golding', J. J. Roe, 'Stella Maria(n) Sarah Miles Franklin', *ADB* 1891−1939; *Cyclopaedia of New South Wales*, pp. 672B−C; Lucy Frost, 'Barbara Baynton: An Affinity with Pain' and Frances McInherny, 'Miles Franklin, *My Brilliant Career*, and the Female Tradition', in Shirley Walker (ed.), *Who Is She? Images of Women in Australian Fiction*, UQP, Brisbane, 1983, pp. 56−70, 71−83; Verna Coleman, *Miles Franklin in America: Her Unknown (Brilliant) Career*, Angus & Robertson, Sydney, 1981; Wilde; Wilde and T. Inglis Moore, *Letters of Mary Gilmore*, MUP, 1980, pp. xxi−xxvii.

20 *Dawn*, 5 October 1889, p. 6.

21 W. Nicol, 'Women and the Trade Union Movement in New South Wales, 1890−1900', *LH* 36, 1979, pp. 18−30, esp. 20−21.

22 5 October 1889, p. 6.

23 Nicol; Ray Markey, 'Women and Labour, 1880−1900', in Elizabeth

Windschuttle (ed.), *Women, Class and History: Feminist Perspectives on Australia 1788–1978*, Fontana, Sydney, 1980, pp. 83–111, esp. 92–105.

24 Godden.

25 Kay Daniels, Mary Murnane and Anne Picot (eds), *Women in Australia: an Annotated Guide to Records Edited for the National Research Program*, vol. II, Australian Government Publishing Service, Canberra, 1977, p. 179; Dianne Scott, 'Woman Suffrage: The Movement in Australia', *JRAHS* 53, 4, 1967, pp. 299–322, esp. 310–11; Dora B. Montefiore, *From a Victorian to a Modern*, E. Archer, London, 1927, pp. 31–41. For influence of literary societies on a relatively conservative woman, see Judith Godden, 'Portrait of a Lady: A Decade in the Life of Helen Fell (1849–1935)', in Bevage *et al.*, pp. 33–48.

26 Montefiore, pp. 30–1; Anne Summers, *Damned Whores and God's Police: The Colonization of Women in Australia*, Penguin, Melbourne, 1975, p. 358.

27 Nicol, pp. 23–4. An Early Closing Bill was introduced in December 1890 by Alfred Allen, husband of Amelia, a founder of WSL and the Female Employees Union. A later version was said to be drafted in Rose Scott's home; see Summers, p. 354.

28 Ann-Mari Jordens, 'Rose Scott: Making a Beginning' in James Walter and Raija Nugent (eds), *Biographers at Work*, Institute of Modern Biography, Griffith University, Brisbane, 1984, pp. 26–35, esp. 28; Rose Scott, 38/27, f. 347; Summers. Quotation Rose Scott papers, A3376, f. 63a, 2 November 1892.

29 Personal communication, Miss Beatrice Proust, 18 November 1987; Sydney directories.

30 Heather Radi, 'Dame Constance Elizabeth D'Arcy', *ADB* 1891–1939; *PSJ*, 1 April 1918, pp. 17–18. For Charles Fry, telegraph operator and editor of the *Transmitter*, see *Transmitter*, 18 September 1896, p. 3; for Edith Fry and Millie Fry (later Muscio) see Norman, pp. 215, 232; for Edith see Godden, Philanthropy, table pp. 335–6; for Millie see Meredith Foley and Gillian Fulloon, 'Florence Mildred Muscio', *ADB*, ibid..

31 59 Vic. No. 25, s. 35; *PD*, 1895, p. 1821, 17 October.

32 ibid., pp. 1883–4.

33 ibid., p. 1643, 10 October.

34 For telephonists see PSB *Report* 1896, V & P 1896, vol. II, p. 11; *Transmitter*, 27 July, 18 September, 19 October, 1896; *GG*, 2 September. For typing and shorthand see PSB *Report* 1897, V & P 1898, vol. 1, p. 7; *Report* 1898, V & P 1899, 3rd sess., vol. I, pp. 14–15. For post and telegraph assistant see *GG*, 1899, p. 3385, 1900, p. 6077; PSB *Report* 1899, V & P 1900, vol. II, pp. 18–19; *Transmitter*, 17 April 1899, p. 7. For junior attend-

ants see PSB *Report* 1899, pp. 10–11, 59; H. C. L. Anderson, 'Women as Library Assistants', *Library Record of Australasia*, 1902, pp. 98–9. For clerks see PSB *Report* 1898, pp. 14–15; *Report* 1899, pp. 18–19; *GG*, 1899, pp. 5066, 9167–9, 1900, p. 964; *PSJ*, 3 September 1900, pp. 1–2.

35 For the introduction of the typewriter see Gail Reekie, 'Female Office Workers in Western Australia, 1895–1920: The Process of Feminization and Patterns of Consciousness', in Lenore Layman (ed.), *The Workplace, Time Remembered* Special Issue 5, Murdoch University, 1982, pp. 1–35. For Barling see RCPS, V & P 1894–5, vol. III, *Minutes of Evidence*, p. 226. For Mrs Bennett's family see Norman, pp. 201–2; Ann Curthoys, 'Agnes Elizabeth Lloyd Bennett', *ADB* 1891–1939; Robert Johnson, 'William Christopher Bennett', *ADB* 1851–1890. She was dismissed 1896; see *PD*, 1896, p. 1030, 24 June. Mary Collins's starting salary as a typist was £50; Dora Murphy's as a shorthand writer and typist was £120. *Public Service List* gives Dora Murphy's date of birth as 1860 but her granddaughter gives the correct date as 1853; see Proust, 27 Oct. 1987.

36 H. Randle-Hancock, 'Shorthand as an Art', *AJE*, 2 November 1903, p. 14.

37 Robinson to the under-secretary for public works, 29 December 1886, V & P 1887, vol. II, p. 108.

38 Fry, p. 4.

39 *TCJ*, 20 October 1909.

40 Evidence from Barling, RCPS, *Minutes of Evidence*, p. 231.

41 *PSJ*, September 1916, p. 15.

42 Fry, pp. 2, 87, 127, 181.

43 *Western Australian*, 21 December 1889, quoted Reekie, p. 6–7.

44 Fry, p. 121.

45 Suzy Baldwin, 'Dora, Typist and Heroine', *Bulletin*, 5 January 1988, pp. 26–27.

46 *Dawn*, May 1889, p. 24, 28.

47 ibid., 1 February 1895; *SMH*, 18 October 1895; National Council of Women of New South Wales, *Report of a Public Meeting to Consider the Formation of the National Council of Women of New South Wales*, quoted Daniels *et al*, p. 169.

48 Fry, p. 171.

49 May Hickman, Flo Peisley, Dora Elphinstone (who died), Sarah Nicoll, Annie Gray, Mabel Smith; see Fry, p. 183.

50 Baldwin, p. 26.

51 Fry, pp. 176–7.

52 Fry, p. 183.

53 *Dawn*, 1 February 1895; *SMH*, 18 October 1895.

54 Burgmann, pp. 51–5.

55 Florence Wearne to Mary Booth, 2 December 1924, Anzac Fellow-
    ship of Women papers, ANL MS 2864, courtesy Heather Radi.
    Information on Wearne's friendship with Scott from Judith Allen.
56 Scott, 38/28, ff. 67—91; A2271; ibid., A2280, f. 74; Handbill for
    WPEL, 19 January 1903, ibid., 38/43, f. 1; ibid., A 2277, f. 362.
57 ibid., 38/41, f. 1. Dora Murphy's granddaughter, who lived with
    her from 1919 until her death in 1933, remembers that she 'did
    not share the militancy of the feminists'; Proust, 18 November
    1987.
58 Scott, A2277, f. 227, 24 July 1899.
59 PSJ, 1 September 1921, pp. 27—8.
60 Scott, A2277, ff. 283—5; 38/46, ff. 353—73, courtesy Heather
    Radi.
61 The other women were Annie Frank, Government Printing Office,
    Clara Jones, Public Works, Alice Thompson, Registrar General's
    office, Ethel Goggin and Jessie Carlisle, PSB.
62 Proust, 27 October 1987, 18 November; Public Service. (Information
    Respecting Clerk at the Botanic Gardens.), V & P, 1901, pp. 693—4.
63 Scott, A2277, f. 227, 24 July 1899. Daniels et al., p. 178 note that
    League was 'insisting that women be...allowed to contest pos-
    itions in the Public Library and Public Service' by 1900.
64 Report 1898, pp. 14—15.
65 GG, 1899, pp. 9167—9, 1900, p. 964.
66 Anderson; Arnot; Transmitter, 20 February 1892, p. 3.
67 Private communications, E. L. Ellis (nephew), 12 November
    1987, 9 January 1988, Mrs S. C. Foote (niece), 17 February 1988;
    Michael Roe, Nine Australian Progressives: Vitalism in Bourgeois
    Social Thought 1890—1960, UQP, Brisbane, 1984, p. 255.
68 Scott, 38/27, ff. 347ff., 12 April 1921.
69 7 May 1902, Coghlan papers, ANL MS 6335.
70 Scott, A2277, f. 236, 22 Nov. 1901.
71 John S. Baker, 'Louisa Margaret Dunkley', ADB 1891—1939;
    Transmitter, various issues 16 August 1900 to 17 November 1902.
    Louisa Dunkley married Kraegen in December 1903.
72 For PSA see PSJ, 4 January 1900, 1 October 1921, p. 6, 15
    August 1928, p. 177.
73 Report 1899, pp. 18—19.
74 Report 1896, p. 11.
75 Wearne to Booth.
76 Scott, A2277, f. 227.
77 Dawn, 1 July 1900 reported a PSB promise to treat men and
    women alike. For Murphy see Public Service. Her granddaughter
    doubted that Coghlan influenced her promotion; Proust, 18
    November 1987.
78 19 November 1896, p. 1.

79 Wearne to Booth.
80 'The Typists' Examination', Fry, p. 115.
81 7 February 1900, p. 11
82 T. A. Coghlan, *Childbirth in New South Wales: a Study in Statistics*, Government Printer, Sydney, 1900; *The Decline of the Birth-Rate of New South Wales and Other Phenomena of Childbirth: an Essay in Statistics*, Government Printer, Sydney, 1903; Neville Hicks, *'This Sin and Scandal': Australia's Population Debate 1891– 1911*, ANU Press, Canberra, 1978.
83 Arky Parkes, 'Fair Lady Clerk', *PSJ*, 9 April 1904, p. 11.
84 9 March 1889, p. 4; cf. 1 October 1887, p. 4. See also Sylvia Lawson, pp. 196–7, 200–201; Marilyn Lake, 'The Politics of Respectability: Identifying the Masculinist Context', *HS* 22, 86, 1986, pp. 116–31.

7 *Masculinizing merit*

1 *SMH*, 5 August 1904, p. 7, quoted Joan Rydon and R. N. Spann, *New South Wales Politics 1901–1910*, Cheshire, Melbourne, 1962, p. 49.
2 Between 1898 and 1904 Labor increased its share of the vote from 11% to 23%, at the expense of both alternative parties, and shook off or incorporated independents; see Colin A. Hughes and B. D. Graham; *A Handbook of Australian Government and Politics 1890–1964*, ANU Press, Canberra, 1968. For a summary of the period see P. Loveday, A. W. Martin and Patrick Weller, 'New South Wales', in Peter Loveday, A. W. Martin and R. S. Parker (eds), *The Emergence of the Australian Party System*, Hale & Iremonger, Sydney, 1977, p. 172–248, esp. 216–33.
3 S. F. Macintyre, 'Labour, Capital and Arbitration 1890–1920', in Brian W. Head (ed.), *State and Economy in Australia*, OUP, Melbourne, 1983, pp. 98–114; B. E. Mansfield, 'The State as Employer: An Early Twentieth Century Discussion', *AJPH* 3, 2, 1958, pp. 183–96; R. B. Walker, 'Australia's Second Arbitration Act', *LH* 19, 1970, pp. 17–25.
4 H. V. Evatt, *Australian Labor Leader: The Story of W. A. Holman and the Labour Movement*, Angus & Robertson, Sydney, 1940, pp. 118–9; John Rickard, *Class and Politics: New South Wales, Victoria and the Early Commonwealth 1890–1910*, ANU Press, Canberra, 1976, pp. 147–8; J. A. Ryan, An Oxford Liberal in the Freetrade Party of New South Wales, unpubl. MA thesis, Sydney University, 1965, and 'Edward Wise', *ADB* 1851–1890.

5 Neville Hicks, 'Sir Timothy Augustine Coghlan', *ADB* 1851–1890, p. 49.

6 *PD*, 1898, p. 2015, 2 November.

7 Coghlan, 'Autobiography', pp. 10–11, Coghlan papers, ANL MS 6335; V & P 1899, 3rd sess., vol. I, pp. 819–22, 1901, vol. II, pp. 461–72; *PD*, 1899, 3rd sess., p. 2606, 23 November, 1900, pp. 2092–133, 22 August.

8 *PD*, 1899, 3rd sess., pp. 2594–610, 23 November, esp. 2594, 1900, pp. 1633–7, 7 August; for public service comment see *PSJ*, January 1900, pp. 1, 11, February pp. 1, 14; for evidence of Holman's support see *PSJ*, March 1917, p. 19.

9 Delohery was the first chairman of the Public Service Association in 1899. See J. M. Bennett (ed.), *A History of the New South Wales Bar*, Law Book Co., Sydney, 1969, p. 271; *PSJ* January 1900, p. 4, June, pp. 2, 7.

10 *Report*, 1899, V & P 1900, vol. II, pp. 1, 4–5, 19–20, 66–7.

11 Government control of increments was formalized in regulations of 1904. Long absences of Barling (April–November 1901) and Wilson (September–December) may indicate a struggle over this issue; see PSB, *Report* 1900, V & P 1901, vol. II, p. 6, 1902, V & P 1903, vol. II, p. 1, 1904, V & P 1905, 2nd sess., vol. III, pp. 12–18; *PSJ*, June 1900, pp. 1–2, May 1901, p. 1, Oct. 1905, p. 1; *GG*, 31 Dec. 1900, p. 10178, 11 Oct. 1904, p. 7655.

12 Circular 13 June 1901 re shorthand writers, Rose Scott papers, ML MSS 38/25, ff. 41, 43. Conditions governing typists and shorthand writers were not spelled out in regulations; information on typists from a letter to the editor *PSJ*, September 1903, p. 8.

13 *GG*, 18 September 1903, pp. 6958–9.

14 *Report* 1899, pp. 18–19, 18 May 1900.

15 *Transmitter* 19 November 1896, p. 1.

16 *Journal*, September 1900, pp. 1–2.

17 Scott, A2277, f. 236, 22 November. Scott wrote to Vida Goldstein in January 1902 that they were 'indebted to T. Coghlan'; see 38/36, f. 259.

18 Scott, 38/33, f. 236, 11 December 1901, 38/36, f. 217; *Transmitter*, 17 January 1902, p. 5.

19 E. W. O'Sullivan to Rose Scott, 19 December 1901; under-secretary for public works to Scott, 13 March, 15 July, 1902; Coghlan to Scott, 11 July 1902—see Scott, A2277, ff. 237, 243–6. Scott to Coghlan, 7 July 1902—Coghlan papers.

20 Scott, 38/36, f. 217.

21 7 July 1902, Coghlan papers.

22 T. A. Coghlan, *Labour and Industry in Australia: From the First Settlement in 1788 to the Establishment of the Commonwealth in 1901*, OUP, London, 1918, p. 2092.

23 Scott, A2277, f. 244.

24 PSB, *Report* 1902, p. 30, 31 August 1903.

25 Rydon and Spann, p. 47; PSB, *Report* 1904, pp. 12−15, 1905,
    V & P 1906, vol. III, pp. 18−19; *PSJ*, October 1905, p. 1,
    October 1906, p. 1.

26 Carruthers offered Coghlan a position as 'Financial adviser to
    the Treasury with supreme control over all the departments in
    the matter of expenditure' but 'after mature consideration, [he]
    saw fit to decline the offer'. He was also offered the post of
    Federal statistician by Reid; see Coghlan, 'Autobiography',
    pp. 12−13.

27 W. C. Wurth, 'The Public Service Board of New South Wales
    Since 1895', *JRAHS* 45, 6, 1960, pp. 289−313.

28 February 1907, p. 1.

29 Wilshire had been on the council of the PSA in 1900.

30 Saunders was a deputy member of the PSB in 1901 while
    Wilson was on leave. Appointed commissioner of taxation in
    1901, he was under-secretary for finance and trade as well in
    1904, possibly after Coghlan refused the position; see PSB *Report*
    1931, V & P 1930−32, vol. IV, p. 22.

31 Coghlan referred to Neitenstein's letter in his reply of 5 March
    1909; Coghlan's comments in letter to McLachlan 29 April 1910;
    see also Coghlan to Neitenstein 19 March 1909, all in Coghlan
    papers.

32 Coghlan to Neitenstein, 5 March 1909; in a further letter of 19
    March he referred to Neitenstein's independence of his minister
    and to the fact that Williams' place (as under-secretary to Wade)
    was 'no bed of roses', implying this was due to ministerial
    interference; see Coghlan papers.

33 1 January 1910, p. 1.

34 *PSJ*, 1 September 1910, p. 1, 2 January 1911, p. 1; *PD*, 1910,
    1251 ff., 28 July, 1756 ff., 16 August; Rydon and Spann, p. 124.

35 See Coghlan to McKay 3(?) March 1910, Coghlan to McLachlan,
    29 April 1910, McKay to Coghlan, 18 April 1910, Coghlan
    papers; Brian Fitzpatrick, *The British Empire in Australia: An
    Economic History 1834−1939,* 2nd edn, MUP, 1949, p. 266.

36 See Bruce McFarlane, 'Professor Irvine's Economics in Australian
    Labour History, 1913−1933', Australian Society for the Study
    of Labour History, Canberra, 1966; PSB *Report* 1911, V & P
    1912, vol. II, p. 1; Michael Roe, *Nine Australian Progressives:
    Vitalism in Bourgeois Social Thought 1890−1960*, UQP, Brisbane,
    1984.

37 Coghlan to Neitenstein, 19 March 1909, Coghlan papers; PSB,
    1911 and 1912, V & P 1913, vol. II, p. 1.

38 For Hanna see *Cyclopaedia of New South Wales*, p. 214. For Taylor see *PSJ*, March 1912, p. 20.
39 *PSJ*, 1 September 1914, p. 18.
40 *PSJ*, 1 January 1916, p. 22; Evatt, p. 380. The cost of living rose 1914—20 by 68%; see Evatt, p. 358.
41 Evatt, pp. 417—30.
42 *PSJ*, 1 December 1916, p. 27.
43 See Holman's statement, *PSJ*, March 1917, p. 18.
44 *PSJ*, March 1916, p. 5. For a résumé of the campaign see March 1919, pp. 3—4; for the beginning see November 1914, p. 1.
45 V. G. Childe, *How Labour Governs: A Study of Workers' Representation in Australia*, Labour Publishing Co., London, 1923, pp. 147—210; Evatt, pp. 371—436; D. T. Sawkins, *The Living Wage in Australia*, MUP, 1933, pp. 18—19; Ian Turner, *Industrial Labour and Politics: The Dynamics of the Labour Movement in Eastern Australia, 1900—1921*, ANU Press, Canberra, 1965, pp. 35—67 and '1914—19', in Frank Crowley (ed.), *A New History of Australia*, William Heinemann, Melbourne, 1974, pp. 312—56. For Holman and *PSJ* see *PSJ*, March 1917, pp. 18—19, April, pp. 19—20, August, p. 1.
46 The Public Service Amendment Act of 22 December 1919 confirmed changes in the Board's administration. See Evatt, pp. 441—3; Barbara Page, The Mason Allard Inquiry into the Administration of the New South Wales Public Service 1917—1918, unpubl. MEc. thesis, University of Sydney, 1980; *PSJ*, January 1919, March, April, September, November, December; Royal Commission on the Public Service of New South Wales (RCPSNSW), *First Sectional Report; Letter to the Premier from the Public Service Board Regarding Sectional Report; Report of the Public Service Board on Sectional Report*; and *Public Service Board Appointment Bill—Petition from W. J. Hanna, E. H. Wilshire, and J. M. Taylor*, V & P 1918, vol. IV; Turner, '1914—19', pp. 341—2.
47 *PSJ*, October 1906, p. 1.
48 Rydon and Spann, p. 86.
49 Scott, 38/25, ff. 41—3, 47, 57, 359. A Petition of 9 October was signed M. Collins, F. Wearne, A. Frank, A. Thompson, C. Taylor, J. Thompson, F. Beardsmore; cf. Florence Wearne to Mary Booth: 'By this time some more women had come in—I think there were 7 of us in 1900 who regarded ourselves as 'seniors'; after a good deal of talking I drafted a circular letter to the Board and got them (the 7) to sign it protesting against the £150.00 maximum; then the 6 girls went back to their respective departments and talked to the man there in whom they had the

most confidence, and in half a day I had a telephone message or note from the whole six to say that they had talked the matter over with Mr So and So and he had advised them to withdraw their signature as he was sure the PSB would view them with disservice etc etc. So in the end I fought the matter out alone with the Board and got an increase to £175 a year'; See Anzac Fellowship of Women papers, ANL, MS 2864. For taxation see Rydon and Spann, pp. 63−75; *Statistical Register.*

50 Scott, 38/21, f. 327.

51 Rydon and Spann, p. 42 for WOC, PLL, p. 47 for WPA's advocacy of equal pay, p. 61 for the equal pay resolution at a PLL conference in 1905 when women participated for the first time.

52 ibid., pp. 96−125; Turner, *Industrial Labour and Politics.*

53 Desley Deacon, 'Taylorism in the Home: The Medical Profession, the Infant Welfare Movement and the Deskilling of Women', *ANZJS*, 21, 2, pp. 161−73; Neville Hicks, *'This Sin and Scandal': Australia's Population Debate 1891−1911*, ANU Press, Canberra, 1978; Rosemary Pringle, 'Octavius Beale and the Ideology of the Birthrate', *Refractory Girl* 3, 1973, pp. 19−27; Edna Ryan, *Two-thirds of a Man: Women and Arbitration in New South Wales 1902−08*, Hale & Iremonger, Sydney, 1984. There is no definitive study of domestic science in NSW; for Victoria see Kerreen M. Reiger, *The Disenchantment of the Home: Modernizing the Australian Family 1880−1940*, OUP, Melbourne, 1985, pp. 56−82; for SA see Jill Matthews, 'Education for Femininity: Domestic Arts in South Australia', *LH* 45, 1983, pp. 30−53.

54 *PSJ*, January 1911, pp. 1−2.

55 ibid., June, pp. 22−3; September, p. 7, October, p. 3, November, p. 4, December, pp. 4, 25. Wearne reports that 'In 1912 by pegging away we had managed to get the "living wage" the same for men as for women at 21 years of age (£110 a year)'; see Wearne to Booth.

56 *PSJ*, June 1911, p. 23, quoting *DT.*

57 PSB *Report* 1913, V & P 1914−15, vol. IV, p. 4; *GG*, 1912, p. 3654; *PSJ*, February 1912, p. 2. For increased tax receipts see Evatt, pp. 297, 343; Rydon and Spann, pp. 108−9; *Statistical Register.*

58 PSB *Report* 1914, V & P 1915−16, vol. V. p. 4; starting salary £50; automatic increments to £155.

59 For Annie Golding see *Cyclopaedia of New South Wales*; Beverley Kingston, 'Annie Mackenzie and Isabella Theresa Golding', *ADB* 1891−1939; Bruce Mitchell, *Teachers, Education and Politics: A History of Organizations of Public School Teachers in New South Wales*, UQP, Brisbane, 1975, pp. 25−6; *PSJ*, 1 February

1915, p. 15. She had long fought for superannuation justice for women—see *Transmitter*, 13 April 1895, p. 2; *PSJ*, June 1912, p. 4, April 1913, p. 3.

60 ibid., September 1911, pp. 3, 7, October, p. 3.; for activity on superannuation see *PSJ*, August 1912, p. 23.

61 For Belle Golding see Kingston; *Cyclopaedia of New South Wales*; *PSJ*, May 1922, p. 18.

62 For May Matthews see Lyn Brignell and Heather Radi, 'Susan May Matthews', *ADB* 1891—1939; *PSJ*, October 1915, p. 8; *Progressive Journal*, 7 August 1935, p. 5.

63 Scott, A2277, ff. 253a, 444—8.

64 *PSJ*, August 1912, pp. 8, 23, and December 1913, p. 13. For other organizations, private communication, E. L. Ellis, 9 January 1988 and Mrs S. C. Foote, 17 February 1988.

65 *PSJ*, October 1913, p. 25.

66 ibid., December 1913, p. 29.

67 ibid., January 1911, p. 1, November, p. 4, December, pp. 4, 25, April 1912, p. 12, July 1914, p. 7, August, pp. 2, 22—6, September, p. 11.

68 ibid., January 1914, pp. 23—4.

69 ibid., August 1914, pp. 22—6.

70 ibid., September 1914, p. 11.

71 ibid., July 1915, p. 16. See also May, pp. 2—5, June, pp. 3—5, July, pp. 2, 6, 9, 28, September, p. 12, October, p. 13, November, p. 7.

72 ibid., September 1915, p. 3, October, p. 4; November, pp. 6—7, December, pp. 4, 7, 18—22; *GG*, 20 October 1915, p. 6075.

73 *PSJ*, January 1916, pp. 3—6, 15, 22—4, February, p. 2, March, pp. 3, 5, 10.

74 ibid., April 1916, p. 5, May, pp. 3, 6, 14.

75 ibid., August 1916, pp. 4—20 esp. 18.

76 ibid., p. 20.

77 PSB *Report* 1915, V & P 1916, vol. IV, pp. 5—8, 21 September 1916. PSA response *PSJ*, November 1916, p. 7, December pp. 6, 11; women's comments p. 27.

78 ibid., November 1916, p. 7, December, p. 6.

79 ibid., March 1917, p. 32.

80 ibid., pp. 12—19, esp. 16.

81 ibid., May 1917, p. 39, referring *Sun*, 24 April.

82 *GG*, 10 August 1917, p. 4520; *PSJ*, September 1917, p. 5.

83 RCPS NSW, pp. 216—7.

84 *PSJ*, August 1917, p. 5.

85 ibid., May 1918, p. 6, July p. 9.

86 ibid., October 1917, p. 8, December, p. 41.

87 Evatt, pp. 348−50; Sawkins, pp. 18−23, esp. 21.
88 Industrial Arbitration Act, 23 December 1919; *PSJ*, April 1919, pp. 7−8, June, pp. 3−4.
89 Ibid., January 1920, pp. 3, 9, 12, 21, 23, 36, February, pp. 36−7; RCPS NSW, pp lxi, lxiv; for petition see V & P 1919, vol. III, p. 1201; for junior officers see *PSJ*, March 1920, pp. 5, 11−15, 27, May, pp. 23, 34. For a detailed account of the cost of living and public service salaries see PSB *Report* 1918−19, V & P 1920, 2nd sess., vol. IV, pp. 7−12.
90 *PSJ*, September 1920, p. 23, October, p. 10. Wearne wrote in 1924: '5 or 6 years ago I managed to form up a women's section...'. She makes no mention of the previous women's section dismantled in 1918 and portrays herself as a 'lone hand': 'my experience over and over again has been the same as the story of the 7 on the previous page [in 1907]. But if I peg away and get an increase, then it gives the others a precedent for appeals etc'; see Wearne to Booth. This version of events suggests a major rift amongst the women but there is no evidence to illuminate this further.
91 *PSJ*, July 1921, p. 43.
92 ibid., August 1921, pp. 4, 8−13, June 1922, pp. 37−46; PSB *Report* 1921−2, V & P 1922, vol. III, p. 6. For transcript of appeal see *PSJ*, April 1922, pp. 25−37.
93 For judgement see *NSW Industrial Reports* 1921, pp. 189−97, esp. 196−7; for abridged transcript *PSJ*, July 1921, pp. 33, 41−7.
94 ibid., September 1921, pp. 25−34.
95 J. M. Bennett and Martha Rutledge, 'Charles Gilbert Heydon and Louis Francis Heydon', *ADB* 1891−1939; John Rickard, *H. B. Higgins: The Rebel as Judge*, George Allen & Unwin, Sydney, 1984; Sawkins, p. 10; for a discussion of women's cases involving Heydon, Holman, Beeby see Ryan.
96 *NSW Arbitration Reports*, vol. 4, pp. 309−10, quoted Sawkins, p. 12.
97 *NSW Industrial Gazette*, September 1913, pp. 3−6, October, pp. 197−8, March 1914, pp. 100−49; Sawkins, esp. p. 23.
98 For a discussion with special reference to child endowment see Bettina Cass, 'Redistribution to Children and to Mothers; a History of Child Endowment and Family Allowances', in Cora V. Baldock and Bettina Cass (eds), *Women, Social Welfare and the State*, George Allen & Unwin, Sydney, 1983, pp. 54−84.
99 Sawkins, p. 39.
100 Ryan, pp. 162, 173.
101 ibid., title page quoting Beeby in Shop Assistant's case 6 June 1907.

102 See PSB *Report* 1919–20, V & P 1921, vol. III, pp. 15–16 for comparison of pre- and post-1919 salaries. Wearne wrote: 'the arbitration court came along with its man & wife & 2 children, and wiped out our work of a uniform living wage. The arbitration court is no good for the general body of women in the Service; we do better by negotiation with the Board; and I personally find that I do better as a 'lone hand'; see Wearne to Booth.
103 For a review of difficulties which does not acknowledge deskilling women see PSB *Report* 1923–4, V & P 1924, vol. I, p. 6.
104 PSB *Report* 1922–3, V & P 1923, vol. III, p. 9.
105 Jean Arnot, 'Employment of Women in the Civil Service', *PA*(Sydney) 5, 8, 1945, pp. 364–76, esp. 373; PSB *Report* 1924–5, V & P 1925–6, vol. I, p. 10.
106 PSB *Report* 1922–3, p. 3; see also *Report* 1924–5, p. 10.
107 *GG*, 1 July 1923, p. 3764.
108 PSB *Report* 1923–4, p. 15.
109 *PSJ*, March 1922, p. 8.
110 PSB *Report* 1928–9, V & P 1929–30, vol. III, p. 5.
111 Arnot, p. 373.
112 *PSJ*, January 1924, p. 166.
113 ibid., September 1924, p. 524.
114 ibid., November 1925, pp. 3–4, 11–15; *Red Tape*, February 1929, pp. 26–7.
115 ibid., November, pp. 268–70
116 ibid., p. 271, April 1930, p. 92; *Herself*, 17 October 1929, p. ii.
117 *Red Tape*, February 1930, p. 31.
118 ibid., April 1930, p. 92, May, p. 125, July, p. 168.

8 *Managing gender*

1 For law see *Articled Clerks' Journal*, 1889, 1892, 1895; Sir Thomas Bavin (ed.), *The Jubilee Book of the Law School of the University of Sydney 1890–1940*, Halstead Press, Sydney, 1940; J. M. Bennett (ed.), *A History of the New South Wales Bar*, Law Book Co., Sydney, 1969; S. Elliott Napier and E. Newton Daly, *The Genesis and Growth of Solicitors' Associations in New South Wales*, Law Book Co., Sydney, 1937; M. F. Hardie, 'Alexander Oliver', *ADB* 1851–1890; Sir George Houston Reid, *My Reminiscences*, Cassell, London, 1917, p. 172; Stuart Woodman, Lawyers in New South Wales 1856–1914: The Evolution of a Colonial Profession, unpubl. PhD thesis, ANU, 1979. The Medical Act 1898 penalized irregulars who advertised as registered doctors, and was supplemented by two Acts in 1900 giving the Medical Board the right to discipline its own members; the Public Health Act 1896 established regulatory machinery to ensure pure water supply,

sewerage, supervision of food preparation and vending, public cleanliness.

2 For the industrial system see R. B. Walker, 'Australia's Second Arbitration Act', *LH* 19, 1970, pp. 17−25, esp. 21−4; H. V. Evatt, *Australian Labor Leader: The Story of W. A. Holman and the Labour Movement*, Angus & Robertson, Sydney, 1940, pp. 134−6; S. F. Macintyre, 'Labour, Capital and Arbitration 1890−1920', in Brian W. Head (ed.), *State and Economy in Australia*, OUP, Melbourne, 1983, pp. 98−114; *NSW Industrial Gazette*, September 1913, pp. 3−6, October, pp. 197−8, March 1914, pp. 100−49; John Rickard, *Class and Politics: New South Wales, Victoria and the Early Commonwealth, 1890−1910*, ANU Press, Canberra, 1976, pp. 143−57; D. T. Sawkins, *The Living Wage in Australia*, MUP, 1933. For the health system see Brian Dickey, 'The Labor Government and Medical Services in NSW, 1910−1914', in Jill Roe (ed.), *Social Policy in Australia: Some Perspectives 1901−1975*, Cassell, Sydney, 1976, pp. 60−73; Claudia Thame, Health and the State: The Development of Collective Responsibility for Health Care in Australia in the First Half of the Twentieth Century, unpubl. PhD thesis, ANU, 1974. For ministers in professions see Evatt, *Holman*; Bede Nairn, 'Sir George Stephenson Beeby', 'John Daniel Fitzgerald', and 'Daniel Robert Hall', *ADB* 1891−1939.

3 Kerreen M. Reiger, *The Disenchantment of the Home: Modernizing the Australian Family 1880−1940*, OUP, Melbourne, 1985; Michael Roe, *Nine Australian Progressives: Vitalism in Bourgeois Social Thought 1890−1960*, UQP, Brisbane, 1984; Evan Willis, *Medical Dominance: The Division of Labour in Australian Health Care*, George Allen & Unwin, Sydney, 1983.

4 S. P. Hays, *Conservation and the Gospel of Efficiency*, Harvard University Press, 1959, p. 3; G. R. Searle, *The Quest for National Efficiency: a Study in British Politics and Political Thought, 1899−1914*, University of California Press, Berkeley, 1971, pp. 85−6.

5 Harry Braverman, *Labor and Monopoly Capitalism: The Degradation of Work in the Twentieth Century*, Monthly Review Press, New York, 1974; Samuel Haber, *Efficiency and Uplift: Scientific Management in the Progressive Era 1890−1920*, Chicago University Press, 1964; Michael Roe, 'Efficiency: the Fascist Dynamic in American Progressivism', *Teaching History* 8, 2, 1974, pp. 38−55; Frederick Winslow Taylor, *Scientific Management*, Harper, NY, 1947 [1911].

6 B. R. Wise, *The Labour Question; or, Social Revolt and its Causes*, Sydney, c. 1890; and 'What Parliament Can Do For Labour', *Sydney Quarterly Magazine*, 8 September 1891, p. 221.

7 *Bulletin*, 10 September 1887, quoted Woodman, p. 229.

8 Bavin; Reid; Woodman, esp. pp. 223, 230, 251−3. For younger lawyers see Verity Burgmann, *'In Our Time': Socialism and the*

Rise of Labor, 1885–1905, George Allen & Unwin, Sydney, 1985; Evatt, pp. 156–8; L. F. Fitzhardinge, 'William Morris Hughes', and Nairn, 'Beeby', 'Fitzgerald', and 'Hall', *ADB* 1891–1931; Philippa Poole, *The Diaries of Ethel Turner*, Lansdowne, Sydney, 1979 (for Ethel Turner's husband, H. R. Curlewis).

9 *PD* 1916, pp. 1995–8, 21 September. For Holman's socialism see Evatt, pp. 81–9, 118–23; *PD*, 1900, p. 2232, 23 August; Rickard, *Class and Politics*, p. 278; Roe, p. 253.

10 Burgmann, pp. 55, 58–62; Evatt, pp. 159–62, 232–3, 297–8; *PD*, 1900, p. 641 ff.; Roe, p. 19; Nairn, 'Beeby'; Joan Rydon and R. N. Spann, *New South Wales Politics 1901–1910*, Cheshire, Melbourne, 1962, pp. 96–7; Sawkins. Edna Ryan, *Two-Thirds of a Man: Women and Arbitration in New South Wales 1902–08*, Hale & Iremonger, Sydney, 1984, details several cases involving Holman and Beeby.

11 Coghlan papers, *passim*.

12 R. W. Connell, *Gender and Power*, Stanford University Press, 1987, pp. 96 ff. discusses the ability of the state to give consistency to the gender order. For domestic science see Noeline Kyle, *Her Natural Destiny: The Education of Women in New South Wales*, UNSWP, Sydney 1986; for arbitration see Ryan. The role of women in the efficiency movement has barely been explored; J. Godden, Philanthropy and Women's Sphere, Sydney, 1870 to circa 1900, unpubl. PhD thesis, Macquarie University, 1983, and Jan Kociumbus, Children and Society in New South Wales and Victoria 1860–1914, unpubl. PhD thesis, University of Sydney, 1983 discuss upper class ladies' loss of power over the women's sphere and their subordination to and complicity with male professionals at the beginning of the period; Michael Roe makes frequent reference to Dr Mary Booth as one of the female professionals involved in the efficiency movement, but does not discuss her activities in detail; see also J. I. Roe, 'Mary Booth', *ADB* 1891–1939.

13 Dickey; Bede Nairn, 'Fred Flowers', *ADB* 1891–1939. For a detailed discussion see Desley Deacon, 'Taylorism in the Home: The Medical Profession, the Infant Welfare Movement and the Deskilling of Women', *ANZJS* 21, 2, pp. 161–73.

14 N. G. Butlin, A. Barnard and J. J. Pincus, *Government and Capitalism: Public and Private Choice in Twentieth Century Australia*, George Allen & Unwin, Sydney, 1982, p. 19; T. A. Coghlan, 'Is It a Failure?', *Bulletin*, 14 December 1889, p. 6, *Childbirth in New South Wales: a Study in Statistics*, Government Printer, Sydney, 1900, *The Decline of the Birth-rate of New South Wales and Other Phenomena of Childbirth: an Essay in Statistics*, Government Printer, Sydney, 1903, *Labour and Industry in Australia: From the First*

Settlement in 1788 to the Establishment of the Commonwealth in 1901, OUP, London, 1918, p. 2009—10; Neville Hicks, *'This Sin and Scandal': Australia's Population Debate 1891—1911*, ANU Press, Canberra, 1978; Rosemary Pringle, 'Octavius Beale and the Ideology of the Birthrate', *Refractory Girl* 3, 1973, pp. 19—27; Royal Commission on the Decline of the Birth-rate and the Mortality of Infants in New South Wales, *Report*, vol. I, V & P 1904, vol IV, pp. 791—956; *Wealth and Progress 1898—9*, pp. 589, 614. This interest was not shared by all levels of government and population; see Judith Allen, 'Octavius Beale Reconsidered: Infanticide, Babyfarming and Abortion in NSW 1880—1939', in Sydney Labour History Group (eds.), *What Rough Beast? The State and Social Order in Australian History*, George Allen & Unwin, Sydney, 1982, pp. 111—29.

15 J. B. Barrett, *IMJA*, 20 February 1898, pp 94—6, 20 January 1901, p. 26, presidential address to the Medical Society of Victoria; A. Jeffreys Wood, 20 March 1908, pp. 128—34.

16 *CPP* 1929, vol. II, p. 1281.

17 'Women' and 'mothers' displace 'parents' rapidly in the first ten years of the twentieth century; then the almost exclusive focus is on 'mother'.

18 See W. G. Armstrong, 'The Infant Welfare Movement in Australia', *MJA*, 28 October 1939, pp. 641—8, 'Some Lessons from the Statistics of Infantile Mortality in Sydney', in *Transactions of the Seventh Session of the Australasian Medical Congress*, Adelaide, 1905, pp. 385-95; Claudia Thame, Health and the State, and 'William George Armstrong', *ADB* 1891—1939; MOH, *Report* 1903 p. 15; *Report* 1904, p. 15; *Report* 1910, p. 13; *Report* 1913, p. 23; DGPH, *Report* 1915—16, p. 44, 1925, p. 2; *AMG*, 1914, pp. 594—5; *MJA*, 24 April 1915, p. 384, 22 January 1916, pp. 83—4, 22 May, p. 417; 25 November, pp. 462—3; 19 January 1918, pp. 54—5; 23 November p. 436; 13 February 1926, pp. 191—2; 27 August 1927, pp. 295—6, 2 May 1964, pp. 695—6; Department of Trade and Customs Committee Concerning Causes of Death and Invalidity in the Commonwealth, *Report on Infantile Mortality*, CPP, 1917—19, vol. V, pp. 613—52; H. Main and V. Scantlebury, *Report to the Minister of Public Health on the Welfare of Women and Children*, VPP, 1926, vol. II, pp. 32—52; Dame Janet M. Campbell, *Report on Maternal and Child Welfare in Australia*, CPP, 1929—31, vol. II; Royal Commission on Health, *Report*, CPP 1926—8, vol. IV, pp. 1247—301

19 DGPH, *Report* 1927, p. 46; Thame, pp. 222—6.

20 Bonuses for Parentage Bill, introd. Arthur Griffith, *PD*, 1909, 2nd. sess., pp. 1929—51, 14 September; W. G. Spence, *The Child, the Home, and the State*, The Worker Print, Sydney, 1908.

The Labor programme at its most idealistic was concerned 'to work out an entire new system of relations between men and women, that will be free from servitude, aggression, provocation, or parasitism'; see Robert Howe, *CPD*, 1912, p. 3439 quoting H. G. Wells.

21 Maternity Allowances Act; see *CPD*, 1912, pp. 6, 3286–616 *passim*. For other schemes see *AMG*, 1908, p. 383; 1909, pp. 155, 623; 1910, pp. 277–80, 432–3; 1912, p. 673; *AMJ*, 1910, pp. 263, 309–10; *IMJA*, 1908, pp. 260–77, 322.

22 MOH, *Report* 1903, p. 15.

23 *AMG*, 25 January 1901, pp. 43–4, 20 January 1904, p. 24, 20 May, p. 233, 20 October 1908, p. 584, 21 December, pp. 675–6, 6 January 1912, pp. 13–14, 2 March, pp. 218–9, 15 March 1913, pp. 34–5.

24 *MJA*, 25 November 1916, p. 45.

25 DGPH, *Report*, 1914–15, p. 10.

26 Michael Roe, p. 96.

27 J. S. C. Elkington, *Infant Mortality and Its Prevention*, Government Printer, Hobart, 1909, pp. 10–12; DGPH, *Report* 1911, p. 13, 1914–15, p. 47, 1915–16, p. 44.

28 For a discussion of women's response see Kerreen Reiger, 'Mothering De-skilled? Australian Childrearing and the Experts in the Twentieth Century', paper presented at ANZAAS Congress, Canberra, 1984, pp. 16–21.

29 DGPH *Report*, 1927, pp. 6, 46. This characterization was kept alive by a struggle between politicians, paediatricians, voluntary associations and public health officials for control; e.g. campaign against Commonwealth maternity allowance—see *AMJ*, 29 June 1912, p. 568, 13 July, p. 585, *MJA*, 29 May 1920, p. 509, 3 June 1922, pp. 610–12, 29 July, p. 141, 5 August, p. 161, 20 December 1924, pp. 645 ff., 27 December, pp. 673–7, 681–2, 29 August 1925, p. 243, 12 September, pp. 309–12; *CPD* 1912, pp. 3333, 3337, 3414, 3433; Department of Trade and Customs, pp. 1013–14; Royal Commission on Health, p. 1281.

30 Cf. Desley Deacon, 'The Employment of Women in the Commonwealth Public Service: the Creation and Reproduction of a Dual Labour Market', *AJPA* 41, 3, 1982, pp. 232–50; G. C. Morrison, *Report on the Question of Equal Pay for Equal Work in the Department of Public Instruction*, *VPP*, 1914, vol. II, pp. 355–76.

31 V & P 1911–12, vol. II, p. 1137.

32 *AMG*, 15 March 1913, p. 235.

33 6 January 1912, pp. 13–14.

34 *AMG*, 28 February 1914, p. 189; see also M. King. *Truby King the Man. A Biography*, Allen & Unwin, London, 1948.

35 *AMG*, 2 March 1912, p. 219.

36 Heather Radi, '1920–1929', in F. K. Crowley (ed.), *A New History of Australia*, William Heinemann, Melbourne, 1974, pp. 357–414, esp. 396.

37 Michael Roe, pp. 222, 230. See also Kociumbus, pp. 236–48.

38 J. S. Baker, *Communicators and Their First Trade Unions: A History of the Telegraphist and Postal Clerk Unions of Australia*, Union of Postal Clerks and Telegraphists, Sydney, 1980; 'Louisa Margaret Dunkley', *ADB* 1891–1939.

39 Deacon, 'The Employment of Women'.

Select bibliography

Primary sources

A Official Publications

New South Wales

Industrial Arbitration Reports
Industrial Gazette
Parliamentary Debates
Parliamentary Papers, in particular:
> *Blue Book* 1857–94.
> Board of Inquiry in Connection with 'Louisa', *Report*, 1858–9.
> Board of Inquiry into the Post Office Department, *Report*, 1862.
> Board of Inquiry into Retrenchment in Public Expenditure, *Report*, 1865–6.
> Civil Service Board, *Report*, 1885–94.
> Coghlan, T. A., *Reports under the Census and Industrial Returns Act of 1891*, 1891–2.
> ——, *General Report on the Eleventh Census of New South Wales*, Government Printer, Sydney, 1894.
> ——, *Childbirth in New South Wales: a Study in Statistics*, Government Printer, Sydney, 1900.
> ——, *The Decline of the Birth-rate of New South Wales and Other Phenomena of Childbirth: an Essay in Statistics*, Government Printer, Sydney, 1903.
> *Correspondence Concerning Official Post Offices*, 1862.
> *Correspondence Relating to Retrenchment in Public Expenditure*, 1865–6.
> *Correspondence Respecting Removal of W. A. Duncan, Esq. from the Office of Collector of Customs; Further Correspondence; and Correspondence Respecting Removal of Messrs Berney and Jones, and Reinstatement of Mr Duncan*, 1868–9.

Country Postmasters, 1858.

Department of Labour and Industry. Board of Trade, *Transcript of Proceedings of the Inquiry into the Cost of Living of Adult Female Workers*, 1918.

Director-General of Public Health, *Annual Report*, 1913–1939.

——, 'Brief Historical Review of Health Problems and Sanitary Progress in New South Wales, with Especial Reference to the Period 1898–1933', *Annual Report* 1933, p. 115.

Medical Officer of Health, Metropolitan Combined Sanitary Districts, *Annual Report* [from 1913 published as part of *Annual Report* of Director-General of Public Health].

Postmaster-General, *Annual Report*

Public Service Board, *Annual Report*

Public Service Inquiry Commission, *Report on General Post Office, Money Order Office and Electric Telegraph Department*, 1890.

Public Service List, published from 1898.

Return of all the Deputy Postmasters and Postmistresses in New South Wales, 1862.

Royal Commission of Inquiry into Civil Service (see Public Service Inquiry Commission).

Royal Commission of Inquiry into the New South Wales Public Service, *Report and Minutes of Evidence*, 1894–5.

Royal Commission on the Decline of the Birth-rate and on the Mortality of Infants in New South Wales, *Report*, 1904.

Royal Commission on the Public Service of New South Wales, *First Sessional Report*, 1918.

Select Committee on Administration of Justice and Conduct of Official Business in Country Districts, *Progress Report*, 1856.

Select Committee on the Civil Service, *Progress Report*, 1872.

——, *Report and Minutes of Evidence*, 1872–3.

Select Committee on the Customs Department, *Report*, 1858.

Select Committee on Management of Central Post Office, *Report*, 1862.

Select Committee on the Post Office, 1851, 2nd sess..

Select Committee on Retrenchment in the Public Expenditure, *Progress Report*, 1858.

Statistical Register, published from 1850.

The Official Year Book of N. S. W., published from 1904–5.

The Wealth and Progress of New South Wales, 1886–87 to 1900–01.

Queensland

Board of Inquiry into Defalcations in the General Post Office, *Report* and *Papers and Correspondence*, 1865.

Select Committee on Government Departments, *Final Report*, 1860.

Select Committee on Internal Organisation and General Management of the Post Office and Money Order Department, *Report and Minutes of Evidence*, 1865.

Victoria

Hayter, Henry Heylyn, *Census of Victoria* 1881, *General Report*, Government Printer, Melbourne, 1883.
——, *Census of Victoria* 1891, *General Report*, Government Printer, Melbourne, 1893.

Other

Elkington, J. S. C., *Infant Mortality and Its Prevention*, Government Printer, Hobart, 1909.
England and Wales. *Census Reports* 1861–1891.
Great Britain. *Census Report* 1851.
Scotland. *Census Reports* 1861–1891 (in *British Parliamentary Papers*).

B Manuscripts

Sir Timothy A. Coghlan papers, ANL MS 6335; these include correspondence, cuttings and reviews, and two major biographical sources:
- Coghlan, Austin Francis and Eden Willats, 'Reminiscences', transcription of tape recording by Coghlan's surviving children, 1969.
- Coghlan, T. A., 'Autobiography', a short memoir written by Coghlan of his life until about 1905.

Fry family papers, ML MS 1159/2.
Rose Scott papers, ML MSS 38 and A2277.
Anzac Fellowship of Women papers, ANL MS 2864.

C Journals and Newspapers

Australasian Medical Gazette, published 1882–1914, Sydney.
Bulletin, published from 1880.
Daily Telegraph, published from 1879.
Dawn, published 1888–1905.
Medical Journal of Australia, published from 1914, Sydney.
Public Service Journal, published 1900–1926, then continued as *Red Tape*
Red Tape, formerly *Public Service Journal*, published from July 1927.
Sydney Morning Herald.
Town and Country Journal.
Transmitter, published from 1891.

References

Australian Dictionary of Biography, 1788–1850, 1851–1890 and 1891–1939, Melbourne University Press.

Brabazon's New South Wales General Town Directory and Advertiser 1843.

Cyclopaedia of New South Wales, Angus & Robertson, Sydney 1949.

Connolly, C. N., *Biographical Register of the New South Wales Parliament 1856–1901*, ANU Press, Canberra, 1983.

Daniels, Kay, Mary Murnane and Anne Picot (eds), *Women in Australia: an Annotated Guide to Records Edited for the National Research Program*, vol. II, Australian Government Publishing Service, Canberra, 1977.

Hughes, Colin A. and B. D. Graham, *A Handbook of Australian Government and Politics 1890–1964*, ANU Press, Canberra, 1968.

Radi, Heather, Peter Spearritt and Elizabeth Hinton, *Biographical Register of New South Wales Parliamentarians 1901–1970*, ANU Press, Canberra, 1979.

Contemporary books and pamphlets

Blacket, Wilfred, *May it Please Your Honour*, Cornstalk Publishing Co., Sydney, 1927.

Coghlan, T. A., *Labour and Industry in Australia: From the First Settlement in 1788 to the Establishment of the Commonwealth in 1901*, Oxford University Press, London, 1918.

Hancock, W. K., *Australia*, Benn, London, 1930.

Higgins, Henry Bournes, *A New Province for Law and Order*, Constable, Sydney, 1922.

Reid, Sir George Houston, *My Reminiscences*, Cassell, London, 1917.

Sawkins, D. T., *The Living Wage in Australia*, Melbourne University Press, 1933.

Spence, W. G., *The Child, the Home, and the State*, The Worker Print, Sydney, 1908.

Wise, B. R., *The Labour Question; or, Social Revolt and its Causes*, Sydney, c.1890.

Contemporary articles

Armstrong, W. G., 'Some Lessons from the Statistics of Infantile Mortality in Sydney', in *Transactions of the Seventh Session of the Australasian Medical Congress*, Adelaide, 1905, pp. 385–95.

——, 'The Establishment of a Central Health Authority in New South Wales', *Medical Journal of Australia*, 13 March 1937, pp. 400–5.

——, 'The Infant Welfare Movement in Australia', *Medical Journal of Australia*, 28 October 1939, pp. 641–8.

Coghlan, T. A., 'Deaths in Childbirth in New South Wales', *Journal of the Royal Statistical Society* 61, 3, September 1898.

Coghlan, T. A. ['Peter Barkis'], 'The True Basis of Exchange: A

Correction of Mr W. H. Traill's Theories I', *Daily Telegraph*, 1 June 1889, p. 9,

——, 'The True Basis of Exchange: A Correction of Mr W. H. Traill's Theories II', *Daily Telegraph*, 8 June 1889, p. 9.

——, 'The True Basis of Exchange: Labour and Capital', *Daily Telegraph*, 22 June 1889, p. 9.

——, 'The True Basis of Exchange: Money as a Standard of Value', *Daily Telegraph*, 6 July 1889, p. 9.

—— 'Social Economics: The Theory of Wages I', *Daily Telegraph*, 13 July 1889, p.9.

—— 'Social Economics: The Theory of Wages II', *Daily Telegraph*, 7 September 1889, p. 9.

—— 'Social Economics: Henry George's Theory of Wages', *Daily Telegraph*, 14 September 1889, p. 9.

—— ['Henry Siebel'], 'The Reign of Necessity', *Bulletin*, 5 October 1889, p. 6.

——, 'A Lesson from the Leper', *Bulletin*, 12 October 1889, pp. 6–7.

——, 'Fashions in Suicide', *Bulletin*, 19 October 1889, p. 6.

——, 'Drinking—One of the Fine Arts', *Bulletin*, 26 October 1889, pp. 6–7.

——, 'Material Prosperity and Political Wellbeing', *Bulletin*, 2 November 1889, pp. 6–7.

——, 'Profit-Sharing', *Bulletin*, 16 November 1889, p.6.

——, 'What Hanging has Done for Australia', *Bulletin*, 23 November 1889, pp. 6–7.

——, 'The Criminal Neurosis', *Bulletin*, 30 November 1889, p. 6.

——, 'Is It a Failure?', *Bulletin*, 14 December 1889, p. 6.

——, 'The Socialism of Christ', *Bulletin*, 28 December 1889, p. 5.

——, 'Money', *Bulletin*, 4 January 1890, p. 6.

——, 'The New Panacea', *Bulletin*, 18 January 1890, p. 6.

——, 'The Toleration of Adverse Opinion', *Bulletin*, 8 February 1890, p. 6.

——, 'The Future of New South Wales Boys', *Bulletin*, 3 March 1890, p. 6.

——, 'The Morality of the Single-Tax', *Bulletin*, 17 May 1890, p. 6.

Kilminster, G., 'Fifty Years Ago III', *Public Service Journal*, November 1918, p. 9.

Lino, 'Women Who Work. Hard Lot of Farmers' Wives. They Describe Their Lives', *Argus*, 13 January 1902, pp. 5–6.

Manning, May L., 'The Industrial Employment of Women, Thoughts Suggested by the Recent Exhibition of Women's Work in Melbourne and Sydney', *Centennial Magazine* 1, 6, 1889, 408–11.

Randle-Hancock, H., 'Shorthand as an Art', *Australian Journal of Education*, 2 November 1903, p. 14.

Wise, B. R., 'What Parliament Can Do for Labour', *Sydney Quarterly Magazine*, 8 September 1891, p. 221.

Worrall, Ralph, 'The Necessity for Organization in the Profession', *Intercolonial Medical Journal of Australasia*, 20 December 1909, pp. 585–98.

Current articles and chapters

Allen, Judith, 'Breaking into the Public Sphere: The Struggle for Women's Citizenship in NSW 1890–1920', in J. Mackinolty and H. Radi (eds), *In Pursuit of Justice: Australian Women and the Law 1788–1978*, Hale & Iremonger, Sydney, 1979, pp. 107–17.

Althusser, Louis, 'Ideology and Ideological State Apparatuses (Notes Towards an Investigation)', in *Lenin and Philosophy and Other Essays*, Monthly Review Press, New York, 1971, transl. Ben Brewster, pp. 127–86.

Arndt, H. W., 'A Pioneer of National Income Estimates', *Economic Journal* 59, 1949, pp. 236–45.

Arnot, Jean, 'Employment of Women in the Civil Service', *Public Administration* (Sydney) 5, 8, 1945, pp. 364–76.

Aron, Cindy S., '"To Barter Their Souls for Gold": Female Clerks in Federal Government Offices, 1862–1890', *Journal of American History* 67, 4, 1981, pp. 835–53.

Atkinson, Alan, 'Postage in the South-East', *Push from the Bush* 5, 1979, pp. 19–30.

——, 'Women Publicans in 1838', *Push from the Bush* 8, 1980, pp. 88–106.

Baldock, Cora V., 'Public Policies and the Paid Work of Women', in Cora V. Baldock and Bettina Cass (eds.), *Women, Social Welfare and the State*, George Allen & Unwin, Sydney, 1983, pp. 20–53.

Barrett, M., 'Rethinking Women's Oppression: A Reply to Brenner and Ramas', *New Left Review* 146, 1984, pp. 123–8.

Barron, R. D. and G. M. Norris, 'Sexual Divisions and the Dual Labour Market', in Diana Leonard Barker and Sheila Allen (eds), *Dependence and Exploitation in Work and Marriage*, Longman, London, 1976, pp. 47–69.

Bland, Lucy, Trisha McCabe and Frank Mort, 'Sexuality and Reproduction: Three Instances', in Michèle Barrett, Phillip Corrigan, Annette Kuhn and Janet Wolff (eds), *Ideology and Cultural Production*, Croom Helm, London, 1979, pp. 78–111.

Block, Fred, 'Beyond Corporate Liberalism', *Social Problems* 24, 3, 1977, pp. 352–61.

——, 'The Ruling Class Does Not Rule: Notes on the Marxist Theory of the State', *Socialist Revolution* 33, 1977, pp. 6–28.

——, 'Beyond Relative Autonomy: State Managers as Historical Subjects', *Socialist Register*, 1980, pp. 227–42.

Bose, Christine, 'Household Resources and U.S. Women's Work: Factors Affecting Gainful Employment at the Turn of the Century', *American Sociological Review* 49, 4, 1984, pp. 474—90.

Brenner, J., and Maria Ramas, 'Rethinking Women's Oppression', *New Left Review* 144, 1984, pp. 33—71.

Butlin, N. G., 'Colonial Socialism in Australia, 1860—1900', in Hugh G. H. Aitken (ed.), *The State and Economic Growth*, New York, Social Science Research Council, 1959, pp. 26—78.

Cass, Bettina, 'Redistribution to Children and to Mothers; a History of Child Endowment and Family Allowances' and 'Population Policies and Family Policies: State Construction of Domestic Life', in Cora V. Baldock and Bettina Cass (eds), *Women, Social Welfare and the State*, George Allen & Unwin, Sydney, 1983, pp. 54—84, 164—85.

Clegg, Stewart, 'The Policies of Public Sector Administration', in Alexander Kouzmin (ed.), *Public Sector Administration: New Perspectives*, Melbourne, Longman Cheshire, 1983, pp. 1—36.

Connell, R. W., 'Complexities of Fury Leave...A Critique of the Althusserian Approach to Class', 'Crisis Tendencies in Patriarchy and Capitalism' and 'Intellectuals and Intellectual Work', in *Which Way is Up? Essays on Sex, Class and Culture*, George Allen & Unwin, Sydney, 1983, pp. 98—139, 33—49, 231—54.

Davison, Graeme, 'Sydney and the Bush: an Urban Context for the Australian Legend', *Historical Studies*, vol. 18, no. 71, 1978, pp. 191—209.

Deacon, Desley, 'The Employment of Women in the Commonwealth Public Service: the Creation and Reproduction of a Dual Labour Market', *Australian Journal of Public Administration* 41, 3, 1982, pp. 232—50.

——, 'Women, Bureaucracy and the Dual Labour Market: an Historical Analysis', in Alexander Kouzmin (ed.), *Public Sector Administration: New Perspectives*, Longman Cheshire, Melbourne, 1983, pp. 165—82.

——, 'Taylorism in the Home: The Medical Profession, the Infant Welfare Movement and the Deskilling of Women', *Australian and New Zealand Journal of Sociology* 21, 2, 1985, pp. 161—73.

——, 'Political Arithmetic: The Nineteenth Century Australian Census and the Construction of the Dependent Woman', *SIGNS: Journal of Women in Culture and Society* 11, 1, 1985, pp. 27—47.

Dickey, Brian, 'The Labor Government and Medical Services in N.S.W., 1910—1914', *Historical Studies*, vol. 12, no. 48, 1967, pp. 541—55.

Dowse, Sara, 'The Women's Movement's Fandango with the State: the Movement's Role in Public Policy Since 1972', in Cora V. Baldock and Bettina Cass (eds), *Women, Social Welfare and the State*, George Allen & Unwin, Sydney, 1983, pp. 201—22.

Ehrenreich, Barbara and John Ehrenreich, 'The Professional–
    Managerial Class', in Pat Walker (ed.), *Between Labor and Capital*,
    South End Press, Boston, 1979, pp. 5–45.
Fletcher, Brian, 'Administrative Reform in New South Wales under
    Governor Darling', *Australian Journal of Public Administration* 38,
    3, 1977, pp. 246–62.
Fry, E. C., 'Review Article: Labour and Industry in Australia',
    Historical Studies 14, 55, 1970, pp. 430–9.
Game, Ann and Rosemary Pringle, 'Women and Class in Australia:
    Feminism and the Labor Government', in Graeme Duncan (ed.),
    Critical Essays in Australian Politics, Edward Arnold, Melbourne,
    1978, pp. 114–34.
Godden, Judith, 'Portrait of a Lady: A Decade in the Life of Helen
    Fell (1849–1935)' in Margaret Bevage, Margaret James and Carmel
    Shute (eds), *Worth Her Salt: Women at Work in Australia*, Hale &
    Iremonger, Sydney, 1982, pp. 33–48.
Gould, A, 'The Salaried Middle Class in the Corporatist Welfare
    State', *Policy and Politics* 9, 1980, pp. 401–18.
Grimshaw, Patricia and Graham Willett, 'Women's History and
    Family History: an Exploration of Colonial Family Structure', in
    Norma Grieve and Patricia Grimshaw (eds), *Australian Women:
    Feminist Perspectives*, Oxford University Press, Melbourne, 1981,
    pp. 134–55.
——, Charles Fahey, Susan Janson and Tom Griffiths, 'Families
    and Selection in Colonial Horsham', in Patricia Grimshaw, Chris
    McConville and Ellen McEwen (eds), *Families in Colonial Australia*,
    George Allen & Unwin, Sydney, 1985, pp. 118–37.
Hartmann, Heidi, 'Capitalism, Patriarchy and Job Segregation by
    Sex', in Z. Eisenstein (ed.), *Capitalism, Patriarchy and the Case For
    Socialist Feminism*, Monthly Review Press, New York, 1979, pp.
    206–47.
——, 'The Unhappy Marriage of Marxism and Feminism: Towards
    a More Progressive Union', in Lydia Sargent (ed.), *Women and
    Revolution: A Discussion of the Unhappy Marriage of Marxism and
    Feminism*, South End Press, Boston, 1981, pp. 1–41.
Humphries, Jane, 'Class Struggle and the Persistence of the Working
    Class Family', in Alice H. Amsdem (ed.), *The Economics of Women
    and Work*, Penguin, Harmondsworth, 1980, pp. 140–65.
Johnston, T. J., 'The State and the Professions: Peculiarities of the
    British', in Anthony Giddens and Gavin Mackenzie (eds), *Social
    Class and the Division of Labour*, Cambridge University Press, 1982,
    pp. 186–220.
Jordens, Ann-Mari, 'Rose Scott: Making a Beginning', in James
    Walter and Raija Nugent (eds), *Biographers at Work*, Institute for
    Modern Biography, Griffith University, Brisbane, 1984, pp. 26–35.
Knight, Kenneth W., 'Patronage and the 1894 Royal Commission of

Enquiry into the New South Wales Public Service', *Australian Journal of Politics and History* 7, 2, 1961, pp. 166−85.

Lake, Marilyn, 'The Politics of Respectability: Identifying the Masculinist Context', *Historical Studies* 22, 86, 1986, pp. 117−31.

Lamb, P. N., 'Geoffrey Eagar and the Colonial Treasury of New South Wales', *Australian Economic Papers* 1, 1, 1962, pp. 24−41.

——, 'Early Overseas Borrowing by the New South Wales Government', *Business Archives and History* 4, 1, 1964, pp. 44−62.

——, 'Crown Land Policy and Government Finance in New South Wales, 1856−1900', *Australian Economic History Review* 7, 1, 1967, pp. 38−68.

Loveday, Peter, 'Patronage and Politics in New South Wales 1856−70', *Public Administration* 18, 4, 1959, pp. 341−58.

McCuskey, Claire, 'Women in the Victorian Post Office', in Margaret Bevage, Margaret James and Carmel Shute (eds), *Worth Her Salt: Women at Work in Australia*, Hale & Iremonger, Sydney, 1982, pp. 49−61.

Macintyre, Stuart, 'Labour, Capital and Arbitration 1890−1920', in Brian W. Head (ed.), *State and Economy in Australia*, Oxford University Press, Melbourne, 1983, pp. 98−114.

MacKinnon, Catharine A., 'Feminism, Marxism, Method, and the State: Toward Feminist Jurisprudence', *SIGNS: Journal of Women in Culture and Society* 8, 4, 1983, pp. 635−58.

Mansfield, Bruce, 'The Background to Radical Republicanism in New South Wales in the Eighteen-Eighties', *Historical Studies* 5, 20, 1953, pp. 338−48.

——, 'The State as Employer: An Early Twentieth Century Discussion', *Australian Journal of Politics and History* 3, 2, 1958.

Markey, Ray, 'Women and Labour, 1880−1930', in Elizabeth Windschuttle (ed.), *Women, Class and History: Feminist Perspectives on Australia 1788−1978*, Fontana, Sydney, 1980, pp. 83−111.

——, 'The ALP and the Emergence of a National Social Policy, 1880−1910', in Richard Kennedy (ed.), *Australian Welfare History: Critical Essays*, Macmillan, Melbourne, 1982, pp. 103−37.

Matthews, Jill Julius, 'The Proletarian's Wife', *Politics* 18, 2, 1983, pp. 104−7.

——, 'Education for Femininity: Domestic Arts Education in South Australia', *Labour History* 45, 1983, pp. 30−53.

Nichol, W, 'Women in the Trade Union Movement in NSW 1890−1900', *Labour History* 36, 1979, pp. 18−30.

Orloff, Ann Shola and Theda Skocpol, 'Why Not Equal Protection? Explaining the Politics of Public Spending in Britain, 1900−1911, and the United States, 1880s−1920', *American Sociological Review* 49, 6, 1984, pp. 726−50.

Porter, Paige, 'Social Policy, Education and Women', in Cora V. Baldock and Bettina Cass (eds), *Women, Social Welfare and the*

State, George Allen & Unwin, Sydney, 1983, pp. 246—61.

Poulantzas, Nicos, 'The Problem of the Capitalist State', in Robin Blackburn (ed.), *Ideology in Social Science: Readings in Critical Social Theory*, Fontana, Glasgow, 1972, pp. 238—62.

Pringle, Rosemary, 'Octavius Beale and the Ideology of the Birthrate', *Refractory Girl* 3, 1973, pp. 19—27.

Radi, Heather, '1920—1929', in F. K. Crowley (ed.), *A New History of Australia*, William Heinemann, Melbourne, 1974, pp. 357—414.

Reekie, Gail, 'Female Office Workers in Western Australia, 1895—1920: The Process of Feminization and Patterns of Consciousness', in Lenore Layman (ed.), *The Workplace (Time Remembered* Special Issue) 5, Murdoch University, 1982, pp. 1—35.

Rickard, John, 'The Middle Class: What is to be Done,' *Historical Studies* 19, 76, 1981, pp. 446—53.

Roe, Jill, 'The End is Where We Start From: Women and Welfare Since 1901', in Cora V. Baldock and Bettina Cass (eds), *Women, Social Welfare and the State*, George Allen & Unwin, Sydney, 1983, pp. 1—19.

Roe, Michael, 'Efficiency: The Fascist Dynamic in American Progressivism', *Teaching History* 8, 2, 1974, pp. 38—55.

Ross, George, 'Marxism and the New Middle Classes: French Critiques', *Theory and Society* 5, 2, 1978, pp. 163—90.

Ryan, Penny and Tim Rowse, 'Women, Arbitration and the Family', in Ann Curthoys, Susan Eade and Peter Spearritt (eds), *Women at Work*, Society for the Study of Australian History, Canberra, 1975, pp. 15—30.

Skocpol, Theda, 'Political Response to Capitalist Crisis: Neo-Marxist Theories of the State and the New Deal', *Politics and Society* 10, 2, 1980, pp. 155—202.

——, 'Bringing the State Back in', in Peter B. Evans, Dietrich Rueschmeyer and Theda Skocpol, *Bringing the State Back In: Strategies of Analysis in Current Research*, Cambridge University Press, New York, 1986.

Whelan, Dominica, 'Women and the Arbitration System', *Journal of Australian Political Economy* 4, 1979, pp. 54—60.

Wurth, W. C., 'The Public Service Board of New South Wales Since 1895', *Journal of the Royal Australian Historical Society* 45, 6, 1960, pp. 289—313.

Current books

Abercrombie, Nicholas and John Urry, *Capital, Labour and the Middle Classes*, George Allen & Unwin, London, 1983.

Alford, Katrina, *Production or Reproduction? An Economic History of Women in Australia, 1788–1850*, Oxford University Press, Melbourne, 1984.

Aron, Cindy Sondik, *Ladies and Gentlemen of the Civil Service: Middle-Class Workers in Victorian America*, Oxford University Press, New York, 1987.

Baker, J. S., *Communicators and Their First Trade Unions: A History of the Telegraphist and Postal Clerk Unions of Australia*, Union of Postal Clerks and Telegraphists, Sydney, 1980.

Barrett, Michèle, *Women's Oppression Today: Problems in Marxist Feminist Analysis*, Verso, London, 1980.

Berlant, J. L., *Profession and Monopoly: A Study of Medicine in the United States and Great Britain*, University of California Press, Berkeley, 1975.

Braverman, Harry, *Labor and Monopoly Capitalism: The Degradation of Work in the Twentieth Century*, Monthly Review Press, New York, 1974.

Bruce-Briggs, B. (ed.), *The New Class?* Transaction Books, New Brunswick, NJ, 1979.

Burgmann, Verity, *'In Our Time': Socialism and the Rise of Labor, 1885–1905*, George Allen & Unwin, Sydney, 1985.

Butlin, Noel, *Investment in Australian Economic Development 1861–1900*, Cambridge University Press, 1964.

Carchedi, G., *On the Economic Identification of Social Classes*, Routledge and Kegan Paul, London, 1977.

Cockburn, Cynthia, *Brothers: Male Dominance and Technological Change*, Pluto, London, 1983.

Cohn, Samuel, *The Process of Occupational Sex-Typing: the Feminization of Clerical Labor in Great Britain*, Temple University Press, Philadelphia 1985.

Connell, R. W., *Ruling Class, Ruling Culture: Studies of Conflict, Power and Hegemony in Australian Life*, Cambridge University Press, Melbourne, 1977.

—— and T. H. Irving, *Class Structure in Australian History: Documents, Narrative and Argument*, Longman Cheshire, Melbourne, 1980.

——, *Gender and Power*, Stanford University Press, 1987.

Cullen, Michael J., *The Statistical Movement in Early Victorian Britain: the Foundations of Empirical Social Research*, Harvester Press, Hassocks, Sussex, 1975.

Davies, Margery W., *Woman's Place is at the Typewriter: Office Work and Office Workers 1870–1930*, Temple University Press, Philadelphia, 1982.

Dye, Nancy Shrom, *As Equals and as Sisters: Feminism, the Labor Movement, and the Women's Trade Union League of New York*, University of Missouri Press, Columbia, 1980.

Evatt, H. V., *Australian Labour Leader: The Story of W. A. Holman and the Labour Movement*, Angus & Robertson, Sydney, 1940.

Eyler, John M., *Victorian Social Medicine: The Ideas and Methods of William Farr*, Johns Hopkins University Press, Baltimore, 1979.

Freidson, Eliot, *Professional Dominance*, Aldine, Chicago, 1970.

Giddens, Anthony, *The Class Structure of the Advanced Societies*, 2nd edn, Hutchinson, London, 1981.

Golder, Hilary, *Divorce in 19th Century New South Wales*, University of New South Wales Press, Sydney, 1985.

Goodwin, Craufurd D. W., *Economic Enquiry in Australia*, Duke University Press, Durham, NC, 1966.

——, *Image of Australia: British Perception of the Australian Economy from the Eighteenth to the Twentieth Century*, Duke University Press, Durham, NC, 1974.

Gouldner, Alvin, *The Future of Intellectuals and the Rise of the New Class*, Oxford University Press, New York, 1979.

Haber, Samuel, *Efficiency and Uplift: Scientific Management in the Progressive Era 1890—1920*, Chicago University Press, 1964.

Hays, Samuel P., *Conservation and the Gospel of Efficiency: The Progressive Conservation Movement, 1890—1920*, Harvard University Press, Cambridge, 1959.

Head, Brian W. (ed.), *State and Economy in Australia*, Oxford University Press, Melbourne, 1983.

Hicks, Neville, *'This Sin and Scandal': Australia's Population Debate 1891—1911*, ANU Press, Canberra, 1978.

Jervis, James, *The Cradle City of Australia: A History of Parramatta 1788—1961*, Parramatta City Council, Sydney, 1961.

Jordens, Ann-Mari, *The Stenhouse Circle: Literary Life in Mid-Nineteenth Century Sydney*, Melbourne University Press, 1980.

Kanter, Rosabeth Moss, *Men and Women of the Corporation*, Basic Books, New York, 1977.

Kelly, Max, *Nineteenth-Century Sydney: Essays in Urban History*, Sydney University Press, 1978.

Kessler-Harris, Alice, *Out to Work: A History of Wage-Earning Women in the United States*, Oxford University Press, New York, 1982.

Kingsley, John Donald, *Representative Bureaucracy: An Interpretation of the British Civil Service*, Antioch Press, Yellow Springs, Ohio, 1944.

Kolko, Gabriel, *The Triumph of Conservatism: a Reinterpretation of American History, 1900—1916*, Free Press of Glencoe, New York, 1963.

Kyle, Noeline, *Her Natural Destiny: The Education of Women in New South Wales*, University of New South Wales Press, Sydney, 1986.

Larson, Magali Sarfati, *The Rise of Professionalism: a Sociological Analysis*, University of California Press, Berkeley, 1977.

Lasch, Christopher, *Haven in a Heartless World: The Family Besieged,* Basic Books, New York, 1977.

Lawson, Sylvia, *The Archibald Paradox: A Strange Case of Authorship,* Allen Lane, Melbourne, 1983.

Lewis, Jane, *The Politics of Motherhood: Child and Maternal Welfare in England 1900–1939,* Croom Helm, London, 1980.

Loveday, Peter and A. W. Martin, *Parliament, Factions and Parties: The First Thirty Years of Responsible Government in New South Wales, 1856–1889,* Melbourne University Press, 1966.

McMartin, Arthur, *Public Servants and Patronage: The Foundation and Rise of the New South Wales Public Service, 1786–1859,* Sydney University Press, 1983.

Mansfield, Bruce, *Australian Democrat. The Career of Edward William O'Sullivan 1846–1910,* Sydney University Press, 1965.

Martin, A. W., *Henry Parkes: A Biography,* Melbourne University Press, 1980.

Matthews, Brian, *Louisa,* McPhee Gribble, Melbourne, 1987.

Matthews, Jill Julius, *Good and Mad Women: The Historical Construction of Femininity in Twentieth Century Australia,* George Allen & Unwin, Sydney, 1984.

Miliband, Ralph, *The State in Capitalist Society,* Basic Books, New York, 1969.

Mills, C. Wright, *White Collar: The American Middle Classes,* Oxford University Press, New York, 1951.

Nadel, George, *Australia's Colonial Culture. Ideas and Institutions in Mid-Nineteenth Century Eastern Australia,* Cheshire, Melbourne, 1957.

Norman, Lilith, *The Brown and Yellow: a History of Sydney Girls' High School,* Oxford University Press, Melbourne, 1983.

Normington-Rawling, J., *Charles Harpur, An Australian,* Angus & Robertson, Sydney, 1962.

Parkin, Frank, *Marxism and Class Theory: A Bourgeois Critique,* Tavistock, London, 1979.

Parry, N. and J. Parry, *The Rise of the Medical Profession,* Croom Helm, London, 1976.

Pensabene, T. S., *The Rise of the Medical Practitioner in Victoria,* Health Research Project and ANU Press, Canberra, 1980.

Poulantzas, Nicos, *Classes in Contemporary Capitalism,* New Left Books, London, 1975.

Reiger, Kerreen M., *The Disenchantment of the Home: Modernizing the Australian Family 1880–1940,* Oxford University Press, Melbourne, 1985.

Richardson, Henry Handel, *The Fortunes of Richard Mahony,* Book I, William Heinemann, London, 1954.

——, *Myself When Young,* London, Heinemann, 1948.

Roe, Michael, *Quest for Authority in Eastern Australia 1835–1851*, Melbourne University Press, 1965.

——, *Nine Australian Progressives: Vitalism in Bourgeois Social Thought 1890–1960*, University of Queensland Press, Brisbane, 1984.

Rowse, Tim, *Australian Liberalism and National Character*, Kibble Books, Melbourne, 1978.

Ruggie, Mary, *The State and Working Women: A Comparative Study of Britain and Sweden*, Princeton University Press, 1984.

Ryan, Edna, *Two-thirds of a Man: Women and Arbitration in New South Wales 1902–08*, Hale & Iremonger, Sydney, 1984.

Searle, G. R., *The Quest for National Efficiency: a Study of British Politics and Political Thought, 1899–1914*, University of California Press, Berkeley, 1971.

Skowronek, Stephen, *Building a New American State: The Expansion of Administrative Capacities 1877–1920*, Cambridge University Press, 1982.

Sydney Labour History Group, *What Rough Beast? The State and Social Order in Australian History*, George Allen & Unwin, Sydney, 1982.

Thompson, E. P., *The Making of the English Working Class*, rev. edn, Penguin, Harmondsworth, 1968.

Tilly, Louise A. and Joan W. Scott, *Women, Work, and Family*, Holt, Rinehart and Winston, New York, 1978.

Walker, Pat (ed.), *Between Labor and Capital*, South End Press, Boston, 1979.

Walker, R. B., *Old New England: A History of the Northern Tablelands of New South Wales 1818–1900*, Sydney University Press, 1966.

——, *The Newspaper Press in New South Wales, 1803–1920*, Sydney University Press, 1976.

Weinstein, James, *The Corporate Ideal in the Liberal State, 1900–1918*, Beacon Press, Boston, 1968.

Willis, Evan, *Medical Dominance: The Division of Labour in Australian Health Care*, George Allen & Unwin, Sydney, 1983.

Wilson, Elizabeth, *Women and the Welfare State*, Tavistock, London, 1977.

Wood, W. Allan, *Dawn in the Valley: The Story of Settlement in the Hunter River Valley to 1833*, Wentworth Books, Sydney, 1972.

Theses and unpublished papers

Caiden, G. E., 'The Study of Australian Administrative History', paper delivered at APSA Conference, Melbourne, 1963.

Cordell, Joan M., T. A. Coghlan: Government Statist of New South Wales 1886–1905, unpublished manuscript, 1960, copy in possession of writer.

Fry, E. C., 'T. A. Coghlan as an Historian', paper delivered at ANZAAS Congress, Hobart, August 1965.

Godden, J., Philanthropy and the Women's Sphere, Sydney, 1870–circa 1900, PhD thesis, Macquarie University, 1983.

Knight, Kenneth, W., The Development of the Public Service of New South Wales from Responsible Government (1856) to the Establishment of the Public Service Board (1895), MA thesis, University of Sydney, 1954.

Kociumbus, Jan, Children and Society in New South Wales and Victoria 1860–1914, PhD thesis, University of Sydney, 1983.

Lamb, P. N. The Financing of Government Expenditure in New South Wales, PhD thesis, Australian National University, 1963.

McCuskey, Claire, The History of Women in the Victorian Post Office, MA thesis, La Trobe University, 1984.

Martin, A. W., Political Developments in New South Wales 1894–6, MA thesis, University of Sydney, 1952.

Page, Barbara, The Mason Allard Inquiry into the Administration of the New South Wales Public Service 1917–18, MEc thesis, University of Sydney, 1980.

Ryan, J. A., B. R. Wise: An Oxford Liberal in the Freetrade Party of New South Wales, MA thesis, University of Sydney, 1965.

Sernak Cruise, M. L., Penal Reform in New South Wales: Frederick William Neitenstein 1896–1909, PhD thesis, University of Sydney, 1980.

Thame, Claudia, Health and the State: the Development of Collective Responsibility for Health Care in Australia in the First Half of the Twentieth Century, PhD thesis, Australian National University, 1974.

Woodman, Stuart, Lawyers in New South Wales 1856–1914: The Evolution of a Colonial Profession, PhD thesis, Australian National University, 1979.

Sources of illustrations

'Arrival of the Weekly Mail', *Illustrated Australasian News,* 12 August 1871, National Library of Australia; 'Arrival of the Mail', *Illustrated Sydney News*, 16 August 1865, National Library of Australia; B. O. Holtermann's Staff, from the original negative in the Mitchell Library, State Library of NSW, ML Neg. 18443, Box 5; by courtesy of Australia Post; by courtesy of Australia Post; Post Office, West Maitland, National Library of Australia; 'Sketches in the General Post Office Sydney', *Australasian Sketcher*, 30 March 1879, National Library of Australia; Leichhardt Post Office and Town Hall, copied from a postcard dated August 1907, by courtesy of Australia Post; by courtesy of Australia Post; *Gibbs, Shallard, & Co.'s Guide to Sydney*, 1882, National Library of Australia; *Gibbs, Shallard, & Co.'s Guide to Sydney*, 1882, National Library of Australia; *Gibbs, Shallard, & Co.'s Guide to Sydney*, 1882, National Library of Australia; *Bulletin*, 30 June 1883, National Library of Australia; Barling, National Library of Australia; *Town and Country Journal*, 25 January 1896, State Library of NSW; *Town and Country Journal*, 21 March 1896, State Library of NSW; G. S. Beeby (1903?), Mitchell Library, State Library of NSW; Australia, Parties, National Library of Australia; *Gibbs, Shallard, & Co.'s Guide to Sydney*, 1882, National Library of Australia; *Town and Country Journal*, 12 June 1880, National Library of Australia; Sir Timothy Coghlan papers, National Library of Australia (all reasonable attempts to discover copyright were made); *Public Service Journal*, 10 October 1903, Mitchell Library, State Library of NSW; from the Archives of the Metropolitan Business College, Sydney,

NSW; State Labour Exchange, Elizabeth Street, interior, 22 February 1918, Archives of the NSW Government Printing Office; Private collection of Miss Beatrice Proust; Private collection of Mrs Nancy Foote; Mitchell Library, State Library of NSW; *Public Service Journal*, 15 January 1924, Mitchell Library, State Library of NSW; *Public Service Journal*, 10 December 1913, Mitchell Library, State Library of NSW; *Public Service Journal*, 1 October 1914, Mitchell Library, State Library of NSW; *Red Tape*, 5 November 1927, Mitchell Library, State Library of NSW, drawn by Fred Patrick (all reasonable attempts to discover copyright holder were made); National Library of Australia.

Index

WIDENER UNIVERSITY-WOLFGRAM LIBRARY

CIR   HN850.Z9 S642 1989
Managing gender : the state, the new mid

3 3182 00308 5682

WIDENER UNIVER...
WOLF...
LIBRA...
CHESTER...